Living With High Blood Pressure: The Hypertension Diet Cookbook

Living With High Blood Pressure: The Hypertension Diet Cookbook

Joyce Daly Margie, M.S.
James C. Hunt, M.D.

HLS Press
Bloomfield, New Jersey

The production staff of *Living With High Blood Pressure*
included the following persons:
Editor: Robert Offergeld
Art Director: Victor Mazurkiewicz
Illustrator: Mel Klapholz
Photography: Earl Moline/Glen Peterson

ISBN 930618

Library of Congress Catalog Card Number: 77-84368

Printed in the United States of America.

Contents

PREFACE _____ VII
INTRODUCTION _____ IX

PART ONE: High Blood Pressure
Chapter   1. Nutritional Therapy in High Blood Pressure _____ 3
Chapter   2. The Medical Problem _____ 9
Chapter   3. The Medical Treatment of High Blood Pressure _____ 17
Chapter   4. Your Controlled Sodium Meal Plan—The Use of Food Groups _____ 25
Chapter   5. Sample Programs and Menus: 40 and 90 mEq Sodium
at Three Caloric Levels _____ 39

PART TWO: The Recipes
Chapter   6. Appetizers and Beverages _____ 59
Chapter   7. Soups, Sandwiches, and Eggs _____ 69
Chapter   8. Breads _____ 81
Chapter   9. Salads _____ 101
Chapter 10. Main Dishes _____ 117
Chapter 11. Vegetables _____ 157
Chapter 12. Desserts _____ 169
Chapter 13. Pies, Cakes, and Cookies _____ 183
Chapter 14. Use of Herbs and Spices _____ 205
Chapter 15. Measuring Ingredients, Rules for Good Baking,
and Tips Regarding Special Products _____ 215
Chapter 16. Handy Chart of Kitchen Math _____ 217
Chapter 17. High Altitude Cooking _____ 221
Chapter 18. Glossary of Cooking Terms _____ 225

PART THREE: Appendices
Appendix   1. Nutritive Value of Food Groups _____ 228
Appendix   2. Conversion Tables _____ 229
Appendix   3. How to Make Up a Meal Plan from the Foods and
Recipes in This Book _____ 230
Appendix   4. How to Calculate the Nutritive Value of Recipes
Not Found in This Book _____ 233
Appendix   5. How to Modify the Amount of Sodium in Your Dietary Program _____ 235

(continued overleaf)

VI

Appendix **6.** Eating Away From Home ———————————————— 236
Appendix **7.** Names and Addresses of Companies Supplying
Special Dietary Products ———————————————— 239
Appendix **8.** Nutritive Value Charts:
Nutritive Value of Common Foods Not Found in This Book ————— 244
Nutritive Value of The Recipes in This Book ———————— 247
INDEX ———————————————————————————— 301

Preface

I T IS difficult to overemphasize the magnitude and impact of high blood pressure on the health care of this nation. More than 23 million Americans (fifteen percent of the adult population) have hypertension. High blood pressure is the most important factor contributing to the development of strokes that each year kill almost 200,000 persons and disable over 250,000 persons below age 65. High blood pressure accelerates the development of atherosclerosis in the vessels of the heart (the coronary vessels) and is thus a very significant factor in the 1.25 million heart attacks and the 650,000 heart attack deaths that occur each year.

Despite these grim statistics, today there is much hope for the patient with high blood pressure. Although we still do not understand the causes of high blood pressure in over nine out of ten cases (and thus call the high blood pressure essential or idiopathic), we do have effective treatment regimes. Treatment that not only will lead to a normalization of blood pressure, but will also prevent the usual consequences of high blood pressure: stroke, heart failure, and kidney failure.

Dietary change is the cornerstone of safe, effective, long-term blood pressure control. As is emphasized in the early chapters of this book, not only will weight reduction and/or salt restriction (alone or in combination) result in normalization of blood pressure in some individuals, but when normalization requires the addition of drugs, attention to diet will reduce the amount and strength (and hence risk of side effects) of required medications.

The National High Blood Pressure Education Program was initiated almost five years ago. The program was conceived principally in response to three factors: the magnitude of the problem, its treatability, and the fact that high blood pressure usually is *silent*—without signs until its effects on the vascular system are manifest as stroke, kidney failure, heart attack, or heart failure. Six years ago, only fifty percent of Americans with high blood pressure were aware of their problem. Few realized the seriousness of high blood pressure or that it could be treated, and in fact less than one-sixth of those with high blood pressure were on adequate therapy.

During the past six years, the National Heart, Lung, and Blood Institute has participated—along with voluntary health agencies, medical societies, members of the pharmaceutical industry, and other groups—in a nationwide campaign aimed at the better detection and treatment of high blood pressure. The effort coordinated by the Institute has been successful. We have seen a major change in the detection, evaluation, and treatment of hypertensive persons. Over six million previously undiagnosed patients with high blood pressure have been discovered. The number of patient visits to physicians for high blood pressure has increased over fifty percent in the past five years. The number of hypertensives whose blood pressure is now normal on treatment has increased by 100 percent to almost eight million, and both the general public and the health-care professionals are much more aware of the perils of high blood pressure and the promises offered by treatment. Of even greater importance, this new awareness of and behavior toward high blood pressure appears to be paying big dividends. Since 1972, heart attack deaths in this country are down by more than ten percent, and deaths from stroke have declined by more than twenty percent. These unprecedented gains have (despite an ever increasing and aging population) reduced the number of cardiovascular deaths in this country to less than a million in both 1975 and 1976—after more than a decade of above a million deaths each year. With these gains, the average life expectancy of Americans has increased by more than two years in the past five years, and we now have the lowest death rate in our nation's history.

Despite these prodigious steps forward, it is obvious that we still have a long way to go. Almost eleven million Americans are aware of their high blood pressure but are on inadequate or no therapy, and there are still some seven million Americans totally unaware of their problem. Since high blood pressure is so silent, and patients often feel well until hypertension produces its consequences, it is often difficult for a patient to follow a dietary and/or drug regime. All too often initial success in therapy is equated with cure, whereas diet and drugs have only the effect of normalizing the blood pressure, and their discontinuation causes high blood pressure to reappear. Finally, physicians and other health care personnel can only recommend appropriate therapy. It requires the concern, commitment, and motivation of the patient with high blood pressure to long-term maintenance therapy if high blood pressure and its dreadful consequences are to be prevented.

This book significantly increases our armament in the fight against high blood pressure and its consequences. The clear presentation of dietary modifications and their rationale; the plain evidence that these diet changes are manageable, reasonable, and consistent with a highly palatable and varied diet; and the attractive display of menus and food plans—all these go a long way in helping the patient conceptualize high blood pressure control through dietary change as a gain rather than a chore.

This book will help all of us achieve a much desired therapeutic alliance against high blood pressure. It promises to help the physician to help the patient help himself control high blood pressure and maintain optimal health. I strongly commend this book to physicians to give to their patients with hypertension. The individual with high blood pressure and his or her family should read and use this book as part of an effective blood pressure control program.

Robert I. Levy, M.D.
Director, National Heart, Lung,
and Blood Institute

Introduction

HIGH BLOOD pressure (hypertension) is probably the single most common chronic disease in the United States today. The National High Blood Pressure Education Program of the Heart, Lung, and Blood Institute has reported that 20 to 30 million Americans have high blood pressure. Hypertension occurs in all age groups—children, young adults, middle-aged individuals, and it is found with even greater frequency in older persons. It has been estimated that one in every eight adults has high blood pressure.

It is important for the person with high blood pressure to realize that this disease produces few if any symptoms. This point is strongly emphasized in Galton's excellent book, *The Silent Disease: Hypertension,* which we recommend as supplementary reading. High blood pressure is painless and it is therefore often ignored until there is a complicating event. Untreated high blood pressure causes damage to small and medium-sized blood vessels (arteries) with acceleration of atherosclerosis (hardening of the arteries). When symptoms do appear, they usually are secondary symptoms resulting from damage to vital organs such as the kidney, heart, or brain. By the time a person with high blood pressure is aware of any symptoms, serious damage to the blood vessels and these "target organs" already has taken place. Major complications resulting from untreated high blood pressure include heart failure, kidney failure, heart attack, and stroke.

In most cases the cause of high blood pressure is unknown. This type of hypertension is referred to as primary or "essential" and cannot be cured. Yet with proper diet and medical treatment, high blood pressure can be controlled and its complications prevented. In approximately ten percent of cases, hypertension results from glandular (endocrine) disorders, or from blockage of an artery to the kidney (renal artery stenosis), and may be curable. Therefore, when indicated, your physician will undertake various diagnostic tests to determine if you have a correctable condition.

Treatment of hypertension, as it is currently available, requires a change in lifestyle—particularly in terms of your dietary habits. Since a significant change in lifestyle may be necessary for some individuals with high blood pressure, it is most important that the person with hypertension understand his or her problem and how to achieve and maintain blood pressure control. Hypertension—what it is and how it is controlled—will be discussed in some detail in the following chapters. However, the most important reading for *you,* the patient with high blood pressure, will concern the specific things that *you* can do to control *your* blood pressure. It is especially important that you *remain* under close medical supervision, that you *take* the medicines prescribed by your doctor, and that you be *concerned* with your diet and understand its role in helping you to *maintain* a normal blood pressure.

The consequences of high blood pressure can be avoided or postponed in most people with hypertension through the combined efforts of physicians and patients. These efforts should be aimed at the entire family because the children of a person with high blood pressure are at a greater risk of developing hypertension than the general population. The quality of life need not be drastically changed, and with proper treatment the person with high blood pressure should enjoy a normal life expectancy. But the hypertensive patient must carefully follow instructions concerning his health: He must remain under close medical supervision, maintain prescribed drug regimens, and adhere to a nutritional program that not only reflects his medical problem but is aimed at the maintenance of good health.

In this book we have attempted to provide a variety of appetizing, fully-tested recipes that are intended for use by the entire family. For the first time the person with hypertension can eat the same good-tasting food enjoyed by the family and still follow the nutritional program necessary to control blood pressure and to maintain optimum health.

The nutritional programs and recipes outlined in this book were originally developed for the treatment programs of hypertensive patients seen by the authors in their practice. Because they have been successful, we have decided to publish these programs and recipes in book form so that—hopefully—all persons with high blood pressure may benefit from them. The book is written in practical terms for individuals who do not have extensive training in dietetics, nutrition, or medicine. It is intended for distribution to patients with high blood pressure who, with the counsel and support of their physicians and dietitians, wish to develop dietary patterns necessary for general good health despite the necessity to control the intake of certain foods and nutrients.

A book of this type could not have been written without the help and support of many other individuals and institutions. It is the result of many people and disciplines working together toward the common goal of making the diet of people with high blood pressure more enjoy-

able. We are indebted to our colleagues at the Mayo Clinic for their advice, support, and contributions, especially Dr. Ralph A. Nelson, Dr. Clifford F. Gastineau, Mrs. Janice Grainer, Miss Esperanza Briones, and Mrs. Dianne Wellick. We would like to thank the students and faculty of the College of St. Elizabeth, Convent Station, New Jersey for their help in recipe development, especially Miss Emelia Salek. We are grateful to Dr. Robert Levy, Director of the National Heart, Lung, and Blood Institute, and to the leadership of the National High Blood Pressure Education Program, particularly Mr. Graham Ward, for their advice and review.

This book also reflects the growing concern of industry for the health problems of this country. To its great credit, a remarkable industrial complex has participated herewith in a joint venture with medical personnel aimed at controlling a major public health problem. There were many companies that assisted in the development of this manuscript. In particular, we would like to thank the Avoset Corporation and Smith Kline & French Laboratories, divisions of SmithKline Corporation, and the Betty Crocker Kitchens and the Nutrition Department of General Mills Inc., for their substantial and active contributions. In addition, we wish to thank the Department of Citrus, Florida Citrus Commission, the Idaho Potato Commission, Thomas J. Lipton, Inc., the McIlhenny Company, the Banana Bunch, the Tuna Research Foundation, Inc., and the United Fresh Fruit and Vegetable Association for giving us access to their recipe files.

Finally we would like to thank our patients for their contribution and encouragement, our families for their patience—and most particularly our publisher, without whose sympathetic support (and sorely tried endurance) this manuscript might never have been completed.

Joyce Daly Margie, M.S.
James C. Hunt, M.D.

Part One:
High Blood Pressure

1. Nutritional Therapy in High Blood Pressure

IN HEALTH, blood pressure is kept within desirable limits by automatic mechanisms that regulate the amount of blood pumped by the heart, the size of the blood vessels, and the amount or volume of blood within the blood vessels. These regulating mechanisms work through the autonomic or sympathetic nervous system to control the rate of the heartbeat, the amount of blood pumped with each beat of the heart, and the size of the blood vessels. The kidney, in response to signals from a number of hormones produced in the adrenal gland and the kidney itself, adjusts the volume of water and the amount of sodium in the body. When these mechanisms are working well, the pressure of the blood is optimum, the blood is delivered to the tissues in the needed amounts, and the blood vessels will have the least wear and tear. But, as you will discover in these pages, an elevated blood pressure produces a strain on the system—and, if untreated, can lead to disastrous results.

Only your physician can determine the manner of treatment which will be most appropriate for you. But there are certain precautions in diet which everyone who has hypertension should observe—mainly dietary control of sodium,* calories, and fats. For the most part, the basic programs outlined in this book can be used without modification for most persons having hypertension. In some instances your doctor may wish to modify these plans because of a particular problem.

Changing one's eating habits is not easy, so we have attemped to include in these nutritional programs as wide a variety and selection of food as possible. We would encourage the user of this book to try to vary his selection of foods from day to day, both for the purpose of enhancing enjoyment of eating and also for improving the nutritive qualities of the diet. A monotonous diet is not only unpleasant but often tends to be less nutritious. Your taste for certain foods and seasonings can be modified by time. For example, the taste for salt will gradually disappear over a period of a few months when the intake of salt is reduced. Herbs and spices can be used to replace salt to enhance the taste of food and can introduce a new and exciting taste sensation.

If you combine the information your physician has given you with that given in this book, you should be able to observe the necessary dietary precautions, even when eating away from home. Learning the diet prescription is something like learning the multiplication tables. A little time and effort are necessary at first, but with usage the selection of kinds and amounts of foods is accomplished easily and quickly. The recipes in this book were developed to be used by the entire family, and you should notice little difference from the foods you are accustomed to eating. We have substituted a variety of flavorings to take the place of the salt that other cookbooks call for. You and your family probably would never notice the difference if you didn't know the sodium content of these recipes had been reduced.

*Many people are confused about the difference between *sodium* and *salt*. Sodium is not salt. But salt (sodium chloride) contains a good deal of sodium. In fact, it is nearly half sodium (see next page).

The sodium content of your diet not only has a direct relationship to your blood pressure, but it is also intimately related to the way in which some of the medication used to control hypertension works (see Chapter 3). The effectiveness of a given medication program may be greatly enhanced by proper dietary measures. Therefore you should understand something about the nutrients involved in your nutritional program and the reason for regulating these nutrients.

SODIUM

Sodium is a naturally occurring mineral and it is found in a great variety of foods. Americans tend to eat large amounts of sodium, consuming up to 200-400 mEq (approximately 4-9 grams) of sodium a day. Probably the single biggest contributor of sodium to any diet is sodium chloride—common table salt, which is composed of approximately 50 percent sodium. High levels of sodium can cause hypertension to develop in people who have a predisposition (tendency) to this disorder. For that reason it is important for your family to reduce their sodium intake too. Large amounts of sodium can also aggravate high blood pressure, causing it to become more severe. Control of sodium intake will frequently lower the blood pressure, sometimes to within normal limits. The manner in which the restriction of sodium does this is not entirely clear, and some persons may have greater benefits from reducing their sodium intake than others.

To reduce the sodium consumption to 90 milliequivalents (approximating 2 grams or 2000 milligrams) or less per day, it should not be necessary to buy special dietary products, but special salt-free foods—such as salt-free margarine or bread—may be required to reduce the sodium content of the diet below 90 mEq. Reduction in the consumption of sodium not only facilitates the treatment of hypertension but is beneficial if there is any weakness of the pumping action of the heart or a trend toward accumulation of fluid.

If the body accumulates too much sodium, there is a tendency for the amount of fluid within the body to increase. This in turn increases the volume of blood within the blood vessels, and the blood pressure rises. Excessive amounts of sodium may also have a direct effect on the blood vessel wall. Reduction of the amount of sodium in the body—by decreasing consumption of sodium and through the use of diuretics (sometimes referred to as fluid or water pills) which cause the kidneys to eliminate sodium—is often helpful. Since the diuretic and the dietary control of sodium work together, it follows that it is difficult for the physician to regulate the dose of the diuretic properly if the consumption of sodium is not regulated at the same time. In other words, the effects of the diuretic on blood pressure will not be consistent if the person is consuming varying amounts of sodium.

Sodium is not found only in salt. It is also a preservative, and it is used in many different forms in canned, frozen, commercially preserved, and convenience foods. Baking powder, baking soda, monosodium-glutamate, meat sauces, flavorings, condiments, koshered foods, some tooth paste, and water that is chemically softened contain large amounts of sodium (see Chapter 4). So a person on a controlled sodium intake should be aware of the ingredients in a product he eats. Look at labels. If the sodium content of the product is not given, look at the list of ingredients. Ingredients are listed according to the amount contained in the product. The first item listed is the one which the product contains the most of. Therefore if salt or sodium is given at the beginning of a product's list of ingredients, or is not listed in this book, you probably had better avoid that product or check with a dietitian or health care professional before using it. Appendix 8 contains the sodium content of many foods not included in the basic food groups. If you want to use these foods, be sure to add the sodium content of the food into your diet plan for the day.

Since your sodium intake has a direct relationship to your blood pressure, it is important to follow the instructions of your meal plan regarding it. If you faithfully follow the regimen in this book prescribed by your doctor, you need not worry about consuming too much sodium.

CALORIES

Excessive body weight also increases your risk of developing the complications of hypertension. Therefore we recommend that you maintain a normal body weight. The person with hypertension should avoid gaining weight, and if he is already overweight should try to lose weight and thereafter maintain a normal weight. Since hypertension occurs most commonly in persons over 40 years of age, and many persons beyond that age are overweight, control of calories is usually an important part of the dietary treatment of hypertension. A person has the maximum amount of muscle development at ages 20 to 25, and after that there is a gradual decrease in the amount of muscle. A person will lose five to fifteen pounds of muscle during the years from young adult life until age fifty or sixty, and there is a shift in the proportions of muscle and fat in the body. In addition, the weight of bone also decreases as people become older. Ideally, most people (if they are to retain the same proportion between fat and muscle throughout life) should weigh less at age fifty than they did in their twenties. Most height-weight tables are reasonably good guides to ideal weight for people in their twenties, but usually permit excessive weight for persons in

later life. If you are overweight, the combination of controlling both the sodium and calorie content of your diet may have a very substantial effect in lowering blood pressure. Weight reduction not only helps the blood pressure but can have a beneficial effect on the blood fats as well.

Your physician will determine what is a normal weight for you and will prescribe a regime that will help you either to reach or to maintain your ideal weight. Since you may need to control your calorie intake, the calories per serving are given at the bottom of each recipe. Also, the foods in each food group contain approximately the same number of calories when used in the specified portions.

FATS

Since we are concerned with the effect of hypertension on the blood vessel wall, we must also be concerned with other factors which adversely affect the lining of the blood vessel. Hypertension is a major risk factor for heart disease. Elevated levels of cholesterol and triglycerides (another form of fat) in the blood may lead to deposit of cholesterol in the linings of the blood vessels and contribute to the weakness of the blood vessel wall or narrowing of the channel. If the level of fats within the blood is excessive, there will be specific diet restrictions that your physician or dietitian will explain to you. Even if one has normal levels of cholesterol and triglycerides, current research indicates it is still appropriate for persons with high blood pressure to control the type and amount of fat in their diet in order to avoid the risk of developing heart disease. For this reason, we have incorporated fat and cholesterol control into your meal plans. This is done by selecting meat and fish which are lower in fat, using polyunsaturated margarine and oils, skim milk, and substitutes for eggs whenever possible. In order to cut down your fat intake, we encourage you to select fish, white meat of chicken, and lean meats; to trim away skin and visible fat from your meats; and to limit eggs to two or three a week. Save your fresh eggs for sunny-side-up eggs and substitute with imitation eggs whenever possible. We have attempted to show you how to do this in the recipe chapters of this book.

These nutritional considerations are also built into the programs given in other chapters, and you should not have to take further steps to accomplish a reasonable fat intake. If you have a specific problem, your physician or dietitian may direct you to take additional measures.

POTASSIUM

Sometimes potassium is lost from the body as a consequence of the action of medications (diuretics) used in the treatment of high blood pressure. When the potassium levels in the body are reduced or low, weakness may develop because muscles don't work as well as they should. You may have some muscle cramping. This can be very dangerous in certain situations—especially if there has been heart damage, because the heart muscle will not work as it should. Since not all patients develop these problems, your doctor will periodically check your blood for potassium levels. If a problem develops he may add a potassium-sparing diuretic to your drug regimen, prescribe a medication that is a potassium supplement, or ask you to add foods to your diet that are high in potassium. Lists of these foods may be obtained from him. If there is a need to increase the amount of potassium substantially, most physicians prefer to accomplish this by giving medications and by lowering the sodium content of the diet, since "potassium rich" foods are usually high in calories.

WATER

Water need not be controlled. In fact, it is generally desirable to be generous in the consumption of water. Except under unusual circumstances, swelling or "fluid retention" is not a consequence of excessive water intake. It results from excessive accumulation of sodium in the body, and it is controlled by diet or a combination of diet and diuretics. As mentioned earlier, chemically softened water may be a source of excessive sodium, so check the sodium content of your water supply.

VITAMINS

If you eat a balanced diet, you should be getting the vitamins that your body requires. Your physician or dietitian can advise you whether any supplementary vitamins are desirable in your particular dietary program.

PROTEIN

Control of dietary protein is necessary where there is reduced kidney function. But even for the normal person there is no virtue in having extra protein in the diet. Many forms of protein contain generous amounts of saturated fat, cholesterol and sodium. Some attention to the protein intake is therefore appropriate, and the serving size of meat may not be as large as you might wish. In general, six ounces of meat a day is sufficient to fulfill the nutritional needs of most adults for protein. It is important to keep in mind that processed or commercially prepared meats are high in both fat and sodium, and should be avoided.

BALANCED NUTRITION

Good nutrition means a balanced intake of all the nutrients necessary to maintain general good health. Professionals in the field of nutrition have developed guidelines to follow in order to assure the adequate intake of the nutrients essential for health. These guidelines are referred to as the *Basic Four Food Groups*: Meat and meat substitutes, dairy products, bread and cereals, and fruits and vegetables. It is recommended that adults eat a minimum of two servings of meat and meat substitutes; four of bread and cereal; two of dairy products; and four of fruits and vegetables. Because of the additional dietary considerations necessary for the person with high blood pressure, we employ slightly different food groups in these pages. But we carry through the same general principles of balanced nutritional intake. We strongly recommend that you eat a variety of foods and follow a nutritionally balanced meal plan.

2. The Medical Problem

THE MEDICAL problems of high blood pressure are best understood in relation to the nature of the circulatory system, which is a complex network within the body composed of the heart, arteries, capillaries, and veins. Blood is the fluid in the circulatory system that transports oxygen from the lungs, nutrients from the intestinal system, and other essential components needed by the cells or the organs and tissues throughout the body. The blood also carries waste products (carbon dioxide, metabolic by-products, and other wastes) from the tissues to various organs so that they can be eliminated from the body.

The heart and blood vessels have been compared to a plumbing system (see Figure 1). The heart functions much like a pump by providing the pressure necessary to drive the blood and its contents through the arteries (the pipes). The arterioles, small artery branches, act as control valves (faucets) by adjusting the flow of the blood to the smallest vessels, the capillaries, which are the tiny outlets to the tissues and cells. The blood is then returned to the heart by way of the veins (collection drains). Blood coming from the heart is under a higher pressure as it is transported through the arteries to the organs, and under a lower pressure as it returns to the heart by way of the veins. The circulatory system was first described in 1628 by the British physician William Harvey, who studied the circular flow of the blood within the vessels of the body. A century later an English clergyman, the Rev. Stephen Hales, proved the existence of blood pressure by inserting a long glass tube into one of the large arteries of a horse and measuring the pressure generated in the blood vessel. In 1819 a French physician, René Laennec, invented the stethoscope. Before that time the physician, in order to hear the heart sounds, had to place his ear directly on the patient's chest. The stethoscope made it possible to hear the interior sounds generated by the opening and closing of the heart valves, thereby determining the rhythm of the heart.

For over a hundred years now, a column of mercury has been used by scientists and physicians to measure the pressure of blood within the circulatory system. And for about fifty years it has been possible to measure the blood pressure by external means (outside the body). This is done by wrapping around the arm a blood-pressure cuff which is attached to a mercury column as a pressure-measuring device, meanwhile using the stethoscope to pick up the sounds of the pulse. This blood pressure machine is called a sphygmomanometer (see Figure 2).

The existence of high blood pressure in disease states has been recognized since late in the 19th century, when it was noted that people with high blood pressure had damaged arteries. Yet it is only since the 1930's that physicians have become aware that high blood pressure is the *cause*, rather than a *result*, of diseased arteries. Prior to that time it was believed that the diseased arteries caused the heart to pump harder in order to drive the blood through the narrowed and rigid vessels—with the end result being a higher blood pressure.

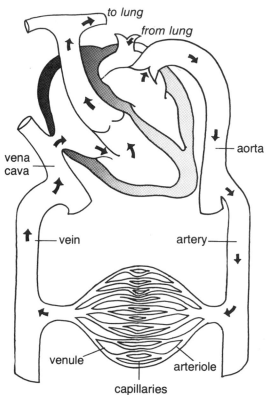

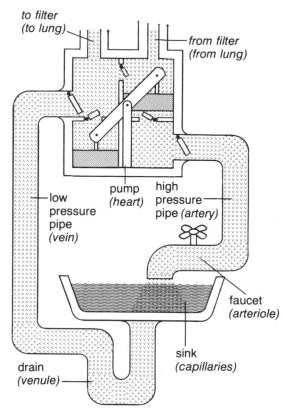

Figure 1

Taking Your Blood Pressure

Since high blood pressure, especially in the early stages, has no characteristic symptoms (it is called asymptomatic), the only practical way to tell if you have this condition is to have your blood pressure checked. This is done with the sphygmomanometer—either a graduated glass tube filled with mercury or an aneroid or dial gauge. Both of these operate on a simple principle of physics. This principle states that if pressure is exerted at any point in a system, that pressure will be equally transmitted to all other points in that system, including the walls. Think of the artery as an enclosed cylinder filled with fluid (blood). We know that blood pressure is the force exerted by the blood against the walls of the arteries as it is pumped from the heart through the circulatory system. By measuring the pressure exerted upon the walls of the artery, therefore, we will know the pressure of the blood within the artery.

In taking your blood pressure the physician or nurse first feels for the underlying artery of the arm—the brachial artery. Then an inflatable rubber cuff is wrapped around the arm and connected to the sphygmomanometer (see Figure 2). When the rubber bulb is squeezed, the cuff is inflated with air. As the cuff gets tighter, it compresses the brachial artery. Since the compression from the air pressure in the cuff is greater than the push of the blood in the artery, this temporarily shuts off the flow of blood. At this point, the mercury is high in the glass tube and the numbers next to the column of mercury show the height of air pressure in the cuff (measured in millimeters of mercury).

Next, the air is gradually released from the cuff, and the examiner listens with a stethoscope over the compressed artery for the first sound of blood rushing through the artery. This is the point at which the air pressure in the cuff is slightly lower than the blood pressure in the artery. The pressure on the gauge at that moment is noted and recorded. It is the point at which blood begins to flow through the artery with each heart beat, and it is called the "systolic" pressure—the maximum pressure produced by the heart (see Figure 3). The release of the air from the cuff is continued. At the point where the sound becomes muffled or disappears, pressure in the gauge is again noted. This is the "diastolic" pressure—the lowest pressure within the artery, which occurs when the heart is at rest (between beats). Both levels are important and both are recorded. First, the systolic or level of maximum pressure; then the diastolic or level of least pressure. For example, if 130 over 90 is recorded, 130 is the systolic pressure and 90 is the diastolic pressure.

What is hypertension?

As described earlier, the blood pressure is the force exerted by the blood against the walls of the arteries. There are several factors which influence the blood pressure: the amount of blood pumped by each beat of the heart, the amount of blood within the entire system of vessels, and the capacity, caliber, and tone of the arteries.

High blood pressure, or hypertension, is a sustained (persistent) elevation of the blood pressure. The body has an extensive and complicated regulatory system which normally maintains a variable blood pressure within a narrow range. The blood pressure changes when there is an increased need for blood flow. During exercise, for example, the blood pressure rises, and when you are resting the blood pressure in the system is lower.

There are several major factors which regulate the blood pressure. The force of the constriction of the heart largely determines how high the pressure develops in the arteries—the stronger the force of the contraction, the greater the pressure. The pressure generated by the contraction of the heart is maintained in the circulatory system by the expansion and contraction of the arteries and by the opening and closing of the smallest arteries, the arterioles. The arterioles feed the capillaries, which in turn nourish the body tissues with oxygen and nutrients. Imagine an arteriole as the nozzle of a

Sphygmomanometer

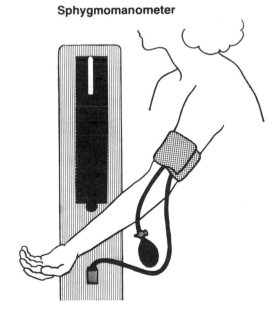

Figure 2

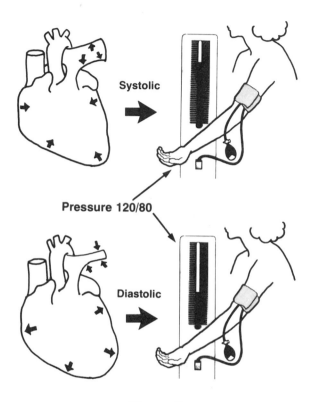

Systolic

Pressure 120/80

Diastolic

Figure 3

garden hose. If the nozzle is open, the water flows freely. But if for some reason the nozzle is narrowed, the pressure inside the hose builds up. The arterioles act like nozzles causing the heart to work harder to force the flow of blood through these narrow passages. This stronger pumping action of the heart results in an elevation in blood pressure.

The volume (amount) of blood in the circulatory system also exerts a major influence on blood pressure. When the blood volume is increased, the heart will have to pump more blood, and since the greater volume of blood is forced into a vessel of relatively fixed size, the blood pressure increases. Similarly, when the blood volume is decreased, the pressure in the artery is lowered. To a large extent, the volume of blood in the circulatory system is influenced both by the amount of sodium in the diet, and the amount of sodium eliminated from the body primarily through the kidneys (see Figure 4). Too much salt in the diet can result in the retention of fluid by the body and can produce an increase in the circulating blood volume. This is a particularly important factor in individuals with hypertension, because in such persons the mechanism for elimination of salt from the body may be impaired. In this circumstance the blood volume may increase and the blood pressure rises.

Another factor which can influence blood pressure is the capacity and tone of the arteries, which are regulated by the activity of the nervous system. This activity may change the blood pressure by altering the pumping action of the heart and by varying the peripheral vascular resistance. (By this we mean the resistance of the arterioles, for whatever reason, to the flow of blood.)

Generally speaking, 120/80 is considered normal blood pressure in the adult. Consistent pressures of 140/90, and higher, in a relaxed and resting person, mean that that individual has hypertension. As people get older, their blood vessels become less resilient (less elastic) and the pressure exerted by the heart in order to maintain proper circulation becomes higher. Physicians are less concerned about mild elevations of systolic blood pressure in older persons, and the acceptable limits of "normal" are somewhat higher for older persons—140/90 in a 60-year-old is not uncommon. On the other hand, normal blood pressure tends to be lower in younger people. Thus a pressure of 140/90 in a six-year-old child would be considered a significant elevation of the blood pressure.

Does a *single* measurement of blood pressure with levels of 140/90 or more mean the adult has hypertension? No, not at all. Blood pressure fluctuates throughout the day. Various emotions—stress, excitement, and physical activity—can cause the pressure to rise. But emotions, like physical activity, are temporary, and usually the blood pressure drops back to normal. Because of these fluctuations, the *trend* of the blood pressure over a period of time (weeks or months) is usually more important than one isolated reading. When the blood pressure is *consistently* elevated, usually at levels of 150/100 or more, almost all physicians now recommend medical treatment. In a person less than 50 years old, we would advocate treatment of even less severe elevations of blood pressure.

To assure adequacy of treatment, more and more physicians now recommend that their hypertensive patients take and record their own blood pressure at home. These readings are generally more reliable than those obtained in the environment of the physician's office, and they provide valuable information for your physician when it is necessary to adjust your individual treatment program.

Who Gets High Blood Pressure?

Actually, no one is immune. But long-term (epidemiological) studies have demonstrated that certain population groups are more likely to be affected. Hypertension is more common in black males and black females, and when it strikes them, it is usually more severe. White males have a greater frequency of hypertension than do white females. Older individuals, regardless of race or sex, have a higher prevalence of high blood pressure than do younger persons. When there are several members of a family with hypertension, the probability of developing high blood pressure increases for the other family members. If hypertension is discovered in *one* member of the family, it is extremely important that the blood pressure of *all* members of the family be measured. A good rule to follow is to have your pressure checked at least once a year—and more frequently if you have been diagnosed as having high blood pressure.

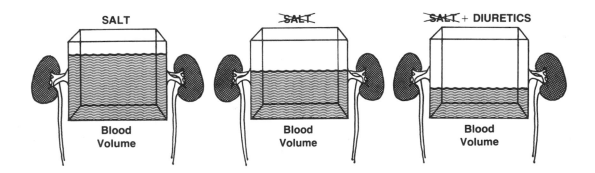

Figure 4

Complications of
Untreated High Blood Pressure

No matter what the cause of high blood pressure, it is primarily the circulatory system which is affected, especially the blood vessels supplying the kidneys, brain, and heart. The earliest changes are in the small arteries and arterioles. In order to protect the organs and tissues from the elevated pressure, the arterioles constrict, and as a result suffer the full effects of the elevated pressure. The higher the elevation of blood pressure, the greater the damage to the blood vessels. The lining of the arterioles becomes thick (proliferation) and the vessels narrow. If the pressure is extremely high, tearing and fragmentation of the lining of the vessel and the underlying elastic fibers and muscle occur. This is followed by cell destruction (necrosis) with scar formation. This scar tissue causes blockage of the vessels and interferes with blood flow to the various organs. Because of the decreased blood flow, the organs and tissues are deprived of their supply of oxygen and nutrients, and carbon dioxide and other waste products cannot be properly removed. The end result is that these organs and tissues cannot function properly.

With high blood pressure of long duration, changes in the medium-sized and large arteries also can occur. The vessel walls become thick and hardened, and deposits of cholesterol and other lipids (fats) accumulate and obstruct the flow of blood. This accumulation of cholesterol and other fats is called atherosclerosis (hardening of the arteries). Once set in motion by an elevated blood pressure, the atherosclerotic process slowly progresses, even after the blood pressure is returned to normal.

Damage to the arteries and arterioles of the vital organs (kidney, heart, and brain) is common in the hypertensive process, and they are therefore referred to as "target organs" (see Figure 5). Unfortunately, by the time inadequate circulation to these target organs produces symptoms, the process is irreversible. For this reason physicians are anxious to detect high blood pressure early and to begin as soon as possible an effective treatment program for lowering the blood pressure. *Untreated high blood pressure can lead to congestive heart failure, kidney failure, heart attack, and stroke.*

Consequences of
Untreated High Blood Pressure

In a 1959 study of more than 4 million people undertaken by the life insurance industry, it was found that the higher the blood pressure, the greater the risk of early death or heart attack. Even when the blood pressure was only mildly elevated at levels of 140/90, there was an increased mortality (death rate). In a federally supported study in Framingham, Massachusetts that began in 1948, detailed observations were made on approximately 5,000 people who had no evidence or sign of heart disease or atherosclerosis Continuing close observation of these individuals showed that the risk of developing heart failure, heart attack, or stroke is three to five times greater in persons with high blood pressure than in persons with normal blood pressure. The Framingham study also showed that there is an increase in stroke, sudden death, and heart attack in individuals who are obese, smoke cigarettes, have elevated cholesterol and uric acid levels, and live sedentary lifestyles (lack exercise).

The major complications of high blood pressure are not inevitable, nor should it be assumed, once an individual with hypertension has suffered a complication, that prompt treatment should not be started. Whatever the degree of elevation of the blood pressure, and despite the presence or absence of damage to the "target organs" (heart, kidney, brain), an effective antihypertensive program can result in a greatly improved life expectancy, diminished symptoms, and lower rate of complications.

The atherosclerotic process can be prevented, or long deferred, if treatment of hypertension is begun early—*before* the development of atherosclerotic changes.

Risk Factors

For several decades the National Heart, Lung, and Blood Institute, the American Heart Association, and the National Kidney Foundation have called the public's attention to the increased probability of early death from heart attack, stroke, and kidney failure for individuals who have one or more of several health problems. The scientific validity for these concerns has been proved by the reports of the life insurance study, the Framingham study, and a variety of other medical investigations. Cigarette smoking, obesity, diabetes, elevated blood cholesterol levels, lack of exercise, and especially high blood pressure can result in target organ damage and early death. These risk factors appear to be cumulative, and the Framingham study makes this point very succinctly: At middle age, the man with high blood pressure runs twice the risk of coronary heart disease as the man with normal pressure. If he is also a heavy cigarette smoker his risk is nearly three times as great. And if, in addition, he has high blood cholesterol, his risk is over five times as great as the man with none of these three risk factors.

There are other risks that should be considered. The person with diabetes is even more prone to many of these problems. Overweight, stress, and lack of exercise are also risk factors and also increase the odds against you. But you can decrease those odds and increase your chances for a longer, healthier life. For exam-

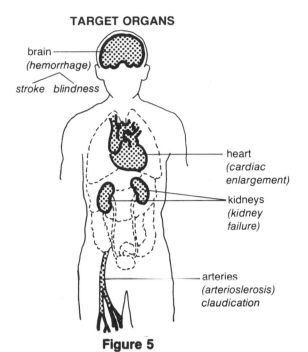

TARGET ORGANS

brain
(hemorrhage)

stroke   blindness

heart
*(cardiac
enlargement)*

kidneys
*(kidney
failure)*

arteries
*(arterioslerosis)
claudication*

Figure 5

ple, if you are overweight, lose weight. Weight loss often lowers blood pressure and reduces the level of blood cholesterol. Engage in a regular exercise program. There is good evidence that exercise, in moderation, can improve the heart function. If you smoke, stop smoking. Cigarette smoking constricts the blood vessels and increases blood pressure. In addition, nicotine causes the release of adrenalin into the blood stream. Adrenalin, in turn, acutely speeds up the heart rate, which may raise the blood pressure further.

If you have any or all of these risk factors, it justifies careful health care planning with a view to making the necessary changes in your life style. Few things are more important for you to remember than this: The proper changes in your lifestyle can increase your protection against the complications of high blood pressure and *you* can significantly increase your life expectancy.

3. The Medical Treatment of High Blood Pressure

THE PURPOSE of this chapter is to help you understand your high blood pressure problem and its treatment so you will be better equipped to assist in your care. The information provided is medical in nature and may be more technical than many people feel to be necessary. But we have found that a well-informed patient is better able to follow a good treatment program. High blood pressure is unlike other diseases. Although in most cases there is no cure, it can be controlled with proper treatment. But successful treatment involves lifelong therapy and a complete understanding and cooperation between the patient and the physician.

Once diagnosed, the major problem in the treatment of high blood pressure is poor adherence to a treatment program. In other words, many people simply don't follow their doctor's recommendations. The probable reason for this is that high blood pressure doesn't hurt—at least not for many years. If you have a pain, in most cases you see your physician and he gives you something to alleviate that pain. If you have hypertension, you may visit your doctor and say that you're feeling well, but the physician tells you that you have high blood pressure, gives you a medication—and at first you may not feel as well. No wonder there is a tremendously high treatment drop-out rate among hypertensives. Yet drug therapy, when necessary, can be tailored to fit the individual patient's needs and physiological makeup so that he or she suffers few if any side effects. The

more you know about high blood pressue itself, and about the need for initial testing, repeated examinations, and lifelong therapy, the more motivated you will be to follow your doctor's advice in controlling what has been so aptly called the *silent killer*.

THE PRE-DRUG ERA

As recently as 30 years ago, the life expectancy of the individual with moderate to severe high blood pressure was strikingly reduced. The patient could expect inevitable complications which included heart failure, kidney failure, or stroke. Since there was little that the physician could do to control the high blood pressure itself, he had to concern himself primarily with the treatment of the complications of the disease.

Congestive heart failure was treated with bed rest, salt restriction, digitalis, and mercurial diuretics that temporarily improved heart function, increased elimination of sodium and water from the body, and reduced the blood pressure. On most occasions, however, the blood pressure would again increase, and soon the heart would be unable to maintain the pumping action necessary for adequate circulation. Generally the patient would sooner or later return to the physician in a still more severe state of heart failure. The treatment would be started again, but the end result was inevitably an early death.

Prior to the advent of modern drug therapy, severe high blood pressure often resulted in the rupture of blood vessels (stroke), especially to the brain, causing paralysis or death. Similar damage to the blood vessels in the kidney caused "uremic poisoning" (kidney failure). If the patient survived an episode of heart failure, kidney failure, or brain hemorrhage, he usually died from a recurrent stroke, kidney failure, or heart failure.

Two methods of controlling severe high blood pressure were developed in the 1940's. One was Spartan and the other radical, but neither was regularly successful. The first was the "Kempner Rice Diet," originally developed for the treatment of kidney failure. This method utilized a strict diet of rice and fresh fruit while avoiding meat and meat products. The diet almost completely eliminated sodium and reduced the dietary protein intake from a daily average of 100 or 125 grams to 20 grams. Kempner observed that when patients could be maintained on this extremely Spartan nutritional program, their blood pressure was reduced and their overall state of health was greatly improved. Unfortunately, few physicians understood or were committed to the concept of such rigid dietary sodium and protein control, and even though it was an important scientific contribution, Kempner's concept and approach was interpreted by many as a dietary fad.

An alternate to the rice diet was a surgical procedure called a sympathectomy. In this procedure the sympathetic trunk nerves in the chest and abdomen were severed, thus preventing abnormal constriction of the blood vessels. Although it resulted in dilation (relaxation) of the arteries and lowering of blood pressure, this operation had many serious side effects and was seldom successful in lowering the blood pressure for more than a few years. Today, because of the development of a variety of drugs that act as "chemical surgeons" in preventing abnormal constriction of the arteries, the sympathectomy is seldom used.

THE MODERN DRUG ERA

The era of antihypertensive drug therapy began in 1950 with the development of hexamethonium, a drug that exerted a powerful effect on the sympathetic nervous system. The sympathetic nervous system is a part of the involuntary (automatic) nervous system that regulates tissues not under voluntary control—such as the glands, the heart, and the smooth muscles. Spontaneous nerve impulses and chemical messengers originating in the sympathetic nervous system also regulate the functions of the arterioles and the flow of blood within them. In some people, these impulses do not function normally and they cause the arterioles to constrict, thereby increasing the resistance to the flow of blood and raising the blood pressure. Hexamethonium blocked the nerve signals by interfering with the chemical messengers before they reached the arterioles. This caused the arterioles to relax and kept the blood pressure down. In effect, this drug performed a chemical sympathectomy. Hexamethonium could be administered by injection or taken as a tablet by mouth. When injections were used, it was necessary to give the medication several times daily, and when it was taken by mouth its absorption in the intestinal tract was not predictable. Side effects included blurring of vision, dry mouth, and constipation. This drug was invaluable for treating severe hypertension, but the severity of the side effects limited its usefulness for less severe cases of high blood pressure.

By this time, however, many pharmaceutical companies had begun a search for effective hypertensive drugs, and before long many new agents with different modes of action were available for testing. Today there is an impressive array of antihypertensive drugs available to the physician to help in the treatment of mild, moderate, or severe high blood pressure.

In the United States there are six major drugs, or types of drugs, that are commonly used. These include diuretics, reserpine, propranolol, hydralazine, methyldopa, and guanethedine. Since each of these drugs may cause varying degrees of adverse reactions, it is important for the patient to promptly report side effects to his physician. Many times the dosage or the medication can be changed, thereby reducing or eliminating undesirable side effects. Since some of these medications are marketed by more than one pharmaceutical company, we have chosen to use generic names whenever possible, rather than to identify the trade names used by the manufacturers.

DIURETIC ANTIHYPERTENSIVE AGENTS

The cornerstone and mainstay of most antihypertensive drug therapy is the oral diuretic. Thiazide diuretics are the most frequently used oral diuretic in the treatment of hypertension. Diuretics increase the elimination of sodium and water through the kidney, which results in a lowering of the blood pressure. The first of the oral diuretics used for this purpose was chlorothiazide. Today thiazide diuretics, either alone or in combination with one or more other drugs, are frequently used to reduce the blood pressure.

There are a number of non-thiazide diuretics, such as triamterene and spironolactone (which are potassium-sparing diuretics), and furosemide and ethacrynic acid, which physicians consider to have special roles in the treatment of hypertension. But the usual approach in the treatment of high blood pressure is to start antihypertensive drug therapy with a thiazide diuretic, and to add additional medications when necessary to control the elevated blood pressure. In some cases it may be preferable to start treatment with a potassium-sparing diuretic, or to use a so-called loop diuretic such as furosemide.

Side effects of continued diuretic therapy are fairly common but rarely serious enough to discontinue therapy. The most common side effect is loss of potassium (hypokalemia), which may cause fatigue and muscle weakness. The development of hypokalemia can be minimized by the reduction of sodium in the diet and by the use of one of the potassium-sparing diuretics. Some physicians prefer to add potassium-rich foods to the diet, or to give the patient potassium chloride supplements. Many patients with mild to moderate high blood pressure are able to control their blood pressure through the use of diet and diuretic therapy.

PROPRANOLOL

Propranolol is a widely used antihypertensive agent employed by physicians as a supplement when dietary sodium control and diuretics do not adequately control blood pressure. Propranolol has a number of pharmacologic effects which result in lowering the blood pressure. It causes the blood vessels to relax and the heart to slow, thus reducing the blood pressure. Since this medication also acts on the bronchial tubes, it should not be used by patients with asthma. Also, because the pumping effectiveness of the heart may be impaired by a very slow pulse, propranolol should be used with caution in persons with congestive heart failure. Among other actions, propranolol interferes with the automatic nervous system, and is more effective in slowing the heart rate than a number of other drugs with somewhat similar actions, such as methyldopa, guanethedine, and reserpine. For this reason, and because of other antihypertensive actions, many physicians now consider propranolol the supplemental agent of choice.

HYDRALAZINE

If the combination of diet, a diuretic, and propranolol fails to reduce the blood pressure adequately, a third drug, hydralazine, is commonly added. Hydralazine lowers the blood pressure by directly dilating the arterioles. This is a mode of action quite different from other antihypertensive drugs. In dilating the arteries, hydralazine also sets off reflexes within the circulatory system that increase the pumping action of the heart. If used alone, this drug may cause a fast heart beat, palpitations, aggravation of angina, and headaches. The side effects are reduced when hydralazine is used in combination with diuretics and propranolol. It is seldom used alone for the treatment of chronic high blood pressure.

METHYLDOPA

Methyldopa is frequently used for treating patients with moderate or moderately severe hypertension, and it is usually given in combination with a thiazide diuretic. Its action is not completely understood, but we do know that it has a central nervous system effect. A number of side effects may be experienced, and they include a feeling of tiredness, sleepiness, dizziness upon standing, and interference with liver function and the blood forming system. Most of the side effects are transient in nature and disappear after the first few weeks of treatment. Nevertheless, your physician will probably wish to monitor your response to this medication.

RESERPINE

If diuretic antihypertensive therapy, alone or in combination with previously described agents, is unsuccessful in establishing a normalized blood pressure, your physician may desire to add reserpine to the treatment regimen. Reserpine, a drug purified from the Indian plant, rauwolfia serpentina, was the first drug to which the term "tranquilizer" was applied. It acts in the central nervous system, reducing the flow of exciting impulses which causes the arterioles to constrict and raise the blood pressure. Besides having a mild sedative effect, reserpine may cause other side effects, including nasal stuffiness, aggravation of a peptic ulcer, or mental depression. The primary advantage of the drug is its low cost. However, it is used less extensively as more effective and less hazardous drugs become available.

GUANETHEDINE

Guanethedine is an extremely potent antihypertensive drug. It interferes with the usual action of the sympathetic nervous system and causes dilation of the veins, pooling of blood in the venous system, and decreased work action by the heart. Since the heart rate is slowed, less blood is pumped into the system and the blood pressure decreases.

Since guanethedine causes the veins to relax and store the blood, it is more effective when the person is in the upright position. Low blood pressure (postural hypotension) may be experienced when a person using this drug is standing or walking. Another troublesome side effect is diarrhea, which may be a particular problem when high dosages of this drug are necessary. Men may also notice indirect interference with sexual function when high doses of guanethedine are necessary. These side effects can usually be avoided or eliminated when the dosage of guanethedine is small, and it therefore is usually used to supplement other drugs in the treatment of severe hypertension.

OTHER DRUGS

There are a number of other antihypertensive drugs currently on the market with similar or different modes of action. Among these are clonidine and prazosin. Clonidine is a potent compound that acts mainly on the brain centers that regulate the autonomic (automatic) nerves, and it reduces heart output and constriction of the blood vessels. Clonidine and prazosin have been introduced relatively recently, and their modes of action and side effects are not as well described as the previously mentioned antihypertensive agents.

COMBINATION THERAPY

Each of the drugs used in antihypertensive therapy, depending on its potency, how much is given, and how well you respond to its actions, produces a certain effect in lowering the blood pressure. Because people respond to medication in a very individual way, it is not always possible for your physician to inform you in advance what effect, if any, the drug will have on you. Therefore a trial period of weeks or even months may be necessary before you and your doctor can determine what may be the best drug or combination of drugs for your individual problem. The goal is to return your blood pressure to a normal level. It is extremely important that your blood pressure be maintained at a normal level for the indefinite future in order to prevent the complications of hypertension.

In the treatment of high blood pressure, most physicians start their patients with a diet emphasizing control of sodium intake. For persons with mild hypertension, diet and diuretics will usually result in a normal blood pressure. If the blood pressure is not properly controlled, the diuretic will usually be continued along with a diet, and other blood-pressure-lowering medications will be added to your treatment program. Most if not all antihypertensive drugs work better if good dietary sodium control is maintained. Too much salt in the diet is the single greatest cause for drug treatment failure.

The fact that you may be taking two or more antihypertensive drugs should not worry you.

Some people require more medications than others to control their hypertension. The important concern is that you have sufficient treatment to keep your blood pressure normal and at the same time experience as few side effects as possible from your treatment program.

DRUG-DRUG INTERACTIONS

When drugs are given alone, they may have different effects than when two or more medications are used for the same or different problems. Sometimes the result is desirable, as in the use of a thiazide diuretic in combination therapy. That is, the thiazide diuretic may cooperate with other drugs to enhance the antihypertensive effect. On other occasions, the combination of two different drugs may result in an undesired action.

An example of a potentially serious drug-drug reaction is the use of a thiazide diuretic for antihypertensive therapy in a patient who requires digitalis for the management of a co-existent heart problem. Abnormal heart rhythms are more frequent when digitalis and thiazide diuretics are used. This is especially true if the serum potassium level becomes low. Therapy under these circumstances must be carefully tailored to the individual patient's needs.

The American public commonly uses medications for tension, anxiety, or depression. Some of the tranquilizer drugs have the potential for adverse drug-drug interactions with antihypertensive agents. The frequently used tricyclic antidepressants when used in combination with guanethedine may negate the effect of the guanethedine. Another example is the interaction between salicylates and spironolactone—the diuretic antihypertensive effect of spironolactone may be ameliorated or even lost as a result of aspirin therapy.

The greater the number of drugs being used

by a patient, the greater the potential for a possible drug-drug interaction. So it is extremely important that you report to your physician any prescription drug or any so-called "over the counter" drug that you may be taking.

NUTRITIONAL APPROACH TO BLOOD PRESSURE CONTROL

Is drug therapy *always* necessary in controlling high blood pressure? The answer is obviously "no." As was pointed out earlier, obese people with high blood pressure can sometimes reduce their blood pressure by losing weight. The hypertensive who consumes 300 mEq of sodium a day may have his blood pressure return to normal or near-normal level when he follows a diet of 90 mEq or less of sodium (2 grams). Ninety (90) mEq of sodium probably represents the maximum desirable intake for any individual with high blood pressure. When drug therapy is required, as it is in most patients with moderate or severe hypertension, a controlled sodium diet is the foundation upon which your physician prefers to build an appropriate drug therapy program. If the sodium content of your diet is kept at a reasonable level, you probably will need less medicine.

There are other aspects of a non-drug treatment of high blood pressure that are of major importance. Cigarette smoking, high cholesterol, lack of exercise, and tension, alone or in combination, may play a part in making your high blood pressure problem more dangerous. It is very important that consideration be given to all these risk factors as you and your physician develop your individualized treatment program. Most importantly, drug treatment should not be considered as a substitute for good health habits.

Notice the priorities: First, a change in lifestyle; then subsequent drug therapy as necessary to get the blood pressure down to a normal level and keep it there. The objective of every physician, with patient cooperation, is an individualized approach to each particular person, so that the blood pressure is lowered as safely as possible with a minimum amount of therapeutic manipulation. Unfortunately, this objective is not always attained, usually because of failure to establish a satisfactory nutritional approach, alone or in conjunction with drug therapy.

Good nutrition is a difficult goal in our mobile society, which stresses "fast food" preparation and eats more and more meals away from the home. It is becoming apparent that the education of the patient and his family in good nutrition is an important part of the treatment program. Until recently, physicians have not had readily available an easy-to-follow nutritional program that would allow the patient to control his calories, sodium, cholesterol, and dietary fat intake without drastically changing his lifestyle. Now most physicians start antihypertensive therapy by urging the development of good health habits, especially a sound nutritional program, and then adding an oral thiazide diuretic agent. When necessary, the physician will use additional therapy in a step-by-step fashion in order to tailor the program for the individual patient.

Remember, the purpose of the diuretic is to increase the elimination of excess salt and water. But it has been demonstrated that if the patient consumes 150 mEq (about 3.5 grams) or more of sodium a day, the average dose of an oral diuretic is unlikely to result in a normal blood pressure. If the diuretic dosage must be increased, side effects and complications from the drug increase in frequency and severity. In a series of studies at the Mayo Clinic in which patients failed to maintain a normal blood pressure with two or more antihypertensive agents, we found that the average sodium intake was

250 mEq per day. Furthermore, a large percentage of patients with mild hypertension could maintain a normal blood pressure without *any* medication when their dietary sodium intake was consistently less than 90 mEq (2 grams) per day.

Most patients with high blood pressure could achieve a good, if not excellent, response if they could adapt to the lifestyle necessary for adherence to the Spartan rice and fruit diet advocated by Kempner. But few of us are willing to make this degree of commitment. So we compromise by following a total therapeutic program which includes proper nutritional *and* drug therapy. It is a program that really isn't that difficult to follow. It does call for a change in lifestyle, but it is successful for those who follow it.

A NATIONWIDE PROBLEM

The challenge is quite clear. Hypertension is easily diagnosed and it can be controlled with modern nutritional and drug therapy. When high blood pressure is reduced to normal levels, premature death from heart attack, kidney failure, and stroke can be prevented. Yet, too many people with high blood pressure do not achieve good treatment results.

Unfortunately, the dropout rate for hypertensive patients is discouragingly high. Successful patient adherence to a good treatment program requires proper education and motivation. The person with hypertension must understand the importance of *staying* on his regimen and visiting his doctor or clinic regularly.

High blood pressure is a nationwide problem afflicting more than 23 million Americans of all ages. Of these 23 million, more than 15 million are not being treated adequately, and many do not even know that they have hypertension.

Tackling this nationwide problem calls for a nationwide program. This has been undertaken with good success by the National High Blood Pressure Education Program, a joint effort between the National Heart, Lung, and Blood Institute, several volunteer agencies, the principal medical societies, the pharmaceutical industry, and other health-related groups. The major goals of this national program have been to alert the public to the magnitude of the problem of high blood pressure and to improve therapeutic compliance for those hypertensives who know they have the condition.

The National High Blood Pressure Education Program will be successful only if you, the person with high blood pressure, are more informed about the nature of your problem and the measures necessary to control the disease.

SUMMARY

A better understanding of the nutritional approach to the management of high blood pressure will assist you and your physician in the treatment of your problem. We recommend to you the nutritional programs outlined in this book with the hope that they will be of assistance to you in the development of a dietary program suited to your individual needs.

You must see your physician regularly. You must follow your diet faithfully. And you must use the medications prescribed by your physician even when you feel well. Above all, you must learn more about your high blood pressure problem and assume individual responsibility for your own health maintenance. Remember, uncontrolled high blood pressure can lead to stroke, heart attack, or kidney failure. Yet high blood pressure *can* be controlled with proper treatment. And though this treatment must be daily and lifelong, successful treatment can mean a long and healthy life. *It's up to you.*

4.Your Controlled Sodium Meal Plan–The Use of Food Groups

TO ASSURE a balanced nutritional intake, and for ease of understanding and for flexible meal planning, all food considered here is divided into seven categories. These are as follows:
1. Meat and meat substitutes
2. Milk and milk products
3. Bread, cereals and starchy vegetables
4. Fats
5. Vegetables
6. Fruits
7. Caloric Supplements
We call each of these categories a Food Group and they form the basis of your nutritional program. Foods listed in each Food Group contain approximately the same amount of sodium when the correct serving portions are used. Portions of foods are often just as important as the kind of food. This is all part of the concept of controlled food intake. Be sure to check the portion size listed next to each food item in the food groups and at the bottom of each recipe. In addition, each food group contains approximately the same amount of sodium, fat, and calories, as well as similar minerals and vitamins. Therefore, for all practical purposes, the foods included in each group are interchangeable when served in the portion specified. Examples are given below.

Meat Group: 1 serving equals ¾ cup cottage cheese OR 3 ounces of beef.

Vegetable Group: 1 serving equals ½ cup green beans OR ½ small head of lettuce.

Bread Group: 1 serving equals 1 slice of bread OR 1 small potato.

Fruit Group: 1 serving equals ½ cup orange juice OR ½ small grapefruit.

Fat Group: 1 serving equals 1 teaspoon polyunsaturated margarine OR 1 teaspoon polyunsaturated cooking oil.

No one Food Group can supply all the nutrients needed for a well-balanced diet. The food in each group contributes different necessary nutrients. It takes all of them working together as a team to supply the nutritional needs for good health. A balanced diet will contain poultry, fish, and meat, vegetables and fruit, breads and cereals, and some dairy products. Each person is an individual with his own particular needs, so your physician or dietitian will instruct you on the exact make-up of your individual diet. If you do not find certain foods included in the Food Groups, it is because these foods contain excessive sodium, saturated fat, cholesterol, or calories. So in some instances, your meal plan may not allow you the kinds and amounts of foods you may be accustomed to eating and you may have to make some minor adjustments in your life style. But there is evidence that if you change and adopt a lifestyle that reflects your concern for your condition (hypertension), you can expect to live a *longer*, more enjoyable life with less chance of developing the consequences of hypertension.

All this does not mean you have to give up all the good things in life or live a life devoid of good foods and good cheer. It may involve some changes in your way of living, but it can be relatively painless if you follow the advice and recipes given in this book. It cannot be a hit-or-miss affair, but involves a commitment to yourself and to your family that you are going to live a *long*, full life. A normal life expectancy is well worth making the effort.

If you follow your meal plan carefully, you need not worry about getting too much or not enough of the controlled nutrients. All this is taken care of for you, because it is built into your program. We hope that you will soon be devising your own meal plans to fit your personal tastes and changing life patterns. For example, your eating schedule will be different when you are traveling or vacationing than when you are eating three meals a day at home. Once you know your program well and understand the reasons for it, you should be able to adjust your plan to meet your needs. Check the Appendices of this book for such things as ways to adapt meal plans, recipes, and eating away from home to your particular program, and to find out how to include in your program foods not contained in the Food Groups or in this book. The Appendices will also give you information on where to find special dietary foods and how to change the amount of sodium in your diet.

DIET PRESCRIPTION

Here is your diet prescription for a controlled sodium intake. These instructions are intended for you and no one else. Remember that a diet that may help one person may harm another.

Sodium _____ mEq or _____ mg.
Calories _____ kcal
Potassium _____ mEq or _____ mg.

Fat _____ grams

YOUR WEIGHT

Your physician has estimated your ideal weight to be _____ pounds. (_____ kilograms.) You should weigh yourself in the morning before breakfast without clothes. If your scale registers a difference of _____ pounds or more from the morning before, follow your physician's instructions concerning changes in weight.

MEASURING FOOD

Standard measuring equipment is all that is needed for measuring food portions unless you are instructed otherwise by your physician or dietitian.

MILLIEQUIVALENTS

A milliequivalent (mEq) is a unit of measure used for calculating sodium and potassium content of foods. It is not a unit that you will be measuring, but it is important for you to be able to convert milligrams (mg—the form in which many labels state sodium and potassium) into milliequivalents in order to facilitate incorporating foods into your particular dietary program.

$$\text{mEq sodium} = \frac{\text{mg sodium (x 1)}}{23}$$

$$\text{mEq potassium} = \frac{\text{mg potassium (x 1)}}{39}$$

$$\text{mg sodium} = \frac{\text{mEq sodium x 23}}{1}$$

$$\text{mg potassium} = \frac{\text{mEq potassium x 39}}{1}$$

WATER SUPPLY

Softened water and some water supplies are very high in sodium content. This may or may not be a problem, depending on the degree of sodium control in your diet. If your program calls for less than 40 mEq Sodium (1 gram), check with your physician or dietitian. The local water company will be able to answer your questions about the sodium content of local water.

FOOD GROUPS DETAILED

The seven (7) Food Groups are detailed in the following pages. Your physician or dietitian will outline your nutritional program as it involves these groups. If these spaces have not been filled in, please request your physician, dietitian, or health professional to do so. Sample nutritional programs incorporating the Food Groups begin on Page 39.

LEAN MEAT (and Meat Substitutes) GROUP

Meat, poultry, fish and eggs are important sources of protein, iron, vitamin B$_{12}$, and other B-complex vitamins. Liver and eggs also contain vitamin A. Oysters and peanut butter contain magnesium. Liver is a good source of iron and both liver and peanut butter contain folacin. Zinc is found in lean beef, crab, liver, peanut butter, oysters, and dark meat of turkey.

Be certain to select lean cuts of meat and trim off *all* visible fat and skin. Measure meat after it has been cooked. A three ounce serving of cooked meat is equal to approximately four ounces of raw meat.

Each controlled serving in this group is equivalent to 3 ounces of meat and contains approximately:

- 3 mEq sodium, unsalted (70 mg sodium)
- 9 mEq sodium salted (¼ tsp salt per pound) (207 mg sodium)
- 200 calories

If meat is prepared with fat, omit the equivalent number of fat servings.

_____servings from the Meat Group each day.

Divide as follows:

BREAKFAST	NOON MEAL	EVENING MEAL

FOOD	AMOUNT
Beef	3 ounces
Egg Substitutes*	3 tablespoons (47 grams)
Egg White	2
Lamb	3 ounces
Pork	3 ounces
Veal	3 ounces
Poultry: Capon, Chicken, Guinea Hen, Pheasant, Turkey	3 ounces
Fish: Any fresh or frozen	3 ounces
Mackerel, Salmon, Tuna, canned, water pack	¾ cup

Peas, dried, cooked	¾ cup
Dried beans	¾ cup
Peanut butter, unsalted or fresh ground	
(omit 1 fat serving)	2 tablespoons

Do not use the following for more than 2 servings per week:

Heart	3 ounces
Kidneys	3 ounces
Liver	3 ounces
Sweetbreads	3 ounces
Crab, fresh, cooked	3 ounces
Clams, fresh	3 ounces
Lobster, fresh, cooked	3 ounces
Oyster, fresh	3 ounces
Scallops, fresh	3 ounces
Eggs, fresh, whole (75 calories)	1 egg

Avoid: canned, commercially prepared, salt-cured and koshered meats

*Check individual labels for nutrient comparison information. Currently, according to their labels, the three nationally available products contain:

	SODIUM	CALORIES
3 Tablespoons Egg Beaters	3.5 mEq	78
3 Tablespoons Second Nature Imitation Eggs	3.0 mEq	37
3 Tablespoons Scramblers	5.1 mEq	55

Egg Substitutes
Note: In developing and testing the recipes in this book, considerations of accuracy, reliability, and nutrient composition dictated the use of a single egg substitute. If this product is unavailable in your area, you may try others—but adjustments may need to be made. Check labels for nutrient composition and cooking instructions.

MILK (and Dairy Products) GROUP

Milk is the leading source of calcium. It is a good source of phosphorus, protein, some of the B-complex vitamins, including folacin and vitamin B_{12} and vitamins A and D. Magnesium is also found in milk.

The milk shown on your meal plan can be used to drink, to add to cereal, in coffee or tea, or with other foods.

Each controlled serving in this group is equivalent to 1 cup of milk and contains approximately:
$\begin{cases} \text{6 mEq sodium} \\ \text{(115 mg sodium)} \\ \text{70 or 150 calories} \end{cases}$

_____Servings from Milk Group each day.

Divide as follows:

BREAKFAST	NOON MEAL	EVENING MEAL

FOOD	AMOUNT
I 70 calories	
Skim Milk	1 cup
Skim Milk, powdered, dry	2 tablespoons
2% milk	½ cup
1% milk	¾ cup
Parmesan cheese	1 heaping tablespoon
Creamed cottage cheese	¼ cup
II 150 calories	
Whole Milk	1 cup
Evaporated milk, unsweetened, canned	½ cup
Low fat yogurt	1 cup
Chocolate skim milk	¾ cup
Sour ½ & ½	½ cup
Ice cream	½ cup
Ice milk	¾ cup
Whole chocolate milk	¾ milk

BREAD (Cereal and Starchy Vegetables) GROUP

Whole grain or enriched breads and cereals are good sources of iron and some of the B vitamins, as are dried beans and peas and the vegetables on this list. Magnesium is found in dried cooked beans and whole grain cereals. Dried beans, peas, and lentils are sources of zinc. Dried peas and beans, and whole grain breads and cereals are excellent sources of fiber.

Each controlled serving from this group is equivalent to 1 slice of bread and contains approximately:
{ 1, 5 or 10 mEq sodium
(23, 115 or 230 mg sodium)
70 calories

_____Servings from Bread Group each day.

Divide as follows:

BREAKFAST	NOON MEAL	EVENING MEAL	SNACK

FOOD	AMOUNT
1 mEq sodium (23 mg sodium)	
Unsalted corn flakes	½ cup
Puffed rice, unsalted	¾ cup
Puffed wheat, unsalted	¾ cup
Shredded wheat, unsalted	½ ounce
Oatmeal, cooked, no salt	½ cup
Corn grits, cooked, no salt	½ cup
Popcorn, plain, no salt	1 cup
Tortilla	3
Salt free soda crackers	2
Unsalted bread	1 slice
Spaghetti, cooked, no salt	3 cup
Egg noodles, cooked, no salt	⅓ cup
Macaroni, cooked, no salt	⅓ cup
Rice, cooked, no salt	⅓ cup
Cornmeal, dry	2 tablespoons
Flour	2½ tablespoons
Wheat germ	3 tablespoons
Corn, fresh cooked	⅓ cup

Corn, canned, low sodium	⅓ cup
frozen, cooked	⅓ cup
on the cob	1 small
Lima beans, fresh cooked	⅓ cup
canned, low sodium	⅓ cup
Parsnips, cooked	½ cup
Potatoes, baked	1 small
pared, boiled	½ cup
Potatoes, french fried, no salt	
(omit 1 fat serving)	5
Pumpkin, canned	¾ cup
Peas, canned, low sodium	½ cup
Squash, winter, baked	½ cup
Sweet potato, baked in skin	¼ cup

II 5 mEq sodium (115 mg sodium)

Puffed rice, honey coated	¾ cup
Graham crackers	2
Bread, white	1 slice
French	1 slice
Italian	1 slice
whole wheat	1 slice
rye	1 slice
raisin	1 slice
Muffin, plain	1 small
Bread crumbs, dry	¼ cup
English muffins	½ muffin
Corn, regular, canned	⅓ cup
Peas, frozen, cooked	½ cup
Mixed vegetables, frozen, cooked	½ cup
Sweet potato, vacuum pack	⅓ cup
Dried beans, peas, lentils	¼ cup

III 10 mEq sodium (230 mg sodium)

Wheat flakes	⅝ cup
Wheat and malted barley flakes	¾ cup
Bran flakes	½ cup
Corn flakes	¾ cup
Puffed oats	¾ cup
Oat flakes	½ cup
Oatmeal, cooked	½ cup
Corn grits, cooked	½ cup

Corn bread	1½ inch piece
Roll, plain	1 large
Hamburger buns	1 bun
Lima beans, regular, canned	⅓ cup
Potatoes, rice, noodles, macaroni, spaghetti, (cooked with ⅛ teaspoon salt)	½ cup

VEGETABLE GROUP

Dark green and deep yellow vegetables are leading sources of vitamin A. Some vegetables such as asparagus, broccoli, brussel sprouts, cauliflower, cabbage, green peppers, greens and tomatoes contain vitamin C. Green leafy vegetables contain folacin, and broccoli, cabbage, carrots, spinach and tomatoes are good sources of vitamin B_6. Brussel sprouts, greens, tomatoes and broccoli contain potassium. Spinach is a source of zinc, and magnesium is found in green beans, broccoli and tomatoes. Vegetables are good sources of fiber.

Serve vegetables cooked or raw. If fat is added in preparation, omit the equivalent number of fat exchanges. If salt is used in preparation, use ⅛ teaspoon per ½ cup and add 11 mEq (253 mg) sodium per ½ cup cooked vegetable.

Each controlled serving from this group is equivalent to ½ cup beans and contains approximately:
{
1 mEq sodium, unsalted (23 mg sodium)
12 mEq sodium salted (275 mg sodium)
(⅛ teaspoon salted per ½ cup)
25 calories

_____servings from the Vegetable Group each day.

Divide as follows:

NOON MEAL	EVENING MEAL

FOOD	AMOUNT
Asparagus, fresh cooked	½ cup
canned, low sodium	½ cup
Bean sprouts	½ cup
Broccoli, fresh, cooked	½ cup
frozen, cooked	½ cup

Beans, snap, fresh, cooked	½ cup
canned, low sodium	½ cup
frozen, cooked	½ cup
Brussel sprouts, fresh cooked	½ cup
frozen cooked	½ cup
Cabbage, cooked	½ cup
Cauliflower, fresh, cooked	½ cup
frozen cooked	½ cup
Cucumbers, raw	1 cup
Eggplant, cooked	½ cup
Chicory greens, raw	1 cup
Endive	1 cup
Romaine or escarole	1 cup
Lettuce, head type	1 cup
Green peppers	½ cup
Greens: collard	½ cup
mustard	½ cup
Kohlrabi, raw	½ cup
Mushrooms	½ cup
Okra, raw	½ cup
cooked	½ cup
Onion, raw	½ cup
Parsley	½ cup
Peas, fresh, cooked	⅓ cup
Radishes	½ cup
Rhubarb, raw	1 cup
Rutabagas, cooked	½ cup
Summer squash, cooked	¾ cup
Tomatoes, raw	½ cup
Tomato juice, canned, low sodium	½ cup
Turnips, cooked	½ cup
Vegetable juice cocktail (unsalted)	1 cup
Zucchini, cooked	1 cup

Do not use the following for more than 1 serving per day:

Artichokes, cooked	½ cup
Beets, fresh, cooked	⅓ cup
canned, low sodium	⅓ cup
Carrots, raw	½ cup
fresh cooked	½ cup
Celery	½ cup
Chinese cabbage, raw	1 cup

Greens: beet	½ cup
chards	½ cup
dandelion, raw	½ cup
Kale	½ cup
Spinach	1 cup
Turnips	½ cup
Watercress	1 cup

Starchy vegetables are contained in the Bread Group.

FRUIT GROUP

Fruits are valuable for vitamins and minerals and fiber. Oranges, tangerines, grapefruit, strawberries, cantaloupe and honeydew melons are good sources of vitamin C. Apricots and peaches contain vitamin A. Mangoes and papaya contain both vitamin A and vitamin C. Bananas, nectarines, oranges, plums, and dried fruits are sources of potassium. Cantaloupe, oranges and strawberries contain folacin. Magnesium and vitamin B_6 are found in bananas.

Each controlled serving in this group is equivalent to ½ cups orange juice and contains approximately:
- trace sodium
- 40 calories

_____Servings from the Fruit Group each day.

Divide as follows:

BREAKFAST	NOON MEAL	EVENING MEAL	SNACK

FOOD	AMOUNT
Apple	1 small
Apple juice	⅓ cup
Applesauce, unsweetened	½ cup
Apricots raw	2 medium
Apricots, dried	4 halves
Banana	½ small
Blackberries, canned, artificially sweetened	½ cup
Raspberries, fresh	½ cup
Blueberries, fresh	½ cup

Strawberries fresh	¾ cup
Cherries, fresh	10
Cranberries	½ cup
Dates	2
Figs, fresh	1 large
Figs, dried	2
Grapefruit	½ medium
Grapefruit juice	½ cup
Grapes, fresh	12
Grape juice	¼ cup
Mangoes	½ small
Melon: Cantaloupe	¼ small
Honeydew melon	⅛ medium
Watermelon	1 cup
Nectarines	1 large
Orange	1 small
Orange juice	½ cup
Papaya	1 medium
Peach	1 medium
Pear	1 small
Persimmon	1 medium
Pineapple	½ cup
Pineapple juice	⅓ cup
Plums	2 medium
Prunes	2 medium
Prune juice	¼ cup
Raisins	2 tablespoons
Rhubarb, raw	1½ cups
Tangerine	1 large

FAT GROUP

Since all fats are high in calories, foods on this list should be measured carefully to control weight. Margarine, butter, cream and cream cheese contain vitamin A.

Each controlled serving from this group is equi- { less than 1 mEq sodium (23 mg)
valent to 1 teaspoon vegetable oil and contains { 45 calories
approximately:

_____Servings from the Fat Group each day

FOOD	AMOUNT
Avocado (4 inches in diameter)	⅛
Margarine, unsalted	1 teaspoon
Mayonnaise, unsalted	1 teaspoon
Salad dressing, mayonnaise type, unsalted	2 teaspoons
Oil, corn, cottonseed, safflower, soy, sunflower	1 teaspoon
Oil, olive	1 teaspoon
Oil, peanut, unsalted	1 teaspoon
Almonds, unsalted	10 whole
Pecans, unsalted	2 large whole
Peanuts	
Spanish	20 whole
Virginia	10 whole
Walnuts, unsalted	6 small
Nuts, other, unsalted	6 small

The following are equal to 2 mEq sodium (46 mg)

Margarine, regular	1 teaspoon
soft	1 teaspoon
Mayonnaise, regular	1 teaspoon
Salad dressing, commercial, mayonnaise type	2 teaspoons

CALORIC SUPPLEMENT GROUP (including Beverages)

The listed foods and beverages contain only trace amounts of sodium. The calories per listed serving are given next to each item. Since coffee and tea contain only negligible calories, you may use them as desired unless otherwise directed by your physician.

If your caloric intake is controlled, calculate each item into your daily intake.

FOOD	AMOUNT	CALORIES
Sugar	1 teaspoon	20
Honey	1 teaspoon	20
Hard candy	1 piece	20
Jelly	1 tablespoon	40
Jam	1 tablespoon	40
Gingerale	1 cup	75
Colas	1 cup	95
Fruit flavored sodas	1 cup	110
Root beer	1 cup	100
Sherbet	½ cup	120
Fruit ice	½ cup	75
Popsicle	1 twin bar	95
Kool-aid	1 cup	90
Syrup, cane,	2 tablespoons	90
Syrup, corn	2 tablespoons	100
Syrup, maple (2 mEq Sodium)	2 tablespoons	90
Molasses, cane, medium	2 tablespoons	80
Beer, 3.6*	12 ounces	150
Alcohol, 80 proof	1½ ounces	105
86 proof	1½ ounces	115
90 proof	1½ ounces	120
94 proof	1½ ounces	125
100 proof	1½ ounces	130
	6 ounces	245
Wine,* Dessert	6 ounces	150
Table		

*The sodium in beer and wine must be calculated into your daily intake (approximate content: 1 mEq [23 mg] sodium per cup).

5.Sample Programs & Menus: 40 & 90 mEq Sodium at Three Caloric Levels

I N THE following pages, suggested 40 and 90 mEq sodium dietary programs are outlined. These programs are calculated at three caloric levels: 1000, 1500, and 2000 calories. Dietary programs begin on page 43.

Please note that the first three charts in this chapter (on pages 40, 41, and 42) are left blank for your personal use as determined by your physician and dietitian.

The sample menus begin on page 49.

DAILY MEAL PLAN FOR: _____

DATE: _____

DIETITIAN: _____

DAILY ALLOWANCE

Sodium _____ mEq

Calories _____ kcal

Food Group	Breakfast	Noon Meal	Evening Meal	Snack
Meat or Substitute serving				
Milk or Substitute servings				
Bread or Substitute servings				
Vegetables servings				
Fruits servings				
Fat servings				
Caloric supplements extra calories per day				
Salt teaspoons per day				

DAILY MEAL PLAN FOR: _____

DATE: _____

DIETITIAN: _____

DAILY ALLOWANCE

Sodium _____ mEq

Calories _____ kcal

Food Group	Breakfast	Noon Meal	Evening Meal	Snack
Meat or Substitute serving				
Milk or Substitute servings				
Bread or Substitute servings				
Vegetables servings				
Fruits servings				
Fat servings				
Caloric supplements extra calories per day				
Salt				

DAILY MEAL PLAN FOR: _____

DATE: _____

DIETITIAN: _____

DAILY ALLOWANCE

Sodium _____ mEq

Calories _____ kcal

Food Group	Breakfast	Noon Meal	Evening Meal	Snack
Meat or Substitute serving				
Milk or Substitute servings				
Bread or Substitute servings				
Vegetables servings				
Fruits servings				
Fat servings				
Caloric supplements extra calories per day				
Salt teaspoons per day				

40 mEq (1000 mg) SODIUM, 1000 CALORIES DIETARY PATTERN

DAILY MEAL PLAN FOR: _____

DATE: _____

DIETITIAN: _____

DAILY ALLOWANCE

Sodium	40 mEq
Calories	1010 kcal

Food Group	Breakfast	Noon Meal	Evening Meal	Snack
Meat or Substitute 2 servings		1	1	
Milk or Substitute 2 servings	1 (Group I)	1 (Group I)		
Bread or Substitute 3 servings	1 (Group I)	1 (Group II)	1 (Group II)	
Vegetables 2 servings		1	1†	
Fruits 3 servings	1	1	1	
Fat 2 servings		1	1	
Caloric supplements extra calories per day				
Salt teaspoons per day				

†Salted.
90 mEq sodium—add ½ teaspoon salt and use salted margarine.

90 mEq SODIUM (2000 mg), 1000 CALORIES DIETARY PATTERN

DAILY MEAL PLAN FOR: _____

DATE: _____

DIETITIAN: _____

DAILY ALLOWANCE

Sodium   87 mEq

Calories   1010 kcal

Food Group	Breakfast	Noon Meal	Evening Meal	Snack
Meat or Substitute 2 servings		1†	1†	
Milk or Substitute 2 servings	1 (Group I)	1 (Group I)		
Bread or Substitute 3 servings	1 (Group III)	1 (Group II)	1 (Group II)	
Vegetables 2 servings		1	1†	
Fruits 3 servings	1	1	1	
Fat 2 servings		1†	1†	
Caloric supplements extra calories per day				
Salt ¼ teaspoons per day				

†Salted.

40 mEq SODIUM (1000 mg), 1500 CALORIES DIETARY PATTERN

DAILY MEAL PLAN FOR: _____

DATE: _____

DIETITIAN: _____

DAILY ALLOWANCE

Sodium   39.5

Calories   1500

Food Group	Breakfast	Noon Meal	Evening Meal	Snack
Meat or Substitute 3 servings	1 egg or egg substitute*	1	1	
Milk or Substitute 1½ servings	1 (Group I)	½ (Group I)		
Bread or Substitute 4 servings	1 (Group I)	2 (Group II)	1 (Group II)	
Vegetables 3 servings		1	2	
Fruits 4 servings	1	2	1	
Fat 4 servings	1†	1†	2	
Caloric supplements 225 extra calories per day				
Salt teaspoons per day				

*This may be exchanged for 1 ounce of meat.
†Salted.
90 mEq sodium—add ½ teaspoon salt and salted margarine, or use salted meat and vegetables and unsalted margarine.

90 mEq SODIUM (2000 mg), 1500 CALORIES DIETARY PATTERN

DAILY MEAL PLAN FOR: _____

DATE: _____

DIETITIAN: _____

DAILY ALLOWANCE

Sodium	91.5 mEq
Calories	1505 kcal

Food Group	Breakfast†	Noon Meal	Evening Meal	Snack
Meat or Substitute 3 servings	1 egg or egg substitute*	1†	1†	
Milk or Substitute 1½ servings	1 (Group I)	½ (Group II)		
Bread or Substitute 5 servings	2 (1 Group I) (1 Group III)	2 (Group II)	1 (Group II)	
Vegetables 3 servings		1	2†	
Fruits 3 servings	1	1	1	
Fat 4 servings	1†	1†	2†	
Caloric supplements 200 extra calories per day				
Salt teaspoons per day				

*This may be exchanged for 1 ounce of meat.
†Salted.

40 mEq SODIUM (1000 mg), 2000 CALORIES DIETARY PATTERN

PROGRAMS, MENUS **47**

DAILY MEAL PLAN FOR: _____

DATE: _____

DIETITIAN: _____

DAILY ALLOWANCE

Sodium _____ 39.5 mEq

Calories _____ 2000 kcal

Food Group	Breakfast	Noon Meal	Evening Meal	Snack
Meat or Substitute 3 servings	1 egg or egg substitute*	1	1	
Milk or Substitute 1½ servings	1 (Group I)	½ (Group II)		
Bread or Substitute 6 servings	2 (Group I)	2 (Group II)	2 (1 Group I) (1 Group II)	
Vegetables 5 servings		2	3	
Fruits 6 servings	2	1	1	2
Fat 5 servings	1	2	2	
Caloric supplements 410 extra calories per day				
Salt teaspoons per day				

*This may be exchanged for 1 ounce of meat
90 mEq sodium—add ½ teaspoon salt and use salted margarine.

90 mEq SODIUM (2000 mg), 2000 CALORIES DIETARY PATTERN

DAILY MEAL PLAN FOR: _____

DATE: _____

DIETITIAN: _____

		DAILY ALLOWANCE	
		Sodium	91.5 mEq
		Calories	2000 kcal

Food Group	Breakfast	Noon Meal	Evening Meal	Snack
Meat or Substitute 3 servings	1 egg or egg substitute*	1†	1†	1†
Milk or Substitute 1½ servings	1 (Group I)	½ (Group II)		
Bread or Substitute 6 servings	2 (1 Group I) (1 Group III)	2 (Group II)	2 (1 Group I) (1 Group II)	
Vegetables 4 servings		2	2†	
Fruits 5 servings	1	2	1	1
Fat 5 servings	1†	2†	2†	
Caloric supplements 475 extra calories per day				
Salt teaspoons per day				

*This may be exchanged for 1 ounce of meat.
†Salted.

SAMPLE MENUS

40 mEq (1000 mg) SODIUM
1000 CALORIES

An asterisk preceding an entry indicates a recipe in this book. A dagger following an entry indicates a food salted in preparation.

MENU I

Breakfast:
½ grapefruit
¾ cup puffed rice
1 cup skim milk
coffee, 1 teaspoon sugar

Lunch:
*1 Hamburger
*1 serving Herbed Tomatoes
1 slice rye bread†
1 pear
coffee or tea

Dinner:
*1 serving Easy Grilled Chicken
*1 serving Tart Coleslaw
*1 serving Roastin' Ears
*1 serving Minted Pineapple
coffee or tea
plus ¼ scant teaspoon salt per day

MENU II

Breakfast:
½ cup orange juice
½ cup oatmeal†

1 cup skim milk
coffee or tea

Lunch:
*1 serving Chilled Melon Balls
*1 serving Potato Omelet
*1 serving Spinach Salad
½ cup skim milk

Dinner:
*1 serving Homestyle Pot Roast
½ cup broccoli†
*1 serving Double Fruit Whip
coffee or tea

MENU III

Breakfast:
½ cup grapefruit juice
*1 serving Poached Egg (imitation eggs)
1 slice toast†
1 teaspoon margarine†
coffee or tea

Lunch:
*1 serving Vegetable Soup
open face sandwich:
  1 slice bread
  lettuce, tomato
  2 ounces sliced turkey
  1½ teaspoons mayonnaise†
coffee or tea

Dinner:
*1 serving Baked Fish, lemon wedge
½ cup green beans†
*1 serving Cresson Salad
½ cup fresh blueberries
coffee or tea

SAMPLE MENUS

90 mEq (2000 mg) SODIUM
1000 CALORIES

MENU I

Breakfast:
⅛ medium honeydew melon
*1 serving Mushroom Omelet
1 slice toast†
1 teaspoon margarine†
coffee or tea

Lunch:
*1 serving Chicken Soufflé
*1 serving Tossed Green Salad
1 corn bread (1½" square)†
½ teaspoon margarine†
coffee or tea

Dinner:
3 ounce lamb chop†
*1 serving Parsleyed Potatoes
½ cup asparagus†
½ cup sliced tomatoes
coffee or tea
plus ½ scant teaspoon salt per day

MENU II

Breakfast:
½ cup orange juice
¾ cup cornflakes†
½ cup skim milk
1 slice toast†
1 teaspoon margarine†
coffee or tea

Lunch:
Salad:
  ½ cup cottage cheese
  1 tomato
  ½ head lettuce
*1 tablespoon Old Fashioned French Dressing
*2 Honey Whole Wheat Pan Rolls
coffee or tea

Dinner:
*1 serving Caribbean Chicken
*½ cup Mixed Green Salad
*1 teaspoon Zero Salad Dressing
1 cup zucchini†
¾ cup strawberries
coffee or tea
plus scant ½ teaspoon salt

MENU III

Breakfast:
½ small banana, sliced
½ cup bran flakes†
½ cup skim milk
*1 Cinnamon Roll (with salt)
coffee or tea

Lunch:
*1 serving Tomato Stuffed with Chicken Salad
1 large roll†
1 teaspoon margarine†
ice tea

Dinner:
1 serving grilled fish
*1 serving Tart Coleslaw
*1 serving Zippy Potato Salad
½ cup fresh fruit cup
coffee or tea
plus ½ teaspoon salt

SAMPLE MENUS

40 mEq (1000 mg) SODIUM
1500 CALORIES

MENU I

Breakfast:
½ grapefruit
1 poached egg
1 slice toast†
2 teaspoons margarine
coffee or tea, 1 teaspoon sugar

Lunch:
roast beef sandwich:
    2 slices rye bread†
    3 ounces roast beef
    lettuce, tomato
    2 teaspoons mayonnaise†
1 large apple
1 cup skim milk

Dinner:
1 cup fresh fruit cup
*1 serving Flounder with Lemon and Almonds
1 small baked potato
2 tablespoons sour cream
*1 serving Broiled Tomato
*1 serving Green Beans with Dill
*1 serving Emerald Ice
coffee or tea

MENU II

Breakfast:
½ cup orange juice
*Supernog (with imitation eggs)
1 slice whole wheat bread†
1 teaspoon margarine†
coffee or tea

Lunch:
*1 Fruit 'n' Tuna Sandwich
*1 Brownie
1 peach
1 cup skim milk

Dinner:
*1 serving Chilled Melon Balls
3 ounces roast turkey†
½ cup whipped potato†
⅓ cup fresh peas
1 teaspoon margarine†
*1 serving Cranberry Gelatin
*1 serving Zabaglione
coffee or tea

MENU III

Breakfast:
⅓ cup apple juice
½ cup cooked cereal†
*1 Cranberry Orange Muffin
1 teaspoon margarine†
1 cup skim milk
coffee or tea

Lunch:
Salad Plate:
    *1 serving Egg Salad
    *1 serving Asparagus Salad
    1 tomato, sliced
    on ¼ head lettuce
*2 teaspoons French Dressing
coffee or tea

Dinner:
*1 serving Meaty Spaghetti Sauce
¼ cup spaghetti, cooked†
*1 serving Tossed Green Salad
*1 tablespoon Vinaigrette Dressing
1 slice Italian bread†

1 small slice melon
coffee or tea

SAMPLE MENUS

**90 mEq (2000 mg) SODIUM
1500 CALORIES**

MENU I

Breakfast:
1 orange, sliced
½ cup bran flakes†
1 slice toast†
1 teaspoon margarine†
1 teaspoon jelly
½ cup skim milk
coffee, 2 teaspoons sugar

Lunch:
sandwich:
  2 slices rye bread†
  3 ounces turkey†
  lettuce, tomato
  1 tablespoon mayonnaise†
1 apple
½ cup skim milk

Dinner:
*1 serving Oven Poached Haddock
½ cup carrots, cooked†
*1 serving Broccoli Polonaise
*1 serving Zesty Lettuce Salad
coffee or tea, 2 teaspoons sugar
plus ¼ teaspoon salt for the day

MENU II

Breakfast:
½ cup orange juice

1 poached egg
1 slice toast†
1 teaspoon margarine†
¾ cup cornflakes†
½ cup skim milk
coffee, 2 teaspoons sugar

Lunch:
*1 serving Spanish Lobster Salad
1 roll†
1 teaspoon margarine†
¾ cup ice milk
ice tea, lemon

Dinner:
*1 serving Roast Lamb
1 potato, roasted†
1 teaspoon margarine†
*1 serving Grilled Eggplant
lettuce wedge
*2 tablespoons Zero Salad Dressing
1 slice honeydew melon
coffee or tea
plus ¼ teaspoon salt for the day

MENU III

Breakfast:
½ cup grapefruit sections
½ cup cooked cereal†
1 slice raisin toast†
1 teaspoon margarine†
1 cup skim milk
coffee, 2 teaspoons sugar

Lunch:
*1 serving Baked Tuna Fondue
*1 serving Fresh Bean Salad
1 tomato, sliced
1 teaspoon salad dressing†
1 peach, sliced
coffee or tea

Dinner:
*1 serving Meat Loaf
*1 serving Parsleyed Potatoes
*1 serving Exemplary Beets
½ cup tossed salad
*1 tablespoon Lemon Dressing
*1 serving Baked Apple
coffee or tea
plus scant ¼ teaspoon salt

SAMPLE MENUS

40 MEq (1000 mg) SODIUM
2000 CALORIES

MENU I

Breakfast:
⅔ cup apple juice
*1 serving Scrambled Egg
1 English muffin†
2 teaspoons margarine†
1 tablespoon jelly
1 cup skim milk
coffee, 1 teaspoon sugar

Lunch:
*1 serving Hamburger with Pepper and Onion
  Topper
*1 serving Zippy Potato Salad
¼ cup carrot sticks
¼ cup celery sticks
¾ cup fresh strawberries
*1 Brownie
1 cup skim milk

Dinner:
*1 serving Swedish Broiled Lamb Chops
*1 serving Crisscross Potato
1 teaspoon margarine†

*1 serving Green Beans with Dill
*1 serving Sunshine Salad
*1 serving Blueberry Lime Sundae
coffee or tea, 1 teaspoon sugar

MENU II

Breakfast:
½ cup orange juice
*2 slices French Toast (low sodium bread)
2 teaspoons margarine
½ cup maple syrup
1 cup skim milk
coffee, 2 teaspoons sugar

Lunch:
Sandwich:
  3 ounces roast beef
  lettuce, tomato
  2 teaspoons mayonnaise†
  2 slices whole wheat bread†
1 apple
*3 Lemon Squares
1 cup skim milk

Dinner:
*1 serving Bluefish Hampton
  lemon wedge
1 small baked potato
3 teaspoons margarine
*1 serving Italian Green Beans
*1 serving Mixed Green Salad with Lemon
  Dressing
*1 serving French Plums
coffee or tea, 1 teaspoon sugar

MENU III

Breakfast:
½ grapefruit
¾ cup puffed rice

*1 serving Streusel Coffee Cake
1 cup skim milk
1 teaspoon margarine†
coffee, 2 teaspoons sugar

Lunch:
*1 serving Chicken Noodle Soup
*1 serving Tuna Salad
1 plain muffin
1 teaspoon margarine†
*1 serving Golden Pound Cake
1 peach, sliced
½ cup skim milk

Dinner:
*1 serving Golden Banana Bowl
*1 serving Chicken in Mushroom Sauce
⅓ cup cooked rice
*1 serving Broiled Tomato
½ cup green beans†
⅛ honeydew melon with a lime wedge
coffee or tea

SAMPLE MENUS

90 mEq (2000 mg) SODIUM
2000 CALORIES

MENU I

Breakfast:
¼ cantaloupe
*2 Pancakes
2 teaspoons margarine
2 tablespoons pancake syrup
1 cup skim milk
coffee, 1 teaspoon sugar

Lunch:
½ cup fruit cup

3 ounces broiled fish†
lemon wedge
1 small baked potato
½ cup broccoli†
½ cup mixed green salad
2 teaspoons salad dressing†
1 roll
2 teaspoons margarine†
coffee or tea

Dinner:
*¼ cup Curry Dill Dip
1 cup assorted fresh vegetable sticks
3 ounces steak†
*1 serving Tomato Macaroni
⅓ cup frozen peas, cooked
*1 serving Minted Fruit Salad
plus ¼ teaspoon salt per day

MENU II

Breakfast:
1 cup orange juice
1 soft boiled egg
2 slices whole wheat toast†
2 teaspoons margarine†
1 tablespoon jelly
1 cup skim milk
coffee, 1 teaspoon sugar

Lunch:
1 hamburger (3 ounces)†
1 hamburger bun†
lettuce, tomato, onion slice
½ cup coleslaw†
½ cup vanilla ice cream
1 cup skim milk

Dinner:
*1 serving Ginger Fruit Cup
*1 serving Apple Pork Chop Roast

The recipe for Beer Crab Dip is on page 59.

The recipes for breads begin on page 81.

1 small baked sweet potato
2 teaspoons margarine†
½ cup spinach†
1 tomato, sliced
*2 teaspoons Old-Fashioned French Dressing
*1 serving Gingerbread
coffee or tea

MENU III

Brunch:
*1 serving Brunch Float
*1 serving Sizzling Grapefruit
*1 serving Ratatouille Omelet
1 English Muffin†
2 teaspoons margarine†

1 tablespoon jam
1 cup skim milk
coffee, 1 teaspoon sugar

Dinner:
*1 serving Macedoine of Winter Fruit
  with Glaze
4 ounces roast beef†
½ cup whipped potatoes†
½ cup asparagus†
*1 serving Caesar Salad
1 dinner roll†
2 teaspoons margarine†
*1 serving Apple Pie (¹/₆ of 8″ pie)
coffee or tea
plus ⅛ teaspoon salt for the day

Part Two:
The Recipes

6.Appetizers&Beverages

There is no real need to settle for routine or humdrum meals when these simple but effective recipes can be used to give them an appetizing extra dimension.

HAWAIIAN DIP

1 fresh pineapple
1 carton (8 ounces) low-fat orange yogurt
2 tablespoons brown sugar
1 pint strawberries

Cut thick slice from bottom and top of pineapple. Cut remaining pineapple into 1-inch slices; remove rind and core. Cut ¾ of rings into cubes; place in bowl. Cover and refrigerate.

Finely chop remaining rings. Mix chopped pineapple, the yogurt and sugar in small bowl. Cover and refrigerate to blend flavors.

Insert wooden picks in pineapple cubes. Arrange strawberries (with hulls) and pineapple cubes on serving plate. Place bowl with yogurt mixture in center. Guests spoon some of the yogurt mixture onto dessert plates, then dip pineapple and strawberries into mixture.

4 servings.

1 serving = ¼ milk, 2 fruit
145 calories

BEER CRAB DIP

1½ cups low-sodium mayonnaise
1 teaspoon Mustard (page 150)
¼ teaspoon Tabasco pepper sauce
Dash lemon juice
2 tablespoons beer or ale
1 package (6 ounces) frozen Alaska king crab meat, thawed and broken apart
Vegetable sticks

Mix mayonnaise, mustard, pepper sauce, lemon juice, and beer until smooth. Stir in crab meat. Serve with vegetable sticks.

4 servings.

1 serving (2 tablespoons) = ⅓ meat, 3 fat
110 calories

CURRY DILL DIP

½ cup low-sodium mayonnaise
½ cup dairy sour half-and-half
1 teaspoon fresh lemon or lime juice
1 teaspoon grated onion
1 teaspoon curry powder
½ teaspoon dill weed
½ teaspoon dry mustard
Vegetable sticks

Mix all ingredients except vegetable sticks. Cover and refrigerate at least 1 hour. Serve with vegetable sticks.

1 cup.

1 serving (1 tablespoon) = 1½ fat
45 calories

BLUSHING GRAPEFRUIT

1 medium grapefruit
1 teaspoon red currant jelly
1 teaspoon honey

Cut grapefruit in half; remove seeds. Cut around edges and sections to loosen fruit; remove centers. Mix jelly and honey and spread on grapefruit halves.

Set oven control at broil and/or 550°. Broil grapefruit with tops about 4 inches from heat until hot and bubbly, about 8 minutes. Serve hot.

2 servings.

Note: Add a sprinkle of nutmeg or cinnamon if you wish.

1 serving = 1 fruit
65 calories

SIZZLING GRAPEFRUIT

1 medium grapefruit
2 teaspoons unsalted margarine
2 teaspoons sugar
¼ teaspoon cinnamon
2 maraschino cherries

Cut grapefruit in half; remove seeds. Cut around edges and membranes of halves to loosen fruit; remove centers. Dot halves with margarine. Mix sugar and cinnamon and sprinkle on halves.

Set oven control at broil and/or 550°. Place halves in shallow baking pan. Broil with tops 4 to 6 inches from heat until juice bubbles and edge of peel turns light brown, about 8 minutes. Serve hot, topped with cherries.

2 servings.

1 serving = 1 fruit, 1 fat
105 calories

CHILLED MELON BALLS

1 large cantaloupe, chilled
1 lime, sliced

Scoop out balls from cantaloupe with melon ball cutter. Make 5 balls for each serving. Place in sherbet dishes and garnish with a slice of lime.

4 servings.

1 serving = ½ fruit
15 calories

MINTED MELON BALLS

3 cups cantaloupe and watermelon balls
¼ cup kirsch
½ cup sugar
1 tablespoon snipped mint
1 tablespoon crème de menthe

Mix all ingredients. Serve immediately.

6 servings.

1 serving = 1 fruit
115 calories

SPICED HONEYDEW MELON

2 cans (8 ounces each) pineapple chunks,
drained (reserve syrup)
1 teaspoon ginger
1 teaspoon cloves
1 honeydew melon

Heat reserved pineapple syrup, ginger, and cloves just to simmering. Cut off top of melon; remove seeds. Pour warm pineapple syrup into melon. Refrigerate 2 hours.

Drain melon, reserving syrup. Fill melon with pineapple chunks; pour In as much reserved syrup as possible.

6 servings.

1 serving = 1½ fruit
80 calories

TROPICAL FRUIT AND WINE COMPOTE

1 can (13½ ounces) pineapple chunks,
drained
1 medium grapefruit, pared and sectioned
2 small bananas, sliced
1 cup seeded Malaga grapes
¼ cup sugar
⅓ cup sherry
2 tablespoons Madeira

Gently mix fruits, sugar and wine. Cover and refrigerate.

6 servings.

1 serving = 1½ fruit
155 calories

GOLDEN BANANA BOWL

½ pineapple, cut into pieces
2 oranges, pared and sectioned
½ cup orange juice
1 tablespoon slivered crystallized ginger
2 bananas

Combine pineapple pieces, orange sections and ginger in bowl. Pour orange juice on fruits. Cover and chill.

Just before serving, slice bananas into bowl and mix lightly.

4 servings.

Note: To cut pineapple, twist out top; cut pineapple in half, then into quarters. Hold pineapple quarter securely, slice fruit from rind. Cut off pineapple core and remove any "eyes." For pieces, slice quarters lengthwise, then cut crosswise.

1 serving = 2 fruit
125 calories

MACEDOINE OF WINTER FRUIT WITH GLAZE

2 red apples
2 pears
1 pineapple, pared, cored, and cut into spears
2 grapefruit, pared and sectioned
4 oranges, pared and sectioned
Seedless green grapes and Tokay grapes
1 cup red currant jelly
2 tablespoons orange juice
¼ cup Galliano® liqueur

Slice unpared apples and pears into large bowl. Add remaining fruits.

Melt jelly in small saucepan over low heat, stirring constantly. Remove from heat; stir in orange juice and liqueur. Pour on fruit, carefully lifting fruit with fork so that all pieces will be glazed.

8 servings.

Note: If desired, dessert can be prepared ahead. Dip apple and pear slices into lemon or lime juice. Cover bowl of fruit and refrigerate. Glaze can be refrigerated and heated at serving time.

1 serving = 2 fruit
    220 calories

FRUIT KEBABS

12 pineapple chunks
12 cantaloupe balls
12 honeydew melon balls
12 strawberries
6 thin melon wedges

Place pineapple chunk, cantaloupe ball, honeydew melon ball and strawberry on each of 12 wooden skewers. Insert 2 skewers in each melon wedge.

6 servings.

1 serving = 1 fruit
    45 calories

GINGER FRUIT CUP

2 cans (8 ounces each) pineapple chunks in unsweetened pineapple juice
4 navel oranges, pared and sectioned
2 large pieces crystallized ginger, finely chopped
4 bananas

Place pineapple chunks (with juice), orange sections and ginger in bowl. Cover and refrigerate 8 hours.

Slice ½ banana into each sherbet dish. Spoon pineapple mixture and juice on slices. Serve with decorative picks.

8 servings.

1 serving = 2 fruit
    110 calories

STUFFED CHERRY TOMATOES

Cut off tops of cherry tomatoes and remove pulp, leaving a ¼-inch wall. Stuff each with Chicken Salad (page 111), Tuna Salad (page 115), or Egg Salad (page 109).

4 tomatoes with Chicken Salad = ½ vegetable, ¼ meat
60 calories

4 tomatoes with Tuna Salad = ½ vegetable, ¼ meat
55 calories

4 tomatoes with Egg Salad = ½ vegetable ¼ meat
40 calories

MIDDLE EASTERN MEATBALLS

1½ pounds ground lamb
2 cloves garlic, minced
3 tablespoons Second Nature imitation eggs*
Freshly ground pepper
1 tablespoon dry mustard
½ cup snipped parsley
2 tablespoons olive oil
Vegetable oil
Curry Dip (page 60)

Mix meat, garlic, imitation eggs, parsley, mustard and pepper. Moisten mixture with 1 tablespoon of the olive oil. Shape mixture into 48 small balls.

Heat remaining 1 tablespoon olive oil and just enough vegetable oil in large skillet to cover bottom. Brown meatballs in skillet, shaking skillet briskly to cook meatballs evenly. Serve with Curry Dip.

8 servings.

2 meatballs = ⅓ meat
120 calories

ARTICHOKES

Allow 1 artichoke for each serving. Remove any discolored leaves and the small leaves at base of artichoke; trim stem even with base of artichoke. Cutting straight across, slice 1 inch off top; discard top. Snip off points of the remaining leaves with scissors. Rinse artichoke under cold water.

Cook artichokes in large kettle. For 4 medium artichokes, heat 6 quarts water, 1 teaspoon salt and juice of 1 lemon to boiling. Add artichokes; heat to boiling. Reduce heat; simmer uncovered until leaves pull out easily and bottom is tender when pierced with a knife, 30 to 40 minutes. Remove artichokes carefully from water (use tongs or 2 large spoons); place upside down to drain. Remove choke (fuzzy center) from centers with a teaspoon. Serve with Lemon-Margarine Sauce (below).

Lemon-Margarine Sauce: Mix ½ cup unsalted margarine, melted, and 2 tablespoons lemon juice.

½ cup (enough for 4 artichokes).

1 serving = 1 vegetable
25 calories

* If this ingredient is not available in your market area, see page 29 for substitutes.

HOT MEATBALLS

Substitute ground round steak for lean ground beef in Hamburgers (page 118) and shape mixture into 1-inch balls.

Heat just enough vegetable oil in large skillet to cover bottom; brown meatballs in hot oil but do not cook through. Turn meatballs into chafing dish; keep warm. Serve with Dijon-type Mustard (page 150) and provide wooden picks for guests to spear meatballs.

2 meatballs = ¼ meat
75 calories

STEAMED CLAMS

Wash 6 pounds shell clams ("steamers") thoroughly, discarding any broken shell or open (dead) clams. Place in steamer with ½ cup boiling water. Cover and steam until clams open, 5 to 10 minutes. Serve hot in shells with melted unsalted margarine and cups of unsalted broth.

6 servings.

Note: If steamer is not available, add 1 inch water to kettle with clams. Cover tightly.

1 serving = 1 meat
100 calories

RAINBOW FLOAT

1 cup unsweetened tangerine or orange juice
1 cup cranberry cocktail
1 cup unsweetened pineapple juice
2 bottles (20 ounces each) ginger ale or club soda, chilled
Mint leaves

Pour each fruit juice into refrigerator tray; freeze to make 10 cubes of each juice. To serve, place 2 cubes of each juice in each of 5 tall glasses; pour ½ cup ginger ale into each. Serve with colored straws.

5 servings (about ¾ cup each).

Note: Flavor develops as juice cubes melt.

1 serving = trace sodium
150 calories

BRUNCH FLOAT

¼ cup lemon ice (1 small scoop)
⅓ cup orange juice
2 tablespoons carbonated lemon-lime beverage
Orange slice

Place lemon ice in 6-ounce glass. Pour in orange juice and lemon-lime beverage. Garnish with orange slice and serve immediately.

1 serving (about 1 cup).

1 serving = ½ fruit
115 calories

GLOW WINE

1 bottle (25 ounces) claret
½ cup plus 2 tablespoons sugar
¼ cinnamon stick
1 whole clove

Heat all ingredients, stirring until sugar is dissolved, just to simmering. Serve hot.

5 servings (about ⅔ cup each).

1 serving = trace sodium
230 calories

WINTER WARMER

1 bottle (25 ounces) claret
¾ cup sugar
Peel of 2 oranges (cut with vegetable parer)
¼ teaspoon cinnamon

Heat all ingredients, stirring until sugar is dissolved, just to simmering. Serve hot.

5 servings (about ⅔ cup each).

1 serving = trace sodium
250 calories

SUMMER COOLER

2 bottles (25 ounces each) Moselle, chilled
1 bottle (8 ounces) club soda, chilled
2 tablespoons sugar
1 lemon peel (cut from lemon in single spiral curl)
Juice of 1 lemon

Combine all ingredients; refrigerate until serving time.

10 servings (about ¾ cup each).

1 serving = trace sodium
140 calories

MULLED PINEAPPLE JUICE

3 cups pineapple juice
½ cup water
1 tablespoon honey
1 teaspoon lemon juice
Two 2-inch sticks cinnamon
4 whole cloves
¼ teaspoon allspice
Lemon twists
Stick cinnamon stirrers

Heat pineapple juice, water, honey, lemon juice, cinnamon sticks, cloves and allspice just to simmering; simmer 30 minutes. Remove cinnamon sticks and whole cloves with slotted spoon. Serve hot in mugs with lemon twists and cinnamon stirrers or chill and serve in glasses with ice cubes.

4 servings (about ¾ cup each).

1 serving = 1½ fruit
125 calories

LIME-APPLE COOLER

½ pint lime ice
¾ cup apple juice, chilled

Soften lime ice. Gradually stir in apple juice until mixture is smooth. Pour into chilled glasses. Nice served with stick cinnamon stirrers.

2 servings (about 1 cup each).

1 serving = 1 fruit
105 calories

TROPICAL FIZZ

**2 cups unsweetened grapefruit juice,
chilled**
1 cup unsweetened orange juice, chilled
½ cup unsweetened pineapple juice, chilled
1 bottle (12 ounces) club soda, chilled
Mint leaves

Mix fruit juices and soda. Serve in glasses with ice cubes or crushed ice and garnish with mint leaves.

6 servings (about ¾ cup each).

Note: If you do not have fresh mint, substitute a thin slice of orange, lemon or lime.

1 serving = 1 fruit
             60 calories

TANGY FRUIT JUICE COCKTAIL

⅔ cup water
⅔ cup sugar
3 cups unsweetened grapefruit juice
1½ cups unsweetened pineapple juice
1 cup lime juice
Mint leaves

Heat water and sugar to boiling, stirring until sugar is dissolved. Cool.

Mix sugar, water and juices. Pour into chilled glasses and garnish with mint leaves.

8 servings (about ¾ cup each).

Note: Sugar water and juices can be mixed in blender.

1 serving = 1 fruit
             130 calories

BANANA SNACK SHAKE

⅓ cup dry milk powder
½ cup iced water
1 banana, cut into pieces
2 teaspoons sugar
¼ teaspoon vanilla
4 ice cubes

Measure dry milk powder and iced water into blender container. Blend on low speed until mixed. Add banana pieces, sugar and vanilla; blend on high speed until smooth. Add ice cubes and blend on high speed until cubes are melted.

2 servings.

1 serving = 1 milk
             150 calories

BANANA-ORANGE DRINK

Place 1 banana, cut up, and 1 cup orange juice in blender container. Blend on high speed until smooth.

2 servings.

1 serving = 2 fruit
             105 calories

EGGNOG

**¼ cup Second Nature
  imitation eggs***
1 cup skim milk
1 tablespoon sugar
½ teaspoon vanilla

Mix all ingredients in tall glass.

1 serving.

1 serving = 1 milk, 1½ meat
             200 calories

* If this ingredient is not available in your market area, see page 29 for substitutes.

BANANA SHAKES

Banana Nog

¾ cup skim milk
1 banana, cut into pieces
1 egg white or 2 tablespoons Second Nature imitation eggs*
½ teaspoon vanilla

Place all ingredients in blender container. Blend on high speed until foamy.

1 serving.

1 serving = ¾ milk, ¾ meat
200 calories

Orange Shake

½ cup orange juice
½ cup skim milk
1 banana, cut into pieces
2 tablespoons Second Nature imitation eggs*
¼ cup crushed ice

Place all ingredients in blender container. Blend on high speed until foamy.

1 serving.

1 serving = ½ milk, ¾ meat
225 calories

Coffee Shake

½ cup skim milk
¼ teaspoon instant coffee
1 banana, cut into pieces
2 tablespoons Second Nature imitation eggs*
¼ cup crushed ice

Place all ingredients in blender container. Blend on high speed until foamy.

1 serving.

Note: If blender is not available, mash banana and beat all ingredients with rotary beater.

1 serving = ½ milk, ¾ meat
170 calories

SUPER NOG

2 cups skim milk
3 bananas, cut up
¼ cup wheat germ
2 tablespoons honey
¼ cup plus 2 tablespoons Second Nature imitation eggs* or 2 eggs

Measure all ingredients into blender container. Blend on highest speed 1 minute.

3½ cups.

½ cup = ½ milk, ½ meat
235 calories (with eggs)
215 calories (with Second Nature imitation eggs*)

* If this ingredient is not available in your market area, see page 29 for substitutes.

ORANGE EGGNOG

**3 tablespoons Second Nature
   imitation eggs***
**3 tablespoons thawed frozen orange
   juice concentrate**
1 cup skim milk
Nutmeg

Measure imitation egg, orange concentrate and milk into blender container. Cover and blend about 30 seconds. Pour into glasses and sprinkle with nutmeg.

2 servings.

**1 serving = ½ milk, ½ meat
             110 calories**

HONEYED TEA

6 cups boiling water
6 orange pekoe tea bags
¼ cup plus 2 tablespoons honey
1 stick cinnamon
½ cup lemon juice

Pour boiling water on tea bags in saucepan. Cover; let steep 5 minutes. Stir and remove tea bags. Stir in remaining ingredients; heat to boiling. Reduce heat and simmer 5 minutes. Remove stick cinnamon and serve hot.

6 servings (about 1 cup each).

**1 serving = trace sodium
             75 calories**

*If this ingredient is not available in your market area, see page 29 for substitutes.

7. Soups, Sandwiches, Eggs

Many of these hearty soups and sandwiches are perfect for quick use as entrées—and the headline news included here is the marvelous recipes using palatable egg substitutes.

VEGETABLE SOUP

3-pound beef knuckle bone
1 large onion, chopped
3 quarts water (12 cups)
6 unsalted beef bouillon cubes
2 cups cut fresh green beans
1 large potato, pared and diced
2 cups coarsely chopped cabbage
1 pound tomatoes, peeled and coarsely
  chopped
3 small carrots, sliced
¼ teaspoon lemon juice
Bouquet garni (1 bay leaf, 1 sprig thyme,
  2 sprigs parsley, 1 sprig rosemary)*

If necessary, trim fat from bone. Heat bone, onion, water and bouillon cubes in 4-quart Dutch oven or covered large kettle to boiling. Reduce heat; cover and simmer 2 hours. Add remaining ingredients; simmer 1 hour longer. Remove bone.

10 servings.

1 serving = 1 vegetable
             50 calories

*If using dry herbs, tie in cheesecloth.

VEGETABLE RING SOUP

⅓ cup uncooked macaroni rings
1 cup cut-up cooked unsalted beef
2 cups unsalted beef broth
½ cup sliced carrot
¼ cup chopped celery
¼ cup finely chopped onion
2 medium tomatoes, peeled and
  cut up
1 teaspoon lemon juice
¼ teaspoon marjoram leaves
¼ teaspoon thyme

Cook macaroni rings as directed on package except—omit salt.

Heat remaining ingredients to boiling, stirring occasionally. Reduce heat; cover and simmer 15 minutes. Stir in macaroni rings and heat.

8 servings (½ cup each).

1 serving = 1 vegetable
             70 calories

CREAM OF CAULIFLOWER SOUP

2 tablespoons finely chopped onion
2 tablespoons unsalted margarine
1 tablespoon flour
⅛ teaspoon white pepper
½ teaspoon dill weed
½ cup water
1 cup unsalted chicken broth
½ cup skim milk
1 package (10 ounces) frozen cauliflower,
  thawed and cut into bite-size pieces
½ cup diced cooked potato
1 tablespoon finely chopped pimiento
1 tablespoon lemon juice

Cook and stir onion in margarine in medium saucepan until tender. Stir in flour, pepper and dill weed. Cook over low heat, stirring until mixture is bubbly. Stir in remaining ingredients.

Heat to boiling, stirring constantly. Boil and stir 1 minute. Reduce heat and simmer uncovered 10 minutes, stirring occasionally.

Six ½-cup servings.

1 serving = ½ vegetable
      70 calories

MULLIGATAWNY SOUP

¼ cup unsalted margarine
6 ounces cut-up cooked unsalted chicken
¼ cup sliced carrot (1 medium)
¾ cup sliced unpared apple (1 medium)
1 small onion (2 inches in diameter), sliced
¼ cup diced celery
½ cup water
2 tablespoons flour
1 teaspoon curry powder
⅛ teaspoon mace
1 can (16 ounces) unsalted tomatoes
2 whole cloves
1 sprig parsley, snipped
1 bay leaf
1 tablespoon lemon juice
¾ cup diced green pepper (1 medium)

Melt margarine in 2-quart saucepan. Cook and stir chicken, carrot, apple, onion and celery in margarine 10 minutes. Reduce heat; cover and simmer until carrot is tender, about 20 minutes.

Mix water, flour, curry powder and mace until smooth. Stir flour mixture, tomatoes (with liquid) and remaining ingredients except green pepper into saucepan. Heat to boiling, stirring constantly. Boil and stir 1 minute. Stir in green pepper. Reduce heat; simmer uncovered 10 minutes.

4 servings (1 cup each).

1 serving = 1 vegetable, ½ meat
      275 calories

GAZPACHO

1 cup unsalted tomato juice
1 unsalted beef or chicken bouillon cube
½ cup chopped peeled tomato
⅓ cup diced unpared cucumber
2 tablespoons diced green pepper
2 tablespoons chopped onion
2 tablespoons white vinegar
½ cup uncooked macaroni rings

Heat tomato juice in small saucepan to boiling. Add bouillon cube and stir until cube is dissolved. Stir in vegetables and vinegar; heat to boiling. Remove from heat; cool and refrigerate at least 4 hours.

Cook macaroni rings as directed on package except—omit salt.

Divide macaroni rings among 4 soup bowls; spoon soup on top.

4 servings.

Note: Soup with macaroni rings can be covered and refrigerated up to 3 days. It will thicken as rings absorb liquid. To serve, stir in unsalted tomato juice to desired consistency.

1 serving = ½ vegetable, 1 bread I
              90 calories

CHICKEN NOODLE SOUP

3 tablespoons uncooked spaghetti
2 cups unsalted chicken broth*
½ cup cut-up cooked unsalted chicken
1 teaspoon onion powder
¼ teaspoon sage
⅛ teaspoon pepper
¼ teaspoon lemon juice

Cook spaghetti as directed on package except—omit salt.

Drain spaghetti and return to saucepan. Stir in remaining ingredients. Heat to boiling, stirring occasionally.

2 servings (1 cup each).

1 serving = ⅓ meat, ½ bread I
              110 calories

*Unsalted chicken broth can be made by dissolving 2 unsalted chicken bouillon cubes in 2 cups boiling water.

CHICKEN CLUB SANDWICH

1 slice low-sodium bread
1 teaspoon unsalted margarine
1 ounce sliced cooked unsalted chicken
2 tomato slices
2 tablespoons low-sodium bread crumbs
½ teaspoon oregano
1 tablespoon unsalted margarine, melted

Set oven control at broil and/or 550°. Toast bread on 1 side. Spread untoasted side of bread with 1 teaspoon margarine. Arrange chicken and tomato slices on bread. Sprinkle 1 tablespoon of the bread crumbs and the oregano on tomato slices. Drizzle melted margarine on top and sprinkle with remaining bread crumbs. Broil 5 inches from heat until crumbs are golden brown, 3 to 5 minutes.

1 serving.

1 serving = ¼ meat, 1 bread I
380 calories

SANDWICH IDEAS

Spread each slice bread with softened unsalted margarine or low-sodium mayonnaise. Add crisp lettuce leaves, spinach leaves or alfalfa sprouts topped with thin slices roast beef, roast chicken, turkey, Tuna Salad (page 115) or Chicken Salad (page 111) for filling; if you like, add thin slices cucumber, tomato, radish or green pepper. Serve sandwich with carrot curls.

Note: Check food groups and individual receipes for sodium and calorie information.

OPEN-FACED SALMON SANDWICH

½ cup drained canned unsalted salmon
1½ teaspoons cranberry-orange relish
1½ teaspoons low-sodium mayonnaise
1 teaspoon chopped onion
2 slices low-sodium bread
1 tablespoon snipped parsley

Mix salmon, relish, mayonnaise and onion. Spread on bread slices; sprinkle with parsley.

2 servings.

1 serving = ½ meat, 1 bread I
190 calories

FRUIT 'N' TUNA SANDWICH

1 slice low-sodium bread or
 1 low-sodium English muffin
1 ounce drained unsalted tuna
2 tablespoons well-drained crushed
 pineapple
1 teaspoon lemon juice
¼ teaspoon ginger
2 tablespoons low-sodium mayonnaise

Set oven control at broil and/or 550°. Toast bread on 1 side (do not toast muffin). Mix tuna, pineapple, lemon juice, ginger and mayonnaise with fork. Spread untoasted side of bread with tuna mixture. Broil 5 inches from heat until light brown, about 3 minutes.

1 serving.

1 serving = ⅓ meat, 1 bread I
300 calories

BEEF AND MUSHROOM SANDWICH

1 slice low-sodium bread
1 teaspoon unsalted margarine
2 radishes, sliced
1 ounce chopped cooked unsalted beef
¼ cup Sauce Stroganoff (below)
¼ cup sliced fresh or canned unsalted
  mushrooms

Spread bread with margarine and toast in oven. Arrange radish slices on margarine. Heat remaining ingredients in small saucepan over low heat just to simmering. Spoon beef mixture over radish slices. Serve hot and, if desired, with radish roses.

1 serving.

1 serving = 1 bread I, ⅓ meat, ¼ milk
            305 calories

Sauce Stroganoff

½ cup water
2 tablespoons flour
1 teaspoon onion powder
2 teaspoons imitation roast beef flavor
  paste
¼ teaspoon garlic powder
½ cup dairy sour cream

Mix water, flour and onion powder in small saucepan until smooth. Add flavor paste. Heat to boiling, stirring constantly. Boil and stir 1 minute. Remove from heat; stir in sour cream.

About 1 cup.

WESTERN EGG SANDWICH

1 tablespoon unsalted margarine
¼ cup chopped onion
¼ cup chopped green pepper
½ cup Second Nature
  imitation eggs*
4 slices white or whole wheat bread,
  toasted

Melt margarine in small skillet. Cook and stir onion and green pepper in margarine until onion is tender. Pour in imitation eggs. As egg mixture begins to set at bottom and side, gently lift cooked portion with spatula so that thin uncooked portion can flow to bottom. When almost set, cover skillet and cook until set, about 2 minutes. Cut egg mixture in half; place each half on piece of toast and top with remaining toast piece.

2 servings.

1 serving = 1½ meat, 2 bread II
            275 calories

*If this ingredient is not available in your market area, see page 29 for substitutes.

PIZZA

1 low-sodium English Muffin (page 88)
 split and toasted
2 teaspoons unsalted margarine, softened
1 tablespoon unsalted tomato paste
1 tablespoon water
1 tablespoon finely chopped green pepper
⅛ teaspoon basil leaves
⅛ teaspoon oregano
Dash each garlic powder and pepper
½ teaspoon parsley flakes
2 onion rings
1 fresh mushroom, sliced

Heat oven to 400°. Spread toasted side of each muffin half with 1 teaspoon margarine. Mix remaining ingredients except parsley flakes, onion rings and mushroom; spread on muffin halves. Sprinkle with parsley flakes and top each with an onion ring and mushroom slices. Place on ungreased baking sheet. Bake until bubbly, 3 to 5 minutes.

1 serving.

1 serving = 1 bread I
**   305 calories**

QUICK MIX PIZZA

1 can (10 ounces) unsalted tomatoes
1 can (6 ounces) unsalted tomato paste
⅛ teaspoon garlic powder
⅛ teaspoon red pepper
¼ teaspoon basil leaves
½ teaspoon oregano leaves
1 pound lean ground beef
½ cup chopped onion
2 cups sliced fresh mushrooms
2 tablespoons unsalted margarine
1 package active dry yeast
1 cup warm water (105 to 115°)
1 teaspoon sugar
2 tablespoons vegetable oil
2½ cups all-purpose flour
1 medium green pepper, cut into rings

Heat tomatoes, tomato paste and seasonings to boiling, breaking up tomatoes with fork. Reduce heat; simmer uncovered about 10 minutes.

Cook and stir ground beef, onion and mushrooms in margarine until meat is brown and onion is tender. Drain off fat; set meat mixture aside.

Dissolve yeast in warm water. Stir in sugar, oil and flour. Beat vigorously about 20 strokes. Allow dough to rest about 5 minutes.

Heat oven to 425°. Divide dough in half. Pat each half on lightly greased baking sheet into 12-inch circle. (Flour fingers frequently when patting dough into circles.) Spread tomato sauce on each circle. Sprinkle with meat mixture. Arrange green pepper rings on top.

Bake 25 to 30 minutes or until crust is brown and topping is hot and bubbly.

2 pizzas.

⅛ of pizza = 1 bread I
**   190 calories**

OMELET

1 tablespoon unsalted margarine
1 cup Second Nature imitation eggs*

Stir Method: Melt margarine in 8-inch skillet or omelet pan over medium heat. Pour imitation eggs into skillet. With left hand, start sliding skillet back and forth rapidly over heat. At the same time, stir quickly with fork to spread imitation egg continuously over bottom of skillet as it thickens. Let stand over heat a few seconds to cook.

Tilt skillet; run fork under edge of omelet, then jerk skillet sharply to loosen omelet from bottom of skillet. If filling is used, spoon on center. With fork, fold portion of omelet nearest you just to center.

Grasp skillet handle with hand; turn omelet onto warm plate, flipping folded portion of omelet over so far side is on bottom.

Lift Method: Melt margarine in 8-inch skillet or omelet pan over medium heat. Pour imitation eggs into skillet. Do not stir. As mixture begins to set at bottom and side, gently lift cooked portion with spatula so that thin uncooked portion can flow to bottom. When almost set, cover pan and cook until top of omelet is set, 2 minutes. If desired, spoon filling on half of omelet. Fold other half onto filling. With large spatula, lift or slide omelet onto warm plate.

2 servings.

1 serving = 2½ meat
        155 calories

Variations

Ratatouille Omelet: Fill omelet with 1 cup Ratatouille (page 164).

1 serving = 2½ meat, ½ vegetable
        220 calories

Herb Omelet: Before pouring imitation eggs into skillet, sprinkle 1 tablespoon each snipped chives and snipped parsley on margarine in skillet.

1 serving = 2½ meat
        155 calories

Mushroom Omelet: Before pouring imitation eggs into skillet, cook and stir ¼ cup chopped mushroom and 1 tablespoon snipped parsley in margarine 1 minute.

1 serving = 2½ meat, ½ vegetable
        160 calories

Green Pepper Omelet: Before pouring imitation eggs into skillet, cook and stir ¼ cup chopped green pepper and 2 tablespoons minced onion in margarine 1 minute.

1 serving = 2½ meat, ¼ vegetable
        165 calories

Apple Omelet: Before pouring imitation eggs into skillet, cook and stir 1 small apple, sliced, in margarine. Stir in 1 teaspoon sugar and ¼ teaspoon cinnamon. Remove apple mixture and set aside. Before removing omelet, spoon apple mixture on half the omelet.

1 serving = 2½ meat, ¼ fruit
        185 calories

Cheese Omelet: Before pouring imitation eggs into skillet, sprinkle 1 tablespoon snipped chives and 1 tablespoon snipped parsley on margarine. Sprinkle ¼ cup shredded skim milk mozzarella cheese on omelet when rolling it.

1 serving = 3 salted meat
        195 calories

* If this ingredient is not available in your market area, see page 29 for substitutes.

MUSHROOM OMELET

½ pound fresh mushrooms, sliced
½ cup thinly sliced onion
¼ cup finely chopped green pepper
2 tablespoons vegetable oil
4 eggs
Freshly ground pepper

Cook and stir mushrooms, onion and green pepper in oil until onion is tender, 3 to 4 minutes. Mix eggs with fork until whites and yolks are just blended. Pour on vegetables in skillet. Slide skillet back and forth rapidly over heat. At the same time, stir quickly with fork to spread egg mixture continuously over bottom of skillet as it thickens. Let stand over heat a few seconds to lightly brown bottom of omelet; do not overcook. (Omelet will continue to cook after folding.)

Tilt skillet; run fork under edge of omelet, then jerk skillet sharply to loosen egg mixture from bottom of skillet. With fork, fold portion of omelet nearest you just to center. (Allow for portion of omelet to slide up side of skillet.)

Grasp skillet handle with hand; turn omelet onto warm plate, flipping folded portion of omelet over so far side is on bottom. If necessary, tuck sides of omelet under. Season with pepper.

4 servings.

1 serving = 1 meat, 1 vegetable
       175 calories

OMELET AUX FINES HERBES

3 eggs
2 tablespoons snipped parsley
1 teaspoon snipped fresh or ½ teaspoon
    dried tarragon leaves
½ teaspoon snipped fresh or ¼ teaspoon
    dried thyme leaves
⅛ teaspoon pepper
2 teaspoons chopped shallots or green
    onions
1 tablespoon unsalted margarine

Beat eggs with fork until whites and yolks are just blended. Stir in parsley, tarragon leaves, thyme leaves, pepper and shallots. Heat margarine in 8-inch skillet or omelet pan over medium-high heat. As margarine melts, tilt skillet in all directions to coat side thoroughly. When margarine just begins to brown, skillet is hot enough to use.

Quickly pour egg mixture all at once into skillet. With left hand, start sliding skillet back and forth rapidly over heat. At the same time, stir quickly with fork to spread eggs continuously over bottom of skillet as they thicken. Let stand over heat a few seconds to lightly brown bottom of omelet; do not overcook. (Omelet will continue to cook after folding.)

Tilt skillet; run fork under edge of omelet, then jerk skillet sharply to loosen eggs from bottom of skillet. With fork, fold portion of omelet nearest you just to center. (Allow for portion of omelet to slide up side of skillet.)

Grasp skillet handle with hand; turn omelet onto warm plate, flipping folded portion of omelet over so far side is on bottom. If necessary, tuck sides of omelet under.

3 servings.

1 serving = 1 meat
       125 calories

POTATO OMELET

1 small potato, pared and cubed
1 tablespoon vegetable oil
1 egg
1 tablespoon snipped chives
Freshly ground pepper

In small skillet, cook and stir potato cubes in oil until tender but not brown. Remove from skillet; drain and cool to lukewarm. Beat egg with fork until white and yolk are just blended; stir in potato cubes, chives and pepper. Heat skillet. Pour egg mixture into skillet. Slide skillet back and forth rapidly over heat. At same time, stir quickly with fork to spread egg mixture continuously over bottom of skillet as it thickens. Let stand over heat a few seconds to lightly brown bottom of omelet; do not overcook. (Omelet will continue to cook after folding.)

Tilt skillet; run fork under edge of omelet, then jerk skillet sharply to loosen egg mixture from bottom of skillet. With fork, fold portion of omelet nearest you just to center. (Allow for portion of omelet to slide up side of skillet.)

Grasp skillet handle with hand; turn omelet onto warm plate, flipping folded portion of omelet over so far side is on bottom. (If necessary, tuck sides of omelet under.)

1 serving.

1 serving = 1 meat, 1 bread I
           270 calories

PUFFY OMELET

4 eggs, separated
2 tablespoons water
Dash pepper
1 teaspoon unsalted margarine

In small mixer bowl, beat egg whites until stiff but not dry. Beat egg yolks, water and pepper until thick and lemon colored. Fold into egg whites.

Heat oven to 325°. Heat margarine in large skillet with ovenproof handle until just hot enough to sizzle a drop of water. Pour egg mixture into skillet; level surface gently. Reduce heat; cook slowly until puffy and light brown on bottom, about 5 minutes. (Lift omelet at edge to judge color.)

Place in oven; bake until knife inserted in center comes out clean, 12 to 15 minutes. Tip skillet and loosen omelet by slipping pancake turner or spatula under. Fold omelet in half, being careful not to break it; slip onto warm platter. Serve immediately.

4 servings.

1 serving = 1 meat
           90 calories

FRITTATA OMELET

½ green pepper, chopped
3 to 4 tablespoons vegetable oil
4 fresh mushrooms, sliced
¼ cup chopped pimiento
2 eggs
Freshly ground pepper

In small skillet, cook and stir green pepper in half the oil until tender. Stir in mushrooms and pimiento; cook and stir 1 to 2 minutes. Remove from heat and cool.

Heat oven to 325°. Beat eggs until fluffy. Stir in vegetable mixture. Heat remaining oil in skillet until just hot enough to sizzle drop of water. Pour egg mixture into skillet. Reduce heat; cook slowly until puffy and light brown on bottom, about 5 minutes. (Lift omelet at edge to judge color.)

Place in oven; bake until knife inserted in center comes out clean.

2 servings.

1 serving = 1 meat, 1 vegetable
330 calories

OMELET FRANÇAISE

4 eggs
¼ cup skim milk
2 teaspoons unsalted margarine
1 tablespoon strawberry jam or jelly
1 teaspoon powdered sugar

Beat eggs until light and fluffy. Stir in milk. Heat margarine in large skillet until just hot enough to sizzle drop of water. As margarine melts, tilt pan to coat bottom. Pour egg mixture into skillet. Cook over medium heat, lifting edge to allow uncooked portion to flow to bottom, until omelet is light brown on bottom.

Drop jam by small amounts on half the omelet. Tip skillet and loosen omelet by slipping pancake turner or spatula under. Fold omelet in half, being careful not to break it. Slip onto heated platter; sprinkle sugar on top.

4 servings.

1 serving = 1 meat
155 calories

POACHED EGGS (Imitation Eggs)

For each serving, pour 3 tablespoons Second Nature imitation eggs* into an oiled egg-poaching cup. Place cup over simmering water; cover and cook until egg substitute is set, about 7 minutes.

1 serving = 1 meat
40 calories

* If this ingredient is not available in your market area, see page 29 for substitutes.

POACHED EGG

2 teaspoons vinegar
1 egg
1 slice low-sodium bread, toasted
1 teaspoon unsalted margarine
Freshly ground pepper

Heat 1½ inches water in small skillet to boiling; reduce to simmer and add vinegar. Break egg into cup or saucer; slip into water, holding cup or saucer close to surface of water.

Cook to desired doneness, 3 to 5 minutes. Remove egg from water with slotted spoon. Place on toast and dot with margarine. Season with pepper and, if desired, with dash curry powder, sage or dry mustard.

1 serving.

1 serving = 1 meat
              230 calories

EGGS AND PEPPERS

½ cup chopped onion
1 cup chopped green pepper
3 tablespoons vegetable oil
8 eggs
Freshly ground pepper

In large skillet, cook and stir onion and green pepper in oil until tender. Beat eggs until blended; pour on onion and green pepper. As mixture begins to set at bottom and side, gently lift cooked portion with spatula so that thin uncooked portion can flow to bottom. Avoid constant stirring. Cook until eggs are thickened throughout but still moist, 3 to 5 minutes. Sprinkle with pepper.

8 servings.

1 serving = 1 meat, ½ vegetable
              140 calories

EGGS AND TOMATOES

½ cup chopped green pepper
2 tablespoons chopped onion
2 tablespoons vegetable oil
½ cup chopped peeled tomato (seeds removed)
Small bay leaf
2 teaspoons basil leaves
1 teaspoon sugar
Dash paprika
3 eggs

Cook and stir green pepper and onion in oil until onion is tender, 3 to 4 minutes. Stir in tomato, bay leaf, basil leaves, sugar and paprika. Heat just to boiling, stirring constantly. Reduce heat; break eggs into skillet and stir with fork until eggs are set. Remove bay leaf.

4 servings.

1 serving = ¾ meat, ½ vegetable
              150 calories

SCRAMBLED EGGS (Imitation Eggs)

**2 teaspoons salad oil or
unsalted margarine
1 pint (2 cups) Second Nature
imitation eggs***

Heat oil in large skillet over medium heat. Pour imitation eggs into skillet. Cook, stirring frequently with spatula until set, about 2 minutes.

4 servings.

**1 serving = 2½ meat
120 calories**

Variations

1. Before cooking, add 2 tablespoons snipped parsley, 1 teaspoon chopped chives or ¼ teaspoon tarragon leaves, dill weed, basil or fines herbes to imitation eggs.

**1 serving = 2½ meat
125 calories**

2. Before removing from heat, sprinkle ½ cup shredded skim milk mozzarella cheese on top.

**1 serving = 3 salted meat
165 calories**

SCRAMBLED EGGS

**4 eggs
2 tablespoons water
¼ teaspoon dry mustard
Dash pepper
1 tablespoon unsalted margarine**

Mix eggs, water, mustard and pepper with fork, stirring thoroughly for a uniform yellow, or mixing just slightly if streaks of white and yellow are preferred.

Heat margarine in skillet over medium heat until just hot enough to sizzle a drop of water. Pour egg mixture into skillet. As mixture begins to set at bottom and side, gently lift cooked portions with spatula so thin uncooked portion can flow to bottom. Avoid constant stirring. Cook until eggs are thickened throughout but still moist, 3 to 5 minutes.

4 servings.

**1 serving = 1 meat
110 calories**

Variation

Herbed Scrambled Eggs: Substitute snipped chives, snipped parsley, tarragon leaves or chervil leaves for the dry mustard.

---

*If this ingredient is not available in your market area, see page 29 for substitutes.

8.Breads

These recipes present dramatic evidence of a big change in the hypertension diet—a grand variety of breads heretofore unavailable to the person on a controlled sodium intake.

TRADITIONAL WHITE BREAD

2 packages active dry yeast
½ cup warm water (105 to 115°)
1¾ cups warm water
3 tablespoons sugar
1½ teaspoons salt**
2 tablespoons vegetable oil
6 to 7 cups all-purpose flour
Unsalted margarine, softened

Dissolve yeast in ½ cup warm water in large bowl. Stir in 1¾ cups water, the sugar, salt, oil and 3½ cups of the flour. Beat until smooth. Mix in enough remaining flour to make dough easy to handle.

Turn dough onto lightly floured board; knead until smooth and elastic, about 10 minutes. Place in greased bowl; turn greased side up. Cover and let rise in warm place until double, about 40 minutes. (Dough is ready if an impression remains when touched.)

Punch down dough; divide in half. Roll each half into rectangle, 18x9 inches. Roll up, beginning at short side. Press each end with side of hand to seal. Fold ends under loaf. Place seam side down in greased loaf pan, 9x5x3 inches. Brush loaves lightly with margarine. Let rise until double, about 25 minutes.

Heat oven to 425°. Place loaves on low rack so that tops of pans are in center of oven. Pans should not touch each other or sides of oven. Bake 25 minutes or until deep golden brown and loaves sound hollow when tapped. Remove from pans. Brush loaves with margarine; cool on wire rack.

2 loaves.

1 serving (1 slice) = 1 bread II
110 calories
**1 serving (1 slice) = 1 bread I (without salt)
110 calories

STREAMLINED BATTER BREAD

1 package active dry yeast
1¼ cups warm water (105 to 115°)
2 tablespoons vegetable oil
2 tablespoons sugar
½ teaspoon salt
2⅔ cups all-purpose flour
Unsalted margarine

Dissolve yeast in warm water in large mixer bowl. Add oil, sugar, salt and 2 cups of the flour. Blend on low speed ½ minute, scraping bowl constantly. Beat on medium speed 2 minutes, scraping bowl occasionally. (By hand, beat 300 vigorous strokes.) Stir in remaining flour until smooth. Scrape batter from side of bowl. Cover; let rise in warm place until double, about 30 minutes.

Stir down batter by beating about 25 strokes. Spread evenly in greased loaf pan, 9x5x3 inches. Smooth out top of batter with floured hand. Let rise uncovered until double, about 25 minutes.

Heat oven to 375°. Bake 45 minutes or until loaf sounds hollow when tapped. Brush top with margarine. Remove loaf from pan; cool on wire rack.

1 loaf.

1 serving (1 slice) = ½ bread II
100 calories

HOT BREAD IN FOIL

Heat oven to 400°. Cut 1 loaf (1 pound) low-salt French bread into 1-inch slices, cut low-salt rye bread into ½-inch slices or split 8 large individual low-salt club rolls. Spread generously with ½ cup unsalted margarine or with one of the Margarine Spreads(opposite).

Reassemble loaf or rolls; wrap in 28x18-inch piece of heavy-duty aluminum foil and seal securely. Heat loaf 18 to 20 minutes, rolls 10 to 12 minutes.

1 serving (1 slice) = 1 bread I
180 calories

CORN BREAD

1 cup yellow cornmeal
1 cup all-purpose flour
2 tablespoons low-sodium baking powder
2 tablespoons sugar
1 cup skim milk
¼ cup unsalted margarine, softened
¼ cup Second Nature imitation
eggs*

Heat oven to 425°. Grease baking pan, 8x8x2 inches. Measure all ingredients into bowl; stir until dry ingredients are moistened, about 20 seconds. Beat vigorously 1 minute. Pour into pan. Bake 20 to 25 minutes or until golden brown.

9 to 12 servings.

1 serving = 1 bread I
145 calories

Corn Muffins: Fill 12 greased medium muffin cups (2¾ inches in diameter) ⅔ full. Bake 15 minutes.

12 muffins.

1 muffin = 1 bread I
145 calories

*If this ingredient is not available in your market area, see page 29 for substitutes.

GARLIC FRENCH BREAD

Heat oven to 350°. Cut 1 loaf (1 pound) low-salt French bread horizontally in half. Mix ½ cup unsalted margarine, softened, and ¼ teaspoon garlic powder; spread generously on cut sides of loaf. Reassemble loaf; cut crosswise into 2-inch slices. Wrap securely in heavy-duty aluminum foil. Heat 15 to 20 minutes.

24 to 28 slices.

1 serving (1 slice) = 1 bread I
95 calories

FRENCH BREAD

1 package active dry yeast
1¼ cups warm water (105 to 115°)
¾ teaspoon salt**
1 tablespoon vegetable oil
3½ to 4 cups all-purpose flour
1 tablespoon cornmeal
1 egg white
2 tablespoons water

Dissolve yeast in warm water in large mixing bowl. Stir in salt, oil and 1½ cups of the flour. Beat until smooth. Stir in enough remaining flour (first with spoon, then by hand) to make dough easy to handle.

Turn dough onto lightly floured board; knead until smooth and elastic, about 5 minutes. Place in greased bowl; turn greased side up. Cover with damp cloth; let rise in warm place until double, about 1 hour. (Dough is ready if an indentation remains when touched.)

Punch down dough; round up and let rise until almost double, about 20 minutes. Punch down; cover and let rest 15 minutes.

Lightly grease baking sheet; sprinkle with cornmeal. Roll dough into rectangle, 15x10 inches. Roll up tightly, beginning at long side.

Pinch edge to seal. Roll gently back and forth to taper ends.

Place loaf on baking sheet. Make ¼-inch slashes across loaf at 2-inch intervals or make 1 slash lengthwise. Brush top of loaf with cold water.

Let rise uncovered about 35 minutes. Brush with cold water.

Heat oven to 375°. Bake 20 minutes. Beat egg white and 2 tablespoons cold water slightly; brush on loaf. Bake 25 minutes longer. Remove from baking sheet; cool on wire rack.

1 loaf (about 15 slices).

1 serving (1 slice) = 1 bread II
125 calories

**1 serving (1 slice) = 1 bread I (without salt)
125 calories

Margarine Spreads

Mix ½ cup unsalted margarine, softened, and one of the following—

Garlic: 1 medium clove garlic, minced.

Tarragon: 1 teaspoon tarragon leaves and ¼ teaspoon paprika.

Onion: 2 tablespoons minced onion or snipped chives.

Seeded: 1 to 2 teaspoons dill or sesame seed.

Basil: 1 teaspoon basil leaves.

HONEY WHOLE WHEAT BREAD

2 packages active dry yeast
½ cup warm water (105 to 115°)
⅓ cup honey
¾ teaspoon salt**
¼ cup vegetable oil
1¾ cups warm water
3 cups whole wheat flour
3 to 4 cups all-purpose flour
Unsalted margarine

Dissolve yeast in ½ cup warm water in large mixing bowl. Stir in honey, salt, oil, 1¾ cups warm water and the whole wheat flour. Beat until smooth. Mix in enough white flour to make dough easy to handle.

Turn dough onto lightly floured board. Knead until smooth and elastic, about 10 minutes. Place in greased bowl; turn greased side up. Cover; let rise in warm place until double, about 40 minutes. (Dough is ready if an indentation remains when touched.)

Punch down dough; divide in half. Flatten each half into rectangle, 18x9 inches. Fold crosswise into thirds, overlapping the 2 sides. Roll dough tightly toward you, beginning at one of the open ends. Press with thumbs to seal after each turn. Pinch edge firmly to seal. With side of hand, press each end to seal; fold ends under loaf. Place seam side down in greased loaf pan, 9x5x3 inches. Brush lightly with margarine and sprinkle with whole wheat flour.

Cover; let rise until double, 20 to 25 minutes.

Heat oven to 375°. Place loaves on low rack so tops of pans are in center of oven. Bake 40 to 45 minutes or until deep golden brown and loaves sound hollow when tapped. Remove from pans. Brush with margarine and cool on wire rack.

2 loaves.

1 slice = ½ bread II
**1 slice (no salt) = trace sodium
                    110 calories

Honey Whole Wheat Rolls: After punching down dough, divide into thirds. Use one third dough in each of the Variations (below). Brush with soft margarine. Cover and let rise 20 to 25 minutes before baking.

Heat oven to 375°. Bake rolls 35 to 40 minutes or until golden brown.

Variations

Pan Rolls: Grease layer pan, 9x1½ inches. Cut dough into fourths; cut each fourth into 6 pieces. Shape pieces of dough into smooth balls. Place in pan.

24 rolls.

1 roll = 1 bread I
**1 roll (no salt) = trace sodium
                    45 calories

Cloverleaf Rolls: Grease 12 muffin cups. Cut dough into thirds; cut each third into 12 pieces. Shape pieces into smooth ball. Place 3 balls in each muffin cup.

12 rolls.

1 roll = ½ bread II
**1 roll = trace sodium
                    85 calories

NUT BREAD

2½ cups all-purpose flour
1 cup sugar
1 tablespoon plus 2 teaspoons low-sodium
   baking powder
3 tablespoons vegetable oil
1¼ cups skim milk
¼ cup Second Nature imitation
   eggs*
1 cup chopped pecans

Heat oven to 350°. Grease and flour loaf pan, 9x5x3 inches. Measure all ingredients into large mixer bowl: beat on medium speed ½ minute, scraping side and bottom of bowl constantly.

Pour into prepared pan. Bake 55 to 65 minutes or until wooden pick inserted in center comes out clean. Remove from pan; cool thoroughly before slicing.

1 loaf (about 16 servings).

1 serving (1 slice) = 1 bread I
                    210 calories

Variations

Banana Nut Bread: Reduce milk to ¾ cup and add 1 cup mashed ripe banana (2 to 3 medium). Bake 70 to 75 minutes.

1 serving = 1 bread I
                220 calories

Date Nut Bread: Substitute date mixture for the milk. For date mixture, add 1½ cups boiling water to 1½ cups cut-up dates. Stir and cool. Bake 65 to 70 minutes.

1 serving (1 slice) = ½ bread I
                       250 calories

Cranberry-Orange Nut Bread: Decrease milk to 1 cup. After beating, stir in 1 cup chopped fresh or frozen cranberries, well drained, 2 teaspoons grated orange peel and 2 tablespoons orange juice. Bake 70 to 75 minutes.

1 serving (1 slice) = 1 bread I
                    215 calories

DOUBLE-QUICK DINNER ROLLS

1 package active dry yeast
1 cup warm water (105 to 115°)
2 tablespoons sugar
½ teaspoon salt
¼ cup Second Nature
   imitation eggs*
2 tablespoons vegetable oil
2¼ cups all-purpose flour

Dissolve yeast in warm water in large mixer bowl. Add sugar, salt, imitation eggs, oil and 1 cup of the flour; beat until smooth. Mix in remaining flour until smooth, scraping batter from side of bowl. Cover and let rise in warm place until double, about 30 minutes.

Grease 12 large muffin cups. Stir down batter and spoon into muffin cups, filling each about ½ full. Let rise uncovered until batter reaches tops of cups, about 20 minutes.

Heat oven to 400°. Bake 15 minutes or until golden brown.

12 rolls.

1 serving (1 roll) = 1 bread II
                     125 calories

*If this ingredient is not available in your market area, see page 29 for substitutes.

TRADITIONAL ROLL DOUGH

1 package active dry yeast
¼ cup warm water (105 to 115°)
¾ cup lukewarm skim milk (scalded
 then cooled)
¼ cup sugar
¼ cup Second Nature imitation
 eggs*
¼ cup vegetable oil
3½ cups all-purpose flour

Dissolve yeast in warm water in large mixing bowl. Stir in milk, sugar, imitation eggs, oil and 2 cups of the flour. Beat until smooth. Mix in enough remaining flour to make dough easy to handle.

Turn dough onto lightly floured board; knead until smooth, about 5 minutes. Place in greased bowl; turn greased side up. Cover; let rise in warm place until double, about 50 minutes. (Dough is ready if an indentation remains when touched.)

Punch down dough; divide in half. Shape only half the dough at a time into desired rolls (below). Cover; let rise until double, about 20 minutes.

Heat oven to 400°. Bake rolls 12 to 15 minutes.

Cloverleaf: Shape bits of dough into 1-inch balls. Place 3 balls in each greased muffin cup. Brush with soft unsalted margarine.

12 rolls

1 serving (1 roll) = 1 bread I
                210 calories

Crescents: Roll dough into 12-inch circle, about ¼ inch thick. Spread with soft unsalted margarine. Cut into 12 wedges. Roll up, beginning at rounded edge. Place rolls with point underneath on greased baking sheet. Curve slightly. Brush with soft unsalted margarine.

12 rolls.

1 serving (1 roll) = 1 bread I
                210 calories

STIR 'N' ROLL BISCUITS
(with salt and regular baking powder)

2 cups all-purpose flour
3 teaspoons regular baking powder
¼ teaspoon salt
⅓ cup vegetable oil
⅔ cup skim milk
Unsalted margarine

Heat oven to 450°. Measure flour, baking powder and salt into bowl. Pour oil and milk into measuring cup (do not stir); pour into flour mixture. Stir with fork until mixture cleans side of bowl and forms a ball.

To knead dough: turn onto waxed paper. Lift paper by one corner and fold dough in half; press down firmly and pull paper back. Repeat until dough looks smooth. Pat or roll dough ½ inch thick between 2 sheets of waxed paper. Cut with unfloured 2-inch biscuit cutter. Place on ungreased baking sheet.

Bake 10 to 12 minutes or until golden brown. Serve hot with margarine and, if desired, with jelly, honey, jam or syrup.

16 biscuits.

1 biscuit = 1 bread II
                110 calories

*If this ingredient is not available in your market area, see page 29 for substitutes.

The recipe for French Toast is on page 89.

The recipe for Sunshine Salad is on page 107.

The recipe for Spanish Lobster Salad is on page 114.

The recipes for hamburgers begin on page 118.

STIR 'N' ROLL BISCUITS (no salt)

2 cups all-purpose flour
1 tablespoon plus 1½ teaspoons
low-sodium baking powder
⅓ cup vegetable oil
⅔ cup skim milk
Unsalted margarine

Heat oven to 450°. Measure flour and baking powder into bowl. Pour oil and milk into measuring cup (do not stir); pour into flour mixture. Stir with fork until mixture cleans side of bowl and forms a ball.

To knead dough: turn onto waxed paper. Lift paper by one corner and fold dough in half. Press down firmly and pull paper back. Repeat until dough looks smooth. Pat or roll dough ½ inch thick between 2 sheets of waxed paper. Cut with unfloured 2-inch biscuit cutter. Place on ungreased baking sheet.

Bake 10 to 12 minutes or until golden brown. Serve hot with margarine and, if desired, with jelly, honey, jam or syrup.

16 biscuits.

1 serving (1 biscuit) = ½ bread I
110 calories

Variations

Herb Biscuits: Add 1¼ teaspoons caraway seed, ½ teaspoon crumbled leaf sage and ¼ teaspoon dry mustard to flour mixture.

1 serving (1 biscuit) = ½ bread I
110 calories

Drop Biscuits: Increase skim milk to 1 cup. Omit kneading and drop dough by spoonfuls onto greased baking sheet.

1 serving (1 biscuit) = ½ bread I
120 calories

SWEDISH LIMPA RYE BREAD

2 packages active dry yeast
1½ cups warm water (105 to 115°)
2 tablespoons molasses
⅓ cup sugar
1½ teaspoons salt**
2 tablespoons vegetable oil
Grated peel of 1 orange
2½ cups medium rye flour
2¼ to 2¾ cups all-purpose flour
Cornmeal

Dissolve yeast in warm water in large mixing bowl. Stir in molasses, sugar, salt, oil, orange peel and rye flour. Beat until smooth. Mix in enough white flour to make dough easy to handle.

Turn dough onto lightly floured board. Cover; let rest 15 minutes. Knead until smooth, about 5 minutes. Place in greased bowl; turn greased side up. Cover; let rise in warm place until double, about 50 minutes. Punch down dough; round up, cover and let rise again until double, about 40 minutes.

Grease baking sheet; sprinkle with cornmeal. Punch down dough; divide in half. Shape each half into round, slightly flat loaf. Place loaves on opposite corners of baking sheet. Cover; let rise 25 minutes.

Heat oven to 375°. Bake 30 to 35 minutes.

2 loaves.

1 slice = 1 bread II
**1 slice (no salt) = trace sodium
185 calories

ENGLISH MUFFINS

1 package active dry yeast
1 cup warm water (105 to 115°)
½ teaspoon salt
1 teaspoon sugar
¼ cup vegetable oil
3 cups all-purpose flour
2 tablespoons cornmeal

Dissolve yeast in warm water in large mixing bowl. Stir in salt, sugar, oil and flour until smooth. Roll dough ¼-inch thick on floured board. Cut into 3½-inch circles.

Sprinkle ungreased baking sheet with 1 table-spoon cornmeal; place circles on baking sheet. Sprinkle remaining cornmeal on circles. Cover; let rise in warm place until light, about 35 minutes. (Dough is ready if an indentation remains when touched.)

Heat ungreased electric griddle or skillet to 375°. Transfer circles to griddle. Cook 7 minutes on each side; cool. To serve, split, toast and spread with margarine and marmalade.

10 to 12 muffins.

1 muffin = 1 bread II
180 calories

WATER BAGELS

1 package active dry yeast
1 cup warm water (105 to 115°)
2 tablespoons sugar
¼ teaspoon salt**
2¾ cups all-purpose flour
2 quarts water

Dissolve yeast in 1 cup warm water in large mixing bowl. Stir in sugar, salt and 1¼ cups of the flour. Beat until smooth. Mix in remaining flour.

Turn dough onto lightly floured board. Knead until smooth and elastic, about 10 minutes. Place in greased bowl; turn greased side up. Cover; let rise in warm place until double, about 15 minutes. (Dough is ready if an indentation remains when touched.)

Punch down dough; divide into 8 equal parts. Roll each part into a rope 6 inches long; moisten ends with water and pinch to form a bagel. Or shape each part into a smooth ball, punch hole in center and pull gently to enlarge hole and make uniform shape. Let rise 20 minutes.

Heat oven to 375°. Heat 2 quarts water to boiling in large kettle. Reduce heat; add 4 bagels. Simmer 2 minutes, turning once (1 minute on each side). Drain on kitchen towel. Repeat with remaining bagels. Bake on greased baking sheet 30 to 35 minutes or until golden brown. Cool. To serve, toast and spread with marmalade.

8 bagels.

1 bagel = ½ bread II
**1 bagel (no salt) = trace sodium
180 calories

CRANBERRY-BANANA TOAST

1 slice low-sodium bread
1 teaspoon unsalted margarine, softened
1 tablespoon cranberry sauce
¼ banana, sliced
1 teaspoon brown sugar
¼ teaspoon cinnamon

Set oven control at broil and/or 550°. Toast bread on one side. Spread untoasted side of bread with margarine, then with cranberry sauce. Arrange banana slices on cranberry sauce. Mix sugar and cinnamon; sprinkle on top. Broil about 5 inches from heat until bubbly, ½ to 1 minute.

1 serving.

1 serving = 1 bread I
                    220 calories

APPLESAUCE TOAST

1½ teaspoons unsalted margarine, melted
2¼ teaspoons sugar
½ cup unsalted applesauce
⅛ teaspoon nutmeg
⅛ teaspoon cinnamon
8 slices low-sodium bread

Set oven control at broil and/or 550°. Mix margarine, sugar, applesauce, nutmeg and cinnamon. Spread about 1 tablespoon applesauce mixture to edges of each bread slice. Broil 5 inches from heat until hot and edges are light brown, 1 to 2 minutes. Watch closely.

8 servings.

Note: Applesauce mixture can be covered and stored in refrigerator.

1 serving (1 slice) = 1 bread I
                    125 calories

FRENCH TOAST

1 cup Second Nature
  imitation eggs*
½ cup skim milk
1 loaf (1 pound) French bread or
  12 slices day-old bread
2 tablespoons unsalted margarine
Syrup, jam or honey

Mix imitation eggs and milk in shallow dish. If using French bread, cut into 1-inch slices.

Melt margarine in large skillet. Dip bread slices into imitation egg mixture, coating both sides and arrange in skillet. Cook over medium heat until light brown. Turn and cook until light brown on other side. Serve with syrup.

4 to 6 servings.

Note: Salt-free bread can be used.***

1 serving (1 slice) = ½ meat, 1 bread II
                    125 calories

***1 serving (1 slice) = ½ meat, 1 bread I**
                    125 calories

*If this ingredient is not available in your market area, see page 29 for substitutes.

BERGMAN'S HOMEMADE GRANOLA

6 cups oats
1 cup regular wheat germ
1 cup shredded coconut
1 cup chopped nuts (soya, peanuts, al-monds)
¼ cup dried sunflower seed
2 tablespoons sesame seed
4 dates, chopped
½ cup honey
½ cup vegetable oil
1 cup raisins

Heat oven to 425°. Mix oats, wheat germ, coconut, nuts, sunflower seed, sesame seed and dates in large bowl. Blend honey and oil; pour over oat mixture and toss until ingredients are coated. Spread in ungreased jelly roll pan, 15½x10½x1 inch.

Bake until mixture is light brown, stirring frequently. Remove from oven and stir in raisins. Cool. Store in covered container. Serve with milk and fresh fruit if desired.

About 10 cups.

½ cup = ¼ bread I
260 calories

HERB-SEASONED CROUTONS

4 cups ½-inch low-sodium bread cubes (about 4 slices)
1 tablespoon thyme leaves
2 teaspoons parsley flakes
¼ teaspoon pepper
⅛ teaspoon garlic powder
⅛ teaspoon sage
½ cup unsalted margarine
½ cup finely chopped onion

Heat oven to 325°. Measure bread cubes and seasonings into bowl. Melt margarine in small skillet over low heat. Cook and stir onion in margarine until tender. Pour over bread cubes and toss. Spread in ungreased baking pan, 13x9x2 inches. Bake until golden brown, about 30 minutes.

4 cups.

1 serving (¼ cup) = 1 bread I
170 calories

DUMPLINGS

1½ cups all-purpose flour
3 teaspoons low-sodium baking powder
3 tablespoons vegetable oil
¾ cup skim milk

Measure flour and baking powder into mixing bowl. Mix in oil. Stir in milk. Drop dough by spoonfuls onto hot meat or vegetables in boiling stew. (Do not drop directly into liquid.) Cook uncovered 10 minutes; cover and cook 10 minutes longer.

8 to 10 dumplings.

1 serving (1 dumpling) = 1 bread I
120 calories

GOLDEN WAFFLES

½ cup Second Nature
   imitation eggs*
1¾ cups skim milk
½ cup unsalted margarine, melted
2 cups all-purpose flour
2 tablespoons low-sodium baking powder
1 tablespoon sugar

Heat waffle iron. Measure all ingredients into mixing bowl. Beat with rotary beater until batter is smooth.

Pour batter from cup or pitcher onto center of hot waffle iron. Bake until steaming stops, about 5 minutes. Remove waffle carefully.

Three 10-inch waffles.

One 10-inch waffle = 1 bread II
725 calories

Variations

Orange Waffles: Stir in 1 tablespoon grated orange peel. Serve waffles with Orange Margarine: Beat ½ cup unsalted margarine, softened, 1 tablespoon powdered sugar and ¼ teaspoon grated orange peel until fluffy.

One 10-inch waffle = 1 bread II
1035 calories

Nut Waffles: Sprinkle 2 tablespoons coarsely chopped pecans on each waffle before baking.

One 10-inch waffle = 1 bread II
770 calories

PANCAKES

2 cups all-purpose flour
¼ cup sugar
2 tablespoons low-sodium baking powder
½ cup Second Nature imitation
   eggs*
1½ cups skim milk
¼ cup vegetable oil

Measure flour, sugar and baking powder into mixing bowl. Mix imitation eggs, milk and oil; add to dry ingredients. Beat only until large lumps disappear.

Pour batter from tip of large spoon or from pitcher onto hot lightly greased griddle. Turn pancakes when bubbles break and edges are cooked. Bake other side (total time 6 to 7 minutes). Serve immediately.

Sixteen 4-inch pancakes.

1 pancake = 1 bread I
120 calories

*If this ingredient is not available in your market area, see page 29 for substitutes.

TOPPERS FOR PANCAKES, WAFFLES

Maple Syrup: Measure 1 cup light corn syrup, ½ cup brown sugar (packed) and ½ cup water into small saucepan. Cook and stir until sugar is dissolved. Stir in few drops maple flavoring and 1 tablespoon unsalted margarine.

¼ **cup = 2 mEq sodium**
245 calories

Whipped Margarine: Beat ½ cup unsalted margarine in small mixer bowl until fluffy.

2 tablespoons = trace sodium
215 calories

Honey Margarine: Beat ½ cup unsalted margarine in small mixer bowl until fluffy. Continue beating, adding ¼ cup honey gradually, until smooth. If desired, stir in 2 teaspoons grated orange peel.

2 tablespoons = trace sodium
185 calories

Cranberry-Orange Margarine: Place 1 cut-up small orange (with peel), ¼ cup cranberries and ¼ cup sugar in blender container. Blend on high speed 40 seconds. Beat ½ cup unsalted margarine in small mixer bowl until fluffy. Fold in cranberry mixture.

2 tablespoons = trace sodium
140 calories

Blueberry Sauce: Empty 1 can (16 ounces) blueberries into small saucepan. Stir in 2 teaspoons cornstarch. Cook, stirring constantly, until mixture thickens and boils. Boil and stir 1 minute. Stir in 1 teaspoon lemon juice.

¼ **cup = trace sodium**
65 calories

Orange Sauce: Heat ½ cup unsalted margarine, 1 cup sugar and ½ cup frozen orange juice concentrate in small saucepan just to boiling, stirring occasionally.

¼ **cup = trace sodium**
455 calories

BLUEBERRY BLINTZES

Crêpes
½ cup blueberries
1 tablespoon sugar
¼ teaspoon cinnamon
2 teaspoons lemon juice
2 teaspoons water
½ cup dry cottage cheese
2 tablespoons unsalted margarine

Prepare Crêpes as directed on page 173 except—brown only on one side. Cool, keeping crêpes covered to prevent them from drying out.

Heat blueberries, sugar, cinnamon, lemon juice and water in small saucepan to boiling, stirring occasionally. Reduce heat; simmer 5 minutes. Remove from heat; stir in cottage cheese.

Place about 2 tablespoons cheese mixture in center of browned side of each crêpe. Fold sides of crêpe up over filling, overlapping edges; roll up.

Melt margarine in skillet until bubbly. Place blintzes seam side down in skillet. Cook, turning once, to golden brown. Serve with dairy sour cream if desired.

5 blintzes.

1 blintz = 1 bread I, ½ milk I
165 calories

GERMAN STOLLEN

1 package active dry yeast
¾ cup warm water (105 to 115°)
½ cup sugar
¼ teaspoon salt
¾ cup Second Nature
 imitation eggs*
½ cup unsalted margarine, softened
3½ cups all-purpose flour
½ cup chopped blanched almonds
¼ cup cut-up citron
¼ cup raisins
1 tablespoon grated lemon peel
¼ cup plus 2 tablespoons unsalted
 margarine, softened
1 egg white
1 tablespoon water
Quick White Icing (below)
Blanched almond halves
Gumdrops

Dissolve yeast in warm water in large mixer bowl. Add sugar, salt, imitation eggs, ½ cup margarine and 1½ cups of the flour. Blend on low speed ½ minute, scraping bowl constantly. Beat on medium speed 10 minutes, scraping bowl occasionally.

Stir in remaining flour, the chopped almonds, citron, raisins and lemon peel. Scrape batter from side of bowl. Cover; let rise in warm place until double, about 1 hour.

Stir down batter by beating 25 strokes. Cover bowl tightly; refrigerate at least 8 hours.

Turn dough onto well-floured board; turn to coat with flour. Divide dough in half. Press each half into oval, about 10x7 inches. Spread each with 3 tablespoons margarine. Fold lengthwise in half; press only folded edge firmly. Place on greased baking sheet. Beat egg white slightly; beat in 1 tablespoon water and brush on stollen. Let rise until double, about 35 minutes.

Heat oven to 375°. Bake 20 to 25 minutes or until golden brown. While warm, frost with Quick White Icing; decorate with almond halves and gumdrops. Or, if desired, dust stollen with powdered sugar.

2 stollen.

1 serving (1 slice) = 1½ bread I
 165 calories

Quick White Icing: Mix 1½ cups powdered sugar and 1½ tablespoons skim milk until smooth.

SWEET DOUGH

1 package active dry yeast
¼ cup warm water (105 to 115°)
¼ cup lukewarm skim milk (scalded then
 cooled)
¼ cup sugar
¼ cup Second Nature
 imitation eggs*
¼ cup vegetable oil
2¼ to 2½ cups all-purpose flour

Dissolve yeast in warm water in mixing bowl. Stir in milk, sugar, imitation eggs, oil and half the flour. Beat until smooth. Mix in enough remaining flour to make dough easy to handle. Turn onto lightly floured board. Knead until smooth and elastic, about 5 minutes. Place in greased bowl; turn greased side up. (At this point, dough can be refrigerated 2 to 3 days.) Cover; let rise in warm place until double, about 1 hour. (Dough is ready if an indentation remains when touched.)

Punch down dough. Shape dough for desired rolls or coffeecakes. Cover; let rise until double. Heat oven to 375°. Bake as directed.

1 roll = ½ bread I
 125 calories

*If this ingredient is not available in your market area, see page 29 for substitutes.

STREUSEL COFFEE CAKE

1½ cups all-purpose flour
¾ cup sugar
3½ teaspoons low-sodium baking powder
¼ cup unsalted margarine, softened
¾ cup skim milk
¼ cup Second Nature
  imitation eggs*
Streusel Mixture (below)

Heat oven to 375°. Grease round layer pan, 9x1½ inches. Measure all ingredients into large mixing bowl. Blend thoroughly with fork; beat vigorously ½ minute. Spread half the batter in pan. Sprinkle half the Streusel Mixture on batter in pan. Top with remaining batter and Streusel Mixture. Bake 25 to 30 minutes or until wooden pick inserted in center comes out clean. Serve warm.

16 servings.

1 serving = ½ bread I
180 calories

Streusel Mixture: Mix ½ cup brown sugar (packed), 2 teaspoons cinnamon, ½ cup finely chopped pecans and 2 tablespoons unsalted margarine, melted.

GOLDEN PUFFS

2 cups all-purpose flour
¼ cup sugar
1 tablespoon plus 1½ teaspoons
  low-sodium baking powder
1 teaspoon nutmeg or mace
¼ cup vegetable oil
¾ cup skim milk
¼ cup Second Nature imitation
  eggs*
½ cup sugar
1 teaspoon cinnamon

Heat oil (3 to 4 inches) in deep fat fryer or heavy kettle to 375°. Measure flour, ¼ cup sugar, the baking powder and nutmeg into mixing bowl. Add oil, milk and imitation eggs; beat with fork until smooth.

Drop batter by teaspoonfuls (too large puffs will not cook through) into hot oil. Fry until golden brown on both sides, about 3 minutes. Drain.

Mix ½ cup sugar and the cinnamon. Roll warm puffs in sugar-cinnamon mixture or, if desired, glaze puffs with a powdered sugar glaze.

2½ dozen puffs.

1 puff = ½ bread I
75 calories

*If this ingredient is not available in your market area, see page 29 for substitutes.

PINEAPPLE COFFEE CAKE

**1 can (13¼ ounces) crushed pineapple,
   drained (reserve 1 tablespoon plus
   1 teaspoon syrup)**
2 tablespoons cornstarch
¼ cup brown sugar (packed)
¼ cup sliced almonds
2 tablespoons unsalted margarine
2 tablespoons brown sugar
¼ cup all-purpose flour
¼ cup sliced almonds
1 recipe Sweet Dough (page 93)
Glaze (opposite)

Mix pineapple, cornstarch and ¼ cup sugar in small saucepan. Cook, stirring constantly, until mixture thickens and boils. Boil and stir 1 minute. Remove from heat; stir in ¼ cup almonds. Cool.

Mix margarine, 2 tablespoons sugar and flour until crumbly. Stir in ¼ cup almonds and set aside.

Roll dough into rectangle, 18x6 inches, on lightly floured board. Spread pineapple mixture on rectangle to within ½ inch of edges. Roll up, beginning at long side. Pinch edge of dough into roll to seal well. Stretch roll to make even. Place roll seam side down on lightly greased baking sheet to form horseshoe shape. With scissors, make lengthwise cut through top layers of dough. Fold back layers to completely expose filling and double width of coffee cake. Sprinkle with crumbly mixture. Cover; let rise until double, about 30 minutes.

Bake about 20 minutes or until golden brown. While warm, drizzle with Glaze.

18 servings.

**1 serving = ½ bread I
              200 calories**

Glaze: Mix ½ cup brown sugar (packed) and the reserved 1 tablespoon plus 1 teaspoon pineapple syrup until smooth.

BLUEBERRY COFFEE CAKE

2 cups all-purpose flour
¾ cup sugar
3½ teaspoons low-sodium baking powder
¼ cup unsalted margarine, softened
¾ cup skim milk
**¼ cup Second Nature
   imitation eggs***
1 cup well-drained blueberries
Crumb mixture (below)

Heat oven to 375°. Grease round layer pan, 9x1½ inches. Measure flour, sugar, baking powder, margarine, milk and imitation eggs into large mixing bowl. Blend thoroughly with fork; beat vigorously ½ minute. Carefully stir blueberries into batter. Pour into pan. Sprinkle Crumb Mixture on top. Bake 45 to 50 minutes or until wooden pick inserted in center comes out clean. Serve warm.

16 servings.

**1 serving = ½ bread I
              200 calories**

Crumb Mixture: Mix ½ cup sugar, ⅓ cup all-purpose flour, ½ teaspoon cinnamon and ¼ cup unsalted margarine, softened.

*If this ingredient is not available in your market area, see page 29 for substitutes.

BLUEBERRY-LEMON COFFEE CAKE

1 cup fresh or frozen blueberries
3 tablespoons sugar
1 tablespoon cornstarch
1 tablespoon lemon juice
1 recipe Sweet Dough (page 93)
Lemon Icing (below)

Mix blueberries, sugar, cornstarch and lemon juice in small saucepan. Cook, stirring constantly, until mixture thickens and boils. Boil and stir 1 minute. Cool.

Roll dough into rectangle, 18x6 inches, on lightly floured board. Spread blueberry mixture on rectangle to within ½ inch of edges. Roll up, beginning at long side. Pinch edge of dough into roll to seal well. Stretch roll to make even. Place roll seam side down on lightly greased baking sheet to form horseshoe shape. Cover; let rise until double, about 30 minutes.

Bake about 20 minutes or until golden brown. While warm, frost with Lemon Icing.

18 servings.

1 serving = ½ bread I
135 calories

Lemon Icing: Mix ½ cup powdered sugar, 1 tablespoon grated lemon peel and 2 teaspoons lemon juice until smooth.

SWEDISH TEA RING

1 recipe Sweet Dough (page 93)
2 tablespoons unsalted margarine,
  softened
½ cup brown sugar (packed)
2 teaspoons cinnamon
½ cup raisins
Powdered Sugar Icing (page 97)

Roll dough into rectangle, 15x9 inches. Spread with margarine and sprinkle sugar, cinnamon and raisins on rectangle. Roll up, beginning at long side. Pinch edge of dough into roll to seal well. Stretch roll to make even. With sealed edge down, shape into ring on lightly greased baking sheet. Pinch ends together. With scissors, make cuts ⅔ of the way through ring at 1-inch intervals. Turn each section on its side. Let rise until double, about 30 minutes.

Bake 20 to 25 minutes. While warm, frost with Powdered Sugar Icing. Serve warm.

17 servings

1 serving = ½ Bread I
190 calories

SUGAR CRISP ROLLS

1 recipe Sweet Dough (page 93)
3 tablespoons unsalted margarine, melted
1 cup sugar
1 cup finely chopped pecans

Turn dough onto lightly floured board; roll into rectangle, 18x9 inches. Brush with margarine. Mix sugar and pecans; sprinkle half the mixture on rectangle. Roll up, beginning at long side. Cut roll into 1-inch slices. Roll and flatten each slice into a 4-inch circle, using remaining sugar-nut mixture in place of flour. Place on greased baking sheet. Cover; let rise until double, about 30 minutes. Bake 10 minutes or until done.

18 rolls.

1 serving (1 roll) = ½ bread I
215 calories

CINNAMON ROLLS (WITH SALT)

1 package active dry yeast
¼ cup warm water (105 to 115°)
¼ cup lukewarm skim milk (scalded then cooled)
¼ cup sugar
¼ teaspoon salt
¼ cup Second Nature imitation eggs*
¼ cup vegetable oil
2¼ to 2½ cups all-purpose flour
2 tablespoons unsalted margarine, softened
¼ cup sugar
2 teaspoons cinnamon

Dissolve yeast in warm water in mixing bowl. Stir in milk, ¼ cup sugar, the salt, imitation eggs, oil and half the flour. Mix with spoon until smooth. Mix in enough remaining flour to make dough easy to handle.

Turn dough onto lightly floured board. Knead until smooth and elastic, about 5 minutes. Place in greased bowl; turn greased side up. (At this point, dough can be refrigerated up to 2 days.) Cover; let rise in warm place until double, about 1 hour. (Dough is ready if an indentation remains when touched.)

Punch down dough. Roll into rectangle, 15x9 inches. Spread with margarine. Mix ¼ cup sugar and the cinnamon; sprinkle on rectangle. Roll up, beginning at long side. Pinch edge of dough into roll to seal well. Stretch roll to make even. Cut into 15 slices; place in greased baking pan, 13x9x2 inches. Let rise about 30 minutes.

Heat oven to 375°. Bake 20 to 25 minutes.

15 rolls.

1 serving (1 roll) = 1½ bread I
           155 calories

CINNAMON ROLLS

1 recipe Sweet Dough (page 93)
2 tablespoons unsalted margarine softened
¼ cup sugar
2 teaspoons cinnamon
Powdered Sugar Icing (below)

Roll dough into rectangle, 15x9 inches. Spread with margarine. Mix sugar and cinnamon; sprinkle on rectangle. Roll up, beginning at long side. Seal well by pinching edge of dough into roll. Cut roll into 15 slices. Place in greased baking pan, 13x9x2 inches. Let rise about 30 minutes. Bake 20 to 25 minutes or until golden brown. While warm, frost with icing.

15 rolls.

1 serving (1 roll) = ½ bread I
           190 calories

Powdered Sugar Icing: Mix 1 cup powdered sugar, 1 tablespoon skim milk and ½ teaspoon vanilla until smooth.

Variation

Butterscotch-Pecan Rolls: Before rolling dough into rectangle, melt ½ cup unsalted margarine in baking pan; sprinkle ½ cup brown sugar (packed) and ½ cup pecan halves over margarine. Roll, slice and bake as directed. Immediately turn pan upside down on large tray. Let pan remain a minute so butterscotch drizzles down over rolls.

1 serving (1 roll) = ½ bread I
           235 calories

*If this ingredient is not available in your market area, see page 29 for substitutes.

FROSTED ORANGE ROLLS

**3 tablespoons unsalted margarine,
softened**
1 tablespoon grated orange peel
2 tablespoons orange juice
1½ cups powdered sugar
1 recipe Sweet Dough (page 93)

Mix margarine, orange peel, juice and sugar until creamy and smooth.

Roll dough into rectangle, 15x9 inches; spread with half the orange frosting. Roll up, beginning at long side. Pinch edge of dough into roll to seal well. Stretch roll to make even. Cut roll into 15 slices. Place in greased baking pan, 13x9x2 inches. Let rise about 30 minutes. Bake 20 to 25 minutes or until golden brown. While warm, frost rolls with remaining frosting.

15 rolls.

**1 serving (1 roll) = ½ bread I
200 calories**

BABKA

½ cup hot water
¼ cup unsalted margarine
½ cup sugar
¾ teaspoon cinnamon
1 tablespoon grated orange peel
1 package active dry yeast
¼ cup warm water (105 to 115°)
½ cup Second Nature imitation eggs*
3½ to 4 cups all-purpose flour
**2 tablespoons unsalted margarine,
melted**
Filling (opposite)

Mix ½ cup water, ¼ cup margarine, the sugar, cinnamon and orange peel in large bowl. Dissolve yeast in ¼ cup warm water. Stir into margarine mixture. Add imitation eggs and 1 cup of the flour; beat until smooth. Beat in enough remaining flour to make dough easy to handle.

Turn dough onto lightly floured board; knead until smooth and elastic, about 10 minutes. Place in greased bowl; turn greased side up. Cover and let rise in warm place until double, 1½ to 2 hours. (Dough is ready if an impression remains when touched.)

Punch down dough; allow to rise again, about 1 hour.

Punch down dough; divide in half. Roll each half into rectangle, 12x8 inches. Brush each with 1 tablespoon of the melted margarine and sprinkle with half the Filling. Roll up, beginning at long side. Cut into ten 1-inch slices. Place 10 slices cut side up in single layer in well-greased 9-inch tube pan. Top with remaining slices and Filling. Let rise until double.

Heat oven to 350°. Bake 35 to 40 minutes or until golden brown. To serve, break rolls apart with 2 forks.

20 rolls.

Filling

½ cup chopped walnuts
½ cup raisins
2 tablespoons sugar
1 teaspoon cinnamon
**2 tablespoons unsalted margarine,
melted**

Mix all ingredients.

**1 roll = ½ bread I
240 calories**

*If this ingredient is not available in your market area, see page 29 for substitutes.

SWEET MUFFINS

¼ cup Second Nature imitation eggs*
½ cup skim milk
¼ cup vegetable oil
1½ cups all-purpose flour
3 teaspoons low-sodium baking powder
½ cup sugar

Heat oven to 400°. Grease bottoms of 12 small or 8 large muffin cups. Measure imitation eggs, milk and oil into mixing bowl. Mix in remaining ingredients just until flour is moistened. Batter should be lumpy.

Fill muffin cups ⅔ full. Bake 20 to 25 minutes or until golden brown. Immediately remove from pan.

12 small or 8 large muffins.

1 small muffin = 1 bread I
145 calories

Variations

Apple Muffins: Stir in 1 cup shredded pared apple to oil mixture and add ½ teaspoon cinnamon with the flour. Bake 25 to 30 minutes. If desired, before baking, sprinkle tops with Nut-crunch Topping: Mix ⅓ cup brown sugar (packed), ⅓ cup chopped walnuts and ½ teaspoon cinnamon.

1 small muffin = 1 bread I
200 calories

Blueberry Muffins: Fold 1 cup fresh blueberries or ¾ cup well-drained frozen blueberries (thawed) into batter.

1 small muffin = 1 bread I
155 calories

Cranberry-Orange Muffins: Fold 1 tablespoon grated orange peel and 1 cup cranberries, cut in half, into batter.

1 small muffin = 1 bread I
150 calories

Surprise Muffins: Fill muffin cups only ½ full; drop 1 teaspoon jelly in center of each and add batter to fill cups ⅔ full.

1 small muffin = 1 bread I
160 calories

*If this ingredient is not available in our market area, see page 29 for substitutes.

9.Salads

In these appealing salads, you'll find daily opportunities for adventurous mealtime variety in texture and color—plus a truly remarkable range of flavorsome dressings.

MIXED VEGETABLE SALAD

2 tablespoons low-sodium mayonnaise
1 tablespoon chopped onion
½ teaspoon dry mustard
½ teaspoon sugar
¼ teaspoon caraway seed
1 cup unsalted mixed vegetables
Lettuce
Paprika

Mix mayonnaise, onion, mustard, sugar and caraway seed; pour on vegetables and toss. Serve on lettuce and sprinkle with paprika.

2 servings.

1 serving = ½ bread II
            140 calories

TOMATO SALAD

½ cup Old-fashioned French Dressing
  (page 112)
1 tablespoon finely snipped parsley
1 teaspoon dill seed
1 teaspoon minced chervil leaves
½ teaspoon rosemary leaves
3 tomatoes, peeled and sliced
1 medium cucumber, thinly sliced
2 medium onions, thinly sliced and
  separated into rings

Mix dressing, parsley, dill seed, chervil leaves and rosemary in large bowl. Add tomatoes, cucumber and onions and toss. Cover and refrigerate to blend flavors.

6 servings.

1 serving = ½ vegetable
            150 calories

HERBED TOMATOES

1 teaspoon basil leaves
1 teaspoon snipped chives
¼ teaspoon tarragon
Freshly ground pepper
Grated peel and juice of 1 lemon
1 teaspoon grated orange peel
1 tablespoon orange juice
3 tablespoons unsalted tomato juice
4 medium tomatoes, peeled and sliced

Shake all ingredients except tomatoes in tightly covered jar. Refrigerate 2 hours. At serving time, pour on tomatoes.

6 servings.

1 serving = 1 vegetable
            25 calories

TOSSED GREEN SALAD

½ clove garlic
3 or 4 lettuce leaves (iceberg, Boston, Bibb, leaf and/or bronze)
1 teaspoon olive oil
1 teaspoon cider or wine vinegar
¼ teaspoon sugar, if desired
Freshly ground pepper

Rub small wooden salad bowl with cut side of garlic. Tear lettuce into bite-size pieces (about 1 cup) into bowl. Drizzle with oil and toss until leaves glisten. Refrigerate until serving time.

Mix vinegar, sugar and pepper; drizzle on lettuce and toss.

1 serving.

1 serving = ½ vegetable
            70 calories

ZESTY LETTUCE SALAD

1 head Boston lettuce
3 sprigs chervil, if desired
3 green onions, chopped
2 tablespoons plus 1½ teaspoons olive oil
1 tablespoon plus 1½ teaspoons vinegar
¼ teaspoon dry mustard
¼ teaspoon freshly ground pepper
3 drops Tabasco pepper sauce

Tear lettuce into bite-size pieces (about 2 cups) into bowl; add chervil and onions. Shake oil, vinegar, mustard, pepper and pepper sauce in tightly covered jar. Pour on vegetables and toss.

2 servings.

1 serving = 1 vegetable
            205 calories

SUPER TOMATO SALAD

¼ cup wine vinegar
1 tablespoon sugar
1 tablespoon basil leaves
1 teaspoon tarragon
1 teaspoon oregano
Freshly ground pepper
¼ cup olive oil
2 large tomatoes, sliced
1 large Spanish onion, sliced

Shake vinegar, sugar, basil leaves, tarragon, oregano, pepper and oil in tightly covered jar. Arrange 1 layer each tomato slices and onion slices in serving bowl; drizzle with 1 to 2 tablespoons dressing. Repeat with remaining tomato slices, onion slices and dressing. Cover and refrigerate until serving time.

4 servings.

1 serving = ½ vegetable
            200 calories

SPINACH AND ENDIVE SALAD

1 clove garlic, peeled and halved
¼ cup olive or vegetable oil
¼ pound spinach
1 head curly endive, washed and chilled
10 cherry tomatoes, cut into halves
¾ teaspoon oregano leaves
¼ teaspoon freshly ground pepper
1 tablespoon wine vinegar
1 tablespoon lemon juice
¼ teaspoon dry mustard

Add garlic to oil and let stand 1 hour.

Wash spinach; remove stems and dry leaves. Remove garlic from oil and rub on inside of salad bowl. Tear spinach leaves into bite-size pieces into bowl. Tear endive into bite-size pieces into bowl. Add tomato halves. Mix remaining ingredients and garlic oil; pour on salad mixture and toss.

8 servings.

1 serving = 1 vegetable
85 calories

MIXED GREEN SALAD WITH LEMON DRESSING

Lemon Dressing (opposite)
Lettuce, washed and chilled
Spinach, washed and chilled
Escarole, washed and chilled

Prepare dressing. Into large salad bowl, tear lettuce and spinach into bite-size pieces to measure 5 cups. Tear escarole into bite-size pieces to measure 1 cup. Pour ⅓ cup dressing on greens and toss.

6 servings.

1 serving = 1 vegetable
95 calories

LEMON DRESSING I

2 tablespoons wine vinegar
⅔ cup vegetable oil
½ teaspoon grated lemon peel
⅓ cup lemon juice
2 tablespoons snipped parsley
1 clove garlic, peeled and split
1 teaspoon sugar
½ teaspoon freshly ground pepper
½ teaspoon dry mustard
¼ teaspoon paprika

Shake all ingredients in jar with tight fitting lid. Let stand 1 hour. Remove garlic and store dressing in refrigerator.

1 cup.

2 tablespoons = 4 fat
190 calories

WATERCRESS AND ROMAINE SALAD

1 bunch watercress, washed and chilled
1 head romaine lettuce, washed and chilled
1 can (11 ounces) mandarin oranges, drained
Shallot Dressing (page 113)

Tear greens into bite-size pieces into bowl. Add oranges; pour dressing on salad mixture and toss.

6 servings.

1 serving = ½ vegetable, ½ fruit
150 calories

SPINACH SALAD

3 tablespoons wine vinegar
¼ cup plus 2 tablespoons vegetable oil
⅛ teaspoon pepper
½ teaspoon dry mustard
2 tablespoons snipped parsley
1 large clove garlic, peeled and halved
1 bag (10 ounces) spinach
½ cauliflower, separated into flowerets
½ red onion, sliced and separated into rings
½ cup sliced radish

Mix vinegar, oil, pepper, mustard, parsley in salad bowl; add garlic and let stand ½ to 1 hour.

Wash spinach; remove stems and dry leaves. Remove garlic from bowl and discard. Tear spinach leaves into bite-size pieces into bowl. Add cauliflowerets and onion rings and toss until vegetables are well coated.

6 servings.

1 serving = 1 vegetable
170 calories

MUSHROOM AND RADISH SALAD

4 medium mushrooms, trimmed
  and thinly sliced
8 radishes, thinly sliced
1 tablespoon lemon juice
3 tablespoons olive oil
Freshly ground pepper
1 tablespoon snipped parsley

Combine mushrooms and radishes in salad bowl. Mix lemon juice, oil, pepper and parsley. Pour over vegetables and toss.

2 servings.

1 serving = 1 vegetable
220 calories

TOSSED SALAD ELEGANTE

2 heads endive, washed
2 heads Bibb lettuce, washed and chilled
½ bunch watercress, washed and chilled
Leaf lettuce, washed and chilled
Shallot Dressing (page 113)

Cut endive into quarters. Place in large bowl; pour lukewarm water over endive and let stand 10 minutes to remove bitterness. Drain and chill.

Tear Bibb lettuce into bite-size pieces into salad bowl. Tear leaf lettuce into bite-size pieces to measure ¼ cup. Add watercress and endive. Pour dressing on greens and toss.

3 or 4 servings.

1 serving = 1 vegetable
190 calories

FRESH BEAN SALAD

2 pounds green beans
2½ cups boiling water
1 tablespoon freshly ground pepper
¾ cup vegetable oil
2 tablespoons wine vinegar
1 tablespoon sugar
1 medium onion, cut into pieces
2 tablespoons snipped parsley

Wash beans and remove ends. Leave beans whole. Pour water on beans; cover and let stand 10 minutes.

Drain beans; place in shallow serving dish. Place remaining ingredients in blender container; blend until smooth. Pour on beans. Cover tightly and refrigerate at least 2 hours. Mix lightly before serving.

8 servings.

1 serving = 1 vegetable
245 calories

CAESAR SALAD

1 clove garlic, split
¼ cup olive oil
3 tablespoons wine vinegar
⅛ teaspoon dry mustard
⅛ teaspoon onion powder
⅛ teaspoon garlic powder
1 teaspoon sugar
Freshly ground pepper
1 head romaine
1 egg, beaten

Rub wooden salad bowl with cut clove of garlic. Measure oil, vinegar and seasonings into bowl and mix thoroughly. Tear romaine into bite-size pieces (about 8 cups) into bowl. Toss until leaves glisten. Add egg and toss until leaves are well coated.

8 servings.

1 serving = 1 vegetable
105 calories

HEARTS OF PALM SALAD

½ head romaine
1 head Boston lettuce
1 can (14 ounces) hearts of palm,
**   drained and cut into ¼-inch slices**
1 avocado, peeled and diced
⅓ cup vegetable oil
2 tablespoons vinegar
1 tablespoon lemon juice
Freshly ground pepper

Tear lettuce into bite-size pieces (about 4 cups) into bowl. Add hearts of palm slices and avocado and toss. Shake remaining ingredients in tightly covered jar; pour on salad and toss.

6 servings.

1 serving = 2 vegetable
135 calories

ASPARAGUS SALAD

5 cooked extra-long asparagus spears
1 lettuce leaf
½ medium tomato
2 teaspoons Lemon Dressing (page 113)

Arrange asparagus spears on lettuce leaf. Cut tomato into 2 wedges and place on either side of asparagus spears. Drizzle with dressing.

1 serving.

1 serving = 1 vegetable
240 calories

TART COLESLAW

1 medium cabbage
¼ cup cider vinegar
½ teaspoon pepper
¼ teaspoon dill weed
¼ teaspoon chervil leaves
¼ cup dairy sour half-and-half
¼ cup low-sodium mayonnaise
Paprika
Snipped parsley

Scoop out center of cabbage, leaving a shell; refrigerate shell. Shred scooped-out cabbage; place in ice and water and let stand 30 minutes.

Drain cabbage thoroughly. Toss cabbage, vinegar, pepper, dill weed and chervil leaves; let stand 1 hour. Drain cabbage thoroughly.

Mix sour half-and-half and mayonnaise; pour on cabbage and toss. Spoon mixture into cabbage shell and sprinkle with paprika and parsley.

8 servings.

1 serving = ½ vegetable
50 calories

SPICED FRUIT MOLD

1 envelope unflavored gelatin
½ cup water
1 can (15¼ ounces) pineapple chunks
  in unsweetened pineapple juice, drained
  (reserve juice)
1 can (11 ounces) mandarin oranges,
  drained (reserve syrup)
2 cups water
1 cinnamon stick (3 inches)
1 teaspoon whole cloves
¼ teaspoon ginger
1 medium red apple, diced

Sprinkle gelatin on ½ cup water to soften. Measure reserved pineapple juice into medium saucepan and add enough reserved orange syrup to measure 1 cup. Add 2 cups water and the spices; heat to simmering and simmer 10 minutes.

Remove cinnamon stick and cloves; pour liquid on gelatin mixture. Stir over low heat until gelatin is dissolved, about 2 minutes. Chill until slightly thickened. Stir in fruit. Pour into 8 individual molds or into 5-cup ring mold. Chill until firm.

8 servings.

1 serving = 1 fruit
        70 calories

GARDEN PATCH SALAD

1 envelope unflavored gelatin
¼ cup sugar
½ cup water
¼ teaspoon Tabasco pepper sauce
¼ cup lemon juice
1 cup water
Choice of Vegetable Combination (below)

Mix gelatin and sugar in saucepan. Stir in ½ cup water. Stir over low heat until gelatin is dissolved. Remove from heat; stir in pepper sauce, lemon juice and 1 cup water. Chill until mixture is slightly thickened.

Fold in vegetable combination. Pour into 3-cup mold or into 6 individual molds. Chill until firm.

6 servings.

Choice of Vegetable Combination

1½ cups shredded carrot
¼ cup chopped cauliflower
¼ cup diced green pepper

1 serving = 1 vegetable
        55 calories

2 cups canned unsalted mixed vegetables
2 tablespoons snipped dill or parsley

1 serving = 1½ vegetable
        80 calories

1½ cups finely shredded cabbage
¼ cup sliced radish
¼ cup minced green onion

1 serving = ½ vegetable
        45 calories

CUCUMBER SALAD

3 medium cucumbers
1 cup dairy sour half-and-half
1 tablespoon lemon juice
1 tablespoon snipped chives
⅛ teaspoon paprika

Pare cucumbers and slice very thinly. Mix remaining ingredients with fork. Cover and refrigerate half-and-half mixture and cucumbers separately.

Just before serving, add cucumbers to half-and-half mixture and toss until all slices are coated.

6 servings.

1 serving = 1 vegetable
            65 calories

CRESSON SALAD

2 bunches watercress
3 green onions, chopped (with tops)
¼ cup slivered green pepper
1 medium navel orange, pared, sectioned, and cut up
½ cup fresh grapefruit sections, cut up
3 tablespoons wine vinegar
1 tablespoon vegetable oil
Freshly ground pepper

Remove imperfect leaves and stems from watercress; discard. Toss watercress leaves, onion and green pepper. Cover with damp towel and refrigerate.

At serving time, add remaining ingredients and toss.

4 servings.

1 serving = ½ vegetable, ¼ fruit
            70 calories

SUNSHINE SALAD

2 envelopes unflavored gelatin
⅓ cup sugar
1 can (1 pound 4 ounces) pineapple chunks, drained (reserve syrup)
⅓ cup lemon juice
1 cup coarsely shredded carrot
1½ cups halved orange sections
Salad greens

Mix gelatin and sugar in saucepan. Add enough water to reserved syrup to measure 2½ cups. Add 1 cup of the syrup mixture to gelatin mixture. Stir over low heat until gelatin is dissolved, about 5 minutes. Remove from heat; stir in lemon juice and remaining syrup mixture. Chill until mixture mounds slightly when dropped from a spoon.

Stir in carrot, orange sections and pineapple chunks. Turn mixture into 5-cup mold. Chill until firm. Unmold onto serving plate and garnish with salad greens.

6 servings.

1 serving = 1 fruit, ¼ vegetable
            145 calories

PINEAPPLE CRANBERRY RELISH MOLD

1 can (18 ounces) pineapple juice
2 envelopes unflavored gelatin
2 tablespoons sugar
½ teaspoon salt
1 can (1 pound 4½ ounces) crushed pineapple
¼ cup vinegar
Juice of 1 lemon (3 tablespoons)
½ cup chopped celery
½ cup chopped green pepper
1 cup chopped cranberries

Measure 1 cup of the pineapple juice into medium saucepan. Sprinkle gelatin on juice to soften. Stir over low heat until gelatin is dissolved, 4 to 5 mintues. Remove from heat; stir in remaining juice, the sugar, salt, pineapple (with syrup), vinegar and lemon juice. Chill until slightly thickened. Stir in celery, green pepper and cranberries. Pour into 6-cup mold. Chill until firm.

8 to 12 servings.

1 serving = 1 fruit, ½ salted vegetable
90 calories

GRAPEFRUIT MOLD

1 tablespoon plus ¾ teaspoon unflavored gelatin
¾ cup sugar
¾ cup boiling water
¾ cup grapefruit juice
¼ cup orange juice
2 tablespoons lemon juice

Mix gelatin and sugar in bowl. Pour boiling water over gelatin mixture and stir until gelatin is dissolved. Stir in remaining ingredients. Pour into 2-cup mold and chill until firm.

4 servings.

Note: This recipe can be doubled.

1 serving = ½ fruit
185 calories

CRANBERRY GELATIN

1 envelope unflavored gelatin
½ cup water
2 cups cranberries
1 cup water
1 cup sugar
⅛ teaspoon mace
½ cup chopped pared apple

Sprinkle gelatin on ½ cup water to soften.

Heat cranberries, 1 cup water, the sugar and mace in large saucepan to boiling, stirring constantly. Cook until cranberries pop, 5 to 10 minutes.

Stir gelatin into hot cranberry mixture. Place pan in bowl of ice and water or refrigerate until mixture mounds slightly when dropped from a spoon. Fold in apple. Pour into 4-cup mold and chill until firm.

6 servings.

1 serving = 1 fruit
160 calories

MINTED FRUIT SALAD

6 navel oranges
3 cups fresh or canned grapefruit sections
2 cans (11 ounces each) mandarin orange
 segments, drained
1 large bunch fresh mint, snipped
½ cup olive oil
¼ cup lemon juice
3 tablespoons cognac
Boston lettuce
Watercress

Pare oranges and cut into slices. Toss orange slices, grapefruit sections, mandarin orange segments and mint. Cover and refrigerate at least 3 hours.

Shake olive oil, lemon juice and cognac in tightly covered jar; pour on fruit. Cover and refrigerate at least 1 hour. Serve on lettuce and garnish with watercress.

8 servings.

1 serving = 2 fruit
                250 calories

EGG SALAD

1 tablespoon unsalted margarine or
 vegetable oil
1 cup Second Nature imitation eggs*
¼ cup chopped onion
½ cup chopped celery
¼ cup low-sodium mayonnaise

Melt margarine in large skillet. Add imitation eggs and cook over low heat until set. (Do not stir.) Turn onto large plate; cool.

Cut egg mixture into small pieces; turn into bowl. Stir in onion, celery and mayonnaise.

4 servings.

1 serving = 1½ meat
                150 calories

*If this ingredient is not available in your market area, see page 29 for substitutes.

SPICED MINTED PEARS

1 can (20 ounces) pear halves, drained
 (reserve syrup)
1 stick cinnamon
6 whole cloves
½ teaspoon ginger
2 tablespoons lemon juice
1 teaspoon sugar
½ teaspoon mint extract
Few drops green food color

Heat reserved pear syrup, cinnamon, cloves, ginger, lemon juice and sugar in large skillet to simmering; simmer uncoverd 3 minutes. Add pears; cover and simmer 5 minutes. Cool pears in syrup. Remove pears to bowl. Stir mint extract and food color into syrup; pour over pears. Cover and refrigerate.

6 servings.

Note: Pears used on greens make a delicious salad. But this recipe is also an excellent garnish for lamb or veal.

1 serving = 1 fruit
                95 calories

SHRIMP GRAPEFRUIT SHELL

1½ quarts water (6 cups)
2 bay leaves
2 teaspoons curry powder
20 frozen unsalted cleaned raw shrimp
2 medium grapefruit
½ cup low-sodium mayonnaise
1 tablespoon grapefruit juice
1 tablespoon apricot jam
1 tablespoon snipped parsley
Grated peel of 1 lemon
1 teaspoon lemon juice

Heat water, bay leaves and curry powder in large saucepan to boiling. Reduce heat and simmer 15 minutes. Add frozen shrimp; cover and heat to boiling. Reduce heat and simmer 5 minutes. Drain; place shrimp in bowl and cool.

Cut each grapefruit in half. Cut around edges and membranes and remove sections; place in bowl with shrimp. Remove membranes from grapefruit shells.

Mix mayonnaise, grapefruit juice, apricot jam, parsley, lemon peel and juice; pour on shrimp mixture and toss. Divide mixture among grapefruit shells. Cover and refrigerate 2 hours.

4 servings.

1 serving = 1 meat, 1 fruit
240 calories

TOMATO STUFFED WITH CHICKEN SALAD

Chicken Salad (below)
2 small tomatoes
2 lettuce leaves
Freshly ground pepper

Prepare Chicken Salad. Cut off stem ends of tomatoes. With cut side down, cut each tomato into sixths, cutting through to within 1 inch of bottom. Carefully spread sections, forming a "flower." Sprinkle inside of each tomato flower with freshly ground pepper and fill with chicken salad. Serve on lettuce.

2 servings.

Chicken Salad

½ green pepper, finely chopped
1 tablespoon finely chopped onion
4 ounces diced cooked unsalted chicken
1 tablespoon low-sodium mayonnaise
1 tablespoon dairy sour cream
½ teaspoon sugar
½ teaspoon dry mustard
¼ teaspoon freshly ground pepper
¼ teaspoon paprika

Combine green pepper, onion and chicken in bowl. Mix mayonnaise, sour cream, sugar, mustard, pepper and paprika; pour on chicken and vegetables and toss.

2 servings.

1 serving = ½ meat, 1 vegetable
195 calories

ZIPPY POTATO SALAD

¼ teaspoon mustard seed
¼ teaspoon dill seed
1 tablespoon water
1½ cups diced unsalted cooked potato
2 tablespoons thinly sliced celery
1 tablespoon sliced green onion
1 teaspoon lemon juice
1 hard-cooked egg, chopped
¼ cup Zippy Cooked Dressing (below)
2 red radishes

Mix mustard seed, dill seed and water; let stand at least 1 hour. Toss seed mixture, potatoes, celery, onion and lemon juice. Stir in egg and dressing. Cover and refrigerate.

Remove stem and root ends from radishes. Cut thin petals around radishes; place in bowl of ice and water to crispen. At serving time, garnish potato salad with radish "roses."

8 servings.

**1 serving = 1 bread I
45 calories**

ZIPPY COOKED DRESSING

1 tablespoon flour
1 tablespoon sugar
¾ teaspoon dry mustard
Dash cayenne pepper
3 tablespoons Second Nature imitation egg*
⅓ cup skim milk
2 tablespoons vinegar
1 teaspoon unsalted margarine

Mix flour, sugar, mustard and cayenne pepper in small saucepan. Stir in imitation eggs and milk. Heat to boiling, stirring constantly, until mixture thickens and boils. Remove from heat; stir in vinegar and margarine. Store in covered container in refrigerator.

About ½ cup.

**2 tablespoons = ½ salted fat
50 calories**

CHICKEN SALAD

2 cups thin strips cooked unsalted chicken
1 cup thin strips pared apple
½ cup thin strips cucumber
¼ cup Lemon Dressing (page 113)
Freshly ground pepper
1 teaspoon dry mustard
½ cup low-sodium mayonnaise
Lettuce leaves
3 tablespoons snipped chives

Combine chicken, apple strips and cucumber strips. Pour Lemon Dressing on chicken mixture and toss. Season with pepper. Mix mustard and mayonnaise; fold into chicken mixture. Line individual salad bowls with lettuce; spoon salad into bowls and sprinkle with chives.

6 servings.

Note: The chicken salad is also tasty as a sandwich filling.

**1 serving = ½ meat
220 calories**

*If this ingredient is not available in your market area, see page 29 for substitutes.

BASIC SALAD DRESSING

¼ cup vegetable oil
1 tablespoon low-sodium mayonnaise
1 tablespoon wine vinegar
⅛ teaspoon pepper
Dash garlic powder.

Mix all ingredients thoroughly. Cover and refrigerate until ready to use.

About ¼ cup.

1 tablespoon = 3 fat
150 calories

FRENCH DRESSING

½ cup vegetable oil
3 tablespoons wine vinegar
2 tablespoons lemon juice
1 tablespoon chopped onion or snipped chives
2 teaspoons snipped parsley
1¾ teaspoons paprika
½ teaspoon basil leaves
⅛ teaspoon pepper
1½ cloves garlic, peeled

Shake all ingrdients in tightly covered jar. Refrigerate at least 12 hours to blend flavors. Remove garlic. Shake before serving.

About ¾ cup.

2 tablespoons = 4 fat
190 calories

OLD-FASHIONED FRENCH DRESSING

1 cup vegetable oil
½ cup cider vinegar
1 tablespoon sugar
1 teaspoon paprika
1 teaspoon lemon juice
½ teaspoon dry mustard
1 clove garlic, peeled

Shake all ingredients in tightly covered jar. Refrigerate. Remove garlic and shake again before serving.

About 1½ cups.

2 tablespoons = 4 fat
185 calories

SPICY FRENCH DRESSING

⅔ cup vegetable oil
⅓ cup lemon juice or vinegar
½ teaspoon Tabasco pepper sauce
1 teaspoon paprika
1 teaspoon dry mustard
½ teaspoon sugar

Shake all ingredients in tightly covered jar. Serve with avocado, tomato and onion salad or with salad greens.

1 cup.

2 tablespoons = 2 fat
95 calories

ZERO SALAD DRESSING

1 teaspoon unflavored gelatin
1¼ cups unsalted tomato juice
2 tablespoons vinegar
1 clove garlic, peeled
¼ teaspoon Tabasco pepper sauce
1 tablespoon vegetable oil

Sprinkle gelatin on ¼ cup of the tomato juice in small saucepan to soften. Stir over low heat until gelatin is dissolved, 2 to 3 minutes. Remove from heat; stir in remaining ingredients. Cover and refrigerate. Shake or stir before using.

1¼ cups.

2 tablespoons = ½ fat
25 calories

SHALLOT DRESSING

¾ cup vegetable oil
1 tablespoon olive oil
2 tablespoons wine vinegar
1 tablespoon sugar
Freshly ground pepper
¼ cup snipped parsley
1 tablespoon tarragon leaves
1 tablespoon snipped chives
1 tablespoon snipped dill
2 shallots, chopped

Measure all ingredients into blender container; blend until smooth.

1½ cups.

2 tablespoons = 3 fat
155 calories

VINAIGRETTE DRESSING

¾ cup olive oil
½ cup tarragon or wine vinegar
¼ teaspoon Tabasco pepper sauce
1 tablespoon snipped chives
1 tablespoon snipped dill or 1
  teaspoon dill weed

Beat all ingredients thoroughly in small bowl. Use as marinade for cooked vegetables or as dressing for tossed salads.

About 1⅓ cups.

2 tablespoons = 4 fat
160 calories

LEMON DRESSING II

¼ cup vegetable oil
2 tablespoons lemon juice
1 tablespoon plus 1½ teaspoons tarragon
  vinegar
1 teaspoon snipped parsley
¼ teaspoon freshly ground pepper

Shake all ingredients in tightly covered jar.

About ¾ cup.

2 tablespoons = 2 fat
90 calories

CURRIED FRUIT SALAD DRESSING

¾ cup low-fat dairy sour cream
¼ cup Mayonnaise (page 115) or
  low-sodium mayonnaise
1 teaspoon sugar
1 teaspoon curry powder
1 teaspoon finely chopped crystallized
  ginger
½ teaspoon lemon juice

Mix all ingredients. Cover and chill at least 2 hours.

1 cup.

2 tablespoons = ½ salted fat
                135 calories

Note: This dressing makes a delicious curried fruit salad.

CURRIED FRUIT SALAD

Arrange banana chunks, pineapple chunks or slices, seedless green grapes, apple slices, and melon wedges on platter. Serve with Curried Fruit Salad Dressing (above).

TROPICAL SALAD DRESSING

½ cup olive oil
½ cup pineapple juice
1 teaspoon brown sugar
1 teaspoon lemon juice
1 banana, cut up
¼ orange, cut up

Place all ingredients in blender container; blend on high speed until smooth. Store in tightly covered jar in refrigerator. Shake before using.

1½ cups.

2 tablespoons = 2 fat
                105 calories

HONEY FRUIT SALAD DRESSING

½ cup honey
2 tablespoons lemon or lime juice
⅛ teaspoon Tabasco pepper sauce

Mix all ingredients.

About ½ cup.

1 tablespoon = trace sodium
                60 calories

SPANISH LOBSTER SALAD

2 quarts water (8 cups)
1 bay leaf
2 packages (8 ounces each) frozen
  lobster tails
2 tablespoons lemon juice
1 apple, pared and diced
1 orange, pared and sectioned
½ cup halved green grapes
¼ cup plus 2 tablespoons low-sodium
  mayonnaise
2 tablespoons skim milk
1 tablespoon Dijon-type Mustard (page 150)
1 tablespoon minced scallion
1 teaspoon tarragon leaves
Lettuce

Heat water and bay leaf in large saucepan to boiling. Add lobster tails and lemon juice; cook over medium heat 15 minutes or cook lobster tails as directed on package. Drain and cool. When cool, remove meat from shell; cut into pieces and chill.

Combine lobster and fruits in bowl. Mix mayonnaise, milk, mustard, scallion and tarragon leaves; pour on salad and mix. Serve in lettuce-lined bowl.

4 servings.

1 serving = 1 salted meat, 1 fruit
                275 calories

TUNA SALAD

**2 cans (7 ounces each) tuna packed in
  water, drained and flaked
½ cup chopped celery
¾ cup chopped onion
½ cup low-sodium mayonnaise
Freshly ground pepper
Salad greens
4 medium tomatoes, quartered
2 cucumbers, sliced
Lemon wedges**

Combine tuna, celery and onion in bowl. Mix mayonnaise and pepper; pour over tuna mixture and toss.

Serve on salad greens with tomato wedges, cucumber slices and lemon wedges.

6 servings.

**1 serving = 1 meat, 1 vegetable
200 calories**

MAYONNAISE

**1 tablespoon plus 2 teaspoons
  white wine vinegar
3 tablespoons Second Nature
  imitation eggs***
**1 teaspoon sugar
1 teaspoon dry mustard
¼ teaspoon white pepper
Dash cayenne pepper
1 cup vegetable oil**

In small mixer bowl, beat vinegar, imitation egg, sugar, mustard, pepper and cayenne pepper until blended. Continue beating, adding oil by the teaspoonful; as mixture thickens, increase amounts of oil. Store in tightly covered container in refrigerator.

About 1½ cups.

**2 teaspoons = 1 fat
55 calories**

*If this ingredient is not available in your market area, see page 29 for substitutes.

10. Main Dishes

Few would suspect that these delicious recipes were prepared for persons on a diet. Use them with confidence for the whole family—with controlled portions for the patient.

SUMMER DINNER PLATTER

3-pound rolled beef rump roast (high quality)
1 pound asparagus
¼ pound mushrooms, thinly sliced
Marinade (below)
16 cherry tomatoes
8 green onions

Place meat fat side up on rack in shallow roasting pan. Insert meat thermometer in center of thickest part of meat, making sure it does not rest in fat. Do not add water. Do not cover. Roast in 325° oven until meat thermometer registers 140° (rare, 1½ to 2 hours; cook longer if desired).

Roasts are easier to carve if allowed to set 15 to 20 minutes after removing from oven. Since meat continues to cook after removing from oven, if roast is to set it should be removed from oven when thermometer registers 5 to 10° lower than the desired doneness.

While meat cools, cook asparagus. Break off ends of asparagus as far down as stalks snap easily. Fill 10-inch skillet ½ full with water; heat to boiling. Add asparagus. Heat to boiling.

Cover and cook until stalk ends are crisp-tender, 8 to 12 minutes. Drain.

Cut meat into ¼-inch slices. Arrange meat, asparagus, and mushrooms in shallow glass dish. Pour Marinade on meat and vegetables. Cover and refrigerate 3 to 4 hours.

Arrange meat and asparagus on serving platter. Spoon mushrooms on meat and garnish with tomatoes and onions.

12 servings.

1 serving = 1 meat, 1 vegetable
375 calories

MARINADE

½ cup vegetable oil
½ cup cider vinegar
2 tablespoons dry mustard
1 tablespoon freshly ground pepper
2 cloves garlic, crushed

Shake all ingredients in tightly covered jar.

HAMBURGERS

1 pound lean ground beef
1 small onion, minced (¼ cup)
½ teaspoon freshly ground pepper
½ teaspoon dry mustard
¼ cup iced water

Mix all ingredients. Shape mixture into 4 patties, each about 3 inches in diameter and 1 inch thick.

To Broil: Set oven control at broil and/or 550°. Broil 3 inches from heat 3 to 4 minutes on each side for rare, 5 to 7 minutes for medium.

To Panfry: Fry in 1 to 2 teaspoons vegetable oil over medium heat, turning frequently, about 10 minutes.

To Grill: Place on grill 4 to 6 inches from hot coals. Cook, turning once, until done, about 12 minutes.

4 servings.

1 serving = 1 meat
270 calories

Variation

Italian-style Hamburgers: Before mixing ingredients, add ¼ teaspoon oregano leaves.

Hamburger Toppers

Smothered Onions: Slice 2 large onions and separate into rings. Cook and stir onion rings in 1 tablespoon unsalted margarine until crisp-tender.

1 serving = 1 meat
315 calories

Pepper and Onion: Slice 1 medium onion. Cut ½ each red pepper and green pepper into thin strips. Cook and stir onion and pepper strips in 1 tablespoon vegetable oil until tender. Season with freshly ground pepper.

1 serving = 1 meat
320 calories

Mashed Potato: Top each hamburger with thin tomato slice and thin slice (½ ounce) low-sodium, low-fat cheese. Spoon on ¼ cup mashed potatoes to which 1 tablespoon chopped onion has been added. Sprinkle with paprika.

1 serving = 1 meat, 1 milk l
325 calories

Hamburgers and Eggplant: Pare and slice eggplant into ¾-inch slices. Season with freshly ground pepper, then coat slices with flour. Cook in hot olive oil until tender. Keep hot while preparing hamburgers. Top each eggplant slice with hamburger, 3 tablespoons hot Tomato Sauce (page 151) and 1 tablespoon grated Parmesan cheese.

1 serving = 1 meat, 1 vegetable
345 calories

Horseradish and Onion: Before cooking hamburgers, heat 2 tablespoons water and 1 tablespoon horseradish powder over low heat. Spoon 1 teaspoon horseradish sauce in center of each hamburger patty. Top cooked patty with Smothered Onions (above).

1 serving = 1 meat
320 calories

The recipe for Meat Balls and Tomato Sauce is on page 120.

The recipe for Pepper Steak is on page 122.

The recipe for Roast Beef is on page 124.

The recipe for Broiled Lamb Chops is on page 128.

BEEF FONDUE

Trim fat from 1½ pounds boneless beef sirloin and cut meat into ¾-inch cubes. Prepare dipping sauces.*

Heat vegetable oil (1½ to 2 inches) in metal fondue pot on top of range to 425°. Transfer pot to source of heat at table.

Spear meat cubes with fondue forks (meat should be at room temperature to prevent splattering). Dip into hot oil and cook to desired doneness. Transfer cooked meat to dinner fork and dip into a sauce.

1 serving = 1 meat
 220 calories

*Select the sauces you prefer from sauces included in this book—or make up your own.

HERBED HAMBURGERS

1 pound lean ground beef
¼ cup finely chopped onion
1 tablespoon olive oil or unsalted
  margarine, melted
1 tablespoon lemon juice
1½ teaspoons snipped parsley
1 teaspoon water
¼ teaspoon garlic powder
⅛ teaspoon marjoram leaves
⅛ teaspoon basil leaves

Mix all ingredients thoroughly. Shape mixture into 4 patties. Set oven control at broil and/or 550°. Broil patties with tops 3 inches from heat 3 to 4 minutes on each side for rare, 5 to 7 minutes for medium.

4 servings.

1 serving = 1 meat
 295 calories

LAZY DAY POT ROAST

1 tablespoon vegetable oil
2-pound beef round steak, 1 inch thick
2 cups water
1 onion, chopped
1 cup canned unsalted tomatoes
1 tablespoon sugar
1 teaspoon allspice
½ teaspoon crushed basil leaves
1 slice lemon

Heat oil in large skillet. Brown meat in oil over medium-high heat. Add remaining ingredients. Reduce heat; cover and simmer until meat is tender, about 3 hours.

6 servings.

1 serving = 1½ meat
 345 calories

CHILI BURGERS

1½ pounds lean ground beef
¼ teaspoon pepper
1 teaspoon chili powder
2 medium tomatoes, peeled and chopped
1 clove garlic, finely chopped
½ cup water

Mix meat and pepper; shape mixture into 4 patties. Brown patties in skillet over medium-high heat; set aside. In same skillet, heat chili powder, tomatoes, garlic and water to boiling. Place patties in sauce; simmer uncovered 15 minutes.

4 servings.

1 serving = 1½ meat
 415 calories

HAMBURGER STROGANOFF

1 pound lean ground beef
1 medium onion, chopped (about ½ cup)
¼ cup unsalted margarine
2 tablespoons flour
1 clove garlic, minced
¼ teaspoon pepper
¾ cup chopped fresh mushrooms
1 cup Medium White Sauce (page 151)
1 cup dairy sour half-and-half
2 cups hot cooked noodles or rice

Cook and stir ground beef and onion in margarine in large skillet until onion is tender and meat is brown. Stir in flour, garlic, pepper and mushrooms; cook and stir 5 minutes. Stir in white sauce; heat to boiling, stirring constantly. Reduce heat; simmer uncovered 10 minutes. Drain off excess fat. Stir in sour half-and-half; heat through. Serve on noodles and, if desired, sprinkle with snipped parsley.

4 servings.

1 serving = 1 meat, 1 bread I
610 calories

MEAT LOAF

1 can (10 ounces) tomato purée
¾ pound lean ground beef
2 tablespoons Second Nature
  imitation eggs*
2 tablespoons skim milk
1 slice low-sodium bread, torn into small
  pieces
Dash red pepper
Dash garlic powder
⅛ teaspoon Italian seasoning
⅛ teaspoon parsley flakes

Heat tomato purée to simmering. Reduce heat and simmer 30 minutes, stirring occasionally.

Heat oven to 350°. Mix remaining ingredients thoroughly. Turn mixture into lightly greased pan and shape into a loaf. Bake 35 minutes. Remove from oven and pour tomato purée over loaf and bake 10 minutes longer.

3 servings.

1 serving = 1½ meat, 1 salted vegetable
310 calories.

MEATBALLS AND TOMATO SAUCE

2 cans (10 ounces each) unsalted tomatoes
1 can (6 ounces) unsalted tomato paste
1 tablespoon sugar
2 teaspoons oregano
⅛ teaspoon pepper
1 pound lean ground beef
1 clove garlic, minced
1 medium onion, finely chopped
1 tablespoon olive oil
1 package (6 or 7 ounces) elbow macaroni

Heat tomatoes, tomato paste, sugar, oregano and pepper to boiling, breaking up tomatoes with fork. Reduce heat and simmer uncovered 30 minutes.

Mix ground beef, garlic and onion. Shape mixture by rounded tablespoonfuls into balls. Slowly brown and cook meatballs in oil in large skillet.

Cook macaroni as directed on package except—omit salt. Serve meatballs and tomato sauce on hot macaroni.

Eight ½-cup servings.

1 serving = ⅓ meat, ½ bread I
280 calories

*If this ingredient is not available in your market area, see page 29 for substitutes.

CHILI CON CARNE

2 medium onions, thinly sliced
½ cup diced green pepper
1 tablespoon vegetable oil
2 pounds lean beef, cut into ½-inch cubes
1 cup chopped peeled tomato
2 cloves garlic, finely chopped
1 tablespoon plus 2 teaspoons chili powder
⅛ teaspoon thyme
⅛ teaspoon oregano
Freshly ground pepper
½ cup water
1 cup canned red kidney beans, rinsed and drained

Cook and stir onions and green pepper in oil over low heat 10 minutes. Add meat; cook and stir until meat is brown. Mix tomato, garlic, chili powder, thyme, oregano, pepper and water; stir into meat mixture. Cover and cook over low heat until meat is tender, about 2 hours. Stir in beans and heat.

6 servings.

1 serving = 2 meat, 1 bread I
390 calories

SPANISH RICE WITH MEAT

¾ cup uncooked regular rice
½ pound lean ground beef
¼ cup chopped onion
¼ cup chopped green pepper
1 can (16 ounces) unsalted tomatoes
½ teaspoon basil leaves
½ teaspoon chili powder

Cook rice as directed on page 148. Cook and stir meat in large skillet until brown. Drain off fat. Add onion, green pepper, tomatoes, basil leaves and chili powder; cook over medium heat, stirring frequently, 15 minutes. Stir in rice and heat.

Three 1-cup servings.

1 serving = ⅓ meat, ½ vegetable,
1 bread I
400 calories

STUFFED GREEN PEPPERS

¼ cup uncooked regular rice
2 medium green peppers
½ pound lean ground beef
¼ cup chopped tomato
2 tablespoons chopped carrot
2 tablespoons chopped celery
1 teaspoon chopped onion
½ teaspoon cinnamon
1 cup unsalted tomato juice
1 teaspoon flour

Cook rice as directed on package except—omit salt.

Heat oven to 350°. Cut green peppers into halves; remove stem, seeds and membranes. Place pepper shells cut sides up in ungreased 1-quart casserole.

Cook and stir meat in skillet until brown. Drain off fat. Stir in tomato, carrot, celery, onion, cinnamon and rice. Spoon meat mixture into pepper shells.

Mix tomato juice and flour in small saucepan until smooth. Heat to boiling, stirring constantly. Boil and stir 1 minute. Pour sauce on pepper shells. Cover and bake until peppers are tender, about 45 minutes.

2 servings.

1 serving = 1 meat, 1 bread I, 1 vegetable
415 calories

PEPPER STEAK

Excellent

2-pound flank steak, scored
Freshly ground pepper
1 tablespoon vegetable oil
2 medium onions, chopped (about 1 cup)
1 can (10½ ounces) unsalted beef broth*
3 tablespoons flour
½ pound mushrooms, trimmed
  and sliced
3 medium green peppers, cut into strips
  (¼ inch wide)
3 tomatoes
1 teaspoon snipped parsley

Cut meat crosswise into ½-inch strips. Season with pepper. Heat oil in large skillet; brown meat in oil over medium heat. Push meat to one section; add onion. Cook and stir until onion is tender, about 3 minutes.

Mix broth and flour until smooth; stir into meat mixture. Heat to boiling, stirring constantly. Boil and stir 1 minute. Reduce heat; cover tightly and simmer 30 minutes.

Stir in mushrooms and green pepper. Cover and simmer 5 minutes. Cut each tomato into eighths and place on meat mixture. Cover and cook over low heat just until tomatoes are heated through, about 2 minutes. Sprinkle with parsley.

8 servings.

1 serving = 1 meat, 1½ vegetable
290 calories

*Unsalted beef broth can be made by dissolving 2 unsalted beef bouillon cubes in 1½ cups boiling water.

STEAK WITH MUSHROOM SAUCE

2 tablespoons lemon juice
2 New York strip steaks (about 6 ounces
  each)
Freshly ground pepper
½ teaspoon vegetable oil
1 tablespoon minced shallot
7 medium or 4 large mushrooms,
  trimmed and thinly sliced (about 1 cup)
½ teaspoon minced garlic
⅓ cup red wine
1 unsalted beef bouillon cube
½ bay leaf
1 tablespoon red wine
1 teaspoon flour
Snipped parsley

Sprinkle steaks with lemon juice; let stand 10 minutes.

Drain steaks; season with pepper. Heat oil in large skillet; brown meat over medium heat, about 4 minutes on each side. Remove meat; set aside.

Cook and stir shallot in skillet until light brown. Add mushrooms and garlic; cook and stir 3 to 4 minutes. Stir in ⅓ cup wine, the bouillon cube and bay leaf. Heat to boiling, stirring constantly. Reduce heat; cover tightly and simmer 5 minutes.

Add meat to mixture in skillet. Cook over medium heat until hot, about 3 minutes. Remove meat to heated platter and keep warm.

4 servings.

Mix 1 tablespoon wine and the flour until smooth; pour into skillet. Heat to boiling, stirring constantly. Boil and stir 1 minute. Pour sauce on meat and sprinkle with parsley.

2 to 4 servings.

One 3-ounce serving = 1 meat
215 calories

BURGUNDY POT ROAST

4-pound rolled beef rump roast
1 clove garlic, halved
¼ cup flour
¼ teaspoon basil leaves
Freshly ground pepper
3 tablespoons vegetable oil
½ cup coarsely chopped tomato
3 onions, quartered
1 cup water
¾ cup red Burgundy or red wine
4 potatoes, pared and quartered
1 carrot, finely chopped

Rub meat with cut sides of garlic. Mix flour, basil leaves and pepper; coat meat with flour mixture. Heat oil in Dutch oven. Brown meat in oil over medium-high heat. Add tomato, onions, water and wine. Cover and simmer until meat is almost tender, 2½ to 3 hours. Add potatoes and carrot; cover and simmer until meat and vegetables are tender, 1 hour.

8 servings.

1 serving = 1½ meat, ½ bread I,
1 vegetable
460 calories

MARINATED FLANK STEAK

1½-pound flank steak, scored
2 tablespoons red wine vinegar
¼ cup plus 2 tablespoons vegetable oil
1 medium onion, chopped (½ cup)
2 cloves garlic, crushed
4 mushrooms, trimmed and chopped
1 teaspoon marjoram leaves
½ teaspoon dry mustard
Freshly ground pepper

Place meat in shallow baking dish. Mix remaining ingredients; pour on meat. Cover tightly and refrigerate at least 1 hour or up to 2 days.

Set oven control at broil and/or 550°. Place baking dish with meat and marinade about 3 inches from heat. Broil until meat is brown, about 5 minutes. Turn meat; broil 5 minutes longer.

Cut meat across grain at a slanted angle into thin slices; serve with onion and marinade.

4 servings.

1 serving = 1 meat
445 calories

HOMESTYLE POT ROAST

1 tablespoon flour
½ teaspoon allspice
¼ teaspoon pepper
3-pound lean beef chuck pot roast
1 tablespoon plus 1 teaspoon vegetable
oil
2 cups water
2 small onions
2 cloves garlic, finely chopped

Mix flour, allspice and pepper; coat meat with flour mixture. Heat oil in large skillet. Brown meat in oil over medium-high heat. Add water, onions and garlic. Reduce heat; cover and simmer until meat is tender, about 3 hours.

8 servings.

Note: If desired, potatoes can be added during last hour of cooking.

1 serving = 1 meat
290 calories

GREEK STUFFADO

2 teaspoons olive oil
½ pound beef stew meat
3 small white onions
½ clove garlic, chopped
¼ cup chopped tomato
2 tablespoons dry red wine
Freshly ground pepper

Heat oil in skillet. Cook and stir meat, onions and garlic in oil over medium heat until meat is brown. Add tomatoes, wine and pepper. Cover and simmer until meat is tender, 2 to 3 hours.

2 servings.

1 serving = 1 meat
310 calories

STEWED BEEF

3 pounds beef shank cross cuts
1 quart water
1 bay leaf
3 peppercorns

Place meat in Dutch oven or large kettle; add water, bay leaf and peppercorns. Heat to boiling. Reduce heat; cover and simmer until meat is tender, about 1¾ hours. Remove meat from broth. Cool broth; skim off fat. Strain broth through cheesecloth. Refrigerate meat and broth separately until ready to use.

One 3-ounce serving = 1 meat
230 calories

ROAST BEEF

Select roast from those listed in chart below. Allow about ½ pound per person—less for boneless roasts, more for roasts with a bone. If desired, season with pepper and cut slits in roast and insert slivers of garlic.

Place meat fat side up on rack in open shallow roasting pan. The rack keeps the meat out of the drippings. (In roasts such as standing rib, the ribs form a natural rack.) It is not necessary to baste.

Insert meat thermometer so tip is in center of thickest part of meat and does not touch bone or rest in fat. Do not add water. Do not cover.

Roast meat in 325° oven. (It is not necessary to preheat oven.) Roast to desired degree of doneness (see timetable), using thermometer reading as final guide.

Roasts are easier to carve if allowed to set 15 to 20 minutes after removing from oven. Since meat continues to cook after removal from oven, if roast is to "set," it should be removed from oven when thermometer registers 5 to 10° lower than the desired doneness.

One 3-ounce serving = 1 meat
200 calories

TIMETABLE FOR ROASTING BEEF (Oven Temperature 325°)

Cut	Approximate Weight	Meat Thermometer Reading	Approximate Cooking Time (Minutes per pound)
Standing Rib	6 to 8 pounds	140° (rare)	23 to 25
		160° (medium)	27 to 30
		170° (well)	32 to 35
	4 to 6 pounds	140° (rare)	26 to 32
		160° (medium)	34 to 38
		170° (well)	40 to 42
Rolled Rib	5 to 7 pounds	140° (rare)	32
		160° (medium)	38
		170° (well)	48
Delmonico* (rib eye)	4 to 6 pounds	140° (rare)	18 to 20
		160° (medium)	20 to 22
		170° (well)	22 to 24
Rolled Rump (high quality)	4 to 6 pounds	150 to 170°	25 to 30
Sirloin Tip (high quality)	4 to 6 pounds	150 to 170°	35 to 40
Tenderloin** (whole)	4 to 6 pounds	140° (rare)	¾ to 1 hour
Tenderloin** (half)	2 to 3 pounds	140° (rare)	¾ to 1 hour

*Roast at 350°
**Roast at 425°

SWEET-AND-SOUR POT ROAST

4-pound rolled beef rump roast
Freshly ground pepper
6 medium onions, chopped
2 tablespoons vegetable oil
2 bay leaves
3 cups unsalted beef bouillon*
2 pounds tomatoes, peeled
½ cup sugar
Juice of 3 lemons

Season meat with pepper. Cook and stir onions in oil in Dutch oven until tender. Remove onions; cover and refrigerate. Brown meat over medium-high heat in Dutch oven. Add bay leaves and bouillon. Reduce heat; cover and simmer until meat is tender, 3 to 3½ hours. Cool meat and refrigerate 8 hours.

Heat oven to 350°. Add onions, tomatoes, sugar and lemon juice to Dutch oven. Bake uncovered 20 to 30 minutes. Cut meat into slices and serve sauce on slices.
8 servings.

1 serving =1 meat, 1 vegetable
450 calories

*Unsalted bouillon can be made by dissolving 3 unsalted beef bouillon cubes in 3 cups boiling water.

SHISH KEBABS

3 ounces lean beef or lamb cubes
1 small onion, quartered
3 cherry tomatoes
3 fresh mushroom caps
½ green pepper, cut into 1-inch pieces
1 ounce unsalted catsup
½ cup white vinegar
1 teaspoon sugar
Pepper

Alternate meat, onion, tomatoes, mushrooms and green pepper pieces on skewers. Mix remaining ingredients and brush on kebabs. Cook on grill or broil to desired doneness.
2 servings.

1 serving = ½ meat, 1 vegetable
145 calories

MEATY SPAGHETTI SAUCE

1 pound lean ground beef
1 medium onion, finely chopped
1 clove garlic, minced
1 can (16 ounces) unsalted tomatoes
6 ounces unsalted tomato paste
1 tablespoon sugar
2 teaspoons oregano leaves
1 teaspoon pepper

Cook and stir meat, onion and garlic in large skillet until meat is brown. Stir in remaining ingredients; break up tomatoes with fork. Simmer uncovered over low heat about 30 minutes.
Four 1-cup servings.

Note: Sauce can be prepared ahead of time. Cover and refrigerate. To serve, heat over medium heat until sauce simmers.

1 serving = 1 meat, ½ vegetable
360 calories

BEEF 'N' BEER CASSEROLE

3 tablespoons olive oil
3 pounds beef stew meat
Freshly ground pepper
¼ cup plus 2 tablespoons unsalted
   margarine
1 cup thinly sliced fresh mushrooms
6 medium onions, thinly sliced
3 tablespoons flour
12 ounces beer
1 teaspoon black pepper
½ to 1 teaspoon Tabasco® pepper sauce

Heat oil in large skillet. Brown meat in oil over medium-high heat. Season with freshly ground pepper. Remove meat to Dutch oven.

Melt margarine in same skillet. Add mushrooms and onions and sprinkle with flour. Cook and stir mushrooms and onions in margarine until onions are tender. Turn into Dutch oven; add beer.

Simmer uncovered over low heat, stirring occasionally, until meat is tender, about 2 hours. Stir in 1 teaspoon pepper and the pepper sauce. Cool. Cover tightly and refrigerate 8 hours.

To serve, heat covered over medium heat until meat mixture simmers.

8 servings.

Note: This casserole can be prepared up to 5 days in advance. The flavor improves with time.

1 serving = 1½ meat, 1 vegetable
        500 calories

CURRIED BEEF

1 tablespoon curry powder
½ cup water
¼ cup unsalted margarine
3 medium onions, chopped or thinly sliced
½ clove garlic, finely chopped
1½ pounds beef chuck or round, cut into
   1-inch cubes
1 tablespoon cornstarch
Freshly ground pepper
3 cups water

Soak curry powder in ½ cup water 1 hour in large saucepan. Melt margarine in large skillet. Cook and stir onions, garlic and meat in margarine until meat is brown and onions are tender. Stir meat mixture into curry mixture.

Cook over medium heat, stirring constantly, 10 minutes. Mix cornstarch, pepper and 3 cups water; stir into meat mixture. Heat to boiling, stirring constantly. Reduce heat; cover and simmer until meat is tender, about 2 hours.

4 servings.

Note: Serve over hot cooked rice.

1 serving = 1½ meat, ½ vegetable
        490 calories

HAMBURGER CASSEROLE

1 pound lean ground beef
1½ cups uncooked elbow macaroni
2 cans (10 ounces each) unsalted tomatoes
¼ cup chopped green pepper
2 teaspoons snipped chives
1½ teaspoons basil leaves

Heat oven to 350°. Cook and stir meat in medium skillet until brown. Cook macaroni as directed on package except—omit salt. Mix meat, macaroni and remaining ingredients in ungreased 2-quart casserole; break up tomatoes with fork. Bake uncovered 15 minutes.

4 servings.

1 serving = 1 meat, 1 vegetable, 1 bread I
495 calories

BROILED LAMB CHOPS

4 lamb loin chops (3 ounces each),
1 inch thick
1 clove garlic, halved
1 tablespoon plus 1 teaspoon lemon juice

Remove "fell" (the paperlike covering) if it is on chops. Diagonally slash outer edge of fat on chops at 1-inch intervals to prevent curling. Rub chops with cut clove garlic; brush with lemon juice.

Set oven control at broil and/or 550°. Broil chops with tops 3 inches from heat 6 to 7 minutes on each side.

4 servings.

Note: For flavor variety, substitute allspice, basil leaves, dill, ginger or oregano for the garlic.

1 serving = 1 meat
175 calories

BONED LEG OF LAMB WITH STUFFING

5- to 6-pound lamb leg, boned
Freshly ground pepper
4 cloves garlic, minced
Juice of 2 lemons
1 cup snipped parsley
¼ cup plus 2 tablespoons low-
sodium bread crumbs
1 tablespoon plus 1 teaspoon thyme
2 medium carrots, sliced
1 medium onion, chopped (about ½ cup)
2 celery ribs, sliced
2 cups unsalted chicken broth*
1 cup white wine

Place meat skin side down; season with pepper. Mix garlic, lemon juice, parsley, bread crumbs and 1 teaspoon of the thyme; spread on meat. Roll up meat; tie securely and place on rack in open shallow roasting pan. Place vegetables in pan; sprinkle with remaining thyme. Pour broth and wine on vegetables.

Roast meat in 325° oven (it is not necessary to preheat oven). Roast meat, basting with broth liquid at 30-minute intervals, until desired doneness, allowing 40 minutes per pound.

Roasts are easier to carve if allowed to set 15 to 20 minutes after removing from oven.

6 to 8 servings.

1 serving = 2½ meat
415 calories

* Unsalted chicken broth can be made by dissolving 2 unsalted chicken bouillon cubes in 2 cups boiling water.

EASTER ROAST LAMB WITH ARTICHOKES

8- to 10-pound lamb leg
2 cloves garlic, split and slivered
¼ cup unsalted margarine, softened
Juice of 2 lemons
2 tablespoons oregano
Freshly ground pepper
4 medium globe artichokes
Juice of 2 lemons
2 tablespoons flour
Snipped fresh dill
Parsley sprigs

Cut 4 or 5 small slits in meat with tip of sharp knife and insert garlic slivers. Rub meat with margarine, then sprinkle with juice of 2 lemons, the oregano and pepper.

Place meat fat side up on rack in open shallow roasting pan. Insert meat thermometer so tip is in center of thickest part of meat and does not touch bone or rest in fat. Do not cover.

Roast meat in 325° oven (it is not necessary to preheat oven), adding boiling water at intervals to drippings in pan so that there will be about 2 cups drippings at end of roasting. Roast meat to rare (150°).

Remove any discolored leaves and the small leaves at base of each artichoke. Trim stem even with base of artichoke. Cutting straight across each artichoke, slice 1 inch off top and discard top. Snip off points of the remaining leaves with scissors. Rinse artichokes under cold water.

Cut each artichoke lengthwise in half; scrape away fuzzy choke from each half. Rub cut sides of halves with part of juice of remaining 2 lemons.

Dissolve flour in small amount of water in large kettle. Stir in remaining lemon juice; add artichoke halves and enough water to cover. Heat to boiling; reduce heat and simmer uncovered 10 minutes.

Remove artichoke halves carefully with tongs or 2 large spoons; drain. Place halves topside down in meat drippings in roasting pan with meat. Bake uncovered until tender, about 30 minutes.

Remove meat to warm platter and surround with artichoke halves. Sprinkle with dill and garnish with parsley sprigs.

8 servings.

1 serving (3 ounces meat / artichoke half) =
1 meat, 1 vegetable
400 calories

ROAST LAMB

3-pound rolled lamb shoulder or leg
1 clove garlic
2 tablespoons rosemary leaves
1 tablespoon freshly ground pepper

Rub meat with cut clove garlic. Cut several slits in meat with tip of sharp knife. Insert some of the rosemary leaves and a sliver of garlic in each. Sprinkle remaining rosemary leaves and the pepper on meat. Place meat fat side up on rack in shallow roasting pan. Insert meat thermometer so tip is in thickest part of meat and does not rest in fat. Roast uncovered in 325° oven until meat thermometer registers 175 to 180°, about 2 hours.

4 servings.

1 serving = 1 meat
245 calories

APPLE-PORK CHOP ROAST

½ cup white wine
¼ cup lemon juice
2 tablespoons vegetable oil
½ teaspoon dry mustard
6 pork rib chops (3 ounces each)
1 teaspoon cumin
1 teaspoon thyme
1 teaspoon basil leaves
Freshly ground pepper
2 apples, cored, pared and cut into 5 slices

Heat oven to 400°. Mix wine, lemon juice, oil and mustard; brush on chops. Season chops with cumin, thyme, basil leaves and pepper.

Alternate pork chops and apple slices to form the shape of a roast; secure with wooden picks. Place in ungreased baking pan, 13x9x2 inches. Bake uncovered 15 minutes.

Reduce oven temperature to 300°. Bake 1 hour longer, basting occasionally with pan juices.

6 servings.

1 serving = 1 meat
300 calories

SWEDISH BROILED LAMB CHOPS

4 lamb loin chops (3 ounces each),
  1 inch thick
½ cup strong coffee
4 teaspoons ginger

Remove "fell" (the paperlike covering) if it is on chops. Diagonally slash outer edge of fat on chops at 1-inch intervals to prevent curling. Dip chops into coffee; rub each with 1 teaspoon ginger.

Set oven control at broil and/or 550°. Broil chops with tops 3 inches from heat, basting occasionally with coffee, 6 to 7 minutes on each side.

4 servings.

1 serving = 1 meat
185 calories

NEAR EAST LAMB

2 cloves garlic, minced
2 medium onions, thinly sliced
2 tablespoons olive oil
1 medium eggplant (about 1½ pounds),
  pared and cut into ½-inch cubes
4 to 5 cups diced cooked lamb
1 teaspoon dill weed
1 teaspoon dry mustard
1 tablespoon curry powder
Freshly ground pepper

In large skillet, cook and stir garlic and onion in oil until onion is tender, about 3 minutes. Add eggplant; cook and stir until eggplant is heated through, 10 minutes. Stir in meat, dill weed, mustard and curry powder. Season with pepper. Cover tightly and cook over low heat, stirring occasionally, 30 to 40 minutes.

6 servings.

1 serving = 1 meat, ½ vegetable
280 calories

BAKED PORK AND APPLES WITH CARAWAY

1 onion, thinly sliced
3 apples, pared and sliced
1 tablespoon honey
1 tablespoon caraway seed
8 pork chops, 1 inch thick
Freshly ground pepper
1 to 2 tablespoons Dijon-style Mustard (page 150)

Heat oven to 350°. Arrange onion slices in ungreased baking pan, 13x9x2 inches. Place apple slices on onion and drizzle with honey. Sprinkle half the caraway seed on mixture.

Trim excess fat from chops. Season chops with pepper and spread each lightly with mustard. Arrange chops in baking pan and sprinkle with remaining caraway seed. Bake uncovered 30 minutes. If no liquid has accumulated in pan, pour in about ¼ cup water. Bake 30 minutes longer or until chops are golden brown.

8 servings.

1 serving = 1 meat, ½ fruit
280 calories

SAVORY LAMB

1 teaspoon olive oil
½ pound lamb stew meat, cubed
½ medium onion, chopped
⅛ teaspoon paprika
Freshly ground pepper
Boiling water
½ cup canned unsalted green beans or ½ cup cut-up fresh green beans
1 medium tomato, peeled and quartered
1 medium potato, pared and quartered
½ green pepper, cut into strips

Heat oven to 325°. Heat oil in medium skillet. Cook and stir meat and onion in oil until meat is brown. Season with paprika and pepper. Pour into ungreased 1-quart casserole; barely cover with boiling water. Cover tightly and bake until meat is tender, about 1 hour. Stir in remaining ingredients. Cover and bake 30 minutes longer.

2 servings.

1 serving = 1 meat, 1 vegetable, ½ bread l
315 calories

PORK CHOPS AND RICE

4 pork loin or rib chops (3 to 4 ounces each)
2 tablespoons uncooked regular rice
1 cup water
1 teaspoon sugar
½ teaspoon rosemary leaves
½ teaspoon sage
8 slices tomato
½ green pepper, sliced
½ teaspoon basil leaves
Freshly ground pepper
1 tablespoon unsalted margarine

Heat oven to 350°. Brown chops in skillet over medium-high heat. Place in ungreased baking dish, 8x8x2 inches. Sprinkle rice on chops. Pour fat from skillet. In same skillet, heat water, sugar, rosemary leaves and sage to boiling; pour on chops and rice. Arrange tomato and green pepper on top. Sprinkle with basil leaves and pepper and dot with margarine. Bake uncovered until chops are tender, 50 to 60 minutes.

4 servings.

1 serving = 1 meat
295 calories

WIENER SCHNITZEL

4 boneless veal cutlets (6 ounces each)
3 tablespoons lemon juice
Freshly ground pepper
¼ cup flour
3 tablespoons Second Nature imitation
 eggs* or 1 egg, beaten
½ cup dry bread crumbs
2 tablespoons unsalted margarine
1 tablespoon vegetable oil
2 large Boston lettuce leaves
1 lemon, cut into fourths

Pound meat until ¼ inch thick. Sprinkle with lemon juice; let stand 10 minutes. Season with pepper and coat with flour. Dip meat into egg, then coat with bread crumbs.

Melt margarine in oil in large skillet. Cook meat over medium heat until brown, 3 to 4 minutes. Turn and cook 3 to 4 minutes longer.

Place meat on lettuce leaves and serve with lemon.

4 servings.

1 serving= 1½ meat
 615 calories

SKILLET PORK CHOPS

6 pork loin or rib chops (3 ounces each)
2 tablespoons flour
2 teaspoons unsalted margarine
1½ cups sliced onion
½ teaspoon sage
½ teaspoon rosemary leaves
⅛ teaspoon pepper
1 cup water
1 cup chopped tomato
½ teaspoon basil leaves

Coat chops with flour. Melt margarine in large ovenproof skillet; brown chops in margarine over medium-high heat. Add onion, sage, rosemary leaves, pepper and water. Cover and simmer 30 minutes.

Heat oven to 400°. Sprinkle tomatoes and basil leaves on chops. Bake uncovered until tender, 30 minutes.

6 servings.

1 serving = 1 meat
 270 calories

EASY GRILLED CHICKEN

3-ounce chicken piece (leg, thigh, breast)
1 tablespoon chopped onion
1 teaspoon snipped parsley
1 teaspoon rosemary leaves
⅛ teaspoon freshly ground pepper

Place chicken on piece of heavy-duty aluminum foil. Sprinkle remaining ingredients on chicken. Fold foil over and seal securely. Cook on grill, turning once, until chicken is tender, about 30 minutes.

1 serving.

1 serving = 1 meat
 120 calories

*If this ingredient is not available in your market area, see page 29 for substitutes.

COQ AU VIN

3- to 3½-pound broiler fryer chicken,
  cut up
1 tablespoon vegetable oil
1 teaspoon unsalted margarine
Freshly ground pepper
¼ cup cognac (2 ounces)
½ pound mushrooms, trimmed and sliced
6 small white onions
2 tablespoons minced shallot
1 clove garlic, minced
1½ cups red wine
1 bay leaf
1 tablespoon red wine
1 teaspoon flour
¼ cup snipped parsley

Wash chicken and pat dry. Season with pepper. Heat oil and margarine in large skillet or Dutch oven. Cook chicken in oil over medium heat until light brown, 15 to 20 minutes. Warm cognac; pour on chicken and flame.

Push chicken to one section. Add mushrooms, onions, shallot and garlic; cook and stir until onions are tender. Drain off fat. Stir in 1½ cups wine and the bay leaf; heat to boiling. Reduce heat; cover tightly and simmer until chicken is tender, about 30 minutes.

Skim off excess fat and remove chicken to heated serving dish. Mix 1 tablespoon wine and the flour until smooth; stir into skillet. Heat to boiling, stirring constantly. Boil and stir 1 minute. Pour sauce on chicken and sprinkle with parsley.

4 servings.

1 serving = 2 meat
            480 calories

VEAL SCALLOPINE WITH LEMON

6 boneless veal cutlets (4 ounces each)
Freshly ground pepper
2 tablespoons flour
2 tablespoons unsalted margarine
¼ cup olive oil
¼ cup white wine
3 tablespoons lemon juice
2 lemons, pared and thinly sliced
1 lemon, cut lengthwise into wedges
Snipped parsley

Pound meat until ¼ inch thick. Season with pepper and coat with flour. Melt margarine in oil in large skillet. Cook meat in oil over medium heat until brown, 3 to 4 minutes on each side. Pour wine and lemon juice on meat and cook over medium heat 3 to 4 minutes.

Arrange meat with lemon slices between meat on heated serving dish. Pour sauce on meat. Arrange lemon wedges around meat and sprinkle with parsley.

4 to 6 servings.

3 ounces = 1 meat
            425 calories

TAHITIAN HASH

2 tablespoons pineapple juice
⅛ teaspoon dry mustard
½ cup finely chopped cooked unsalted pork
½ cup finely chopped cooked sweet potato
1 fresh or canned pineapple slice, quartered
1½ teaspoons brown sugar
1½ teaspoons unsalted margarine

Heat oven to 350°. Mix pineapple juice and mustard in mixing bowl. Stir in meat and sweet potato. Pour into greased 1-quart casserole. Top with pineapple and sprinkle with brown sugar. Dot with margarine. Bake uncovered 30 minutes.

2 servings.

1 serving = ½ meat, ½ bread I
315 calories

CHICKEN CURRY

1 cup uncooked regular rice
3 tablespoons unsalted margarine
¼ cup minced onion
1½ teaspoons curry powder
1 cup water
2 tablespoons flour
¾ teaspoon sugar
⅛ teaspoon ginger
1 unsalted chicken bouillon cube
1 cup milk
1 cup cut-up cooked unsalted chicken
2 teaspoons lemon juice
Accompaniments (opposite)

Cook rice as directed on page 148. Melt margarine in saucepan. Cook and stir onion and curry powder in margarine until onion is tender. Mix water and flour until smooth. Stir flour mixture, sugar, ginger, bouillon cube and milk into saucepan.

Heat to boiling, stirring constantly. Boil and stir 1 minute. Stir in chicken and lemon juice; heat through. Serve chicken mixture on hot rice; sprinkle choice of Accompaniments on top.

4 servings.

1 serving = 1 meat, 1 bread I
390 calories

Accompaniments: Chopped tomato, raisins, pineapple chunks, flaked coconut.

CARIBBEAN CHICKEN

2 tablespoons unsalted margarine
2 chicken breasts, halved
Freshly ground pepper
½ teaspoon tarragon leaves
2 tablespoons lime juice
2 tablespoons water
½ teaspoon Tabasco pepper sauce
Hot cooked rice

Melt margarine in skillet. Place chicken breasts skin side down in skillet; season with pepper and sprinkle with ¼ teaspoon tarragon leaves. Brown chicken over medium heat, about 10 minutes. Turn; season with pepper and sprinkle with remaining tarragon leaves. Brown other side.

Mix lime juice, water and pepper sauce; pour on chicken. Cover and simmer until tender, about 10 minutes. Serve with hot cooked rice.

4 servings.

Note: Recipe can be doubled.

1 serving = 1 meat
290 calories

BAKED CHICKEN

Two 2-pound broiler-fryer chickens, cut into quarters or into pieces
1 tablespoon vegetable oil
¼ cup dry vermouth
¼ teaspoon Tabasco pepper sauce
1 teaspoon snipped chives
Paprika
Freshly ground pepper

Heat oven to 350°. Wash chicken and pat dry. Place chicken skin side down on rack in baking pan. Bake 20 minutes.

Heat oil, wine, pepper sauce and chives in small saucepan 2 or 3 minutes. Turn chicken and brush with wine sauce. Sprinkle with paprika and season with pepper. Bake, basting occasionally with wine sauce, until chicken is tender, about 25 minutes longer.

8 servings.

Note: Orange juice, apple juice or 1 tablespoon lemon juice and 3 tablespoons water can be substituted for vermouth.

1 serving = 1 meat
          225 calories

CHICKEN SOUFFLÉ

1½ cups unsalted chicken broth
¼ cup uncooked cream of rice cereal
2 tablespoons unsalted margarine
1 teaspoon oregano leaves, crushed
¼ teaspoon Tabasco pepper sauce
3 eggs, separated
1 cup diced cooked unsalted chicken

Heat oven to 325°. Heat chicken broth to boiling in saucepan. Sprinkle cereal on broth; cook, stirring constantly, 1 minute. Remove from heat and let stand 4 minutes. Stir in margarine, oregano leaves and pepper sauce.

Beat egg whites until stiff but not dry. Beat egg yolks until thick and lemon colored; gradually mix in warm cereal mixture and chicken. Carefully fold in egg whites.

Pour into ungreased 4-cup soufflé dish or 1-quart casserole. Bake until puffed and golden brown, about 45 minutes. Serve immediately.

6 servings.

1 serving = 1 meat
          150 calories

Note: Nice served with Creole Sauce (page 152).

CHICKEN IN MUSHROOM SAUCE

Four 3-ounce chicken pieces (leg, thigh, breast)
Vegetable oil
Freshly ground pepper
Paprika
½ cup unsalted cream of mushroom soup
½ cup cooking sherry

Set oven control at broil and/or 550°. Place chicken pieces on ungreased baking sheet. Brush with oil and season with pepper and paprika. Broil with top 7 to 9 inches from heat until brown.

Heat oven to 350°. Place chicken in ungreased baking dish, 8x8x2 inches. Mix soup and sherry and pour on chicken. Cover and bake until tender, about 1 hour.

4 servings.

1 serving = 1 meat
          340 calories

CHICKEN OREGANO

Four 3-ounce chicken pieces (leg, thigh, breast)
1 clove garlic, split
¼ cup unsalted margarine, melted
1 tablespoon lemon juice
1½ teaspoons oregano
¼ teaspoon pepper
Parsley sprigs

Set oven control at broil and/or 550°. Rub chicken with cut side of garlic. Mix margarine, lemon juice, oregano and pepper; brush about 2 tablespoons of margarine mixture on chicken. Place chicken skin side down on rack in broiler pan.

Broil with top about 7 inches from heat until brown, about 20 minutes. Turn; brush with about 2 tablespoons of margarine mixture and broil until tender and crisp, about 20 minutes. Turn; brush with remaining margarine mixture and broil a few seconds. Garnish with parsley.

4 servings.

1 serving = 1 meat
285 calories

EASY BROILED CHICKEN

2-pound broiler-fryer chicken, cut up
½ lemon
Freshly ground pepper
Paprika
1 medium onion, thinly sliced
½ cup dry white wine

Set oven control at broil and/or 550°. Rub chicken with cut side of lemon and season with pepper. Arrange skin side down in ungreased baking pan, 13x9x2 inches. Broil with top of chicken 5 inches from heat 10 minutes.Turn; sprinkle with paprika and broil 10 minutes.

Place onion slices on chicken; pour on wine. Broil, basting occasionally with pan juices, until chicken is tender, about 30 minutes longer. Remove to warm platter and pour pan juices on chicken.

4 servings.

1 serving = 1 meat
200 calories

POULET ANDRÉ

4 chicken breasts (6 ounces each)
White pepper
¼ cup vegetable oil
8 medium fresh mushrooms, sliced
3 shallots or 1 medium onion, chopped
1 clove garlic, finely chopped
1 tablespoon snipped parsley
1 medium tomato, peeled and chopped
1 tablespoon lemon juice
½ cup dry white wine

Remove skin and bone from chicken breasts; split each breast and season with pepper.

Heat oil in skillet. Brown chicken in oil over medium-high heat. Add mushrooms, shallots, garlic, parsley, tomato and lemon juice; simmer 5 minutes, stirring once or twice. Pour wine on chicken; cover and simmer until chicken is tender, about 25 minutes. Remove cover for the last few minutes of cooking.

Four 4-ounce servings.

1 serving = 1½ meat
380 calories

STEWED CHICKEN

**4- to 5-pound stewing chicken, cut into
  pieces**
1 sprig parsley
1 celery stalk with leaves, cut up
1 carrot, sliced
1 small onion, sliced
½ teaspoon pepper
1 teaspoon oregano
¼ teaspoon marjoram

Remove skin and excess fat from chicken.
Place chicken in kettle with giblets and neck
and just enough water to cover. Add parsley,
celery, carrot, onion and pepper. Heat to boiling. Reduce heat; cover and simmer 1½ hours.
Add oregano and marjoram; simmer until thickest pieces are tender, 1 to 1½ hours. Allow
chicken to cool in broth if not serving immediately.

Remove meat from bones in pieces as large as
possible. Refrigerate broth and when cold, skim
fat from broth. Refrigerate broth and chicken
pieces separately in covered containers; use
within several days. For longer storage, package chicken in serving portions and freeze.
Freeze broth separately in the same manner.

*About 5 cups cut-up cooked chicken and 5 to 6
cups broth.*

Note: To stew 3- to 4-pound broiler-fryer chick-
en, add oregano and marjoram with other seasonings and simmer until thickest pieces are
tender, about 45 minutes.

*About 3 to 4 cups cut-up cooked chicken and 2
to 3½ cups broth.*

One 3-ounce serving = 1 meat
                     175 calories

CHICKEN TETRAZZINI

1 package (7 or 8 ounces) spaghetti
1 cup water
2 tablespoons flour
1 cup skim milk
1 unsalted chicken bouillon cube
¼ cup unsalted margarine
2 tablespoons red wine vinegar
¼ teaspoon pepper
1½ cups cut-up cooked unsalted chicken*
¾ cup sliced fresh mushrooms
2 tablespoons grated Parmesan cheese

Heat oven to 350°. Cook spaghetti as directed
on package except—omit salt. Mix water and
flour in small saucepan until smooth. Stir in milk
and bouillon cube. Heat to boiling, stirring constantly. Boil and stir 1 minute. Stir in margarine,
vinegar, pepper, chicken, mushrooms and
spaghetti. Pour into ungreased 2-quart casserole. Sprinkle cheese on top. Bake uncovered until bubbly, about 30 minutes.

4 servings.

**1 serving = 1 meat, 1 bread I, ¼ milk
             455 calories**

*Stewed Chicken (opposite) or Broiled Chicken
(page 136) can be used.

ROAST TURKEY

When buying turkeys under 12 pounds, allow ¾ to 1 pound per serving. For heavier birds, 12 pounds and over, allow ½ to ¾ pound per serving.

Wash turkey and pat dry. If desired, rub cavity with lemon juice.

Stuff turkey just before roasting—not ahead of time. (See Bread Stuffing, page 139.) Fill wishbone area with stuffing first. Fasten neck skin to back with skewer. Fold wings across back with tips touching. Fill body cavity lightly. (Do not pack—stuffing will expand while cooking.) Tuck drumsticks under band of skin at tail or tie together with heavy string, then tie to tail.

Heat oven to 325°. Place turkey breast side up on rack in open shallow roasting pan. Brush with unsalted margarine. Insert meat thermometer so tip is in thickest part of inside thigh muscle or thickest part of breast meat and does not touch bone. Do not add water. Do not cover.

Follow Timetable below for approximate total cooking time. Place a tent of aluminum foil loosely over turkey when it starts to turn golden. When ⅔ done, cut band of skin or string holding legs.

One 3-ounce serving = 1 meat
200 calories

Timetable for Roasting Turkey

Ready-to-Cook Weight	Approximate Total Cooking Time	Internal Temperature
6 to 8 pounds	3 to 3½ hours	185°
8 to 12 pounds	3½ to 4½ hours	185°
12 to 16 pounds	4½ to 5½ hours	185°
16 to 20 pounds	5½ to 6½ hours	185°
20 to 24 pounds	6½ to 7 hours	185°

This timetable is based on chilled or completely thawed turkeys at a temperature of about 40° and placed in preheated ovens. Time will be slightly less for unstuffed turkeys. Differences in the shape and tenderness of individual turkeys can also necessitate increasing or decreasing the cooking time slightly. For best results, use a meat thermometer.

A thermometer placed in the thigh muscle should register 185° when the turkey is done. If the bird is stuffed, the point of the thermometer can be placed in the center of the stuffing and will register 165° when done. If a thermometer is not used, test for doneness about 30 minutes before Timetable so indicates. Move drumstick up and down—if done, the joint should give readily or break. Or press drumstick meat between fingers; the meat should be very soft.

When turkey is done, remove from oven and allow to stand about 20 minutes for easiest carving. As soon as possible after serving, remove every bit of stuffing from turkey. Cool stuffing, meat and any gravy promptly; refrigerate separately. Use gravy or stuffing within 1 or 2 days; heat them thoroughly before serving. Serve cooked turkey meat within 2 or 3 days after roasting. If frozen, it can be kept up to 1 month.

ROAST HALVES AND QUARTERS OF TURKEY

Prepare half and quarter turkeys according to the basic instructions for whole turkeys except—skewer skin to meat along cut edges to prevent shrinking from meat during roasting. Place skin side up on rack in open shallow roasting pan. Place meat thermometer in thickest part of inside thigh muscle or thickest part of breast. Be sure it does not touch bone.

Timetable for Roast Halves and Quarters

Ready-to-Cook Weight	Approximate Total Cooking Time	Internal Temperature
5 to 8 pounds	2½ to 3 hours	185°
8 to 10 pounds	3 to 3½ hours	185°
10 to 12 pounds	3½ to 4 hours	185°

BREAD STUFFING

Allow ¾ cup stuffing for each pound of ready-to-cook chicken or turkey.

½ cup chopped fresh mushrooms
1 cup finely chopped onion
½ cup chopped celery (ribs and leaves)
1 cup unsalted margarine
9 cups soft bread cubes
1½ teaspoons crushed sage leaves
1 teaspoon thyme leaves
½ teaspoon pepper

In large skillet, cook and stir mushrooms, onion and celery in margarine until onion is tender. Stir in about ⅓ of the bread cubes. Turn into deep bowl. Add remaining ingredients and toss. Stuff turkey just before roasting.

9 cups (enough for 12-pound turkey).

One ¾-cup serving = 1 bread II, 3 fat
170 calories

Variations

Apple-Raisin Stuffing: Decrease bread cubes to 7 cups and add 3 cups finely chopped apple and ¾ cups raisins with the remaining ingredients.

One ¾-cup serving = 1 bread II, 3 fat, ½ fruit
185 calories

Corn Bread Stuffing: Omit soft bread cubes and substitute Corn Bread cubes (page 82).

One ¾-cup serving = 1 bread III, 3 fat
170 calories

Note: Most holiday stuffings are apt to reflect a highly subjective taste experience, full of nostalgia for the cook's childhood memories. So don't be afraid to experiment with variations of the classic stuffing recipe given here. See Chapter 14.

LEMON SESAME CHICKEN

2½-pound broiler-fryer chicken, cut up
¼ cup lemon juice
2 tablespoons vegetable oil
½ teaspoon dry mustard
¼ teaspoon rosemary leaves
¼ teaspoon thyme
¼ teaspoon marjoram
¼ teaspoon sesame seed
¼ teaspoon pepper

Heat oven to 300°. Arrange chicken in lightly greased broiler pan. Mix remaining ingredients; brush part of mixture on chicken. Bake uncovered, brushing frequently with remaining mixture, 1 hour.

Increase oven temperature to 500°. Bake 15 minutes longer.

4 servings.

1 serving = 1¼ meat
305 calories

SUMMER GARDEN CHICKEN

1 teaspoon vegetable oil
3-ounce chicken piece (leg, thigh, breast)
1 small potato, pared and quartered
1 small tomato
1 small onion
2 fresh mushrooms
2 slices green pepper
2 tablespoons uncooked instant rice
1 tablespoon lemon juice
⅛ teaspoon paprika
⅛ teaspoon dry mustard
Freshly ground pepper

Heat oven to 450°. Heat oil in small skillet. Brown chicken in oil over medium-high heat. Place chicken on piece of double thickness aluminum foil; cover with vegetables and sprinkle with rice. Mix remaining ingredients; drizzle on chicken and vegetables. Fold foil over and seal securely. Place package in shallow baking pan. Bake, turning every 20 minutes, until chicken and vegetables are tender, 1 hour 15 minutes.

1 serving.

Note: Chicken can also be cooked on the grill.

1 serving = 1 meat, 1 vegetable, 1 bread I
420 calories

BROILED FISH

2 pounds fish fillets or steaks,
about 1 inch thick
⅛ teaspoon pepper
¼ cup unsalted margarine, melted
Paprika

Set oven control at broil and/or 550°. Grease broiler pan and place in oven to heat. If fillets are large, cut into serving pieces. Season both sides of fish with pepper. If fish has not been skinned, place skin side up in broiler pan; brush with margarine.

Broil 2 to 3 inches from heat until light brown, 5 to 8 minutes. Brush fish with margarine; turn carefully and brush again with margarine. Broil until fish flakes easily with fork, 5 to 8 minutes longer.

6 servings.

1 serving = 1 meat
320 calories

PANFRIED FISH

2 pounds fish fillets, steaks or
pan-dressed fish
⅛ teaspoon pepper
¼ cup Second Nature
imitation eggs*
1 cup flour or cornmeal
Vegetable oil

If fillets are large, cut into serving pieces. Season both sides of fish with pepper. Dip fish into imitation eggs, then coat with flour.

Heat vegetable oil (⅛ inch) in skillet. Turning fish carefully to brown both sides, cook in oil over medium heat about 10 minutes.

4 to 6 servings.

One 5-ounce serving = 1½ meat
355 calories

*If this ingredient is not available in your market area, see page 29 for substitutes.

OVEN-POACHED HADDOCK

1½ pounds haddock fillets
Juice of 1 lemon
1 bay leaf
1 tablespoon finely chopped onion
1 teaspoon snipped parsley
½ teaspoon thyme
½ teaspoon chervil
½ teaspoon sugar
3 medium tomatoes, sliced
Freshly ground pepper

Cut fish into 4 serving pieces and place in ungreased baking dish, 13½x9x2 inches. Mix remaining ingredients except tomatoes and pepper; spoon onto fish. Cover and refrigerate 3 to 4 hours.

Heat oven to 350°. Arrange tomato slices on fish and season with pepper. Cover and bake until fish flakes easily with fork, about 40 minutes.

4 servings.

1 serving = 1½ meat, ½ vegetable
170 calories

BAKED HADDOCK

2 pounds fresh haddock
3 tablespoons lemon juice
Freshly ground pepper
2 tablespoons unsalted margarine
½ cup vegetable oil
1½ teaspoons water
½ teaspoon dry mustard

Heat oven to 350°. Cut fish into serving pieces and arrange in greased baking dish, 13½x9x2 inches. Brush with 1 tablespoon of the lemon juice; season with pepper and dot with margarine. Mix remaining lemon juice, the oil, water and mustard; pour on fish. Cover and bake 45 minutes.

Increase oven temperature to 500°. Uncover fish and bake until brown, 10 to 15 minutes longer.

4 servings.

1 serving = 1½ meat
345 calories

BARBECUED FISH IN FOIL

2 packages (12 ounces each) frozen haddock fillets, partially thawed
Freshly ground pepper
4 carrots, sliced (about 2 cups)
1 medium onion, sliced
6 green pepper rings
2 cups Tomato Sauce (page 151)
2 tablespoons flour
2 tablespoons lemon juice
2 tablespoons vinegar
2 tablespoons prepared mustard
1 teaspoon sugar

Cut fish into 6 equal serving pieces. Place each on 12-inch square double thickness of aluminum foil. Season with pepper.

Heat 1 inch water to boiling in saucepan. Add carrots and onion. Cover and heat to boiling; cook 12 to 15 minutes or until tender. Drain.

Heat oven to 400°. Top each piece of fish with equal amount of carrot-onion mixture and 1 green pepper ring. Mix tomato sauce, flour, lemon juice, vinegar, mustard and sugar. Spoon mixture on vegetables and fish. Seal foil securely; place packets on baking sheet. Bake until fish flakes easily with fork, about 25 minutes.

6 servings.

1 serving = 1 meat, 1½ vegetable
250 calories

SALMON STEAK ALASKA

**4 fresh or thawed frozen salmon
 steaks, 1 inch thick
2 tablespoons lime or lemon juice
¼ teaspoon Tabasco pepper sauce
Lime slices
Cucumber Sauce (below)**

Heat oven to 350°. Place fish in ungreased baking dish. Mix lime juice and pepper sauce; brush on fish. Bake uncovered until fish flakes easily with fork, 25 to 30 minutes. Garnish with lime slices and serve with Cucumber Sauce.

4 servings.

**1 serving = 1 meat
            270 calories**

To broil salmon steaks: Place fish on greased broiler rack and brush with lime juice-pepper sauce mixture. Broil until fish flakes easily with fork, about 15 minutes.

Cucumber Sauce (with yogurt)

**1 cup low-fat yogurt
¼ teaspoon Tabasco pepper sauce
1 cup chopped seeded cucumber
1 tablespoon snipped fresh dill or
 1 teaspoon dill weed**

Mix yogurt and pepper sauce. Stir in cucumber and dill.

2 cups.

POACHED FISH

**1 medium onion, sliced
3 slices lemon
3 sprigs parsley
1 bay leaf
3 peppercorns
1 pound fish fillets**

Heat to boiling in large skillet 1½ inches water with onion, lemon slices, parsley, bay leaf and peppercorns.

Arrange fish in single layer in skillet. Cover and simmer until fish flakes easily with fork, 4 to 6 minutes.

2 or 3 servings.

**1 serving = 1 meat
            265 calories**

OVEN-FRIED FILLETS

**2 pounds fish fillets or steaks
1 teaspoon white pepper
½ cup skim milk
1 cup dry salt-free bread crumbs
¼ cup unsalted margarine, melted**

Heat oven to 500°. If fillets are large, cut into 6 serving pieces. Stir pepper into milk. Dip fish into milk, then coat with bread crumbs. Place in well-greased baking pan, 13x9x2 inches.

Pour margarine on fish. Place pan on rack that is slightly above middle of oven; bake uncovered until fish flakes easily with fork, 10 to 12 minutes.

6 servings.

**One 4-ounce serving = 1½ meat
                    230 calories**

BLUEFISH HAMPTON

2 pounds bluefish fillets
2 tablespoons unsalted margarine
Freshly ground pepper
¼ cup unsalted margarine
1 tablespoon plus 1½ teaspoons
  instant minced onion
Pinch garlic powder
1 teaspoon dried lemon peel
1 teaspoon freeze-dried chives
1 teaspoon dill weed
1 teaspoon chervil
1 teaspoon parsley flakes
1 teaspoon dry mustard
1 lemon, cut into wedges

Set oven control at broil and/or 550°. Oil broiler pan and place in oven to heat. Season fillets with pepper and arrange in broiler pan. Dot with 2 tablespoons of the margarine.

Broil fillets 3 inches from heat 10 minutes. Mix remaining ingredients except lemon. Spread mixture on fillets and broil until fish flakes easily with fork, about 5 minutes longer. Serve with lemon wedges.

8 servings.

1 serving = 1 meat
      230 calories

BROILED WHITEFISH

1 pound fish fillets or steaks, 1 inch
  thick
½ cup unsalted margarine, melted
Dash pepper
1 tablespoon basil leaves
1 tablespoon snipped chives
1 tablespoon snipped parsley

Grease broiler pan. Cut fillets into serving pieces and, if fish has not been skinned, place skin side up in broiler pan. Mix remaining ingredients; spread half the mixture on fish.

Set oven control at broil and/or 550°. Broil fish with top 2 to 3 inches from heat 5 minutes. Turn carefully and spread remaining mixture on fish. Broil until fish flakes easily with fork, about 5 minutes longer.

4 servings.

Note: Use only unsalted fresh fish or fish you have frozen yourself or that you know is unsalted. Do not use commercially frozen fish fillets unless your sodium intake is unrestricted.

1 serving = 1 meat
      345 calories

BAKED FISH

2 pounds fish fillets or steaks
Freshly ground pepper
2 tablespoons lemon juice
1 teaspoon grated onion
¼ cup unsalted margarine, melted
Paprika

Heat oven to 350°. If fillets are large, cut into serving pieces. Season with pepper. Mix lemon juice, onion and margarine. Dip fish into margarine mixture; place in greased baking pan, 9x9x2 inches. Pour remaining margarine mixture over fish. Bake uncovered until fish flakes easily with fork, 25 to 30 minutes. Sprinkle with paprika.

6 servings.

1 serving = 1 meat
      320 calories

CREOLE FLOUNDER

2 pounds flounder or haddock fillets
1½ cups chopped tomatoes
½ cup chopped green pepper
⅓ cup lemon juice
1 tablespoon vegetable oil
2 teaspoons instant minced onion
1 teaspoon basil leaves
¼ teaspoon coarsely ground
  black pepper
4 drops Tabasco pepper sauce

Heat oven to 500°. Place fish in greased baking dish, 13½x9x2 inches. Combine remaining ingredients; spoon over fish.

Bake 5 to 8 minutes or until fish flakes easily with fork. If desired, garnish with tomato wedges and green pepper rings.

6 servings.

One 4-ounce serving = 1½ meat
                  165 calories

STEAMED HARD-SHELL CRABS

Place 24 live hard-shell blue crabs on rack in large kettle. Add just enough water to cover bottom of kettle. Cover; heat to boiling. Reduce heat and simmer 15 minutes. Remove crabs and serve hot or cold.

To remove meat: With left hand, grasp body of crab with large claws to the right. Break off large claws. Pull off top shell with right hand. Cut or break off legs. Scrape off the gills; carefully remove digestive and other organs located in center part of body.

6 servings.

1 serving = 1¼ salted meat
              110 calories

SALMON WITH DILL SAUCE

1 pound salmon fillets or steaks
½ lemon
Freshly ground pepper
¼ cup unsalted margarine
2 tablespoons snipped dill
Dill Sauce (below)

Set oven control at broil and/or 550°. Oil broiler pan and place in oven to heat. If fillets are large, cut into serving pieces. Squeeze lemon juice on fillets and season with pepper. Arrange fillets in broiler pan and dot with 2 tablespoons of the margarine.

Broil 2 to 3 inches from heat 5 minutes. Spread remaining margarine on fish and sprinkle with dill. Broil 5 minutes longer. Remove fish to heated platter and top with Dill Sauce.

4 servings.

1 serving = 1 meat
          400 calories

Dill Sauce: Heat ¼ cup low-fat dairy sour cream and 2 tablespoons snipped dill over low heat, stirring occasionally.

BARBECUED FISH FILLETS

Clean and fillet a 3-pound fish (such as bass, pike, mackerel or trout). Wash and pat dry with paper towels; brush with vegetable oil. Place in hinged grill or on well-greased grill 3 to 4 inches from medium coals. Grill 5 to 7 minutes on each side or until fish flakes easily with a fork. Baste frequently with mixture of ½ cup unsalted margarine, melted, and ¼ cup lemon juice. Just before serving, season with pepper.

4 to 6 servings.

4-ounce serving = 1 meat
                  355 calories

BROILED LOBSTER TAILS WITH LEMON SAUCE

2 quarts water
1 package (1 pound 8 ounces) frozen South African rock lobster tails
⅓ cup unsalted margarine, melted
Lemon Sauce (below)

Heat water to boiling in large saucepan. Add lobster tails; cover and heat to boiling. Reduce heat and simmer about 15 minutes. Drain.

With kitchen scissors, cut away thin undershell covering meat of lobster tails. To prevent tails from curling, insert long metal skewer from meat side through tail to shell side, then back through shell and meat at opposite end. Place tails meat side up on broiler rack. Brush with margarine.
Set oven control at broil and/or 550°. Broil tails meat side up 3 inches from heat 2 to 3 minutes. Remove skewers and serve with Lemon Sauce in lemon cups.

4 servings.

1 serving = ½ salted meat, 3 fat
160 calories

Lemon Sauce

½ cup unsalted margarine
1 tablespoon lemon juice
1 tablespoon snipped parsley
¼ teaspoon Tabasco pepper sauce

Heat all ingredients over low heat, stirring constantly, until margarine is melted. Keep warm.

BOILED LOBSTER

3 quarts water
2 live lobsters (about 1 pound each)

Heat water to boiling in large kettle. Plunge lobsters headfirst into water. Cover and heat to boiling. Reduce heat and simmer about 10 minutes. Drain.

Place lobster on its back. With a sharp knife, cut lengthwise in half. Remove stomach, which is just back of the head, and the intestinal vein, which runs from the stomach to the tip of the tail. Do not discard the green liver and coral roe. Crack claws.

2 servings.

Note: Serve with lemon juice and melted unsalted margarine.

1 serving = ½ salted meat, 3 fat
160 calories

FLOUNDER WITH LEMON AND ALMONDS

1 pound flounder fillets
1 tablespoon unsalted margarine
Juice of 1 lemon (about 3 tablespoons)
Freshly ground pepper
2 tablespoons sliced almonds
1 tablespoon unsalted margarine
Lemon wedges
Parsley

Cover rack in broiler pan with heavy-duty aluminum foil. If fillets are large, cut into 4 pieces; arrange on foil-covered rack. Dot with 1 tablespoon margarine; sprinkle with lemon juice and season with pepper.

Set oven control at broil and/or 550°. Broil 3 inches from heat 4 minutes. Turn fish; sprinkle with almonds and dot with 1 tablespoon margarine. Broil until fish flakes easily with fork and almonds are light brown, about 4 minutes longer. Serve with lemon wedges and garnish with parsley.

4 servings.

1 serving = 1 meat
185 calories

TUNA GOURMET

1½ cups chopped fresh mushrooms
2 tablespoons unsalted margarine
8 ounces uncooked noodles
2 cans (6½ ounces each) unsalted tuna, drained
1 carton (12 ounces) dairy sour half-and-half (1½ cups)
¾ cup skim milk
¼ teaspoon pepper
¼ cup dry bread crumbs
2 tablespoons unsalted margarine, melted
Paprika

Cook mushrooms in margarine until tender; set aside.

Cook noodles as directed on package except—omit salt and substitute unsalted margarine for the butter. Return noodles to saucepan; stir in tuna, sour half-and-half, milk, mushrooms and pepper. Pour into ungreased 2-quart casserole.

Heat oven to 350°. Mix bread crumbs and melted margarine; sprinkle on tuna mixture. Sprinkle with paprika. Bake uncovered 35 to 40 minutes or until bubbly.

6 to 8 servings.

1 serving = 1 meat, 1 bread I
                425 calories

BAKED TUNA FONDUE

1 can (7 ounces) water-packed tuna, drained
2 cups low-sodium bread cubes, toasted
¼ cup plus 2 tablespoons Second Nature imitation eggs*
1¼ cups skim milk
1 teaspoon instant onion powder
½ teaspoon Italian seasoning
¼ teaspoon oregano
¼ teaspoon garlic powder
¼ teaspoon dill weed
⅛ teaspoon white pepper

Heat oven to 350°. Empty tuna in ungreased 1½-quart baking dish; break tuna apart with fork. Sprinkle bread cubes on top. Mix remaining ingredients and pour over bread cubes. Bake 30 minutes.

5 servings.

1 serving = 1 meat, 1 bread I
                160 calories

COTTAGE CHEESE BAKE

½ cup Second Nature imitation eggs*
1 cup skim milk
1 cup low-fat cottage cheese
2 tablespoons chopped chives
⅛ teaspoon pepper
⅛ teaspoon dill weed

Heat oven to 350°. Mix all ingredients. Pour into 5 oiled custard cups. Place cups in baking pan, 13x9x2 inches. Pour in very hot water to 1½-inch depth. Bake about 50 minutes or until knife inserted in center comes out clean. Remove cups from water and cool.

5 servings.

1 serving = ½ meat, 1 milk I
                75 calories

*If this ingredient is not available in your market area, see page 29 for substitutes.

SPAGHETTI WITH CREOLE SAUCE

1 can (10 ounces) unsalted tomatoes
¼ cup diced celery
2 tablespoons diced green pepper
2 whole cloves or ¼ teaspoon
   ground cloves
1 bay leaf
1 tablespoon white vinegar
1 teaspoon sugar
¼ teaspoon garlic powder
1 tablespoon flour
1½ cups uncooked spaghetti

Combine all ingredients except flour and spaghetti in large saucepan. Mix in flour. Heat to boiling, stirring constantly. Boil and stir 1 minute. Reduce heat and simmer uncovered, stirring occasionally, 20 minutes.

Cook spaghetti as directed on package except—omit salt.

Remove bay leaf and whole cloves from sauce. Serve sauce on hot spaghetti.

3 servings.

1 serving = 1 bread I
              170 calories

VEGETABLE COMBO

¾ cup water
1 tablespoon flour
1 unsalted chicken bouillon cube
1 small potato, pared and cut into
   julienne strips (½ cup)
¼ cup 1-inch pieces fresh green beans
¼ cup 1-inch pieces fresh wax beans
2 tablespoons fresh green peas
1 tablespoon diced green pepper

Heat oven to 350°. Mix water, flour and bouillon cube in small saucepan. Heat to boiling, stirring constantly. Boil and stir 1 minute.

Remove from heat and fold in vegetables gently. Turn into ungreased 20-ounce casserole. Cover and bake until vegetables are tender, 45 minutes.

2 servings.

1 serving = ½ bread I, 1 vegetable
              65 calories

ZUCCHINI-CHEESE CASSEROLE

2 pounds zucchini
2 eggs, beaten
1 carton (16 ounces) low-fat
   cottage cheese
1 cup cooked rice
2 onions, finely chopped
1 teaspoon dry mustard
1 teaspoon marjoram
2 tablespoons snipped chives
Freshly ground pepper
¼ cup grated Parmesan cheese

Wash zucchini; remove stems and blossom ends but do not pare. Cut into ½-inch slices.

Heat 1 inch water to boiling. Add zucchini. Cover and heat to boiling; cook until tender, 12 to 15 minutes. Drain.

Heat oven to 350°. Mix egg, cottage cheese, rice, onion, mustard, marjoram and chives. Season with pepper. Place half the zucchini in greased 1½-quart casserole; top with half the rice mixture. Repeat layers and sprinkle with Parmesan cheese. Bake 45 minutes.

4 servings.

1 serving = ½ meat, 1½ milk,
              1 vegetable, 1 bread I
              250 calories

BASIC RICE

Just follow the directions and use according to the recipe of your choice.

Uncooked regular rice triples in volume—¼ cup uncooked regular rice becomes ¾ cup when cooked.

¼ cup uncooked regular rice
1 teaspoon unsalted margarine
½ cup water

Heat rice, margarine and water, stirring once or twice, in small saucepan to boiling. Reduce heat to simmer; cover pan tightly and cook 14 minutes. (Do not lift cover or stir.) Remove pan from heat. Fluff rice lightly; cover and let steam 5 to 10 minutes.

For converted or instant rice, follow package directions except—omit salt.

¾ cup = 2 bread I
         215 calories

BASIC PILAF

3 tablespoons uncooked regular rice
¼ medium onion, chopped
1 tablespoon olive oil
⅓ cup unsalted chicken broth
Freshly ground pepper

Cook and stir rice and onion in olive oil in small saucepan until onion is tender and rice is golden. Stir in chicken broth and season with pepper. Heat to boiling. Reduce heat to simmer; cover pan tightly and cook until rice is tender and almost all liquid is absorbed, about 14 minutes.

1 serving.

1 serving = 1 bread I
         285 calories

CURRIED RICE

¼ cup uncooked regular rice
2 tablespoons finely chopped onion
½ teaspoon curry powder
1 teaspoon unsalted margarine
½ cup water
Chutney

Heat rice, onion, curry powder, margarine and water in small saucepan, stirring once or twice, to boiling. Reduce heat to simmer; cover pan tightly and cook 14 minutes. (Do not lift cover or stir.) Remove pan from heat. Fluff rice lightly; cover and let steam 5 to 10 minutes. Serve with chutney.

1 serving.

1 serving = 1 bread I
         230 calories

PARTY RICE

1 cup uncooked regular rice
2½ cups water
½ cup chopped onion
¼ cup chopped green pepper
¼ cup shredded carrot
2 tablespoons snipped parsley
½ bay leaf
1 tablespoon unsalted margarine

Heat all ingredients in large saucepan, stirring once or twice, to boiling. Reduce heat to simmer; cover pan tightly and cook until rice is tender, 15 to 20 minutes. (Do not lift cover or stir.)

Remove pan of cooked rice from heat. Remove bay leaf. Fluff rice lightly with fork; cover and let stand 5 to 10 minutes.

4 servings.

1 serving = 1 bread I, ½ vegetable
         225 calories

NEW DELHI RICE

3 cups cooked unsalted rice
½ cup unsalted chicken broth
2 medium tomatoes, peeled and chopped
  (seeds removed)
½ cup chopped onion
2 tablespoons soft unsalted margarine
2 teaspoons curry powder
Freshly ground pepper

Heat oven to 375°. Mix rice, chicken broth, tomatoes and onion in ungreased 1½-quart casserole. Bake uncovered until bubbly, 20 to 30 minutes. Mix margarine and curry powder until smooth; stir into rice mixture. Season with pepper.

8 servings.

1 serving = 1 bread I
        110 calories

MUSHROOM MACARONI CASSEROLE

¼ cup uncooked elbow macaroni
1 tablespoon unsalted margarine
2 tablespoons sliced fresh mushroom
1 tablespoon chopped pimiento
1 teaspoon grated Parmesan cheese

Cook macaroni as directed on package except—omit salt.

Melt margarine in small skillet. Cook and stir mushroom and pimiento in margarine until hot. Stir in macaroni and sprinkle cheese on top.

1 serving.

1 serving = 1 bread I, ½ vegetable
        230 calories

TOMATO MACARONI

¼ cup uncooked elbow macaroni
1 tablespoon unsalted margarine
½ cup cut-up peeled tomato
1 tablespoon diced fresh mushroom

Cook macaroni as directed on package except—omit salt.

Melt margarine in small skillet. Cook and stir tomato and mushroom in margarine until vegetables are hot and bubbly. Stir in macaroni.

1 serving.

1 serving = 1 bread I, 1 vegetable
        255 calories

*If this ingredient is not available in your market area, see page 29 for substitutes.

DIJON-TYPE MUSTARD

1½ cups tarragon vinegar
½ cup water
2 tablespoons sugar
¼ stick cinnamon
5 whole cloves
5 white peppercorns
5 black peppercorns
1 bay leaf
5 cans (2 ounces each) dry English mustard
¼ to ⅓ cup olive oil, if desired

Simmer vinegar, water, sugar, cinnamon stick, cloves, peppercorns and bay leaf in medium saucepan uncovered 5 minutes. Strain and pour on mustard in medium bowl; stir and cover bowl.

Let stand in bowl at room temperature, stirring every other day, about 2 months. (If mustard becomes dry, stir in small amount boiling water or cream sherry.) Stir in olive oil. Pour into jar; cover and store in cool place.

1 tablespoon = ½ fat
65 calories

BASIC BROWN SAUCE

2 teaspoons unsalted margarine
2 teaspoons flour
⅔ cup unsalted beef broth

Melt margarine in saucepan over low heat. Blend in flour. Cook over low heat, stirring until mixture is smooth and bubbly. Cook over medium heat until mixture is brown. Remove from heat. Stir in beef broth. Heat to boiling, stirring constantly. Boil and stir 1 minute. Refrigerate or freeze until ready to use.

About ⅔ cup.

2½ tablespoons = ½ fat
25 calories

BASIC MARINADE

3 parts vegetable oil
1 part acid (vinegar, lemon juice, dry wine)
Enhancements (garlic, herbs, spices, seeds)

Shake all ingredients in tightly covered jar.

1 tablespoon = 2 fat
100 calories

UNSALTED TOMATO PASTE

Heat 1 can (18 ounces) unsalted tomato juice in small saucepan to boiling. Reduce heat; simmer until liquid is evaporated and sauce is consistency of tomato paste, about 45 minutes. Stir in ¾ teaspoon sugar.

½ cup.

1 tablespoon = ½ vegetable
15 calories

The recipe for Easy Grilled Chicken is on page 132.

The recipe for Salmon with Dill Sauce is on page 144.

WHITE SAUCE

Thin White Sauce

Like coffee cream
For creamed vegetables, soup

1 tablespoon unsalted margarine
½ to 1 tablespoon flour*
⅛ teaspoon pepper
1 cup skim milk

Medium White Sauce

Like thick cream
For creamed and scalloped dishes

2 tablespoons unsalted margarine
2 tablespoons flour
⅛ teaspoon pepper
1 cup skim milk

Thick White Sauce

Like batter
For croquettes, soufflés

¼ cup unsalted margarine
¼ cup all-purpose flour
⅛ teaspoon pepper
1 cup skim milk

Melt margarine in small saucepan over low heat. Stir in flour and pepper. Cook over low heat, stirring until mixture is smooth and bubbly. Remove from heat. Stir in milk. Heat to boiling, stirring constantly. Boil and stir 1 minute.

1 cup.

*Use smaller amount of flour with starch vegetables (peas, potatoes), larger amount with nonstarch.

½ cup = ½ milk
Thin   = 110 calories
Medium = 180 calories
Thick = 320 calories

Variations for Medium White Sauce

Curry Sauce (For chicken, lamb, shrimp and rice): Stir in ½ teaspoon curry powder with the flour.

Dill Sauce (For bland meat or fish): Stir in 1 teaspoon finely chopped fresh dill or ½ teaspoon dill weed and dash of nutmeg with the flour.

Cucumber Sauce (For salmon and other fish): Prepare Medium White Sauce and stir in ½ cup shredded or thinly sliced cucumber and dash of cayenne pepper.

TOMATO SAUCE

2 tablespoons unsalted margarine
¼ cup chopped onion
2 medium tomatoes, peeled and
**   chopped**
½ cup unsalted tomato juice
¾ teaspoon basil leaves
¾ teaspoon oregano
¾ teaspoon pepper

Melt margarine over low heat. Cook and stir onion in margarine until tender. Stir in remaining ingredients and simmer uncovered, stirring occasionally, ½ to 1 hour.

About 1 cup.

½ cup = 1 vegetable
**   165 calories**

CREOLE SAUCE

2 tablespoons unsalted margarine
¾ cup chopped green pepper
½ cup chopped onion
2 medium tomatoes, peeled and
  chopped
¼ teaspoon oregano
¼ teaspoon freshly ground pepper

Melt margarine in skillet. Cook and stir green pepper and onion in margarine until onion is tender. Stir in remaining ingredients. Cover and simmer 5 minutes.

4 servings.

Note: Serve on omelet or use as filling for crêpes.

1 serving = ½ vegetable
            80 calories

MEAT-BASTING SAUCE

1 cup red wine
1 cup olive oil
¼ cup wine vinegar
2 medium onions, chopped
2 cloves garlic, peeled
⅛ teaspoon rosemary leaves
⅛ teaspoon cayenne red pepper

Shake all ingredients in tightly covered jar. Refrigerate 24 hours to blend flavors. Remove garlic. Use for basting meat or poultry while roasting or broiling.

About 2¼ cups.

1 tablespoon = 1 fat
              70 calories

LEMON POULTRY-BASTING SAUCE

¾ cup unsalted margarine
2 teaspoons paprika
1 teaspoon sugar
½ teaspoon pepper
¼ teaspoon dry mustard
Dash cayenne red pepper
½ cup lemon juice
½ cup hot water
2 teaspoons grated onion

Melt margarine in saucepan; stir in paprika, sugar, pepper, mustard and cayenne red pepper. Blend in lemon juice, hot water and onion. Use to baste chicken or turkey during grilling or roasting.

About 1¾ cups.

1 tablespoon = 1 fat
              50 calories

BORDELAISE SAUCE

1 teaspoon unsalted margarine
1 teaspoon chopped onion
1 fresh mushroom, chopped
¼ cup Basic Brown Sauce (page 150)
¼ cup red wine

Melt margarine in small skillet; cook and stir onion and mushroom in margarine until onion is tender. Remove from heat and set aside.

Cook Basic Brown Sauce, stirring frequently, until sauce is reduced by half. Stir in wine, onion and mushroom; simmer 2 to 3 minutes. Serve with beef.

⅓ cup.

⅓ cup = trace sodium
           35 calories

SAUCE PROVENÇALE

1 medium tomato
¼ teaspoon sugar
2 teaspoons unsalted margarine
1 tablespoon chopped green onion
2 tablespoons dry sherry
1 small clove garlic, crushed
2 tablespoons unsalted margarine
2 teaspoons snipped parsley
Freshly ground pepper

Peel tomato and cut into 6 to 8 wedges. Sprinkle with sugar and set aside. Melt 2 teaspoons margarine in skillet over medium heat; cook and stir onion in margarine 1 minute. Stir in sherry. Cook, stirring constantly, until liquid is slightly reduced. Stir in tomato wedges and simmer uncovered 2 to 3 minutes.

Stir in garlic, 2 tablespoons margarine, the parsley and pepper; heat until margarine is melted. Serve on beef.

1 cup.

1 tablespoon = ½ fat
25 calories

CUMBERLAND SAUCE

1 cup currant jelly
½ cup Madeira
¼ cup shredded orange peel
1 tablespoon shredded lemon peel
1 small piece crystallized ginger, chopped,
  or ground ginger to taste
½ teaspoon dry mustard
Dash cayenne red pepper

Melt jelly in small saucepan over low heat. Stir in remaining ingredients. Serve warm or cold with meat.

1½ cups.

1 tablespoon = trace sodium
30 calories

KETTLE GRAVY

¼ cup water
2 tablespoons flour
1 cup unsalted beef bouillon
Pepper

Shake water and flour in tightly covered jar. (For a smooth mixture, it is important to measure water into jar first, then the flour.) Stir flour mixture slowly into bouillon in small saucepan. Heat to boiling, stirring constantly. Boil and stir 1 minute. Season with pepper.

1 cup.

2 tablespoons = trace sodium
10 calories

HOLLANDAISE SAUCE

¼ cup plus 2 tablespoons Second Nature
  imitation eggs*
3 tablespoons lemon juice
½ cup unsalted margarine, melted

Measure imitation egg and lemon juice into blender container. Cover and blend on high speed. Remove cover; slowly pour in margarine while mixing on high speed. Mix until smooth and creamy.

About 1 cup.

¼ cup = ½ meat
240 calories

*If this ingredient is not available in your market area, see page 29 for substitutes.

SWEDISH SAUCE

1 cup unsalted mayonnaise
½ cup unsweetened applesauce
1 tablespoon grated horseradish root
Freshly ground pepper

Mix all ingredients; cover and refrigerate. Serve with cold meat.

1½ cups.

1 tablespoon = 2 fat
                    45 calories

QUICK DILL SAUCE

½ cup skim milk
1 cup low-sodium mayonnaise
1 teaspoon lemon juice
¼ teaspoon dill weed or
   ¾ teaspoon snipped dill

Stir milk gradually into mayonnaise in small saucepan. Stir in lemon juice and dill weed. Heat over low heat, stirring occasionally, until heated through, 2 to 3 minutes. Serve on hot vegetables.

1½ cups.

2 tablespoons = 4 fat
                    90 calories

EAST INDIA PEACHES

1 can (16 ounces) peach halves
½ cup Chutney (below)
Grated peel and juice of ½ lemon
1 tablespoon snipped mint

Heat peaches (with syrup) in saucepan. Stir in remaining ingredients and simmer 2 to 3 minutes. Serve warm with meat or poultry.

About 5 servings.

1 serving = 1 fruit
                    120 calories

CHUTNEY

¼ pound pitted dates
¼ pound dried apricots
1 cup cider vinegar
1 hot chili pepper, finely chopped
½ cup sugar
½ cup chopped pared apple
2 medium onions, chopped
¼ teaspoon ginger
¼ teaspoon cloves
¼ teaspoon cinnamon

Soak dates and apricots in vinegar 8 to 12 hours. Chop finely; stir in remaining ingredients. If mixture is too dry, add vinegar, 1 tablespoon at a time. Let stand at least 1 hour. Serve with Curried Rice (page 148).

12 servings.

1 serving = 1 fruit
                    100 calories

HOT PEPPER RELISH

5 green peppers, chopped
½ cup snipped parsley
2 to 4 tablespoons dried hot red peppers
3 tablespoons lemon juice

Mix all ingredients. Cover and refrigerate 2 days to blend flavors.

About 4 cups.

¼ cup = ½ vegetable
25 calories

MEXICAN RELISH

2 cups diced firm tomato
1 cup minced onion
1 cup finely chopped sweet red and green pepper
1 tablespoon garlic or herb vinegar
¼ teaspoon grated lemon peel
2 teaspoons lemon juice
⅛ teaspoon red pepper, if desired

Mix all ingredients thoroughly. Cover and refrigerate 8 hours to blend flavors.

4 cups.

¼ cup = ¼ vegetable
25 calories

HERB MARGARINE

¼ cup unsalted margarine
¼ teaspoon Tabasco pepper sauce
2 tablespoons chopped fresh herbs (parsley, dill or thyme) or 1 tablespoon parsley flakes, dill weed or thyme leaves

Melt margarine; stir in pepper sauce and herbs. Serve on vegetables, broiled fish or meat.

About ¼ cup (4 to 6 servings).

1 teaspoon = 1 fat
35 calories

CRANBERRY-ORANGE RELISH

½ cup water
½ cup orange juice
1 cup sugar
1 pound cranberries
2 tablespoons grated orange peel

Stir water, orange juice and sugar in 3- or 4-quart saucepan until sugar is dissolved. Add cranberries and heat to boiling. Cook, stirring occasionally, until berries begin to pop and are tender but not mushy, 3 to 5 minutes.

Remove from heat and stir in orange peel. Turn relish into bowl and cool. Refrigerate 1 to 2 hours before serving.

4 cups.

¼ cup = ½ fruit
65 calories

SEASONED MARGARINE

½ cup unsalted margarine
¼ teaspoon Tabasco pepper sauce

Mix margarine and pepper sauce until smooth. Serve on hot toasted bread, baked potatoes or vegetables.

½ cup.

1 tablespoon = 3 fat
110 calories

11.Vegetables

Used creatively, these imaginative recipes can be a taste adventure for the entire family—and remember that with vegetables it is always the extra of *freshness* that counts.

POTATO BAKE

4 small baking potatoes
2 tablespoons unsalted margarine,
softened
2 medium onions, sliced
2 medium tomatoes, sliced
Pepper
2 tablespoons snipped parsley

Heat oven to 350°. Pare potatoes and cut into 6 to 8 slices. Spread margarine on slices. Reassemble potatoes, alternating onion and tomato slices between potato slices. Season with pepper.

Wrap each potato in aluminum foil. Bake 1 hour. Open foil and sprinkle parsley on potatoes. Return to oven and bake until tops of potatoes are brown.

4 servings.

1 serving = 1 bread I, ½ vegetable
180 calories

PARSLEYED POTATOES

1 pound potatoes (3 medium)
2 tablespoons unsalted margarine
⅔ cup snipped parsley
2 teaspoons finely chopped onion
¼ teaspoon grated lemon peel
¼ teaspoon sugar
Freshly ground pepper

Pare potatoes and cut into balls with melon ball cutter or cut into ¼-inch slices. Cook potatoes covered in 1 inch boiling water until tender, about 5 minutes. Drain.

Melt margarine in saucepan; stir in parsley, onion, lemon peel and sugar. Season with pepper. Add potatoes and heat, stirring frequently, until potatoes are coated with margarine and hot.

4 servings.

1 serving = 1 bread I
125 calories

GARLIC POTATO BALLS

2 large potatoes
2 tablespoons unsalted margarine
½ teaspoon garlic powder
Freshly ground pepper
2 tablespoons snipped parsley

Pare potatoes and cut into balls with melon ball cutter. Cook potato balls covered in 1 inch boiling water 5 minutes. Drain.

Melt margarine in skillet. Cook and stir potatoes, garlic powder and pepper in margarine until potato balls are golden brown, about 5 minutes. Remove with slotted spoon to serving dish and sprinkle with parsley.

3 servings.

1 serving = 1 bread I
          155 calories

PINEAPPLE SWEET POTATOES

1 can (17 ounces) vacuum-packed sweet
  potatoes, drained
1 can (8 ounces) pineapple chunks in
  unsweetened pineapple juice, drained
  (reserve ¼ cup juice)
½ cup brown sugar (packed)
2 tablespoons brandy
2 tablespoons soft unsalted margarine

Heat oven to 350°. Arrange sweet potatoes and pineapple chunks in greased 1½-quart casserole. Pour on reserve pineapple juice. Mix sugar, brandy and margarine and spread on top. Bake uncovered until hot and bubbly, 30 to 40 minutes.

6 servings.

1 serving = 2 bread I
          225 calories

CRISSCROSS POTATOES

1 large baking potato
2 tablespoons unsalted margarine, melted
Freshly ground pepper
Paprika

Heat oven to 400°. Cut unpared potato lengthwise in half. Make diagonal cuts about ⅛ inch deep in cut surfaces of potato, forming crisscross pattern. Brush with margarine and season with pepper. Place in small shallow baking pan. Bake uncovered 40 minutes. Sprinkle with paprika. Bake until tender, 10 minutes longer.

2 servings.

1 serving = 1 bread I
          180 calories

BAKED GLAZED YAMS

3 yams
1 banana
2 tablespoons sugar
2 tablespoons cinnamon
2 tablespoons lemon juice
¾ cup honey

Heat to boiling enough water to cover yams. Add yams; cover and cook until just tender, 25 minutes. Drain and cool.

Heat oven to 350°. Cut yams lengthwise into halves. Scoop out insides, leaving thin shell. Mash yam, banana, sugar, cinnamon and lemon juice until smooth. Spoon mixture into yam shells. Place shells in ungreased baking dish, 10x6x1½ inches, and drizzle with honey. Bake uncovered, basting occasionally, 15 minutes.

6 servings.

1 serving = 1 bread I
          215 calories

SWEET POTATO AND APPLE BAKE

2 pounds sweet potatoes, cooked, peeled and halved
2 medium cooking apples, pared and sliced
¼ cup molasses
2 tablespoons sugar
2 tablespoons unsalted margarine, melted
⅛ teaspoon ginger
⅛ teaspoon ground cloves
⅛ teaspoon nutmeg
⅓ cup orange juice

Heat oven to 350°. Arrange sweet potatoes and apple slices in layers in ungreased baking pan, 9x9x2 inches. Mix remaining ingredients. Pour over potatoes and apple slices. Bake uncovered 45 minutes, basting occasionally.

8 servings.

1 serving = 1 bread I
            235 calories

ORANGE SWEET POTATOES

4 medium sweet potatoes, pared
½ cup orange juice
2 medium oranges, pared and sectioned
¼ cup brown sugar (packed)
Nutmeg

Heat oven to 375°. Cut a lengthwise gash in each potato. Dip potatoes into orange juice to prevent discoloration. Fill each gash with orange sections and sprinkle top of each potato with sugar and nutmeg. Wrap securely in aluminum foil. Bake until tender, 1 hour.

4 servings.

Note: ½ winter squash can be substituted for each sweet potato.

1 serving = 2 bread I, ½ fruit
            235 calories

PARSLEYED NEW POTATOES

¾ pound small new potatoes
2 tablespoons unsalted margarine, melted
2 tablespoons snipped parsley
1½ teaspoons lemon juice

Cook potatoes covered in 1 inch boiling water until tender, 10 to 15 minutes. Drain and, if desired, peel potatoes.

Mix margarine, parsley and lemon juice and pour on hot potatoes.

3 servings.

1 serving = 1 bread I
            165 calories

CAULIFLOWER PARMESAN

1 large head cauliflower
2 tablespoons unsalted margarine
½ cup bread cubes
1 tablespoon grated Parmesan cheese
1 tablespoon unsalted margarine

Remove outer leaves and stalk of cauliflower. Cut off any discoloration on flowerets. Wash cauliflower and leave whole.

Heat 1 inch water to boiling. Add cauliflower; cover and heat to boiling. Cook until tender, 20 to 25 minutes. Drain.

Melt 2 tablespoons margarine in small saucepan. Stir in bread cubes; cook over low heat, stirring occasionally, until bread cubes are golden brown. Remove from heat; stir in cheese.

Spread 1 tablespoon margarine on hot cauliflower and sprinkle bread cubes on top.

6 servings.

1 serving = ½ vegetable, 1 bread I
            95 calories

ASPARAGUS

Break off tough ends of 1½ pounds asparagus as far down as stalks snap easily. Wash asparagus thoroughly. Remove scales if sandy or tough (if necessary, remove sand particles with vegetable brush). For spears, tie whole stalks in bundles with string or hold together with band of aluminum foil. Or cut stalks into 1-inch pieces.

To cook spears: In deep narrow pan or coffeepot, heat 1 inch salted water (1½ teaspoon salt to 1 cup water) to boiling. Place asparagus upright in pan. Heat to boiling; cook uncovered 5 minutes. Cover and cook 7 to 10 minutes longer or until stalk ends are crisp-tender. Drain.

To cook in skillet: Do not tie stalks in bundles. Fill 10-inch skillet ½ full with water; add 1 teaspoon salt. Heat water to boiling; add asparagus and heat to boiling. Cover; cook until stalk ends are crisp-tender, 8 to 12 minutes. Drain.

4 servings.

**1 serving = 1 vegetable
20 calories**

ONION SLICES SAUTÉED

**2 tablespoons unsalted margarine
1 medium onion, cut into ½-inch slices**

Melt margarine in skillet; cook and stir onion slices in margarine over low heat until onion is tender, about 10 minutes.

1 serving.

**1 serving = 1 vegetable
255 calories**

HERBED ASPARAGUS WITH LEMON

Break off tough ends of 1½ pounds asparagus spears as far down as stalks snap easily. Remove scales if sandy or tough. Tie stalks in bundles with string.

Heat 1 inch water in deep narrow pan or coffeepot to boiling. Place asparagus upright in pan. Heat to boiling; cook uncovered 5 minutes. Cover and cook until stalk ends are crisp-tender, 7 to 10 minutes. Drain. Drizzle with ¼ cup melted unsalted margarine and 3 tablespoons lemon juice. Season with freshly ground pepper or mace, allspice, dill weed, marjoram or savory.

4 servings.

**1 serving = 1 vegetable
85 calories**

SUMMER VEGETABLE SKILLET

**¼ cup unsalted margarine
¼ teaspoon Tabasco pepper sauce
2 small onions, thinly sliced
¾ cup crisp-cooked sliced zucchini*
¾ cup crisp-cooked cut green beans**

Melt margarine in large skillet; add pepper sauce. Cook and stir onion slices in margarine until tender. Add zucchini; cook, stirring occasionally, until heated through, about 5 minutes. Add beans and heat through.

4 servings.

Note: ¾ cup cooked cauliflowerets or ¾ cup cooked peas can be substituted for the zucchini and green beans.

*Cook vegetables in boiling water and ¼ teaspoon pepper sauce just until crisp-tender.

**1 serving = 1 vegetable
125 calories**

BAKED BUTTERNUT SQUASH

**1 large butternut squash, pared and
  cut into 1-inch cubes**
¼ teaspoon cinnamon
¼ teaspoon nutmeg
½ cup brown sugar (packed)
½ cup unsalted margarine, melted
2 teaspoons fresh lemon juice

Heat oven to 375°. Place squash cubes in ungreased 2-quart casserole or baking dish. Sprinkle with cinnamon, nutmeg and brown sugar. Drizzle margarine and lemon juice on top. Bake uncovered until tender, about 45 minutes.

4 servings.

1 serving = ½ vegetable
                390 calories

FRIED CORN

**1 tablespoon plus 1½ teaspoons
  unsalted margarine**
1 cup unsalted cooked corn
¼ green pepper, thinly sliced
½ teaspoon finely chopped onion
1 tablespoon sliced pimiento
Freshly ground pepper
½ teaspoon snipped parsley

Melt margarine in skillet; stir in corn, green pepper and onion. Cover tightly and simmer over low heat, stirring frequently, until green pepper is tender, 20 minutes. Stir in pimiento; season with pepper and simmer 2 to 3 minutes. Garnish with parsley.

3 servings.

1 serving = 1 bread I
                105 calories

ROASTIN' EARS

Heat oven to 450°. Remove husks and silk from corn; reserve husks. Brush each ear of corn with 1 tablespoon unsalted margarine. Dampen husks and wrap around corn. Wrap securely in aluminum foil. Bake until tender, 20 minutes.

1 serving = 1 bread I
                170 calories

CORN ON THE COB

Place corn in enough cold water to cover. Add 1 teaspoon each sugar and lemon juice to each quart of water. Heat to boiling; boil uncovered 2 minutes. Remove from heat; let corn stand about 10 minutes before serving. Serve with Seasoned Margarine (page 155). Allow 1 tablespoon margarine for each serving.

1 serving = 1 bread I
                175 calories

BAKED GREEN PEPPERS

2 medium green peppers
½ clove garlic, finely chopped
1 tablespoon olive oil

Heat oven to 350°. Cut green peppers into quarters; remove stems, seeds and membranes. Mix peppers, garlic and oil in ungreased 20-ounce casserole. Bake uncovered, stirring frequently, 15 to 20 minutes.

2 servings.

1 serving = 1 vegetable
                90 calories

MINTED PEAS

3 pounds green peas or 1 can (15½ ounces) unsalted peas
1 teaspoon dried mint or 7 fresh mint leaves
2 tablespoons unsalted margarine
Freshly ground pepper

If using fresh peas, shell and wash peas just before cooking. Heat 1 inch water to boiling. Add peas and mint. Heat to boiling; cook uncovered 5 minutes. Cover and cook until tender, 3 to 7 minutes. Drain.

If using canned peas, drain liquid into saucepan. Heat to boiling; boil until liquid is reduced to half. Add peas and mint and heat until hot. Drain.

Turn peas into serving dish. Dot with margarine and season with pepper.

4 servings.

1 serving = 1 bread l
140 calories

GRILLED EGGPLANT

Cut medium eggplant (about 1 pound) into ¾-inch slices. Brush both sides of slices with salad oil, then coat with herb-seasoned bread crumbs. Grill 4 inches from heat until tender, turning once, 10 to 15 minutes.

6 servings.

1 serving = 1 vegetable
120 calories

GLAZED MUSTARD PARSNIPS

1½ pounds parsnips
2 tablespoons unsalted margarine
2 tablespoons brown sugar
½ teaspoon dry mustard

Scrape or pare parsnips. Cut lengthwise into ¼-inch strips. Heat 1 inch water to boiling. Add parsnips. Cover and heat to boiling. Cook until tender, about 30 minutes. Drain; turn into ungreased baking dish, 11½x7½x1½ inches.

Heat oven to 400°. Dot parsnips with margarine. Mix brown sugar and mustard; sprinkle on parsnips. Bake until glazed and light brown, about 20 minutes.

4 servings.

1 serving = 1 vegetable
185 calories

PINEAPPLE CARROTS

¾ teaspoon cornstarch
¼ cup pineapple juice
1 cup canned unsalted carrots
¼ cup diced pineapple, canned or fresh
1½ teaspoons unsalted margarine
Freshly ground pepper

Mix cornstarch and pineapple juice until smooth. Cook, stirring constantly, until mixture thickens and boils. Add carrots, pineapple, margarine and heat through. Season with pepper.

2 servings.

1 serving = 1 vegetable
85 calories

EXEMPLARY BEETS

2½ pounds medium beets or 2 cans (15½ ounces each) unsalted whole baby beets
¼ cup tarragon vinegar
¼ cup unsalted bouillon
3 tablespoons sugar
¼ teaspoon freshly ground pepper
1 medium onion, thinly sliced and separated into rings

If using fresh beets, cut off all but 2 inches of beet tops. Wash beets and leave whole with root ends attached. Heat 3 quarts (12 cups) water and 2 tablespoons vinegar (to preserve color) to boiling. Add beets. Cover and heat to boiling; cook until tender, 35 to 45 minutes. Drain; run cold water over beets. Slip off skins and remove root ends. Cut beets into quarters or slice and place in saucepan.

If using canned beets, heat beets (with liquid); drain well.

Add vinegar, bouillon, sugar, pepper and onion slices to beets; heat to boiling, stirring occasionally.

8 servings.

1 serving = 2 vegetable
           70 calories

GLAZED BEETS

1 can (16 ounces) unsalted beets or 1 pound fresh beets, cooked and peeled
1 tablespoon cornstarch
2 tablespoon cider vinegar
1 teaspoon sugar
Few drops red food color
Freshly ground pepper

If using canned beets, drain and measure liquid. Add enough water to measure 1 cup and pour into saucepan. (If using fresh beets, substitute 1 cup water for the liquid.) Mix in cornstarch until smooth. Stir in vinegar and sugar. Cook, stirring constantly, until mixture thickens and boils. Boil and stir 1 minute. Stir in food color, pepper and beets and heat until beets are hot.

6 servings.

1 serving = 1 vegetable
           40 calories

RATATOUILLE

1 small onion, thinly sliced
¼ cup olive oil
3 small zucchini, cut into ⅛-inch slices
4 medium tomatoes, peeled and chopped
2 medium sweet red peppers, chopped
1 clove garlic, finely chopped
½ teaspoon sugar
¼ teaspoon white pepper
⅛ teaspoon dry mustard
1 teaspoon lemon juice
¼ cup snipped parsley

Cook and stir onion slices in oil until tender. Stir in remaining ingredients except parsley. Reduce heat; cover and simmer 3 minutes. Uncover and cook over medium heat, stirring constantly, until liquid is evaporated. (Watch carefully.) Turn into serving dish and sprinkle with parsley.

6 servings.

1 serving = 1 vegetable
130 calories

HONEY-GLAZED ACORN SQUASH

3 medium acorn squash (1 pound each)
¼ cup unsalted margarine, melted
½ teaspoon allspice
¼ cup honey
½ teaspoon nutmeg

Heat oven to 350°. Cut each squash in half; remove seeds and fibers. Place squash cut sides down in ungreased baking pan, 13x9x2 inches. Pour water into pan to ¼-inch depth. Cover with aluminum foil. Bake until tender, 30 to 35 minutes.

Drain; turn squash cut sides up. Mix remaining ingredients; pour 1 tablespoon plus 1 teaspoon honey mixture into each half. Bake uncovered, basting squash twice with honey mixture, until squash is glazed, about 15 minutes.

6 servings.

1 serving = ½ vegetable
170 calories

ORANGE BAKED ACORN SQUASH

1 medium acorn squash
1 tablespoon unsalted margarine, melted
½ cup orange juice

Heat oven to 400°. Cut squash in half; remove seeds and fibers. Brush with margarine. Place cut sides down in ungreased baking pan, 9x9x2 inches. Pour ¼ cup orange juice into pan. Bake uncovered 30 minutes. Turn squash and pour remaining orange juice into halves. Bake, basting frequently with orange juice, until tender, 30 minutes longer.

2 servings.

1 serving = 1 vegetable
165 calories

BROCCOLI

1½ pounds broccoli
2 tablespoons vegetable oil
½ cup unsalted beef broth*
¼ cup unsalted margarine, melted
3 tablespoons lemon juice
Freshly ground pepper

Trim off large leaves of broccoli; remove tough ends of lower stems. Wash broccoli. If stems are thicker than 1 inch in diameter, make lengthwise gashes in each stem.

Heat oil in wok pan or saucepan. Cook and stir broccoli in oil 2 to 3 minutes. Pour in broth; cover and cook over high heat 5 minutes. Drain broccoli; turn into serving dish.

Mix margarine and lemon juice; pour on broccoli and toss. Season with pepper.

4 servings.

*Beef broth can be made by dissolving 1 unsalted beef bouillon cube in ½ cup hot water.

1 serving = 1 vegetable
          210 calories

BROCCOLI WITH LEMON MARGARINE

Cook 1½ pounds broccoli as directed in Broccoli Polonaise (opposite) and omit bread crumb topping. Mix 3 tablespoons unsalted margarine, melted, and 1 tablespoon lemon juice and pour on broccoli. If you wish, garnish with lemon slices.

4 servings.

1 serving = 1 vegetable
          115 calories

BROCCOLI POLONAISE

1½ pounds broccoli
¼ cup unsalted margarine
1 tablespoon lemon juice
¼ cup dry bread crumbs
¼ cup chopped pimiento

Trim off large leaves of broccoli; remove ends of lower stems. Wash broccoli. If stems are thicker than 1 inch in diameter, make lengthwise gash in each stem.

Heat 1 inch water in saucepan to boiling. Add broccoli. Cover and heat to boiling; cook until stems are tender, 12 to 15 minutes. Drain.

Melt margarine; stir in lemon juice, bread crumbs and pimiento. Sprinkle mixture on broccoli.

4 servings.

1 serving = 1 vegetable
          150 calories

BROILED TOMATOES

4 medium tomatoes
¼ cup dry bread crumbs
2 teaspoons minced shallot
3 tablespoons snipped parsley
1 clove garlic, minced
½ teaspoon lemon juice
1 teaspoon basil leaves
2 tablespoons olive oil
Freshly ground pepper

Heat oven to 375°. Wash tomatoes; remove stem ends. Remove pulp from each tomato, leaving 2½-inch wall; chop pulp.

Stir together tomato pulp and remaining ingredients except pepper. Season mixture with pepper. Fill tomatoes with tomato mixture. Place filled tomatoes in ungreased baking dish, 11½x7½x1½ inches. Bake until tomatoes are heated through, about 25 minutes.

4 servings.

1 serving = 1 vegetable, 1 bread I
125 calories.

BAKED TOMATOES WITH SAVORY CRUMB TOPPING

Savory Crumbs (below)
1 can (10 ounces) unsalted tomatoes, drained (reserve 2 tablespoons liquid)
¼ cup unsalted whole kernel corn
2 tablespoons finely chopped green pepper

Heat oven to 425°. Prepare Savory Crumbs. Place tomatoes, reserved liquid, corn and green pepper in ungreased 20-ounce casserole. Top with Savory Crumbs. Bake uncovered until bubbly, 20 minutes.

2 servings.

1 serving = ½ vegetable, ½ bread I
210 calories

Savory Crumbs: Cook and stir 2 tablespoons chopped onion in 2 tablespoons unsalted margarine. Crumble 1 slice low sodium bread into onion. Stir in ½ teaspoon each thyme and parsley flakes and dash each pepper, garlic powder and sage.

TANGY SPINACH

2 pounds spinach or 1 can (15½ ounces) chopped unsalted spinach
1 teaspoon lemon juice
¼ teaspoon basil leaves
Freshly ground pepper

If using fresh spinach, remove imperfect leaves and root ends. Wash greens several times in water, lifting out of water each time so sand sinks to bottom. Drain.

Place greens with just the water which clings to leaves in saucepan. Cover and cook 3 to 10 minutes. Drain. Stir lemon juice, basil leaves and pepper into spinach.

If using canned spinach, drain liquid into saucepan. Heat to boiling; boil until liquid is reduced to half. Add spinach and remaining ingredients and heat over low heat, stirring occasionally.

4 servings.

1 serving = ½ salted vegetable
65 calories

GREEN STRING BEANS

1 pound green beans
¼ cup sliced almonds
2 tablespoons unsalted margarine
2 teaspoons lemon juice
Freshly ground pepper

Wash beans and remove ends. Cut beans crosswise into 1-inch pieces. Place beans in 1 inch water; heat to boiling. Cook uncovered 5 minutes. Cover and cook 3 minutes. Drain.

In small saucepan, cook and stir almonds in margarine until almonds are light brown. Stir in beans and lemon juice. Season with pepper. Cook, stirring frequently, until beans are hot.

4 servings.

1 serving = 1 vegetable
135 calories

ITALIAN GREEN BEANS

1 package (10 ounces) frozen Italian green beans
1 tomato, diced
½ cup diced green pepper
1 tablespoon finely chopped onion
⅛ teaspoon rosemary leaves
⅛ teaspoon basil leaves
⅛ teaspoon oregano

Cook beans as directed on package except— omit salt. Drain, reserving ¼ cup liquid. Place reserved liquid, the tomato, green pepper, onion and seasonings in saucepan. Cook uncovered over low heat until green pepper is tender, about 20 minutes. Stir in beans and heat until hot.

4 servings.

1 serving = 1 vegetable
30 calories

ITALIAN GREENS

2 pounds greens (kale, dandelion greens, turnip greens or collards)
1 clove garlic, crushed
1 tablespoon olive oil
¼ teaspoon sugar
⅛ teaspoon pepper
¼ cup grated Parmesan cheese
Fresh onion rings

Remove imperfect leaves and root ends from greens. Wash greens several times in water, lifting out of water each time so sand sinks to bottom. Drain.

Mix garlic, oil, sugar and pepper in shallow pan. Add greens; cover and heat to boiling. Reduce heat and cook over low heat until tender, 3 to 5 minutes for kale and dandelion greens and 10 to 15 minutes for turnip greens or collards. Turn greens into serving dish; sprinkle with cheese and top with onion rings.

6 servings.

1 serving = ½ vegetable
115 calories

FRENCH GREEN BEANS

1½ pounds fresh green beans
3 medium onions, thinly sliced
3 tablespoons unsalted margarine
¼ teaspoon freshly ground pepper
2 tablespoons snipped parsley
¼ cup red wine vinegar
1 tablespoon lemon juice

Wash beans and remove ends. Cut beans French style, into lengthwise strips or leave whole. Heat 1 inch water to boiling. Add beans; cook uncovered 5 minutes. Cover and cook 5 minutes longer. Drain.

Melt margarine in skillet; cook and stir onions in margarine over medium heat until tender. Add beans and pepper; cook and stir just until beans begin to brown. Turn beans into serving dish. Sprinkle with vinegar, lemon juice and parsley and toss.

6 servings.

1 serving = 1 vegetable
115 calories

GREEN BEANS WITH DILL

1 pound green beans or 1 can (15½ ounces)
unsalted green beans
½ teaspoon dill seed
1 tablespoon unsalted margarine
1 teaspoon lemon juice
Freshly ground pepper

If using fresh beans, wash beans and remove ends. Leave beans whole or cut crosswise into 1-inch pieces. Place beans in 1 inch water; add dill seed and heat to boiling. Cook uncovered 5 minutes. Cover and cook until tender, 10 to 15 minutes. Drain.

If using canned beans, drain liquid into saucepan. Heat to boiling; boil until liquid is reduced to half. Add beans and dill seed and simmer 6 minutes. Drain.

Turn beans into serving dish. Dot with margarine; sprinkle with lemon juice and pepper and toss.

4 servings.

1 serving = 1 vegetable
60 calories

Variation

Green Beans Oregano: Substitute 1 teaspoon oregano and ¼ teaspoon marjoram leaves, crushed, for the dill seed and omit margarine, lemon juice and pepper.

12.Desserts

These unexpectedly glamorous desserts can bring even an average meal to an exciting finale— and many great low-calorie recipes are included to reward the oft-deprived calorie counter.

COMPANY APPLESAUCE

12 medium apples
¾ cup apricot preserves
½ cup sugar
2 tablespoons unsalted margarine
1 tablespoon vanilla
1 tablespoon lemon juice
1 teaspoon cinnamon

Pare, core and quarter apples; cut each quarter into 3 or 4 pieces into saucepan. Cover and cook over low heat, stirring occasionally, about 20 minutes.

Press enough apricot preserves through sieve to measure ½ cup. Stir into apples. Heat, stirring occasionally to simmering and stir in remaining ingredients.

About 2 cups.

Note: This applesauce can be served hot with pork, poultry and other meats, or can be used as a pie filling.

1 serving (½ cup) = 1 fruit
480 calories

BAKED PINEAPPLES

4 medium baking apples
1 teaspoon lemon juice
½ cup chopped fresh pineapple
3 tablespoons honey

Heat oven to 400°. Core apples (do not cut through blossom ends); pare upper ⅓ of each to prevent skin from splitting. Sprinkle with lemon juice. Fill centers with pineapple and drizzle with honey. Place apples upright in baking dish. Pour water (¼ inch deep) into dish.

Bake, basting occasionally, until apples are tender, about 35 minutes. Serve hot or cold.

4 servings.

Note: Try sprinkling with cinnamon, nutmeg or allspice before baking or substitute ½ cup chopped fresh berries for the pineapple.

1 serving = 1 fruit
125 calories

BAKED APPLE

1 baking apple
1½ teaspoons granulated sugar
1 teaspoon raisins
½ teaspoon unsalted margarine
Dash cinnamon

Heat oven to 350°. Core apple; pare upper ⅓ to prevent skin from splitting. Place apple upright in baking dish. Fill center of apple with sugar, raisins, margarine and cinnamon. Pour water (¼ inch deep) into dish.

Bake until apple is tender, 30 to 45 minutes. Serve hot or cold.

1 serving.

Note: 1 tablespoon orange-flavored liqueur can be added to water in baking dish if desired.

1 serving = 1 fruit
135 calories

BAKED BANANAS

2 medium bananas
2 tablespoons lemon or lime juice
2 tablespoons honey

Heat oven to 400°. Cut bananas lengthwise into halves. Place in ungreased baking dish. Mix lemon juice and honey and brush on bananas. Bake uncovered until bananas are golden, 10 to 15 minutes.

4 servings.

Note: For variety, add vanilla, almond, orange or rum extract to taste to the honey-lemon mixture.

1 serving = 1 fruit
90 calories

BANANAS FOSTER

2 tablespoons unsalted margarine
¼ cup brown sugar (packed)
⅛ teaspoon cinnamon
2 bananas
2 tablespoons banana liqueur
¼ cup golden rum

Melt margarine in top pan of chafing dish. Add sugar and cinnamon and stir until sugar is dissolved. Cut bananas lengthwise in half; arrange in pan. Turn bananas to coat with sugar mixture. Pour in liqueur and rum. When mixture is heated, ignite it. Shake pan until flame is extinguished.

4 servings.

1 serving = 1 fruit
175 calories

SPICED FRUIT COMPOTE

1 cup quartered canned pears (with syrup)
1 cup canned red tart cherries
1 cup canned apricot halves
½ cup water
1 tablespoon plus 1 teaspoon sugar
2 tablespoons lemon juice
1 teaspoon ginger
2 sticks cinnamon
4 whole cloves

Heat all ingredients in large skillet just to boiling. Reduce heat and simmer 5 minutes, basting fruit occasionally. Remove from heat and cool, basting fruit occasionally. Remove cinnamon and cloves with slotted spoon. Serve warm or cold.

6 servings.

1 serving = 1 fruit
125 calories

FRESH FRUIT COMPOTE

3 tablespoons sugar
½ cup water
3 tablespoons fresh lemon juice
½ teaspoon vanilla
1 cup diced cantaloupe
1 cup sliced peaches
1 cup blueberries
½ cup seedless green grapes
Fresh mint leaves

Heat sugar and water in small saucepan to boiling; boil ½ minute. Remove from heat; stir in lemon juice and vanilla and cool.

Combine fruits in bowl. Pour sugar syrup on fruit and chill. Serve in sherbet dishes and garnish with mint leaves.

6 servings.

1 serving = 1 fruit
                75 calories

ORANGE COMPOTE

9 medium oranges
2 cups water
1½ cups sugar

Pare oranges, reserving peel from 4 oranges. Remove orange sections and place in bowl.

Cut reserved peel into thin slices; place in saucepan. Add water and sugar and heat to boiling, stirring occasionally. Boil uncovered 20 minutes. Pour hot mixture over orange sections. If you wish, stir in 2 tablespoons rum or liqueur. Cover and refrigerate.

8 servings.

Note: Delicious served warm on crêpes (page 173).

1 serving = 1 fruit
                215 calories

ORANGE SLICES GRAND MARNIER

1 navel orange
1 tablespoon Grand Marnier

Pare orange and cut into thin slices. Arrange slices in dessert dish and sprinkle with liqueur.

1 serving.

1 serving = 1 fruit
                60 calories

STEWED RHUBARB

1 pound rhubarb, cut into ½-inch pieces
¾ cup sugar
½ orange, pared and sectioned
¼ cup orange juice

Combine all ingredients in top of double boiler. Cook over boiling water until rhubarb is tender.

6 servings.

1 serving = ½ fruit
                135 calories

CARRIBEAN JUMBLE

1 banana, sliced
1 package (10 ounces) frozen sliced
  strawberries, thawed, or 2 cups sliced
  fresh strawberries
1 can (8½ ounces) crushed pineapple
1 ounce dark rum

Mix banana, strawberries, pineapple (with syrup) and rum. Cover and refrigerate until ready to serve.

6 servings.

1 serving = 1 fruit
                110 calories

STRAWBERRY SUPREME

2 cups sliced fresh strawberries
2 cups drained crushed pineapple
½ cup powdered sugar
1 ounce kirsch
1 ounce Grand Marnier
**1 medium pineapple, pared, cored and
  sliced**
Grated peel of 1 orange

Mix strawberries, pineapple, sugar, kirsch and
Grand Marnier. Cover and refrigerate, stirring
occasionally, until well chilled. Serve in chilled
bowl. Cut pineapple slices into halves and arrange around bowl. Sprinkle orange peel on
pineapple.

8 servings.

1 serving = 1½ fruit
          120 calories

STRAWBERRY SPARKLER

2 cups fresh strawberries
2 tablespoons sugar
4 splits champagne, chilled

Sprinkle strawberries with sugar and divide
among 4 beakers. Pour champagne over each
and serve immediately.

4 servings.

1 serving = ½ fruit
          355 calories

RASPBERRY MELON BOATS

**1 package (10 ounces) frozen raspberries,
  thawed**
1 tablespoon sugar
1 tablespoon cornstarch
½ cup orange juice
1 small cantaloupe
1 cup raspberry ice

Drain raspberries and reserve ½ cup syrup. Mix
sugar and cornstarch in small saucepan. Stir in
reserved syrup and the orange juice. Cook,
stirring constantly, until mixture thickens and
boils. Cool.

Stir in raspberries. Cut cantaloupe into quarters. Remove seeds and rind. Place scoop of
ice in each quarter. Spoon raspberry sauce on
ice.

4 servings.

1 serving = 1 fruit
          165 calories

BLACK PEARS ELEGANTE

2 medium pears
¼ cup sugar
3 whole cloves
4 thin slices lemon
½ cup port
1½-inch stick cinnamon
Few drops red food color, if desired

Heat oven to 350°. Pare, halve and core pears.
Place in 1-quart casserole. Heat remaining ingredients to boiling and pour on pears. Cover
and bake 20 minutes. Uncover and bake, basting once or twice, until pears are tender, 10
minutes longer. Serve hot or cold.

2 servings.

1 serving = 1 fruit
          255 calories

PEACHES IN PORT

6 peaches
¼ cup sugar
1 to 2 cups port

Peel peaches and slice into serving bowl. Sprinkle with sugar and pour enough wine into bowl to cover peaches. Refrigerate 1 hour.

6 servings.

1 serving = 1 fruit
                        220 calories

MINTED PINEAPPLE

2 cans (13½ ounces each) pineapple chunks, drained
3 tablespoons white crème de menthe
3 tablespoons snipped mint

Divide pineapple chunks among 4 dessert dishes. Drizzle with crème de menthe and sprinkle with mint.

4 servings.

1 serving = 1 fruit
                        60 calories

FRENCH PLUMS

3 cups canned plums
3 tablespoons kirsch
2 tablespoons slivered lemon peel

Heat plums (with syrup); add kirsch and lemon peel. Serve warm or cold.

6 servings.

1 serving = 1 fruit
                        95 calories

CRÊPES

1½ cups all-purpose flour
1 tablespoon sugar
¾ teaspoon low-sodium baking powder
2 cups skim milk
⅓ cup Second Nature imitation eggs*
½ teaspoon vanilla
2 tablespoons unsalted margarine, melted

Measure all ingredients into bowl; beat with rotary beater until smooth.

Lightly grease 7- or 8-inch skillet with margarine; heat over medium heat until margarine is bubbly. For each crêpe, pour scant ¼ cup batter into skillet; immediately rotate skillet until batter covers bottom. Cook until light brown. Loosen around edge with wide spatula; turn and cook other side until light brown. Stack crêpes, placing waxed paper or paper towel between them. Keep crêpes covered to prevent them from drying out.

If desired, spread applesauce, sweetened strawberries, currant jelly or raspberry jam on each crêpe and roll up. (Roll crêpes so most attractive side is on the outside.) Sprinkle with powdered sugar.

12 to 16 crêpes.

1 serving (3 crêpes) = 1 bread I
                        100 calories

---

*If this ingredient is not available in your market area, see page 29 for substitutes.

CANTALOUPE SURPRISE

3 small cantaloupes
1 can (15 ounces) pineapple chunks,
drained (reserve ¾ cup syrup)
6 green maraschino cherries, halved
6 red maraschino cherries, halved
1 tablespoon kirsch

Cut each cantaloupe in half; scoop out seeds. Cut out fruit with melon ball cutter; reserve shells. Place cantaloupe balls and remaining fruit in bowl. Mix reserved pineapple syrup and the kirsch and pour over fruit. Let stand 1 hour. Drain; reserve syrup.

Fill cantaloupe shells with fruit and drizzle 1 tablespoon reserved syrup on each. Refrigerate until serving time.

6 servings.

1 serving = 2 fruit
120 calories

FESTIVE BANANA CRÊPES

Crepes (page 173)
½ cup unsalted margarine
1 cup brown sugar (packed)
1 teaspoon grated lemon peel
1 tablespoon lemon juice
3 medium bananas

Prepare crêpes. Melt margarine in large skillet. Add sugar, lemon peel and juice. Heat over medium heat, stirring until sugar is dissolved. Slice bananas into sugar mixture and heat, stirring carefully. Place 2 tablespoons of banana mixture on center of each crêpe and roll up. Spoon any remaining sauce on crêpes.

6 servings.

1 serving = 1 bread I, ½ fruit
270 calories

BAKED ALASKA

Yellow Cake (below)
1 brick (2 quarts) low-fat
Neapolitan frozen dessert
4 egg whites
½ teaspoon cream of tartar
⅔ cup powdered sugar

Bake Yellow Cake. Cool. Cover baking sheet with aluminum foil. Place cake on baking sheet. Cut brick of frozen dessert lengthwise in half. (Freeze one half for future use.) Place remaining half of frozen dessert on cake. Trim cake around dessert, leaving a 1-inch edge. Freeze cake and dessert.

Heat oven to 500°. Beat egg whites and cream of tartar until frothy. Beat in sugar, 1 tablespoon at a time; continue beating until stiff and glossy. Cover cake and dessert completely with meringue, sealing it to the aluminum foil on baking sheet. (If desired, it can be frozen at this point, up to 24 hours.)

Bake on lowest rack in oven 3 to 5 minutes or until meringue is light brown. Trim aluminum foil to edge of meringue; transfer cake to serving plate. Cut into 6 slices, then cut each slice in half. Serve immediately.

12 servings.

1 serving = 1 bread II, 1 meat
560 calories

Yellow Cake

⅔ cup unsalted margarine, softened
1¾ cups sugar
½ cup Second Nature imitation eggs*
1½ teaspoons vanilla
2¾ cups all-purpose flour
3½ teaspoons low-sodium baking powder
1¼ cups skim milk

Heat oven to 350°. Grease and flour baking

*If this ingredient is not available in your market area, see page 29 for substitutes.

pan, 13x9x2 inches. Mix margarine, sugar, imitation eggs and vanilla in large mixer bowl until fluffy. Beat on high speed 5 minutes, scraping bowl occasionally. On low speed, mix in flour and baking powder alternately with milk. Pour into pan.

Bake 45 to 50 minutes or until wooden pick inserted in center comes out clean.

CRÊPES SUZETTE

3 crêpes (page 173)
2 to 3 tablespoons unsalted margarine
¼ teaspoon grated orange or lemon peel
2 to 3 tablespoons orange juice
1 tablespoon sugar
1 tablespoon orange liqueur (cointreau, curaçao, Grand Marnier)
1 tablespoon brandy
1 teaspoon sugar

Prepare Crêpes as directed on page 173. When removing crêpes from griddle, stack so first baked side is down. Cool, keeping crêpes covered to prevent them from drying out. Use 3 crêpes for this recipe. Remaining crêpes can be stacked with waxed paper between, wrapped in aluminum foil and frozen.

Heat margarine, orange peel and juice and 1 tablespoon sugar in small skillet to boiling, stirring occasionally. Cook 1 minute.

Fold crêpes into fourths; place in hot orange sauce and turn once. Sprinkle with 1 teaspoon sugar. Heat liqueur and brandy but do not boil. Arrange crêpes around edge of skillet. Pour liqueur into center of skillet and ignite. Spoon flaming sauce over crêpes.

1 serving.

1 serving = 3 bread I
          625 calories

BLUEBERRY-LIME SUNDAES

¼ cup sugar
1 tablespoon flour
1 teaspoon grated lemon peel
1 tablespoon water
2 teaspoons lemon juice
1½ cups blueberries
1 pint lime ice

Mix sugar, flour and lemon peel in small saucepan. Stir in water, lemon juice and blueberries. Cook over low heat, stirring constantly, until slightly thickened. Simmer 10 minutes, stirring frequently. Remove from heat and chill.

Scoop lime ice into 4 dessert dishes. Spoon blueberry sauce over ice.

4 servings.

1 serving = ½ fruit
          165 calories

PINEAPPLE GLACÉ

1 pineapple
1 quart orange ice
¼ cup powdered sugar
1 tablespoon kirsch

Remove green top from pineapple. Cut 1-inch slice from top end of pineapple; set aside. With curved knife, cut around edge of pineapple, leaving about 1-inch-thick wall; remove fruit. Fill cavity with orange ice. Replace top slice and freeze until firm, about 8 hours.

Cut fruit into bite-size pieces, removing core. Mix pineapple pieces, sugar and kirsch; cover and refrigerate.

To serve, cut pineapple crosswise into 6 slices. Top slices with pineapple pieces.

6 servings.

1 serving = 1 fruit
          165 calories

QUICK CRANBERRY ICE

1 can (8 ounces) jellied cranberry sauce
1 to 2 drops red food color
½ cup carbonated lemon-lime beverage

Beat cranberry sauce and food color in small mixer bowl until smooth. Mix in lemon-lime beverage gradually on low speed. Pour into refrigerator tray; cover and freeze until firm. Remove from freezer; break into chunks in small mixer bowl. Beat until fluffy and smooth. Return to refrigerator tray; cover and freeze until firm.

4 servings.

1 serving = 1 fruit
       105 calories

RASPBERRY-PINEAPPLE ICE

1 package (10 ounces) frozen raspberries
1 can (13½ ounces) frozen pineapple
  chunks

Break frozen fruits apart with fork. Place fruits, a small amount at a time, in blender container; blend on high speed until smooth. Serve immediately or pour into refrigerator tray and freeze for a short time.

4 servings.

Note: This ice is good served in meringue shells.

1 serving = 2 fruit
       160 calories

FRESH LEMON SHERBET

1 envelope unflavored gelatin
½ cup water
1½ cups sugar
1¾ cups water
2 teaspoons grated lemon peel
½ cup lemon juice
1 teaspoon vanilla
1 egg white

Sprinkle gelatin on ½ cup water in small saucepan to soften. Stir over low heat until gelatin is dissolved. Remove from heat; stir in sugar, 1¾ cups water, the lemon peel, lemon juice and vanilla. Pour into baking pan, 8x8x2 inches, or into freezer tray; freeze until mushy.

Pour mixture into large mixer bowl; add egg white and beat at high speed until fluffy. Return mixture to baking pan and freeze until firm. If desired, garnish with lemon twist and sprig of mint.

1½ quarts.

1 serving (¾ cup) = trace sodium
              155 calories

ICED-ORANGE ICE

4 large oranges
1½ pints orange ice
Lemon leaves or sprigs of mint

Cut 1-inch slice from stem end of each orange; set aside. With curved knife, cut around edge of each orange, leaving about ¼-inch-thick wall; remove fruit and reserve for future use.

Fill cavities with orange ice. Replace top slices and freeze until firm. Serve on lemon leaves.

4 servings.

1 serving = 1 fruit
       165 calories

APRICOT SHERBET

2 cups water
1¼ cups sugar
Juice of 2 lemons
Juice of 2 oranges
12 canned apricot halves
1 egg white

Heat water and sugar in saucepan to boiling, stirring until sugar is dissolved. Cook until thickened, about 20 minutes; cool.

Stir in lemon and orange juices. Press apricots through sieve to make smooth pulp. Stir into juice mixture. Beat egg white until stiff peaks form. Fold in apricot mixture. Pour into refrigerator tray; freeze until mushy. Turn into chilled mixer bowl and beat until smooth. Return to refrigerator tray and freeze until firm.

4 servings.

1 serving = 1 fruit
325 calories

FROSTED FRUIT

1 cup fruit cocktail
½ cup cut-up fresh fruit
1 tablespoon crème de menthe

Place fruits in small bowl; sprinkle crème de menthe on fruits and toss. Place in freezer, stirring occasionally, until chilled, 40 to 50 minutes.

4 servings.

1 serving = 1 fruit
50 calories

EMERALD ICE

1 pint lemon ice
4 tablespoons green crème de menthe

Place ½-cup scoop lemon ice in each of 4 sherbet dishes. Drizzle 1 tablespoon crème de menthe on ice in each dish.

4 servings.

1 serving = trace sodium
85 calories

COUPE LOUISE

2 cups sliced peaches
1 pint orange ice
1½ ounces curaçao

Divide peaches among 4 coupe or dessert dishes. Place ½-cup scoop orange ice in each dish. Drizzle curaçao on each.

4 servings.

1 serving = 1 fruit
120 calories

QUICK ORANGE SOUFFLÉ

1 egg white
1 tablespoon sugar
1 tablespoon orange marmalade

Beat egg white until foamy. Beat in sugar; beat until stiff. Fold in marmalade. Turn into top of double boiler. Place over hot water; cover and cook over low heat 30 minutes. Serve warm and, if desired, with an orange sauce.

1 serving.

1 serving = ¾ meat
110 calories

APPLE SOUFFLÉ

1 egg white
⅓ cup applesauce
Sugar

Heat oven to 350°. Grease 10-ounce custard cup with unsalted margarine. Beat egg white until stiff peaks form. Fold in applesauce. Turn into custard cup. Bake 35 to 40 minutes. Sprinkle with sugar.

1 serving.

1 serving = ¾ meat, 1 fruit
105 calories

PINEAPPLE FLUFF

2 egg whites
2 tablespoons sugar
1 can (4 ounces) crushed pineapple
¼ teaspoon vanilla
2 tablespoons grated orange peel

Beat egg whites until foamy. Beat in sugar, 1 tablespoon at a time; beat until stiff and glossy. Fold in pineapple (with syrup) and vanilla. Divide among 4 dessert dishes; sprinkle orange peel on tops.

Note: This dessert can be baked in a greased casserole and served warm.

4 servings.

1 serving = ¼ meat, ½ fruit
60 calories

APPLE TAPIOCA

⅓ cup quick-cooking tapioca
1 cup brown sugar (packed)
4 cups sliced pared tart apples
2 cups water
2 tablespoons lemon juice
2 tablespoons unsalted margarine
½ teaspoon cinnamon

Measure all ingredients into medium saucepan; let stand 5 minutes. Heat to boiling, stirring constantly. Reduce heat; simmer uncovered until apples are tender, about 12 minutes. Serve warm and, if desired, with sprinkle of nutmeg.

4 servings.

1 serving = 1 fruit
365 calories

LEMON PUDDING

¼ cup water
3 tablespoons flour
¾ cup sugar
1¼ cups water
1 tablespoon unsalted margarine
1 teaspoon grated lemon peel
¼ cup lemon juice
1 to 2 drops yellow food color

Mix ¼ cup water and the flour in small saucepan until smooth. Stir in sugar and 1¼ cups water. Heat to boiling, stirring constantly. Boil and stir 1 minute. Remove from heat; stir in margarine, lemon peel, lemon juice and food color. Pour into 4 dessert dishes; cool slightly and chill about 4 hours.

4 servings.

1 serving = trace sodium
200 calories

VANILLA CREAM PUDDING

⅓ cup sugar
2 tablespoons cornstarch
2 cups skim milk
¼ cup Second Nature imitation eggs*
2 tablespoons unsalted margarine
2 teaspoons vanilla

Mix sugar and cornstarch in saucepan. Stir in milk. Cook over medium heat, stirring constantly, until mixture thickens and boils. Boil and stir 1 minute. Remove from heat. Stir at least half the hot mixture into imitation eggs, then blend into hot mixture in pan. Boil and stir 1 minute. Remove from heat; stir in margarine and vanilla. Pour into dessert dishes. Cool slightly and refrigerate.

4 servings.

1 serving = ½ milk, ½ meat
210 calories

Butterscotch Pudding: Substitute ⅔ cup brown sugar (packed) for the granulated sugar and decrease vanilla to 1 teaspoon.

1 serving = ½ milk, ½ meat
270 calories

RICE PUDDING

½ cup water
½ cup instant rice
¾ cup Second Nature imitation eggs*
½ cup sugar
2 teaspoons vanilla
2½ cups skim milk, scalded
½ cup raisins, if desired
Cinnamon

Heat oven to 350°. Heat water in small saucepan to boiling. Remove from heat; stir in rice. Cover; let stand 5 minutes. Mix imitation eggs, sugar and vanilla in ungreased 1½-quart cas-

serole. Stir in milk slowly. Stir in rice and raisins and sprinkle cinnamon on top. Place casserole in baking pan, 9x9x2 inches; pour very hot water into pan to 1¼-inch depth.

Bake about 70 minutes or until knife inserted halfway between edge and center comes out clean. Remove casserole from water. Serve pudding warm or cold.

6 to 8 servings.

1 serving = ½ milk, ½ meat
250 calories

BREAD PUDDING

Twelve 1-inch slices French bread, cubed
** (about 4 cups)**
2 tablespoons unsalted margarine, melted
½ cup raisins
½ cup sugar
2 cups skim milk
¾ cup Second Nature imitation eggs*
1 teaspoon cinnamon
1 teaspoon vanilla

Heat oven to 350°. Measure bread cubes into ungreased 1½-quart casserole. Pour margarine on bread cubes and mix. Add raisins. Beat remaining ingredients; pour on bread cubes and raisins. Place casserole in pan of very hot water (1 inch deep). Bake until knife inserted in center comes out clean, 45 to 50 minutes. Serve warm or cool.

6 to 8 servings.

1 serving = 1 milk, 1 bread II
240 calories

SNOW PUDDING

1 envelope unflavored gelatin
¾ cup sugar
1 cup water
1 tablespoon grated lemon peel
¼ cup lemon juice
2 egg whites
1 package (10 ounces) frozen
  raspberries, thawed

Mix gelatin and sugar in small saucepan. Stir in water and heat to boiling, stirring until sugar is dissolved. Remove from heat; stir in lemon peel and juice. Refrigerate until mixture is thickened but not set.

Beat egg whites in small mixer bowl until stiff peaks form. Beat gelatin mixture until frothy. Add gelatin mixture to egg whites and beat until mixture holds its shape. Divide among 6 dessert dishes; refrigerate until set. Serve with raspberries.

6 servings.

1 serving = ⅓ meat, ½ fruit
              160 calories

ZABAGLIONE

¾ cup Second Nature imitation eggs*
2 tablespoons sugar
½ cup Marsala

Beat imitation eggs and sugar in top of double boiler until light and fluffy. Continue beating and slowly add wine. Place top of double boiler over simmering water. Cook, beating constantly, until thick and fluffy, about 20 minutes. Mixture will form soft peaks. Serve in sherbet dishes or, if desired, serve as a sauce for fresh fruits.

4½ cups.

1 serving (½ cup) = ½ meat
                      55 calories

DOUBLE FRUIT WHIP

1 envelope unflavored gelatin
1 cup canned unsweetened pineapple juice
½ teaspoon grated lemon peel
3 tablespoons honey
2 cups unsweetened applesauce
Cinnamon or nutmeg

Sprinkle gelatin on pineapple juice to soften. Stir over low heat until gelatin is dissolved. Stir in lemon peel, honey and applesauce. Refrigerate, stirring occasionally, until mixture mounds slightly when dropped from spoon.

Beat until fluffy. Divide among 8 dessert dishes. Refrigerate until firm. Sprinkle each with cinnamon.

8 servings.

1 serving = ½ fruit
              65 calories

*If this ingredient is not available in your market area, see page 29 for substitutes.

CHOCOLATE SAUCE

**2 bars (4 ounces each) sweet cooking
  chocolate**
1 cup water

Heat chocolate and water over medium heat, stirring constantly, until chocolate is melted and mixture is smooth. Stir in 1 teaspoon vanilla if desired.

About 1½ cups.

**2 tablespoons = trace sodium
                105 calories**

RUM SAUCE

3 tablespoons sugar
1½ teaspoons lemon juice
2 tablespoons water
2 tablespoons rum

Heat sugar, lemon juice and water in small saucepan to boiling, stirring until sugar is dissolved. Cool. Stir in rum. Serve on cake or fruit.

About ⅓ cup.

**1 tablespoon = trace sodium
                30 calories**

FRUIT SUNDAE SAUCE

2 teaspoons cornstarch
2 tablespoons water
1 cup crushed pineapple
2 tablespoons honey
½ teaspoon lemon juice

Mix cornstarch and water in small saucepan. Stir in pineapple. Cook, stirring constantly, until mixture thickens and boils. Remove from heat; stir in honey and lemon juice. Cover and refrigerate at least 1 hour.

1 cup.

**2 tablespoons = trace sodium
                30 calories**

13.Pies,Cakes,&Cookies

Like our unprecedented bread recipes, this chapter for the first time brings to the hypertension diet an abundance of fine pastry recipes—including a colorful garland of festive holiday ideas.

DEEP DISH FRUIT PIE

1½ cups sugar
½ cup all-purpose flour
1 teaspoon nutmeg
1 teaspoon cinnamon
12 cups thinly sliced pared apples
  (about 10 medium)
2 tablespoons unsalted margarine
Pastry for 8- or 9-inch One-crust Pie
  (page 188)

Stir together sugar, flour, nutmeg and cinnamon. Mix with apples. Pour into ungreased baking pan, 9x9x2 inches. Dot fruit with margarine.

Heat oven to 425°. Prepare pastry as directed except—roll into 10-inch square. Fold pastry in half; cut slits near center. Unfold over fruit in pan; fold edges under just inside edge of pan.

Bake 1 hour or until juice begins to bubble through slits in crust. Serve warm.

9 servings.
1 serving = 1 bread I, 1 fruit
          455 calories

CHERRY PIE

Pastry for 8- or 9-inch
  Two-crust Pie (page 188)
1⅓ cups sugar
⅓ cup all-purpose flour
2 cans (16 ounces each) pitted red
  tart cherries, drained
¼ teaspoon almond extract
2 tablespoons unsalted margarine

Heat oven to 425°. Prepare pastry. Stir together sugar and flour. Mix lightly with cherries. Pour into pastry-lined pie pan. Sprinkle fruit with extract and dot with margarine. Cover with top crust which has slits cut in it; seal and flute. Cover edge with 2- to 3-inch strip of aluminum foil to prevent excessive browning; remove foil last 15 minutes of baking. Bake 35 to 45 minutes or until crust is brown and juice begins to bubble through slits in crust.

⅛ of pie = 1 fruit
          565 calories

APPLE PIE

8-inch Pie

**Pastry for 8- or 9-inch
  Two-crust Pie (page 188)**
½ cup sugar
3 tablespoons flour
¼ teaspoon nutmeg
¼ teaspoon cinnamon
**5 cups thinly sliced pared tart apples
  (about 5 medium)**
1 tablespoon unsalted margarine

9-inch Pie

**Pastry for 8- or 9-inch
  Two-crust Pie (page 188)**
¾ cup sugar
¼ cup all-purpose flour
½ teaspoon nutmeg
½ teaspoon cinnamon
**6 cups thinly sliced pared tart apples
  (about 6 medium)**
2 tablespoons unsalted margarine

Heat oven to 425°. Prepare pastry. Stir together sugar, flour, nutmeg and cinnamon. Mix lightly with apples. Pour into pastry-lined pie pan. Dot with margarine. Cover with top crust which has slits cut in it; seal and flute. Cover edge with 2- to 3-inch strip of aluminum foil to prevent excessive browning; remove foil last 15 minutes of baking. Bake 40 to 50 minutes or until crust is brown and juice begins to bubble through slits in crust. Serve slightly warm.

$^1/_6$ of 8'' pie = 1 fruit
          540 calories
⅛ of 9″ pie = 1 fruit
          455 calories

FRESH RHUBARB PIE

For mild flavor, choose early pink rhubarb. If tender and pink, do not peel. Cut into ½-inch pieces (1 pound makes 2 cups). Amount of sugar depends on tartness of rhubarb. Early rhubarb requires less sugar. Make pie shallow.

8-inch Pie

**Pastry for 8- or 9-inch
  Two-crust Pie (page 188)**
1 to 1¼ cups sugar
¼ cup all-purpose flour
¼ teaspoon grated orange peel, if desired
3 cups cut-up rhubarb
1 tablespoon unsalted margarine

9-inch Pie

**Pastry for 8- or 9-inch
  Two-crust Pie (page 188)**
1⅓ to 1⅔ cups sugar
⅓ cup all-purpose flour
½ teaspoon grated orange peel, if desired
4 cups cut-up rhubarb
2 tablespoons unsalted margarine

Heat oven to 425°. Prepare pastry. Mix sugar, flour and orange peel. Pour half the rhubarb into pastry-lined pie pan; sprinkle with half the sugar mixture. Repeat with remaining rhubarb and sugar mixture. Dot with margarine. Cover with top crust which has slits cut in it; seal and flute. Sprinkle with sugar. Cover edge with 2- to 3-inch strip of aluminum foil to prevent excessive browning; remove foil last 15 minutes of baking.

Bake 40 to 50 minutes or until crust is brown and juice begins to bubble through slits. Serve warm.

$^1/_6$ of 8″ pie = 1 fruit
          565 calories
⅛ of 9″ pie = 1 fruit
          475 calories

BLUEBERRY PIE

8-inch Pie

**Pastry for 8- or 9-inch
Two-crust Pie (page 188)**
⅓ cup sugar
¼ cup all-purpose flour
½ teaspoon cinnamon, if desired
3 cups fresh blueberries
1 teaspoon lemon juice
1 tablespoon unsalted margarine

9-inch Pie

**Pastry for 8- or 9-inch
Two-crust Pie (page 188)**
½ cup sugar
⅓ cup all-purpose flour
½ teaspoon cinnamon, if desired
4 cups fresh blueberries
1 tablespoon lemon juice
2 tablespoons unsalted margarine

Heat oven to 425°. Prepare pastry. Stir together sugar, flour and cinnamon. Mix lightly with berries. Pour into pastry-lined pie pan. Sprinkle fruit with lemon juice and dot with margarine. Cover with top crust which has slits cut in it; seal and flute. Cover edge with 2- to 3-inch strip of aluminum foil to prevent excessive browning; remove foil last 15 minutes of baking. Bake 8-and 9-inch pies 35 to 45 minutes or until crust is brown and juice begins to bubble through slits in crust.

Variations

Canned Blueberry Pie: Substitute 3 cans (14 ounces each) blueberries, drained, for fresh blueberries.

Frozen Blueberry Pie: Substitute unsweetened frozen blueberries, partially thawed, for fresh blueberries. [1 package (12 ounces) frozen blueberries yields 2½ cups berries.]

Note: If you used canned blueberries, add 100 calories to each serving.

¹/₆ of 8″ pie = 1 fruit
515 calories

⅛ of 9″ pie = 1 fruit
430 calories

CUSTARD PIE

Pastry for 8-inch One-crust Pie (page 188)
¾ cup Second Nature imitation eggs*
⅓ cup sugar
¼ teaspoon nutmeg
1¾ cups skim milk
1 teaspoon vanilla

Heat oven to 450°. Prepare pastry. Measure imitation eggs into bowl; beat in remaining ingredients. Pour into pastry-lined pie pan. Bake 20 minutes.

Reduce oven temperature to 350°. Bake 20 to 25 minutes or until knife inserted halfway between center and edge of filling comes out clean. Serve slightly warm or cold.

¹/₆ pie = ½ bread 1, ½ milk
215 calories

*If this ingredient is not available in your market area, see page 29 for substitutes.

BASIC MERINGUE

8-inch Pie

2 egg whites
¼ teaspoon cream of tartar
¼ cup sugar
¼ teaspoon vanilla

9-inch Pie

3 egg whites
¼ teaspoon cream of tartar
6 tablespoons sugar
½ teaspoon vanilla

Beat egg whites and cream of tartar until foamy. Beat in sugar, 1 tablespoon at a time; beat until stiff and glossy. Do not underbeat. Beat in vanilla.

Heap meringue onto hot pie filling; spread on filling, carefully sealing meringue to edge of crust to prevent shrinking or weeping. Bake in 400° oven until delicate brown, about 10 minutes. Cool away from draft.

Note: Few drops lemon or almond extract or rum or maple flavoring can be added to meringue.

1 serving (8-inch) = ⅓ meat
40 calories

1 serving (9-inch) = ⅓ meat
50 calories

MERINGUE PIE SHELL

4 egg whites
¼ teaspoon cream of tartar
1 cup sugar

Heat oven to 275°. Grease two 9-inch pie pans with unsalted margarine. Beat egg whites and cream of tartar in large mixer bowl until foamy. Beat in sugar, 1 tablespoon at a time; beat until stiff and glossy. Do not underbeat. Divide meringue between pie pans; press meringue against side of pan. Bake 45 minutes. Turn off oven; leave meringue shells in oven with door closed 45 minutes. Remove from oven; cool away from draft.

2 shells (8 servings each).

Note: Meringue shell can be frozen. Wrap carefully in aluminum foil and freeze. To serve, thaw in wrapper at room temperature 15 minutes.

1 serving = ¼ meat
50 calories

COOKIE CRUST

¾ cup all-purpose flour
¼ cup plus 2 tablespoons unsalted margarine, softened
3 tablespoons powdered sugar
¼ teaspoon vanilla

Heat oven to 400°. Mix all ingredients with hands until crumbly. Press mixture firmly and evenly against bottom and side of 8- or 9-inch pie pan. Flute edge and prick well. Bake 10 to 15 minutes or until light brown. Cool.

$1/_6$ of pie crust = trace sodium
185 calories

FRESH PEACH PIE

8-inch Pie

Pastry for 8-inch Two-crust Pie (page 188)
4 cups sliced fresh peaches
  (about 1¾ pounds)
1 teaspoon lemon juice
⅔ cup sugar
3 tablespoons flour
¼ teaspoon cinnamon
1 tablespoon unsalted margarine

9-inch Pie

Pastry for 9-inch Two-crust Pie (page 188)
5 cups sliced fresh peaches
  (about 2½ pounds)
1 teaspoon lemon juice
1 cup sugar
¼ cup all-purpose flour
¼ teaspoon cinnamon
2 tablespoons unsalted margarine

Heat oven to 425°. Prepare pastry. Mix peaches and lemon juice. Stir together sugar, flour and cinnamon; mix with peaches. Pour into pastry-lined pie pan. Dot with margarine. Cover with top crust which has slits cut in it; seal and flute. Cover edge with 2- to 3-inch strip of aluminum foil to prevent excessive browning; remove foil last 15 minutes of baking. Bake 35 to 45 minutes or until crust is brown and juice begins to bubble through slits in crust. Serve slightly warm.

⅛ of pie = 1 fruit
      470 calories

Variations

Brown Sugar: Substitute ¾ cup brown sugar (packed) for the sugar.

¹/₆ of pie = 1 fruit
      565 calories

Apricot: Substitute 5 cups apricot halves for the peaches.

¹/₆ of pie = 1 fruit
      570 calories

LEMON MERINGUE PIE

8-inch Baked Pie Shell (page 188)
1 cup sugar
¼ cup cornstarch
1 cup water
¼ cup Second Nature
   imitation eggs*
2 tablespoons unsalted margarine
1 teaspoon grated lemon peel
⅓ cup lemon juice
2 drops yellow food color, if desired
Meringue for Pie (page 186)

Bake pie shell. Heat oven to 400°. Mix sugar and cornstarch in saucepan. Stir in water. Cook over medium heat, stirring constantly, until mixture thickens and boils. Boil and stir 1 minute. Stir at least half the hot mixture into imitation eggs, then blend into hot mixture in pan. Boil and stir 1 minute. Remove from heat; stir in margarine, lemon peel, juice and color. Pour into baked pie shell.

Heap meringue onto hot pie filling; spread over filling, carefully sealing meringue to edge of crust to prevent shrinking or weeping. Bake about 10 minutes or until a delicate brown. Cool away from draft.

¹/₆ of 8-inch pie = ½ meat
      435 calories

*If this ingredient is not available in your market area, see page 29 for substitutes.

OIL PASTRY

8- or 9-inch One-crust Pie

1 cup plus 2 tablespoons all-purpose flour
⅓ cup vegetable oil
2 to 3 tablespoons cold water

8- or 9-inch Two-crust Pie
or
10-inch One-crust Pie

1¾ cups all-purpose flour
½ cup vegetable oil
3 to 4 tablespoons cold water

Measure flour into mixing bowl. Add oil; stir with fork until mixture looks like meal. Sprinkle water over mixture, 1 tablespoon at a time, mixing with fork until flour is moistened. Mix thoroughly until dough almost cleans side of bowl. (If dough seems dry, add 1 to 2 tablespoons oil. Do not add water.) Gather dough together with hands. Press into ball.

For One-crust Pie, shape dough into a flattened round. Roll out 2 inches larger than inverted pie pan between two long strips of waxed paper crossed in center. (Wipe table with damp cloth to prevent paper from slipping.) Peel off top paper; place pastry paper side up in pan. Peel off paper; fit pastry loosely into pan. If necessary, trim overhanging pastry 1 inch from edge of pie pan. Fold and roll pastry under, even with pan. Flute or fork edge. Fill and bake as directed in recipe. For baked pie shell, flute edge and prick bottom and side well. Bake at 475° for 12 to 15 minutes. Cool. Fill as directed in recipe.

For two-crust pie, divide dough in half. Shape each half into a flattened round. Roll out one part 1½ inches larger than inverted pie pan between two long strips of waxed paper. Peel off paper; fit pastry loosely into pan. If necessary, trim pastry ½ inch from edge of pan.

Roll out other part of pastry 2 inches larger than

pie pan. Place on filling and pull off paper. Make several slits near center of pie to allow steam to escape during baking. If uneven, trim 1 inch from edge of pie pan. Fold and roll edge of top pastry under edge of lower pastry, pressing on rim to seal; flute. Cover edge with 2- to 3-inch strip of aluminum foil to prevent excessive browning; remove foil last 15 minutes of baking. Bake as directed in recipe.

Note: For 9- and 10-inch pies, tape two pieces of waxed paper together.

$^1/_6$ **of one-crust pie = trace sodium**
                                    205 calories
$^1/_6$ **of two-crust pie = trace sodium**
                                    235 calories

STANDARD PASTRY

8- or 9-inch One-crust Pie

1 cup all-purpose flour
⅓ cup plus 1 tablespoon unsalted margarine
2 to 3 tablespoons cold water

10-inch One-crust Pie

1⅓ cups all-purpose flour
½ cup unsalted margarine
3 to 4 tablespoons cold water

8- or 9-inch Two-crust Pie

2 cups all-purpose flour
⅔ cup plus 2 tablespoons unsalted margarine
4 to 5 tablespoons cold water

Measure flour into mixing bowl. Cut in margarine thoroughly. Sprinkle in water, 1 tablespoon at a time, mixing until all flour is moistened and dough almost cleans side of bowl (1 to 2 teaspoons water can be added if needed).

Gather dough into ball; shape into flattened round on lightly floured cloth-covered board.

(For Two-crust Pie, divide dough in half and shape into 2 flattened rounds.) With floured stockinet-covered rolling pin, roll dough 2 inches larger than inverted pie pan. Fold pastry into quarters; unfold and ease into pan.

For One-crust Pie: Trim overhanging edge of pastry 1 inch from rim of pan. Fold and roll pastry under, even with pan; flute. Fill and bake as directed in recipe.

$^1/_6$ **pie = trace sodium**
195 calories

For Baked Pie Shell: Prick bottom and side thoroughly with fork. Bake at 475° for 8 to 10 minutes.

$^1/_8$ **pie = trace sodium**
185 calories

For Two-crust Pie: Turn desired filling into pastry-lined pie pan. Trim overhanging edge of pastry ½ inch from rim of pan. Roll second round of dough. Fold into quarters; cut slits so steam can escape. Place over filling and unfold. Trim overhanging edge of pastry 1 inch from rim of pan. Fold and roll top edge under lower edge, pressing on rim to seal; flute. Cover edge with a 2- to 3-inch strip of aluminum foil to prevent excessive browning; remove foil last 15 minutes of baking. Bake as directed in recipe.

Note: If possible, hook fluted edge over edge of pie pan to prevent shrinking and help keep shape.

$^1/_6$ **pie = trace sodium**
385 calories

ANGEL FOOD CAKE SUPREME

1 cup cake flour
¾ cup plus 2 tablespoons sugar
12 egg whites (1½ cups)
1½ teaspoons cream of tartar
¾ cup sugar
1½ teaspoons vanilla
½ teaspoon almond extract

Heat oven to 375°. Mix flour and first amount of sugar; set aside. Beat egg whites and cream of tartar in large mixer bowl until foamy. Add second amount of sugar, 2 tablespoons at a time, beating on high speed until meringue holds stiff peaks. Fold in flavorings. Sprinkle flour-sugar mixture, ¼ cup at a time, over meringue, folding in gently just until flour-sugar mixture disappears. Push batter into ungreased tube pan, 10x4 inches. Gently cut through batter.

Bake 30 to 35 minutes or until top springs back when touched lightly with finger. Invert tube pan on funnel; let hang until cake is completely cool.

1 serving = ½ bread II
120 calories

FROSTING AN ANGEL FOOD CAKE

1. Invert cooled cake onto waxed paper. If frosting cake, brush loose crumbs off top and side; if glazing, brush crumbs off top only.

2. Coat side of cake with thin layer of frosting to seal in crumbs; swirl more frosting on side, forming a slight ridge above top of cake. Then frost top.

3. To glaze, pour or spoon small amount of glaze at a time on top of cake and spread, allowing some to drizzle unevenly down side.

YELLOW CAKE

⅔ cup unsalted margarine, softened
1¾ cups sugar
½ cup Second Nature imitation eggs*
1½ teaspoons vanilla
2¾ cups all-purpose flour
3½ teaspoons low-sodium baking powder
1¼ cups skim milk

Heat oven to 350°. Grease and flour baking pan, 9x9x2 inches. Mix margarine, sugar, imitation eggs and vanilla in large mixer bowl until fluffy. Beat on high speed 5 minutes, scraping bowl occasionally. On low speed, mix in flour and baking powder alternately with milk. Pour into pan.

Bake 55 to 60 minutes or until wooden pick inserted in center comes out clean.

12 servings.

1 serving = 1 bread I
340 calories

STARLIGHT CAKE

2 cups all-purpose flour
1½ cups sugar
1 tablespoon plus 2 teaspoons low-sodium baking powder
½ cup unsalted margarine, softened
1 cup skim milk
1 teaspoon vanilla
¾ cup Second Nature imitation eggs*

Heat oven to 350°. Grease and flour baking pan, 9x9x2 inches. Measure all ingredients into large mixer bowl. Blend on low speed ½ minute, scraping bowl constantly. Beat on high speed 3 minutes, scraping bowl frequently. Pour into prepared pan.

Bake 50 to 55 minutes or until wooden pick inserted in center comes out clean.

12 servings.

1 serving = 1 bread I
270 calories

CREATIVE CAKES

Cookie Cutter Cake: Frost cake with white frosting. Dip a cookie cutter into liquid food color; press into frosting, making an imprint on top of cake. Repeat around top of cake, dipping cutter into food color each time.

Balloon Cake: Frost cake with white frosting or one that has been delicately tinted with food color. On top of cake, arrange pastel mint-wafer "balloons." Use shoestring licorice for the balloon strings.

Shadow Design: Frost an oblong cake with white frosting. Melt 1 ounce unsweetened chocolate and ¼ teaspoon unsalted margarine. Using teaspoon, drizzle melted chocolate in parallel lines on top of cake. Immediately draw spatula or knife through lines.

---

*If this ingredient is not available in your market area, see page 29 for substitutes.

FILLING AND FROSTING
A TWO-LAYER CAKE

1. Before frosting cake, remove loose crumbs from side and edges of cooled layers. Support cake firmly with one hand and brush gently but thoroughly with the other.

2. Place one layer upside down on plate; spread about ½ cup of frosting to within ¼ inch of edge. (Use a spatula with a flexible blade; a stiff blade may dig into cake.)

3. Place second layer right side up on filling. Coat side with thin layer of frosting; swirl more frosting on side, forming a ¼-inch ridge above top of cake.

4. Spread remaining frosting over top of cake, just meeting the built-up ridge around side. Make attractive swirls or leave top smooth for decoration.

Frosting An Oblong Cake

To frost sides as well as top, place cooled cake right side up on tray (fill sides with frosting to straighten). Or leave cake in the pan and frost only the top.

FRENCH SILK FROSTING

2⅔ cups powdered sugar
⅔ cup unsalted margarine, softened
2 ounces unsweetened chocolate, melted
¾ teaspoon vanilla
2 tablespoons skim milk

Blend sugar, margarine, chocolate and vanilla in small mixer bowl on low speed. Gradually add milk; beat until smooth and fluffy.

Fills and frosts two 9-inch layers or three 8-inch layers.

2 tablespoons = trace sodium
185 calories

WHITE MOUNTAIN FROSTING

½ cup sugar
¼ cup light corn syrup
2 tablespoons water
2 egg whites (¼ cup)
1 teaspoon vanilla

Mix sugar, corn syrup, and water in small saucepan. Cover; heat to rolling boil over medium heat. Uncover; boil rapidly without stirring to 243° on candy thermometer (or until small amount of mixture spins 6- to 8-inch thread when dropped from spoon.

As mixture boils, beat egg whites until stiff peaks form. Pour hot syrup very slowly in a thin stream into egg whites, beating constantly on medium speed. Beat on high speed until stiff peaks form. Stir in vanilla during last minute of beating.

Fills and frosts two 8- or 9-inch layers or frosts a 13x9x2-inch cake.

2 tablespoons = trace sodium
45 calories

MARGARINE FROSTING

⅓ cup unsalted margarine, softened
3 cups powdered sugar
1½ teaspoons vanilla
About 2 tablespoons skim milk

Mix margarine and sugar. Stir in vanilla and milk; beat until smooth and of spreading consistency.

Fills and frosts two 8- or 9-inch layers or frosts a 13x9x2-inch cake.

Note: To fill and frost three 8-inch layers, use ½ cup unsalted margarine, softened, 4½ cups powdered sugar, 2 teaspoons vanilla and about 3 tablespoons skim milk.

2 tablespoons = trace sodium
135 calories

Orange or Lemon Frosting: Omit vanilla and substitute orange or lemon juice for the skim milk. Stir in 2 teaspoons grated orange peel or ½ teaspoon grated lemon peel.

2 tablespoons = trace sodium
135 calories

Cherry Frosting: Stir in 2 tablespoons drained chopped maraschino cherries and 2 drops red food color.

2 tablespoons = trace sodium
140 calories

Maple Nut Frosting: Omit vanilla and substitute ½ cup maple-flavored syrup for the skim milk. Stir in ¼ cup finely chopped walnuts.

2 tablespoons = trace sodium
170 calories

Browned Margarine Frosting: Heat margarine in saucepan over medium heat until a delicate brown. (Margarine browns very slowly.)

2 tablespoons = trace sodium
135 calories

Pineapple Frosting: Omit vanilla and substitute ⅓ cup well-drained crushed pineapple for the skim milk.

2 tablespoons = trace sodium
135 calories

CHOCOLATE CAKE

2 cups all-purpose flour
2 cups sugar
3 teaspoons low-sodium baking powder
¼ cup unsalted margarine, softened
1½ cups skim milk
1 teaspoon vanilla
½ cup Second Nature
    imitation eggs*
4 ounces sweet cooking chocolate, melted
    and cooled
1 cup chopped walnuts

Heat oven to 350°. Grease and flour baking pan, 13x9x2 inches, or 2 layer pans, 8 or 9x1½ inches. Measure flour, sugar, baking powder, margarine, milk and vanilla into large mixer bowl. Beat on medium speed 2 minutes, scraping side and bottom of bowl constantly. Add imitiation eggs and chocolate; beat on high speed 2 minutes, scraping bowl frequently. Stir in nuts. Pour into pan(s). Bake 35 to 40 minutes on until wooden pick inserted into center comes out clean, Cool.

1 serving (2-inch square) = 1 bread I
305 calories

*If this ingredient is not available in your market area, see page 29 for substitutes.

PETITS FOURS

Prepare White Cake (opposite) except—pour butter into greased and floured jelly roll pan, 15½x10½x1 inch. Bake 25 minutes. Cool. Cut cake into small squares, rounds, diamonds, hearts or other fancy shapes.

Glaze cake pieces by placing upside down, a few at a time, on wire rack over large bowl or baking dish. Pour Petits Fours Icing (below) over top so entire cake piece is covered at one time. (Glaze that drips off cakes into bowl can be reheated and used again.) Decorate top with candy flowers, gumdrop roses or with Decorators' Icing (opposite).

About thirty-five 2-inch squares.

Note: Petits Fours can also be glazed by placing each cake piece on a fork over icing (in double boiler) and spooning the glaze on each. With spatula or another fork, push cake off onto wire rack to set glaze.

1 square = 1 bread I
260 calories

Petits Fours Icing

9 cups powdered sugar (about 2 pounds)
½ cup water
½ cup light corn syrup
1 teaspoon vanilla
½ teaspoon almond extract

Combine all ingredients in top of double boiler and heat over boiling water just to lukewarm. (Do not overheat icing or it will become dull.) Remove from heat, leaving icing over hot water to keep it thin. If desired, tint parts of icing delicate pastel colors with food color. If necessary, add hot water, just a few drops at a time, until of spreading consistency.

Decorators' Icing

Mix 2 cups powdered sugar and 1 tablespoon water. Add more water, 1 teaspoon at a time, until icing is of the consistency that can be used easily in a decorators' tube and yet hold its shape.

¾ cup.

WHITE CAKE

2¼ cups all-purpose flour
1½ cups sugar
1 tablespoon plus 2 teaspoons
** low-sodium baking powder**
½ cup unsalted margarine, softened
1 cup skim milk
1 teaspoon vanilla
4 egg whites (½ cup)

Heat oven to 350°. Grease and flour baking pan, 13x9x2 inches, or 2 round layer pans, 8 or 9x1½ inches. Measure flour, sugar, baking powder, margarine, milk and vanilla into large mixer bowl. Blend on low speed ½ minute, scraping bowl constantly. Beat on high speed 2 minutes, scraping bowl occasionally. Add egg whites; beat on high speed 2 minutes, scraping bowl occasionally. Pour into pan(s).

Bake oblong 35 to 40 minutes, layers 30 to 35 minutes or until wooden pick inserted in center comes out clean. Cool.

1 serving (2-inch square) = 1 bread I
220 calories

PINEAPPLE UPSIDE-DOWN CAKE

¼ cup unsalted margarine
½ cup brown sugar (packed)
1 can (8½ ounces)
** pineapple slices, drained**
7 maraschino cherries
6 pecan halves
1 recipe Yellow Cake Batter (page 190)

Heat oven to 350°. Grease and flour one round layer pan, 9x1½ inches. Melt margarine over low heat in another round layer pan, 9x1½ inches. Sprinkle sugar evenly over margarine. Place one pineapple ring in center of pan. Cut remaining rings in half; arrange halves, cut sides out, around pineapple ring in center of pan. Place cherries in center of pineapple rings; arrange pecans around center ring.

Pour half the cake batter (about 2½ cups) into greased and floured layer pan. Pour remaining batter over fruit in layer pan. Bake layer 30 to 35 minutes and pineapple upside-down cake 35 to 45 minutes or until wooden pick inserted in center comes out clean. Invert at once onto serving plate. Leave pan over cake a few minutes. Serve warm.

9 servings.

1 serving = 2 bread I
**   570 calories**

MOCHA SPICE CAKE

2¼ cups all-purpose flour
1½ cups sugar
2 tablespoons cocoa
1½ teaspoons powdered instant coffee
1 tablespoon plus 2 teaspoons low-sodium
** baking powder**
1 teaspoon cinnamon
1 teaspoon nutmeg
½ teaspoon cloves
½ cup unsalted margarine, softened
1 cup skim milk
½ teaspoon vanilla
¾ cup Second Nature
** imitation eggs***
Mocha Icing (below)

Heat oven to 350°. Grease and flour baking pan, 13x9x2 inches. Measure all ingredients except egg substitute and icing into large mixer bowl. Beat on medium speed 2 minutes, scraping side and bottom of bowl constantly. Add imitation eggs and beat on high speed 2 minutes, scraping bowl frequently. Pour into pan. Bake 40 to 45 minutes or until wooden pick inserted in center comes out clean. Cool. Frost with Mocha Icing.

1 serving (2-inch square) = 1 bread I
**   365 calories**

Mocha Icing

2 teaspoons powdered instant coffee
2 tablespoons boiling water
⅓ cup unsalted margarine, softened
3 cups powdered sugar

Dissolve coffee in boiling water; set aside. Blend margarine and sugar. Stir in cooled coffee and beat until smooth and of spreading consistency.

HONEY ORANGE CAKE

½ cup unsalted margarine, softened
½ cup sugar
⅓ cup honey
½ cup Second Nature imitation eggs*
2 cups all-purpose flour
1 tablespoon plus 1 teaspoon low-
  sodium baking powder
⅔ cup skim milk
1 tablespoon grated orange peel
1 tablespoon orange juice

Heat oven to 350°. Grease and flour baking pan, 8x8x2 inches. Mix margarine and sugar thoroughly. Blend in honey and imitation eggs. Mix in flour and baking powder alternately with milk. Stir in orange peel and juice. Pour into pan.

Bake 45 to 50 minutes or until wooden pick inserted in center comes out clean.

9 servings.

1 serving = 1 bread l
             300 calories

POPPY SEED CAKE

½ cup poppy seed
1 cup skim milk
2¼ cups all-purpose flour
1½ cups sugar
6 teaspoons low-sodium baking powder
½ cup unsalted margarine, softened
1½ teaspoons vanilla
4 egg whites (½ cup)

Soak poppy seed in skim milk for 1 hour.

Heat oven to 350°. Grease and flour 2 layer pans, 8 or 9x1½ inches, or a baking pan, 13x9x2 inches. Measure flour, sugar and baking powder into large mixer bowl. Add mar-

garine, a little over half of poppy seed-milk mixture and the vanilla. Beat on medium speed 2 minutes, scraping bowl constantly. Add remaining poppy seed-milk mixture and the egg whites; beat on high speed 2 minutes, scraping bowl frequently. Pour into pan(s). Bake layers 30 to 35 minutes, oblong about 35 minutes or until wooden pick inserted in center comes out clean. Cool.

1 serving (2-inch square) = 1 bread l
                   365 calories

SPICE 'N' RAISIN CAKE

¼ cup Second Nature
  imitation eggs*
⅓ cup unsalted margarine, softened
¾ cup skim milk
1 teaspoon vanilla
1½ cups all-purpose flour
1 cup sugar
2 teaspoons low-sodium baking powder
1 teaspoon cinnamon
½ teaspoon nutmeg
¼ teaspoon cloves
¾ cup raisins

Heat oven to 350°. Grease and flour baking pan, 9x9x2 or 8x8x2 inches. Measure all ingredients in the order listed into blender container. Mix on high speed 30 seconds or just until ingredients are mixed, stopping blender occasionally to scrape sides of container with rubber spatula. (Batter may be slightly lumpy.) Pour into pan. Bake 9-inch cake about 30 minutes, 8-inch cake about 40 minutes or until wooden pick inserted in center comes out clean.

9 servings.

1 serving = 1 bread l
             285 calories

*If this ingredient is not available in your market area, see page 29 for substitutes.

JEWELED FRUITCAKE

1 cup dried apricots (4 ounces)
2 cups pitted dates (8 ounces)
1 cup drained red and green maraschino
** cherries**
1½ cups Brazil nuts (¾ pound)
¾ cup all-purpose flour
¾ cup sugar
¾ teaspoon low-sodium baking powder
¾ cup Second Nature imitation
** eggs***
1½ teaspoons vanilla

Heat oven to 300°. Line loaf pan, 9x5x3 or 8½x4½x2½ inches, with aluminum foil; grease. Leaving apricots, dates, cherries and nuts whole, combine all ingredients in large bowl; mix thoroughly. Spread mixture evenly in prepared pan.

Bake 1 hour 45 minutes or until wooden pick inserted in center comes out clean. If cake becomes too dark, cover with aluminum foil last 30 minutes of baking. Remove from pan; cool. Wrap in plastic wrap or aluminum foil; store in cool place.

1 serving (½-inch slice) = 2 bread I
**   580 calories**

CLEAR LEMON FILLING

¾ cup sugar
3 tablespoons cornstarch
¾ cup water
1 teaspoon grated lemon peel
1 tablespoon unsalted margarine
⅓ cup lemon juice
4 drops yellow food color, if desired

Mix sugar and cornstarch in small saucepan. Stir in water gradually. Cook, stirring constantly, until mixture thickens and boils. Boil and stir 1 minute. Remove from heat; add lemon peel and margarine. Stir in lemon juice and food color. Cool thoroughly. If filling is too soft, refrigerate until set.

Fills an 8- or 9-inch two-layer cake.

2 tablespoons = trace sodium
**   60 calories**

EASY PENUCHE FROSTING

½ cup unsalted margarine
1 cup brown sugar (packed)
¼ cup skim milk
2 cups powdered sugar

Melt margarine in small saucepan. Stir in brown sugar and heat to boiling, stirring constantly. Boil and stir over low heat 2 minutes. Stir in milk; heat to boiling. Remove from heat and cool to lukewarm. Gradually stir in powdered sugar. Place pan of frosting in bowl of ice and water; beat until of spreading consistency. If frosting becomes too stiff, heat slightly, stirring constantly.

Fills and frosts two 8- or 9-inch layers or frosts a 13x9x2-inch cake.

2 tablespoons = trace sodium
**   175 calories**

*If this ingredient is not available in your market area, see page 29 for substitutes.

GOLDEN POUND CAKE

1¾ cups all-purpose flour
1 cup sugar
3 teaspoons low-sodium baking powder
½ cup unsalted margarine, softened
¾ cup skim milk
1 teaspoon vanilla
½ cup Second Nature
  imitation eggs*

Heat oven to 350°. Grease loaf pan, 9x5x3 inches, then line with paper. Measure all ingredients into large mixer bowl. Blend on low speed ½ minute, scraping bowl constantly. Beat on medium speed 2 minutes, scraping bowl occasionally. Pour into pan. Bake 65 to 70 minutes or until wooden pick inserted in center comes out clean.

1 serving (1-inch slice) = 1 bread I
295 calories

APPLE CRISP

4 cups sliced pared tart apples
  (about 4 medium)
⅔ to ¾ cup brown sugar (packed)
½ cup all-purpose flour
½ cup oats
¾ teaspoon cinnamon
¾ teaspoon nutmeg
⅓ cup unsalted margarine, softened

Heat oven to 375°. Place apples in greased baking pan, 8x8x2 inches. Mix remaining ingredients with fork; sprinkle over apples.

Bake 30 minutes or until apples are tender and topping is golden brown. Serve warm.

6 servings.

1 serving = ½ bread I, 1 fruit
300 calories

STRAWBERRY TURNOVER

¼ cup sugar
1 tablespoon plus 1½ teaspoons cornstarch
2 cups sliced fresh strawberries
Pastry for 10-inch One-crust Pie (page 188)
Glaze (below)

Mix sugar, cornstarch and strawberries in small saucepan. Cook over medium heat, stirring constantly, until mixture thickens. Cool.

Heat oven to 425°. Prepare pastry as directed except—place pastry circle on ungreased baking sheet so that one half of circle is centered on sheet. Spread filling over centered half of circle; fold pastry over filling. Seal edges; turn up ½ inch of edge and flute. Cut slits in top. Bake 35 minutes. While warm, frost with Glaze. Serve warm, cut into wedges.

6 servings.

Glaze: Blend ½ cup powdered sugar, 1 tablespoon unsalted margarine, 1 tablespoon skim milk and, if desired, 1 teaspoon grated lemon peel.

1 serving = 1 bread I, ½ fruit
370 calories

*If this ingredient is not available in your market area, see page 29 for substitutes.

APPLE DUMPLINGS

Pastry for 9-inch Two-crust (page 188)
6 baking apples (each about 3 inches in diameter), pared and cored
3 tablespoons raisins
3 tablespoons chopped walnuts
2 cups brown sugar (packed)
1 cup water

Heat oven to 425°. Prepare pastry as directed except—roll ⅔ of dough into 14-inch square and cut into 4 squares. Roll remaining dough into rectangle, 14x7 inches, and cut into 2 squares.

Place an apple on each square. Mix raisins and nuts; fill center of each apple. Moisten corners of squares; bring 2 opposite corners of pastry up over apple and press corners together. Fold in sides of remaining corners (as if wrapping a package); bring corners up over apple and press together. Place dumplings in ungreased baking dish, 11½x7½x1½ inches.

Heat sugar and water to boiling; carefully pour around dumplings. Bake, spooning syrup over dumplings 2 or 3 times during baking, about 40 minutes or until crust is brown and apples are tender when pricked with a fork.

6 servings.

1 serving = 1 bread I, 1 fruit
             750 calories

RUSSIAN TEACAKES

1 cup unsalted margarine, softened
½ cup powdered sugar
1 teaspoon vanilla
2¼ cups all-purpose flour
¾ cup finely chopped walnuts
Powdered sugar

Heat oven to 400°. Mix margarine, ½ cup sugar and the vanilla thoroughly. Work in flour and nuts until dough holds together. Shape dough into 1-inch balls. Place on ungreased baking sheet.

Bake 10 to 12 minutes or until set but not brown. While warm, roll in powdered sugar. Cool. Roll in sugar again.

About 4 dozen cookies.

4 cookies = ½ bread I
             305 calories

SCOTCH SHORTBREAD

¾ cup unsalted margarine, softened
¼ cup sugar
2 cups all-purpose flour

Heat oven to 350°. Mix margarine and sugar until fluffy. Work in flour. If dough is crumbly, mix in 1 to 2 tablespoons soft unsalted margarine. Roll dough ½ to ⅓ inch thick on lightly floured cloth-covered board. Cut into small shapes (leaves, ovals, squares, triangles, etc.). Place ½ inch apart on ungreased baking sheet. Bake about 20 minutes until set. Immediately remove from baking sheet.

About 2 dozen 1½x1-inch cookies.

1 cookie = trace sodium
             100 calories

BROWNIES (Cakelike)

½ cup unsalted margarine, softened
1 cup sugar
¼ cup Second Nature imitation eggs*
2 ounces unsweetened chocolate, melted
  and cooled
1 teaspoon vanilla
¾ cup all-purpose flour
½ cup chopped pecans

Heat oven to 350°. Mix margarine, sugar and imitation eggs thoroughly. Stir in chocolate, vanilla and flour. Stir in nuts. Spread in pan.

Bake 40 to 45 minutes. Cool slightly. Cut into squares, 2x2 inches.

16 brownies.

1 brownie = ¼ bread I
170 calories

BUTTERSCOTCH BROWNIES

¼ cup unsalted margarine
1 cup brown sugar (packed)
¼ cup Second Nature
  imitation eggs*
1 teaspoon vanilla
¾ cup all-purpose flour
1 teaspoon low-sodium baking powder
½ cup chopped walnuts

Heat oven to 350°. Grease baking pan, 8x8x2 inches. Melt margarine in saucepan over low heat. Remove from heat; mix in sugar, imitation eggs and vanilla. Stir in remaining ingredients. Spread in pan. Bake 25 minutes. While warm, cut into 2-inch squares.

16 brownies.

1 brownie = ¼ bread I
125 calories

GINGERBREAD

1 tablespoon vinegar
¾ cup skim milk
2 cups all-purpose flour
3 teaspoons low-sodium baking powder
¼ teaspoon soda
1½ to 2 teaspoons ginger
1 teaspoon cinnamon
¼ teaspoon cloves
⅓ cup unsalted margarine, softened
½ cup sugar
3 tablespoons Second Nature
  imitation eggs*
¾ cup light molasses

Heat oven to 350°. Grease bottom of baking pan, 8x8x2 inches. Measure vinegar into milk and set aside. Mix flour, baking powder, soda and spices; set aside. Mix margarine and sugar thoroughly. Beat in imitation eggs until smooth. Stir in molasses. Stir in flour mixture alternately with milk. Pour into pan. Bake 45 to 50 minutes or until wooden pick inserted in center comes out clean.

9 servings.

1 serving = ½ bread II
295 calories

*If this ingredient is not available in your market area, see page 29 for substitutes.

COOKIE MIX

4 cups all-purpose flour
1¼ cups granulated sugar
1¼ cups brown sugar (packed)
1 tablespoon plus 1½ teaspoons low-
  sodium baking powder
1½ cups unsalted margarine

Mix flour, sugars and baking powder in large bowl. Cut in margarine with pastry blender until mixture is like coarse meal. Do not overmix.

Measure desired amounts of Cookie Mix into jars or plastic containers: 2 cups for about 3 dozen Chocolate Chip Cookies; 2½ cups each for 3 dozen Banana Cookies, Spice Cookies and Chocolate-Nut Cookies. (Can be baked immediately.) Seal tightly, label and refrigerate.

9 to 10 cups mix.

Chocolate Chip Cookies

2 cups Cookie Mix
¼ cup Second Nature
  imitation eggs*
1 cup mini semisweet chocolate pieces
1 cup chopped walnuts

Heat oven to 375°. Mix all ingredients. Drop dough by rounded teaspoonfuls 2 inches apart onto ungreased baking sheet. Bake 12 to 15 minutes or until light brown.

2 cookies = ¼ bread I
                170 calories

Chocolate-Nut Cookies

2½ cups Cookie Mix
¼ cup cocoa
¼ cup Second Nature
  imitation eggs*
1 teaspoon vanilla
1 teaspoon water
1 cup chopped walnuts

Heat oven to 375°. Mix all ingredients. Drop

dough by rounded teaspoonfuls 2 inches apart onto ungreased baking sheet. Bake 12 to 15 minutes or until light brown.

2 cookies = ¼ bread I
                140 calories

Banana Cookies

2½ cups Cookie Mix
½ cup mashed ripe banana
1 teaspoon vanilla
3 tablespoons Second Nature
  imitation eggs*
½ cup chopped walnuts

Heat oven to 375°. Mix all ingredients. Drop dough by rounded teaspoonfuls 2 inches apart onto ungreased baking sheet. Bake 12 to 15 minutes or until light brown.

2 cookies = ¼ bread I
                120 calories

Spice Cookies

2½ cups Cookie Mix
3 tablespoons Second Nature
  imitation eggs*
½ teaspoon cinnamon
½ teaspoon lemon extract
½ cup raisins
½ cup chopped walnuts

Heat oven to 375°. Mix all ingredients. Drop dough by rounded teaspoonfuls 2 inches apart onto ungreased baking sheet. Bake 12 to 15 minutes or until light brown.

2 cookies = ¼ bread I
                125 calories

*If this ingredient is not available in your market area, see page 29 for substitutes.

QUICK PEACH COBBLER

1 can (1 pound 13 ounces) sliced peaches
3 tablespoons cornstarch
½ teaspoon cinnamon
1 cup all-purpose flour
1 tablespoon sugar
2 teaspoons low-sodium baking powder
3 tablespoons vegetable oil
½ cup skim milk

Heat oven to 400°. Combine peaches (with syrup), cornstarch and cinnamon in saucepan. Cook, stirring constantly, until mixture thickens and boils. Boil and stir 1 minute. Pour into ungreased 1½-quart casserole.

Mix flour, sugar and baking powder. Stir in oil and milk until dough forms a ball. Drop mixture by 6 spoonfuls onto hot fruit.

Bake 25 to 30 minutes or until biscuit topping is golden brown. Serve warm.

6 servings.

1 serving = 1 bread I, 1 fruit
265 calories

SPRITZ

1 cup unsalted margarine, softened
½ cup sugar
2¼ cups all-purpose flour
¼ cup Second Nature imitation eggs*
1 teaspoon almond extract or vanilla

Heat oven to 400°. Blend margarine and sugar. Mix in remaining ingredients. Fill cookie press with ¼ the dough at a time; form desired shapes on ungreased baking sheet. Bake 6 to 9 minutes or until set but not brown.

About 5 dozen cookies.

3 cookies = ¼ bread I
160 calories

OATMEAL COOKIES

¾ cup unsalted margarine, softened
1 cup brown sugar (packed)
½ cup granulated sugar
¼ cup Second Nature imitation eggs*
¼ cup water
1 teaspoon vanilla
1 cup all-purpose flour
1 teaspoon cinnamon
½ teaspoon baking soda
½ teaspoon cloves
1 cup raisins
1 cup chopped nuts
3 cups quick-cooking oats

Heat oven to 350°. Mix thoroughly margarine, sugars, imitation eggs, water and vanilla. Stir in remaining ingredients. Drop dough by teaspoonfuls 1 inch apart onto greased baking sheet.

Bake 12 to 15 minutes or until almost no imprint remains when touched with finger. Immediately remove from baking sheet. Store cooled cookies in tightly covered container.

About 5 dozen cookies.

2 cookies = 1 bread I
170 calories

*If this ingredient is not available in your market area, see page 29 for substitutes.

PUMPKIN COOKIES

1½ cups brown sugar (packed)
½ cup unsalted margarine, softened
½ cup Second Nature imitation
    eggs*
1 can (16 ounces) unsalted pumpkin
2¾ cups all-purpose flour
1 tablespoon plus 1½ teaspoons low-
    sodium baking powder
1 teaspoon cinnamon
½ teaspoon nutmeg
¼ teaspoon ginger
1 cup raisins
1 cup chopped pecans

Heat oven to 400°. Mix sugar, margarine and pumpkin. Stir in remaining ingredients.

Drop dough by teaspoonfuls about 2 inches apart onto ungreased baking sheet. Bake until light brown, 12 to 15 minutes. Immediately remove from baking sheet; cool.

About 6 dozen cookies.

1 cookie = ¼ bread I
65 calories

LEMON SQUARES

1 cup all-purpose flour
½ cup unsalted margarine, softened
¼ cup powdered sugar
½ cup Second Nature imitation
    eggs*
1 cup granulated sugar
¾ teaspoon low-sodium baking powder
2 teaspoons grated lemon peel, if desired
2 tablespoons lemon juice

Heat oven to 350°. Mix thoroughly flour, margarine and powdered sugar. Press evenly in ungreased baking pan, 8x8x2 inches, building up ½-inch edge. Bake 20 minutes.

Beat remaining ingredients until light and fluffy. Pour over hot crust and bake about 25 minutes longer or just until no imprint remains when touched in center. Cool and cut into squares.

25 squares.

1 square = ¼ bread I
95 calories

BROWNIES

4 ounces unsweetened chocolate
⅔ cup unsalted margarine
2 cups sugar
½ cup Second Nature
    imitation eggs*
1 teaspoon vanilla
1¼ cups all-purpose flour
1 teaspoon low-sodium baking powder
1 cup chopped walnuts

Heat oven to 350°. Grease baking pan, 13x9x2 inches. Melt chocolate and margarine in large saucepan over low heat. Remove from heat. Mix in sugar, imitation eggs, and vanilla. Stir in remaining ingredients. Spread in pan.

Bake 30 minutes or until brownies start to pull

*If this ingredient is not available in your market area, see page 29 for substitutes.

away from sides of pan. Do not overbake. Cool slightly. Cut into bars, about 2x1½ inches.

32 brownies.

1 brownie = ¼ bread I
150 calories

DATE-NUT SQUARES

¼ cup Second Nature imitation
** eggs***
½ cup sugar
½ teaspoon vanilla
½ cup all-purpose flour
¾ teaspoon low-sodium baking powder
2 cups cut-up dates
1 cup chopped walnuts

Heat oven to 350°. Grease baking pan, 9x9x2 inches. Measure imitation eggs into small mixer bowl. Add sugar and vanilla and beat thoroughly. Mix in flour and baking powder, then stir in dates and nuts. Spread in pan.

Bake 25 to 30 minutes. Cool and cut into squares. If desired, roll squares in powdered sugar.

16 squares.

1 square = ¼ bread I
135 calories

SUGAR COOKIES

¾ cup unsalted margarine, softened
1 cup sugar
¼ cup Second Nature imitation
** eggs***
1 teaspoon vanilla or
** ½ teaspoon lemon extract**
2½ cups all-purpose flour
1½ teaspoons low-sodium baking powder

Mix thoroughly margarine, sugar, imitation

eggs and flavoring. Blend in flour and baking powder. Cover dough and chill at least 1 hour.

Heat oven to 400°. Roll dough ⅛ inch thick on lightly floured cloth-covered board. Cut into desired shapes with cookie cutters. Place on ungreased baking sheet. Bake 6 to 8 minutes or until very light brown.

About 4 dozen 3-inch cookies.

2 cookies = ¼ bread I
140 calories

NUT BARS

2 cups all-purpose flour
1 cup firm unsalted margarine
1 cup ground pecans or walnuts
1 tablespoon water
1 teaspoon vanilla
¾ cup powdered sugar

Heat oven to 375°. Measure flour into bowl; cut in margarine thoroughly. Stir in nuts, water and vanilla. Press evenly in bottom of ungreased baking pan, 9x9x2 inches. Bake 20 to 25 minutes. Cool slightly. Cut into bars, 2x1½ inches, and roll each in sugar.

24 bars.

Note: Few drops of water can be added if mixture is too dry.

1 bar = ½ bread I
170 calories

*If this ingredient is not available in your market area, see page 29 for substitutes.

14. Use of Herbs & Spices

Mastery of the seasoning know-how in this chapter can invest even a controlled diet with taste magic— meanwhile rewarding the rest of the family with new flavor treats both subtle and bold.

YOU CAN MAKE unsalted foods more tasty if you learn to flavor them with spices, herbs, and wine. Herbs can be used as easily as salt and pepper. And cooking with wine can be as simple as cooking with water. When just the right amount of wine is used, it enhances the flavor of the foods you prepare. But be sure to use a good wine for cooking; remember, the whole is only as good as its parts. (Incidentally, you can assure all teetotalers that heating evaporates the alcohol, leaving only the flavor of the wine.)

The spice and herb chart on page 209 suggests which combinations of herbs go best with particular foods. (Because certain spices and herbs are not allowed on a sodium controlled diet, check page 208 for those to avoid.) In cooking with herbs, bear in mind that they should accentuate, not overpower, the flavor of your food. So use them discreetly. If you follow the rules listed below for cooking with herbs and wine, your efforts should be successful. Generally, one strongly seasoned dish per meal is a good rule of thumb.

1. In experimenting with herbs, use no more than ¼ teaspoon of dried herbs or ¾ teaspoon of fresh herbs for a dish that serves four people. At least start with that amount, and then increase it to suit your taste.

2. To soups and stews that are to be cooked a long time, add herbs during the last hour of cooking.

3. To hamburgers, meat loaf, and stuffing, add herbs before cooking.

4. On roasts, sprinkle herbs before cooking, or top with herb-flavored margarine after cooking.

5. On steaks and chops, either sprinkle herbs while the meat is cooking, or 1 hour before cooking brush the meat with oil and then sprinkle with herbs.

6. When cooking vegetables or making sauces and gravies, cook herbs along with them. If you wish, you may first moisten the herbs with a little oil, let the mixture stand for ½ hour and then add the herbs and oil to your food as it cooks.

7. To cold foods such as tomato juice, salad dressing, and cottage cheese, add herbs several hours before serving. You may store these foods in the refrigerator for 3 or 4 hours or overnight.

8. For a subtle seasoning of herbs in your food, put the amount of dried herbs to be used in a tea strainer. Then dip the strainer into piping hot water for 20 seconds. After draining the water off, add the moistened herbs to your food. (Heat and moisture bring out the fragrance and flavor of herbs.)

9. If you do not want bits of herbs in the food, tie the herbs in a small piece of cheesecloth. Then remove the bag before serving.

10. Combine herbs with margarine for use in flavoring steaks, roasts, or vegetables after cooking.

11. If your diet allows it, marinate meats in a wine and herb mixture before cooking to enhance flavor. Check the index of this cookbook for marinade recipes.

12. After measuring dry herbs, crush them in the palm of your hand before adding to your food. This helps hasten the flavor release.

13. When substituting fresh herbs for dried herbs, use three or four times as much fresh herbs.

14. While there are often several herbs or spices that complement the flavor of a given dish, do not combine too many at one time.

The correct combinations of herbs, spices, and wine for any food is the one that tastes best to you. Remember that seasoning foods is not a science but an expressive art—and you are the artist. When experimenting with a new herb, crush some of it and let it warm in your hand; then sniff it and taste it. If it is delicate, you can be bold and adventurous. If it is very strong and pungent, be cautious. Choose a wine that goes best with the food you are cooking—again, according to your personal taste.

TABLE OF SEASONING EQUIVALENTS

For the cook who is temporarily out of a particular seasoning ingredient, and for the cook who wishes to substitute products called for in recipes, here is a convenient guide to equivalents.

ARROWROOT

1 teaspoon	1 tablespoon flour
1 tablespoon	3 tablespoons flour
2 teaspoons	1 tablespoon cornstarch
1 tablespoon	1 tablespoon flour plus 1 teaspoon cornstarch

BAY LEAF

½ teaspoon, cracked	1 whole bay leaf

BELL PEPPERS (GREEN)

1 tablespoon rehydrated	3 tablespoons chopped fresh green pepper

BELL PEPPERS (RED)

1 tablespoon, rehydrated	3 tablespoons chopped fresh red pepper
1 tablespoon, rehydrated	2 tablespoons chopped pimiento

CHIVES (see ONIONS, SHREDDED GREEN)

CORNSTARCH (see ARROWROOT)

GARLIC CHIPS

⅛ teaspoon	1 medium clove garlic
⅛ teaspoon, ground or crushed	⅛ teaspoon garlic powder

GARLIC POWDER

⅛ teaspoon	1 medium clove garlic
⅛ teaspoon	⅛ teaspoon ground or crushed garlic chips

GINGER

1 teaspoon *whole* (Soak in cold water for several hours, then chop finely or grate)	2 teaspoons chopped fresh ginger
2 teaspoons *crystallized* chopped or slivered (wash sugar from ginger or leave on if flavor is compatible)	1 teaspoon chopped fresh ginger
¼ teaspoon *ground*	1 teaspoon chopped fresh ginger
¼ teaspoon *ground*	2 teaspoons chopped *crystallized* ginger

HORSERADISH

1 tablespoon rehydrated in 1 tablespoon water and mixed with 1 tablespoon vinegar and sugar and salt (from daily allowance) to taste	2 tablespoons bottled prepared horseradish

LEMON PEEL

1 teaspoon	1 teaspoon grated lemon peel
1 teaspoon	Grated peel of 1 medium lemon
1 teaspoon	½ teaspoon lemon extract

MINT (see PEPPERMINT or SPEARMINT)

MUSHROOMS (POWDERED)

1 tablespoon	3 tablespoons whole dried mushrooms
1 tablespoon	4 ounces fresh mushrooms for flavor in soups, gravies, sauces, stews

MUSTARD (DRY)

1 teaspoon MILD	1 tablespoon mild prepared mustard in sauces, salad dressings, marinades
1 teaspoon HOT	1 tablespoon hot prepared mustard in sauces, salad dressings, marinades

(use instead of prepared mustard)

ONION POWDER

1 tablespoon, rehydrated	1 medium onion, chopped
1 tablespoon, rehydrated	¼ cup chopped onion

ONION (INSTANT MINCED)

1 tablespoon, rehydrated	1 small onion, chopped
1 tablespoon, rehydrated	2 tablespoons chopped onion
1 tablespoon, not rehydrated	1 tablespoon instant toasted onion

ONION (INSTANT TOASTED)

1 tablespoon	1 tablespoon instant minced onion
As casserole topping or in salads	Use instead of French fried onions

ONION (SHREDDED GREEN)

½ teaspoon	2 teaspoons finely chopped chives
½ teaspoon	2 teaspoons finely chopped green onion tops

ORANGE PEEL

1 tablespoon	1 tablespoon grated orange peel
1 tablespoon	Grated peel of 1 medium orange
2 teaspoons	1 teaspoon orange extract

PARSLEY FLAKES

1 teaspoon	3 teaspoons chopped parsley

PEPPER, CAYENNE

Use equal amount of Nepal pepper

PEPPERMINT

1 tablespoon	¼ cup chopped fresh mint

Pimiento (see BELL PEPPERS, RED)

SPEARMINT

1 tablespoon	¼ cup chopped fresh mint

VANILLA BEAN

1-inch piece, split, and simmered in part of the milk or water called for in recipe	1 teaspoon vanilla
1-inch piece	1 teaspoon vanilla

IMPORTANT: Avoid the seasonings and condiments listed below.

AVOID these seasonings:

Salt (unless permitted on your meal plan)

Salt substitutes (unless permitted by your physician)

Meat tenderizer

Monosodium glutamate

All seasonings containing salt or sodium

AVOID these condiments:

Bottled meat sauce

Catsup

Prepared mustard

DICTIONARY OF HERBS AND SPICES*

Herb or Spice	How it is available	How it tastes	How it is used
ALLSPICE	whole or ground	like a blend of cinnamon, nutmeg and cloves	spices meat, fish, seafood dishes, soups, juices, fruits, spicy sauces, spinach, turnips, peas, red and yellow vegetables
ANISE	whole or ground	aromatic, sweet licorice flavor	sweet rolls, breads, fruit pies, and fillings, sparingly in fruit stews, shellfish dishes, carrots, beets, cottage cheese
BASIL, SWEET	fresh, whole or ground	aromatic, mild mint-licorice flavor	meat, fish, seafood dishes, eggs, soups, stews, sauces, salads, tomato dishes, most vegetables, fruit compotes
BAY	dried whole leaves, ground	aromatic, woodsy, pleasantly bitter	meat, game, poultry, stews, fish, shellfish, chowders, soups, pickled meats and vegetables, gravies, marinades
BURNET	fresh, dried leaves	delicate cucumber flavor	soups, salads, dressings, most vegetables, beverages, as a garnish
CARAWAY	whole or ground, seed	leaves and root delicately flavored, seeds sharp and pungent	beans, beets, cabbage soup, breads, cookies, dips, variety meats, casseroles, dressings, cottage cheese, cheese spreads, sauerbraten
CARDAMOM	whole or ground, seed	mild, pleasant ginger flavor	pastries, pies, cookies, jellies, fruit dishes, sweet potatoes, pumpkin
CAYENNE	ground	blend of hottest chili peppers	sparingly in sauces, meat or seafood dishes, casseroles, soups, curries, stews, Mexican recipes, vegetables, cottage and cream cheeses

*Approximately ⅓ teaspoon ground herbs or 1 teaspoon dried herbs is equal in strength to 1 tablespoon fresh herbs.

DICTIONARY OF HERBS AND SPICES

Herb or Spice	How it is available	How it tastes	How it is used
CHERVIL	fresh, whole	delicate parsley flavor	soups, salads, stews, meats, fish, garnishes, eggs, sauces, dressings, vegetables, cottage cheese
CHILI POWDER	powder	blend of chilies and spices	sparingly in Mexican dishes, meats, stews, soups, cocktail sauces, eggs, seafoods, relishes, dressings
CHIVES	fresh, frozen, dried	delicate onion flavor	as an ingredient or garnish for any dish complemented by this flavor
CINNAMON	whole sticks or ground	warm, spicy flavor	pastries, desserts, puddings, fruits, spiced beverages, pork, chicken, stews, sweet potatoes, carrots, squash
CLOVES	whole or ground	hot, spicy, penetrating	sparingly with pork, in soups, desserts, fruits, sauces, baked beans, candied sweet potatoes, carrots, squash
CORIANDER	whole or ground, seed	pleasant lemon-orange flavor	pastries, cookies, cream or pea soups, Spanish dishes, dressings, spiced dishes, salads, cheeses, meats
CUMIN	ground, seed	warm, distinctive, salty-sweet, reminiscent of caraway	meat loaf, chili, fish, soft cheeses, deviled eggs, stews, beans, cabbage, fruit pies, rice, Oriental meat cookery
CURRY	powder	combination of many spices, warm, fragrant, exotic, combinations vary	meats, sauces, stews, soups, fruits, eggs, fish, shellfish, poultry, creamed and scalloped vegetables, dressings, cream or cottage cheeses
DILL	fresh, whole or ground, seed	aromatic, somewhat like caraway, but milder and sweeter	seafood, meat, poultry, spreads, dips, dressings, cream or cottage cheeses, potato salads, many vegetables, soups, chowders

DICTIONARY OF HERBS AND SPICES

Herb or Spice	How it is available	How it tastes	How it is used
FENNEL	whole or ground, seed	pleasant licorice flavor somewhat like anise	breads, rolls, sweet pastries, cookies, apples, stews, pork, squash, eggs, fish, beets, cabbage
GINGER	fresh, whole root, ground, crystallized	aromatic, sweet, spicy, penetrating	cakes, pies, cookies, chutneys, curries, beverages, fruits, meats, poultry, stews, yellow vegetables, beets, soups, dressings, cheese dishes
MACE	whole or ground	this dried pulp of nutmeg kernel has a strong nutmeg flavor	chicken, creamed fish, fish sauces, cakes, cookies, spiced doughs, jellies, beverages, yellow vegetables, cheese dishes, desserts, toppings
MARJORAM	fresh, whole or ground	faintly like sage, slight mint after-taste, delicate	pork, lamb, beef, game fish, fish sauces, poultry, chowders, soup, stews, sauces, cottage or cream cheeses, omelets, soufflés, green salads, many vegetables
MINT	fresh, dried	fruity, aromatic, distinctive flavor	lamb, veal, fish, soup, fruit, desserts, cottage or cream cheeses, sauces, salads, cabbage, carrots, beans, potatoes
MUSTARD	fresh, whole or ground	sharp, hot, very pungent	salads, dressings, eggs, sauces, fish, spreads, soups, many vegetables
NUTMEG	whole or ground	spicy, sweet, pleasant	desserts of all kinds, stews, sauces, cream dishes, soups, fruits, beverages, ground meats, many vegetables
OREGANO (WILD MARJORAM)	fresh, whole or ground	more pungent than marjoram, but similar, reminiscent of thyme	Italian cooking, Mexican cooking, spaghetti, tomato sauces, soups, meats, fish, poultry, eggs, omelets, spreads, dips, many vegetables, green salads, mushroom dishes

DICTIONARY OF HERBS AND SPICES

Herb or Spice	How it is available	How it tastes	How it is used
PARSLEY	fresh, dried flakes	sweet, mildly spicy, refreshing	as a garnish, ingredient in soups, spreads, dips, stews, butters, all meats, poultry, fish, most vegetables, omelets, eggs, herb breads, salads
POPPY SEED	tiny whole dried seed	nut flavor	breads, rolls, cakes, soups, cookies, dressings, cottage or cream cheeses, noodles, many vegetables, fruits, deviled eggs, stuffings
ROSEMARY	fresh, whole	refreshing, piny, resinous, pungent	sparingly in meats, game, poultry, soups, fruits, stuffings, eggs, omelets, herb breads, sauces, green salads, marinades, vegetables
SAFFRON	whole or ground	exotic, delicate, pleasantly bitter-sweet	expensive but a little goes far; use for color and flavor in rice dishes, potatoes, rolls, breads, fish, stew, veal, chicken, bouillabaisse, curries, scrambled eggs, cream cheese, cream soups, sauces
SAGE	fresh, whole or rubbed	pungent, warm, astringent	sparingly in pork dishes, fish, veal, lamb, stuffings, cheese dips, fish chowders, consommé, cream soups, gravies, green salads, tomatoes, carrots, lima beans, peas, onions, brussels sprouts, eggplant
SAVORY	fresh, whole or ground	warm, aromatic, resinous, delicate sage flavor— winter savory stronger than summer savory	egg dishes, salads, soups, seafoods, pork, lamb, veal, poultry, tomatoes, beans, beets, cabbage, peas, lentils, summer squash, artichokes, rice, barbecue dishes, stuffings
SESAME	whole seed	toasted, it has a nutlike flavor	breads, rolls, cookies, fish, lamb, eggs, fruit or vegetable salads, chicken, thick soups, vegetables, casseroles, toppings, noodles, candies

DICTIONARY OF HERBS AND SPICES

Herb or Spice	How it is available	How it tastes	How it is used
TARRAGON	fresh, whole or ground	licorice-anise flavor, pleasant, slightly bitter	sparingly in egg dishes, fish, shellfish, veal, poultry, chowders, chicken, soups, butters, vinegar, sauces, marinades, beans, beets, cabbage, cauliflower, broccoli, vegetable juices, fresh sprigs in salads
THYME	fresh, whole or ground	strong, pleasant, pungent clove flavor	sparingly in fish, gumbo, shellfish, soups, meats, poultry, tomato juice or sauces, cheeses, eggs, sauces, fricasees, tomatoes, artichokes, beets, beans, mushrooms, potatoes, onions, carrots
TURMERIC	whole or ground	aromatic, warm, mild	substitutes for saffron in salads, salad dressings, butters, creamed eggs, fish, curries, rice dishes without saffron, vegetables, used partially for its orange color
WATERCRESS	fresh	pleasing, peppery	garnish or ingredient in salads, fruit or vegetable cocktails, soups, cottage cheese, spreads, egg dishes, or sprinkled on vegetables or sauces

The recipes for vegetable dishes begin on page 157.

The recipe for Strawberry Sparkler is on page 172.

15.Measuring Ingredients, Rules for Good Baking,&Tips Regarding Special Products

INGREDIENTS AND HOW TO MEASURE THEM

All-purpose flour
Dip from canister with dry measuring cup, then level with spatula.

Granulated sugar
Measure like flour.

Powdered sugar or Cake flour
Spoon lightly into dry measuring cup, then level with spatula. (If necessary to remove lumps in sugar, press sugar through a sieve.)

Brown sugar
Spoon into cup and pack down firmly into dry measuring cup, then level with spatula.

Baking powder
Dip and fill measuring spoon, then level with spatula. Low-sodium baking powder can be purchased in store specializing in dietetic foods or from your pharmacist without a prescription. The formula is:

Tartaric acid .7.5 grams
Potassium bi-tartrate . . . . .56.1 grams
Potassium bi-carbonate . . . . .39.8 grams
Cornstarch .28.0 grams
Measure soda, cream of tartar and spices in the same way.

Yeast
Active dry yeast is bought in small packets. Always check expiration date on the packet before using to assure freshness.

Unsalted Margarine
Use only the regular, unwhipped, unsalted kind bought in sticks. Soften at room temperature.
4 sticks (1 pound) = 2 cups
1 stick (¼ pound) = ½ cup
½ stick (⅛ pound) = ¼ cup
Always use margarine or shortening as recipe specifies. Do not substitute one for another.

Liquids
Pour milk, water, and oil into liquid measuring cup placed on table or counter top. Check measurement at eye level. Measure corn syrup, honey, and molasses in the same way.

Lemon or Orange Peel
To grate, wash fruit and rub in short strokes across small holes of grater onto wax paper. Grate only the colored peel which contains the oil and flavor—the white is bitter. To measure, press grated peel into measuring spoon until level with top.

Eggs and Egg Substitutes
Use medium or large eggs. To separate eggs, tap shell at center with knife blade or against

edge of cup or bowl. Press tips of thumbs into crack and pull shell apart. Shift yolk from one shell half to the other, allowing white to drain into a custard cup. Place yolk in second cup. Remove any particles or yolk or shell from whites with a spoon.

Store extra yolks or whites covered in refrigerator. Use yolks within 2 or 3 days; use whites within 10 days.

To measure egg substitute, read directions carefully and follow package instructions regarding substitutions and storage.

FOR MEASURING

Dry measuring cups
(¼, ⅓, ½ and 1 cup)
Liquid measuring cup
(1 cup)
Measuring spoons
(¼, ½, 1 teaspoon and
1 tablespoon)
Straight-edged spatula

GOOD BAKING RULES

1. Read the recipe carefully to be sure you have all ingredients and equipment on hand.

2. Assemble ingredients on a tray. As you use each one, remove it from the tray. When the tray is empty, you will know you have not omitted any ingredient.

3. Assemble equipment specified in recipe—rotary beater, saucepan, electric mixer, bowls, mixing spoons, baking pan.

4. Measure ingredients over tray or cup rather than over the mixing bowl containing other ingredients, so that overmeasurement will not spoil your baking.

5. Follow recipe directions exactly and in the order directed.

6. For best results, use pans of the size called for in the recipe.

Bread needs a dull aluminum or dark-finished pan to absorb heat for better browning.

Cakes or cookies need a shiny pan for delicate browning.

16. Handy Chart of Kitchen Math

COOKING NEED never erupt into a crisis when you use the handy charts in this book. Need to distinguish between a 4- or 6-cup baking dish? How do you thicken the sauce when you have no cornstarch? Will your fancy mold be the right size for the recipe? See below for the answers—plus much more.

BAKING DISHES	EQUIVALENTS
4-cup baking dish:	8-inch pie pan 8x1½-inch layer pan 7⅛x3⅝x2¼-loaf pan
6-cup baking dish:	8- or 9½-inch layer pan 10-inch pie pan 8½x3⅝x2⅝-loaf pan
8-cup baking dish:	8x8x2-inch baking pan 11x7x1½-inch baking pan 9x5x3-inch loaf pan
10-cup baking dish:	9x9x2-inch baking pan 11¾x7½x1¾-inch baking pan 15½x10½x1-inch jelly roll pan

12-cup and over baking dish:

13½x8¾-inch baking dish	12 cups
13x9x2-inch baking pan	15 cups
14x10½x2-inch roasting pan	19 cups

VOLUME OF VARIOUS BAKING PANS

Tube Pans:

7½x3-inch "Bundt" tube pan	6 cups
9x3½-inch fancy tube or "Bundt" pan	9 cups
9x3½-inch angel cake pan	12 cups
10x3¾-inch "Bundt" or "Crownburst" pan	12 cups
9x3½-inch fancy tube mold	12 cups
10x4-inch fancy tube mold Kugelhupf	16 cups
10x4-inch angel cake pan	18 cups

Melon Mold:

7x5½x4-inch mold	6 cups

Spring-form Pans:

8x3/inch pan	12 cups
9x3/inch pan	16 cups

Ring Molds:

8½x2¼-inch mold	4½ cups
9¼x2¾-inch mold	8 cups

Charlotte Mold:

6x4¼-inch mold	7½ cups

Brioche Pan:

9½x3¼-inch pan	8 cups

DEEP FAT FRYING TEMPERATURE WITHOUT A THERMOMETER

A 1-inch cube of white bread will turn golden brown:

65 seconds	345 to 355°
60 seconds	355 to 365°
50 seconds	365 to 375°
40 seconds	375 to 385°
20 seconds	385 to 395°

CANDY SYRUP TEMPERATURE WITHOUT A THERMOMETER

Drop ½ teaspoon syrup into fresh cold water:

Thread (230 to 234°)	Spins a soft 3-inch thread
Soft Ball (234 to 240°)	Forms a ball when pressed together but does not hold its shape
Firm Ball (242 to 248°)	Forms a ball that holds its shape
Hard Ball (250 to 268°)	Forms a hard but plastic ball
Soft Crack (270 to 290°)	Forms hard but not brittle thread
Hard Crack (300 to 310°)	Forms hard brittle thread that breaks when pressed

MEASUREMENT WITH METRIC EQUIVALENTS

Measure		Equivalent		Metric (ml)	
1	tablespoon	3	teaspoons	14.8	milliliters
2	tablespoons	1	ounce	29.6	milliliters
1	jigger	1½	ounces	44.4	milliliters
¼	cup	4	tablespoons	59.2	milliliters
⅓	cup	5	tablespoons plus 1 teaspoon	78.9	milliliters
½	cup	8	tablespoons	118.4	milliliters
1	cup	16	tablespoons	236.8	milliliters
1	pint	2	cups	473.6	milliliters
1	quart	4	cups	947.2	milliliters
1	liter	4	cups plus 3⅓ tablespoons	1,000.0	milliliters
1	ounce (dry)	2	tablespoons	28.35	grams
1	pound	16	ounces	453.59	grams
2.21	pounds	35.3	ounces	1.00	kilogram

When the recipe calls for:	**You can use:**
1 tablespoon cornstarch	2 tablespoons flour (for thickening)
1 egg	3 tablespoons liquid imitation egg
1 cup milk	1 cup skim milk plus 2 tablespoons unsalted margarine *or* ½ cup evaporated milk plus ½ cup water
1 ounce unsweetened chocolate	3 tablespoons cocoa plus 1 tablespoon unsalted margarine
1 teaspoon baking powder	½ teaspoon cream of tartar plus ¼ teaspoon baking soda
1 cup cake flour	⅞ cup all-purpose flour (⅞ cup is 1 cup less 2 tablespoons)
½ cup unsalted margarine (1 stick)	7 tablespoons vegetable shortening
1 cup buttermilk	1 tablespoon white vinegar plus milk to equal 1 cup
1 clove garlic	1 teaspoon garlic salt *or* ⅛ teaspoon garlic powder
2 teaspoons minced onion	1 teaspoon onion powder
1 tablespoon finely chopped chives	1 teaspoon freeze-dried chives

| 1 teaspoon herb leaves | 1 tablespoon chopped fresh herbs |
| 1 cup dairy sour cream | 1 tablespoon lemon juice plus evaporated milk to equal 1 cup |

When the recipe calls for:	**You start with:**
5½ cups cooked fine noodles	8-ounce package fine noodles
4 cups sliced potatoes	4 medium potatoes
2½ cups sliced carrots	1 pound carrots
4 cups shredded cabbage	1 small cabbage (1 pound)
1 teaspoon grated lemon peel	1 medium lemon
2 tablespoons lemon juice	1 medium lemon
4 teaspoons grated orange peel	1 medium orange
4 cups sliced apples	4 medium apples
2 cups shredded Swiss or Cheddar cheese	8-ounce piece Swiss or Cheddar cheese
1 cup soft bread crumbs	2 slices fresh bread
1 cup egg whites	6 or 7 large eggs
1 cup egg yolks	11 or 12 large eggs
4 cups chopped walnuts or pecans	1 pound shelled walnuts or pecans

17.High Altitude Cooking

HIGH ALTITUDE requires some changes in cooking and baking. One of the first changes you will notice is the lower boiling point of water. At sea level, water boils at 212° F. But at 5000 feet it boils at 202° F; at 7500 feet, 198° F; and at 10,000 feet, 194° F. As the altitude increases, the air pressure decreases. Water will boil more quickly but will not be as hot as it would be at sea level, so the stew will have to simmer longer. Also the rate of evaporation is faster, so liquids may have to be added to foods during cooking. This rapid evaporation will cause sugar solutions to become concentrated sooner than at sea level, so watch the cooking closely to avoid scorching. Flour will dry out faster, so you may need to use less. The lighter air will allow bread doughs and cake batters to expand more and faster, and it may be necessary to reduce baking powder or soda, and sometimes to use larger baking pans.

Most high altitude adjustments are not necessary below 3500 feet, but minor recipe adjustment may be needed as low as 2500 to 3000 feet.

Much of your high altitude cooking, at least initially, will involve experimenting. Try your favorite sea level recipe once before deciding to make high altitude adjustments. Keep a record of problems and solutions. Experience and experiments will make you more adept at high altitude cooking. Make your own charts, and your record of foods, times, temperatures, and baking methods will give you the adjustments needed at your specific altitude.

The local utility company and agricultural extension office in your state can give you help for your particular altitude. Also your experienced friends and neighbors will give you help.

Range-top cooking will require careful attention to prevent scorching and sticking. It is best to use heavy saucepans, such as cast iron or cast aluminum. Tight-fitting covers will help to retain steam when cooking foods in water.

Batters and doughs expand more when they bake, so use larger baking pans or more of them. When a recipe calls for two 8-inch pans at sea level, use two 9-inch or three 8-inch pans. A 9x5x3-inch loaf pan will give better results than a 8½x4½x2½-inch loaf pan. When a 15½x10½x1-inch jelly roll pan is designated in a cake or bar cookie recipe, substitute two 9-inch square pans.

Cakes cause more problems than any other basic baking at high altitudes. Here are some guidelines that will help:

1. Grease and flour pans generously, since cakes have a greater tendency to stick at high altitude. Use at least 1 tablespoon shortening per pan.

2. Increase oven temperature 25° F.

3. Decrease sugar by 2 to 4 tablespoons. For 1 cup sugar at 3500 to 5000 feet, decrease it by 1½ to 2½ tablespoons; at 5000 to 6500 feet, decrease it by 2½ to 3 tablespoons; at 6500 to 8000 feet, decrease it by 3 to 3½ tablespoons.

4. Decrease baking powder. For every 1 teaspoon baking powder at 3500 to 5000 feet, decrease it by ¼ to ½ teaspoon; at 5000 to 6500 feet, decrease it by ½ to ¾ teaspoon; at 6500 to 8000 feet, decrease it by ½ to ¾ teaspoon.

5. Increase liquid by 2 to 4 tablespoons. If buttermilk or sour cream is used, do not increase liquid, as these ingredients have great moisture holding ability.

6. Increase flour by 2 to 4 tablespoons.

Angel food cake is tricky to make at high altitude. We recommend that you use a mix for this cake and follow the high altitude directions on the package, because it has already been tested.

Cookies usually require no adjustment. If problems occur, correct them by reducing baking powder and sugar slightly. For rich cookies, increase flour by 1 tablespoon for each cup required at sea level and increase liquid by ½ tablespoon for each additional one tablespoon flour. Drop cookies are sometimes heavy in texture. To correct this, increase oven temperature by 25° F. and bake the designated time. Cookies that contain only soda for leavening and spread excessively during baking, decrease the amount of soda by at least one half. Keep cookies in an airtight container.

Quick breads have a sturdy structure and require no adjustment. Reduced air pressure offers less resistance to expanding gases in the batters or doughs, so you may want to try reducing the amount of baking powder slightly to slow the expansion.

Muffins: Do not reduce the amount of soda. If necessary, reduce the liquid and flour by 1 to 2 tablespoons.

Biscuits: No adjustments are usually necessary. If dough seems dry, stir in small amount of liquid.

Pancakes: Cook until tops are dry and bottoms are brown, then turn.

Yeast breads can be favorites for baking at high altitude. Reduced air pressure causes the yeast gases to expand faster, so the time needed for dough to rise is shortened and other adjustments are minimal. Use the minimum amount of flour the recipe calls for, since the flour may be dry. If the recipe gives only one measurement of flour, use ½ cup per loaf less than recipe calls for. Check the dough 15 to 30 minutes before recommended sea level time for rising until double.

Desserts usually need no adjustment. For crisps and cobblers at 8000 feet, it may be necessary to precook fruit until just tender to increase doneness. Always use a heavy saucepan for the preparation of custards, cooked rice for rice pudding.

Coffee and tea require a longer brewing time. Set automtic coffee maker for medium to strong coffee. Use rapidly boiling water to make tea. Brew large amounts of coffee and instant tea in range-top percolator, rather than individual cups, since boiling water poured into cups does not generate enough heat to dissolve crystals and release flavor.

Candies and cooked frosting mixture will become concentrated quicker because of the faster evaporation, so watch the cooking time closely to prevent scorching and reduce the recipe temperature by 2° F. for every 1000 feet of elevation.

Rice, pasta, and dried peas or beans should be cooked before adding to casseroles. To cook rice, increase the cooking time and the amount of water. Add 1 tablespoon oil per cup of rice to prevent sticking and boiling over. For pasta, heat water to boiling, then add salt and 1 teaspoon oil per cup of pasta to prevent sticking and boiling over.

Fresh vegetables should be cut into small pieces or cooked before adding to main dishes. It will take longer to cook fresh and frozen veg-etables. At 5000 feet it is not uncommon to have a 50 percent increase in cooking time. Increase the liquid to prevent scorching and add the salt at serving time. Use a pressure cooker to shorten cooking time and follow manufacturer's high-altitude directions.

Meats, poultry, and fish may require a longer cooking time, and it is important to baste meat and poultry frequently. For soups and stews, the liquids and the simmering time may have to be increased.

Pastry may not need an adjustment. If pastry is too dry, increase liquid, 1 teaspoon at a time, until all flour is moistened and pastry almost cleans side of bowl.

18.Glossary of Cooking Terms

TERMS YOU SHOULD KNOW
FOR PREPARING INGREDIENTS

Chop: Cut into pieces with a knife or other sharp tool (hold end of knife tip on board with one hand; move the blade up and down with the other).

Cube: Cut into cubes ½ inch or larger.

Dice: Cut into small cubes less than ½ inch.

Grate: Cut into tiny particles using small holes of grater (lemon peel).

Pare: Cut off outer covering with a knife or other sharp tool (potatoes, apples).

Peel: Strip off outer covering (oranges).

Shred: Cut into thin pieces using large holes on grater or shredder (cheese).

Snip: Cut into very small pieces with a scissors (parsley, chives).

FOR COMBINING INGREDIENTS

Beat: Make mixture smooth by a vigorous over-and-over motion with a spoon, whip or rotary beater.

Blend: Thoroughly combine all ingredients until very smooth and uniform.

Cut in: Distribute shortening in dry ingredients by chopping with knives or pastry blender.

Fold: Combine ingredients lightly by a combination of motions: one motion cuts vertically through mixture, the other slides the spatula or wire whisk across the bottom of the bowl and up the side, turning over (soufflés).

Stir: Combine ingredients with circular or figure-8 motion until of uniform consistency.

Toss: Tumble ingredients lightly with a lifting motion (salads).

FOR COOKING

Brown: Cook until food changes color, usually in small amount of fat over medium heat (meat).

Cook and stir: Cook in small amount of shortening, stirring occasionally, until tender and brown (onion, ground beef).

Simmer: Cook in liquid just below the boiling point. Bubbles form slowly and collapse below the surface.

Boil: Heat until bubbles rise continuously and break on surface of liquid.

OTHER TERMS

Cool: Allow to come to room temperature.

Refrigerate: To store or chill.

Marinate: Let food stand in liquid that will add flavor or tenderize.

Baste: Spoon a flavoring ingredient on food during cooking period.

Toast: Brown in oven or toaster (bread).

Part Three:
Appendices

1.Nutritive Value of Food Groups

Food Group	Sodium mEq (mg)		Calories (kCal)
	Unsalted	Salted	
Meat (and meat substitutes)	3 (70)	9 (207)†	200
Milk (and dairy products)	5 (115)	-	70-150
Bread (and starchy foods)			
I	1 (23)	-	70
II	5 (115)	-	70
III	10 (230)	-	70
Vegetables	1 (23)	12 (275)‡	25
Fruits	trace	-	40
Fats	trace	2 (46)	45
Carbohydrate Supplements	trace	-	varies

† moderately salted during preparation (¼ teaspoon salt per pound of meat)
‡ moderately salted during preparation or processing (⅛ teaspoon salt per serving)

2.Conversion Tables

PLEASE NOTE that as a matter of policy this cookbook does not provide a table for the conversion of conventional recipes to metrical ones. It is the consensus of food editors at this time that such tables are at best misleading, since the kitchenwares industry has not yet provided standard utensils to implement the changeover—a process that in fact is now expected to take many years. Meanwhile the preparation of metrical recipes in nonmetrical utensils is so complex and so chancy that home economists as a class do not advise it. The recipes in this cookbook therefore employ conventional U.S. measurements.

BRITISH CONVERSION TABLE

Ingredient	American	British
Baking powder	1 teaspoon	1½ teaspoons
Margarine	1 cup	8 ounces
Cheese (cheddar)	1 cup shredded	4 ounces
Chocolate	1 square	1 ounce
Chocolate chips	1 cup	6 ounces
Flour	1 cup	4½ ounces
Molasses or syrup	1 cup	8 fluid ounces
Rice	1 cup	6¼ ounces
Sugar, granulated or brown	1 cup	7 ounces
Sugar, powdered	1 cup	4½ ounces
Walnuts	1 cup	4 ounces
Yeast (dry)	1 packet	¼ ounce

Liquid Measurements

American Cups	Fluid ounces	British Tablespoons
2 tablespoons	1 ounce	1¾
¼ cup	2 ounces	3¼
⅓ cup	2¾ ounces	4¼
½ cup	4 ounces	6½
⅔ cup	5½ ounces	9
¾ cup	6¼ ounces	10
1 cup	8 ounces	13

Temperature Conversion Table

Temperature ° Centigrade equals 5/9 (temperature ° Farenheit minus 32)

Temperature ° Farenheit equals 9/5 (temperature ° Centigrade plus 32)

3. How to Make Up a Meal Plan from the Foods & Recipes in This Book

THE NUTRIENT values for food are given for each food group on page 228. The nutrient value of all recipes contained in this book are given in two ways. First, the exact value of the controlled nutrients is given in Appendix 8. Second, each recipe has been calculated to fit into the established food groups which form the basis of your nutritional program. This information is given at the bottom of each recipe and also in Appendix 8. When you are planning your daily menus, unless specifically instructed by your dietitian to use the exact figures for specific foods*, use the food groups in the following manner to quickly calculate amount of sodium and calories in your total menu.

The sample menu on the following page can serve as a guide to you.

*Exact figures for specific foods are given in *Agricultural Handbook #8: Composition of Foods* (see Appendix 4, page 233).

MENU FOR DAILY MEAL PLAN CONTAINING 90 mEq SODIUM. 1500 CALORIES

RECIPE OR FOOD	AMOUNT	Meat	Milk I	Milk II	Bread I	Bread II	Bread III	Vegetable	Fruit	Fat	Caloric Supplement	Calories
BREAKFAST												
Grapefruit	½ medium								1			40
Poached Egg	1	1										75
Toast†	1 slice					1						70
Margarine†	1 teaspoon									1		45
Cornflakes	¾ cup						1					70
Milk	½ cup		½									70
Sugar	2 teaspoons										2	40
Coffee												40
LUNCH												
Sandwich:												
Bread†	2 slices					2						140
Roast Beef†	3 ounces	1†										200
Lettuce and Tomato	½ cup							1				25
Margarine†	1 teaspoon									1†		45
Apple	1 large								2			80
Skim milk	1 cup		1									70
DINNER												
Broiled White Fish*	1 serving	1										200
Sweet Potato	1 small					1						70
*Lemon Sesame Asparagus	1 serving							1				40
Margarine†	2 teaspoons									2		90
*Mixed Green Salad with Lemon Dressing	1 serving							1				85
*Frosted Fruit	1 serving								1			50
Sanka	1 cup											
TOTAL		3	1½	0	0	4	1	3	4	4		1505

Add ¼ teaspoon of salt to this menu to equal 90 in Eq Sodium.

*Denotes recipes from this cookbook.

†Salted

To calculate the sodium in your meal plan, now take the total figure from each column and multiply it by the figure given for that group in Appendix 1. For example, using the menu given, the total intake of sodium for the day would be:

Food Group	Number of Servings	times	mEq of Sodium per serving	= Total
Meat or substitute	2†	X	9	= 18.0 mEq
Egg or substitute	1	X	3	= 3.0 mEq
Milk or substitute	1½	X	5	= 7.5 mEq
Bread or substitute	4 Group II	X	5	= 20.0 mEq
	1 Group III	X	10	= 10.0 mEq
Vegetable	3	X	1	= 3.0 mEq
Fruit	4	X	0	= 0 mEq
Fats	4†	X	2	= 8.0 mEq
¼ teaspoon salt				= 22.0 mEq
				91.5 mEq

† Salted

If planning menus seems a bit complicated at first, don't get discouraged. Calculating your daily intake will get much easier in a week or two. If you find your total sodium too high or too low, a quick look at your chart will tell you where you must add or subtract to arrive at the correct figure. You will find it easiest to use your main dish terms as a basis for menu planning. Then you can fill in the menu with accompanying dishes and dessert. These dishes are easier to adjust to fit into your meal plan. Don't forget to add up your calories if your physician has instructed you to control your caloric intake.

4. How to Calculate the Nutritive Value of Recipes Not Found in This Book

IF YOU have a favorite food or recipe that you would like to eat, but the nutrient value has not been given in this book, you may obtain the information from one of the following sources:

1. *Agricultural Handbook #8: Composition of Foods*
   Superintendent of Documents
   U.S. Government Printing Office
   Washington, D.C. 20402

2. *Food Values of Foods Commonly Used* (by Bowes and Church)
   J. B. Lippincott Company
   Philadelphia, Pennsylvania 19100

3. *The Dictionary of Sodium, Fat, and Cholesterol* (by Barbara Kraus)
   Grosset and Dunlap
   New York, N.Y. 10000

If you consult these sources, you will be using the exact figures for the foods making up a particular recipe. The sodium values are often given in milligrams. Just add up the sodium values for each food item and divide the total by the number of servings that the recipe makes. This number is then divided by 23 to determine the milliequivalents for one serving.

If the data is given for a 100-gram portion keep in mind that 30 grams equals 1 ounce and calculate the sodium content in this way.

A	B	C	D	E
Nutrient value for a specific item per 100 grams	÷ 100 grams =	nutrient value for 1 gram	X gram weight of portion desired	= nutrient value for portion desired

For example: you want chocolate-coated graham crackers that weigh 15 grams (½ ounce). You calculate it like this:

	A		B		C		D		E
Sodium	407 mg	÷	100	=	4.07 times		15	=	61.05
	61.05 mg	÷	23	=	2.6 mEq of Sodium				
Calories	475	÷	100	=	4.75 times		15	=	71 Calories

If you have a favorite recipe, you follow the same procedure for each ingredient. Then add up your nutrient values for each item for the overall value of the recipe. Divide this number by the number of portions or cups specified for the recipe to arrive at the exact sodium and caloric value of one serving.

5. How to Modify the Amount of Sodium in Your Dietary Program

IF YOUR physician directs you to increase or decrease the amount of sodium in your diet, you may do this in one of two ways:

1. You may use more or less table salt.
2. You may eat foods already salted in preparation or you can eat unsalted foods.

Addition or subtraction of table salt
⅛ teaspoon = 11 mEq sodium
¼ teaspoon = 22 mEq sodium
½ teaspoon = 44 mEq sodium
¾ teaspoon = 66 mEq sodium
 1 teaspoon = 88 mEq sodium

Addition or subtraction of foods moderately salted in preparation:
Meat salted in preparation adds 2 mEq per ounce.
Salted vegetables add 11 mEq sodium per serving.
Salted margarine adds 2 mEq per serving.

When using this method, be sure to add up the totals from your food group again for the entire day to make sure you are at the proper level of sodium intake.

6. Eating Away From Home

JUST BECAUSE you need to control your food intake, there is no reason that you cannot eat out. Once you know your nutritional program well, you can pick out foods that you can eat from almost any menu. In some cases, you may not be able to eat the whole portion but be brave, leave some on your plate and ask for a "doggie bag." The chef's feelings may be hurt, but you will feel better! If it is a special occasion, go easy at breakfast and lunch and save a little extra for dinner. We don't recommend that you make this a regular practice but weddings, holidays, anniversaries and birthdays come into the special occasion category.

You will find that if you ask, most restaurants will prepare your food without salt if necessary when you order simple foods such as omelets, steak, lamb chops, fresh fish or pork chops. Ask for oil and vinegar for your salad dressing. Baked potatoes are not salted and ask for unsalted margarine if that is necessary. Have fruit juice or fruit cocktail for an appetizer and fruit ice, sherbet, or fresh fruit for dessert. Remember to plan ahead so that you save a little extra sodium during the day for that something special that catches your eyes.

Here are some menu ideas to help you when you are traveling or having a meal away from home. Keep in mind your menu plan and the portion size given for a serving of each particular food.

BREAKFAST:

Fresh fruit or juice
Melon
Orange Juice
Grapefruit half
Sliced banana
Fruit cup
Prunes
Prune juice
Apple juice
Cranberry juice
Apricot nectar

Cereal or Bread
Shredded wheat
Puffed wheat
Puffed rice
Cooked cereal

If you are allowed a salted bread serving, you may choose any cereal, toast, a doughnut, danish pastry, etc. If not, better stick with unsalted cereals.

Milk
Order skim milk. You can split a milk serving and use half at breakfast and half later in the day.

Egg
Soft cooked egg
Hard cooked egg
Poached egg
Plain omelet
Scrambled egg

Remember—only 2 fresh eggs a week. If possible order an egg substitute. Be sure to specify to cook your egg without salt and in cooking oil if your menu plan calls for unsalted egg.

LUNCH OR SUPPER:

Appetizer
Juice
Fruit cocktail
Grapefruit half

Melon

Avoid soups. They are usually very high in sodium.

Main Dish
Roast beef
Sliced chicken, turkey
Small steak
Hamburger
Fruit salad
Chef's salad with chicken, turkey,
   beef (no ham or cheese).

Salad or Vegetable
Lettuce and tomato
Tossed green
Sliced tomato
Heart of lettuce
Lettuce wedge

Use oil and vinegar dressing. Avoid cooked vegetables unless your meal plan permits it, since they are very high in sodium.

Dessert
Fresh fruit
Fruit compote
Sherbet
Fruit ice
Fruit pie

DINNER:

Appetizer
Fresh fruit cup
Melon
Grapefruit sections

Avoid soups, marinated fish, seafood cocktails, tomato juice, vegetable juice.

Entree
Steak
Center cut of roast
Lamb chops
Turkey
Chopped steak

Fresh fish
Breast of chicken
Pork chop

Remember your portion size and specify cooked without salt if your menu plan calls for unsalted meat. Avoid foods cooked in sauces, casseroles and fried foods.

Vegetables
Vegetables are usually pre-cooked and pre-salted, so unless you are permitted salted vegetables, better avoid them when you are out.

Potato
Order baked potato, most of the others are pre-salted.

Salad
Lettuce hearts
Sliced tomato
Tossed green
Lettuce and tomato
Fruit salad (check to find out what dressing is used)

Oil and vinegar dressing.

Bread
Unless your meal plan specifies unsalted bread, you can have any bread or roll except salted bread sticks or rolls with salted tops. If your meal plan specifies unsalted bread, better skip the bread.

Dessert
Stewed fruit
Fruit ice
Sherbet
Fresh fruit
Fruit cup
Baked apple
Fruit compote
Angel food cake
Check the appropriate food group portion size.

Beverage
Coffee, tea, Sanka, soft drinks, fruit juice, if your meal plan permits.

In this diet-conscious age we live in, restaurants are accustomed to requests for special dietary items so don't be reluctant to ask. Even fast service hamburger restaurants will prepare french fries and hamburgers without salt if you ask. You probably are not the first to make such a request nor likely to be the last! Also, many restaurants will prepare special items for you if you give them a little advance warning. When you are making a reservation, you might mention that you would like to order something that may not be on the menu such as unsalted vegetables or unsalted margarine. They probably will be delighted to accommodate you.

If you frequent a particular restaurant, most likely they will be glad to keep certain items on hand for you if you bring them in, such as unsalted margarine, salad dressings, or fruit ice.

Eating at the home of a friend

Being invited to dinner at the home of a friend need not pose a problem if you tell your hostess in advance that you have a medical problem and are on a special diet. This will save embarrassment for you and for her because she can plan the menu accordingly. It will alleviate the problem of being urged to eat "just a little more" and she will understand if you pass up a dish or don't finish everything on your plate. Ask if you can bring along your own margarine or other items. Think ahead—eat less during the day and save your sodium for the evening meal.

There is no reason to feel ill-at-ease about being on a controlled dietary regime. No one is going to think any less of you because of it, in fact most people will be very happy to help you.

Eating on airplanes

Most airlines offer a variety of meals to meet special medical, religious, or other dietary specifications. All that they ask is that you notify their reservations personnel at least twenty-four hours in advance of your flight so that proper preparation can be made. The special meals are boarded with the rest of the food supplies. Just remind the flight attendant or the gate agent upon check-in that you have ordered a special meal.

7. Names & Addresses of Companies Supplying Special Dietary Products

COMPANY	FOOD PRODUCTS
Adolph's, Ltd. 1800 W. Magnolia Blvd. Burbank, Ca. 91503	Sugar and salt substitutes, seasoned salt substitute, low sodium and low calorie dressing.
Amurol Naperville, Il. 60540	Cookies, candies, gum.
Anderson Clayton Foods P. O. Box 35 Dallas, Tex. 75221	Chiffon margarine (regular and salt-free).
Avoset Foods 80 Grand Avenue Oakland, Ca. 94612	Second Nature Imitation Eggs®
Bernard Food Industries, Inc. 1125 Hartrey Avenue P. O. Box 1497 Evanston, Il. 60204	Low-sodium soups and condiments
Best Foods Division of CPC International, Inc. International Plaza Englewood, Cliffs, N. J. 07632	Low-sodium and cholesterol foods, salt-free margarine
Best of Fish & Seafood Dietetic Dept. Los Angeles, Ca. 90021	Tuna

Breads for Life
P. O. Box 3434
Springfield, Mo. 65804

Sugar-free bread

California Canners & Growers
312 Stockton Avenue
San Jose, Ca. 95126

Low sodium canned vegetables (Diet Delight)

Campbell Soup Company
Campbell Place
Camden, N.J. 08101

Low sodium soups

Chicago Dietetic Supply
405 East Shawmut Avenue
LaGrange, Il. 60525

Low sodium and low cholesterol products (including baking powder). Featherweight and Cellu Products

Chico San
1144 W. First Street
Chico, Ca. 95926

Low sodium rice, millet, buckwheat cakes

Clayco Foods, Inc.
1775 Broadway
New York, N.Y. 10019

Low sodium soups

Corn Products Co.
717 5th Avenue
New York, N.Y. 10022

Corn oil - Mazola

Devonsheer
Melba Corporation
Carlstadt, N.J. 07072

Low sodium melba toast, rye and plain

Diamond Crystal Salt Company
10 Burlington Avenue
Wilmington, Mass. 01887

Sugar and salt substitutes

Edgemar Farms, Inc.
346 Rose Avenue
Venice, Ca. 90291

Low sodium milk and cottage cheese

Ener-G Foods, Inc.
1526 Utah Avenue, South
Seattle, Wash. 98134

Jolly Jean Products, low sodium mixes, low cholesterol egg substitutes

Estee
135 W. Central Blvd.
Palisades Park, N.J. 07650

Low sodium cookies

Fearn Soyo Foods
Richard Foods Co.
Melrose Park, Il. 60616

Low sodium products

Fisher Cheese Co.
Box 409
Wapakoneta, Oh. 45895

Low sodium, low cholesterol cheese

Flavor Tree Foods, Inc.
Franklin Park, Il. 60131

Unsalted soynuts

Geoghegan
8835 S. Greenwood Ave.
Chicago, Il. 60619

Low sodium products

General Foods, Inc.
250 "N" Street
White Plains, N.Y. 10600

Low sodium products D-Zerta pudding

Hain Pure Food Co.
Los Angeles, Ca. 90061

Low cholesterol margarine and mayonnaise

Health Valley Natural Foods
670 Mesquite
Los Angeles, Ca. 90021

Unsalted potato chips

Holgrain
Golden Grain
Seattle Wash. 98103

Low sodium rice and wheat wafers

Hunt Wesson Foods, Inc.
1645 W. Valencia Drive
Fullerton, Ca. 92634

Corn oil

Jays Foods, Inc.
825 E. 99th Street
Chicago, Il. 60628

Corn oil

Keebler Company
One Hollow Tree Lane
Elmhurst, Il. 60126

Low sodium crackers

Kellogg Company
Department of Home Economics
   Services
235 Porter Street
Battle Creek, Mich. 49016

Low sodium cereals

Knox Gelatin
Johnstown, N.Y. 12095

Low sodium and low cholesterol products

Kraft Foods
Institutional Department
500 Peshtigo
Chicago, Il. 60690

Parkay margarine, corn oil, Crisco oil

Loma Linda Company

Soyagen, jellos, gluten meats, gravy mixes

Low-Sodium Dairy Products Corporation
346 Rose Avenue
Venice, Ca. 90291

Milk

Milani Foods, Inc.
12312 W. Olympic Blvd.
Los Angeles, Ca. 90064

Soups, puddings, salad dressings, low calorie, low sodium

Miles Laboratories, Inc.,
Grocery Products Division,
Chicago, Illinois 60638

Low cholesterol egg substitute

Mitchel Foods, Inc.
Fredonia, N.Y. 14063

"Poly Perx" (cream substitute)

Morton Salt Company
110 North Wacker Drive
Chicago, Il. 60606

Salt substitutes

National Biscuit Company
425 Park Avenue
New York, N.Y. 10022

Low sodium crackers and cereal

Presto Food Products, Inc.
P. O. Box 21908
Los Angeles, Ca. 90021

Mocha Mix (cream substitute)

Quaker Oats Co.
Merchandise Mart Place
Chicago, Il. 60654

Low sodium cereal

S and W Fine Foods
San Mateo, Ca. 94402

Salt free vegetables

Savage Laboratories, Inc.
P.O. Box 700
Bellaire, Tex. 77401

Dia-Sal Salt substitute

Seabrook Farms Co., Inc.
Seabrook, N.J. 08302

Low sodium entrees

John Sexton Company
222 S. Riverside Plaza
Chicago, Il. 60606

Low sodium soups

Standard Brands
625 Madison Avenue
New York, N.Y. 10022

Salt free margarine, low cholesterol
egg substitute

Sun-O-Morn, Inc.
P. O. Box 331
Hales Corners, Wis. 53130

Low cholesterol egg

Tillie Lewis
Drawer J
Stockton, Ca. 95201

Low sodium vegetables and dressings

USV Pharmaceutical Corp.
1 Scarsdale Road
Tuckahoe, N.Y. 10707

"Co-Salt" salt substitute

Van Brode Milling Co.
Clinton, Mass. 01510

Low sodium prepared cereals

Webster-Van Winkle Corp.
5 Lafayette Avenue
Summit, N.J. 07901

Low sodium products

Winthrop Laboratories
90 Park Avenue
New York, N.Y. 10016

"Neocurtasol" salt substitute

Wylers Foods
Borden, Inc.
Chicago, Il. 60618

Low sodium bouillon

8.Nutritive Value Charts

Common Foods Not Found in This Book

FOOD	AMOUNT	SODIUM		CALORIES
		mEq	mg	kcal
Bacon	1 strip	2.2	51	30
Baking Powder	1 tsp	14.3	239	5
Baking Soda	1 tsp	59.1	1360	0
Beer	12 oz	1.1	25	150
Biscuits, baking powder	1 2-in. biscuit	9.5	219	130
Bouillon	1 cup	34.0	782	30
Buttermilk	1 cup	13.6	312	85
Cake, commercial, angel food	1 piece	2.9	66	115
Cake, commercial, chocolate frosted	1 piece	5.7	131	170
Cake, commercial, white frosted	1 piece	4.9	113	175
Cake, homemade, angel food	1 piece	5.5	127	120
Cake, homemade, chocolate, frosted	1 piece	5.1	117	185
Cake, homemade, plain, frosted	1 piece	4.9	115	185
Canned Meat	1 oz	16.1	370	88
Canned soup— chicken noodle	1 cup	42.5	979	62
Canned soup—split pea	1 cup	40.0	922	142
Canned soup— vegetable beef	1 cup	44.6	1025	77
Canned spaghetti	1 cup	41.5	955	190
Catsup	1 tbsp	6.8	156	16

FOOD	AMOUNT	SODIUM		CALORIES
		mEq	mg	kcal
Cheese—American	1 oz	9.1	210	119
Brick	1 oz	9.1	210	111
Camembert, domestic	1 oz	9.1	210	89
Cream cheese, natural	1 oz	3.3	75	112
Limburger	1 oz	9.3	213	103
Low-sodium (Cheezola)	1 oz	7.2	165	90
Parmesan	1 oz	9.6	220	118
Pasturized processed:				
American cheese	1 oz	14.8	341	111
Cheese spread	1 oz	21.2	488	86
Roquefort	1 oz	9.1	210	110
Swiss	1 oz	9.3	213	111
Chocolate candy bar, plain	1 bar	1.4	33	182
Chocolate cream candy	1 piece	0.4	9	21
Chow Mein, homemade	½ cup	12.5	287	102
Chow Mein, canned	½ cup	12.6	290	38
Cocoa, mixes	1 tbsp	1.6	38	39
Coconut, dried	2 tbsp	0.1	3	99
Cold cuts	1 oz	17.0	390	91
Cookie, commercial, misc.	1 cookie	2.6	60	71
Cookies, homemade, chocolate chip	1 cookie	3.0	70	103
Cookies, homemade, sugar	1 cookie	1.4	32	44
Crab, canned regular	¼ cup	17.4	400	40
Crackers—Graham	2	4.1	94	54
Saltine	5	7.2	165	65
Soda	2	6.7	154	62
Doughnut	1	7.6	175	137
Dried Beef	1 oz	56.1	1290	60
Fish sticks	1 oz	2.3	53	52
Frankfurters	1	23.9	550	155
French fries, salted	½ cup	12.0	276	233
Ham	1 oz	14.3	330	60
Heinz 57 sauce	1 tbsp	12.3	284	15
Jello	½ cup	2.6	61	71
Lobster, regular, canned	1 oz	2.7	63	28
Mustard, regular, prepared	1 tbsp	8.2	188	11
Olives	3	21.4	493	50
Pancakes	1 4-in. pancake	8.3	191	104
Peanut butter	2 tbsp	8.0	182	175
Pickle, dill, large	1	31.0	714	5

FOOD	AMOUNT	SODIUM		CALORIES
		mEq	mg	kcal
Pickle, sweet, chip	1	3.1	71	1
Pickle relish	2 tsp	5.9	135	1
Pie, fruit	⅛ of pie	19.6	452	385
Pizza, commercial	1 piece	28.1	647	245
Pizza, homemade	1 piece	31.7	729	234
Potato chips	1 oz	4.4	102	170
Pot pie, beef	1	44.5	1024	448
Pot pie, turkey	1	38.1	876	423
Pot pie, chicken	1	38.1	876	510
Pretzels, small	5	11.0	252	58
Pudding, homemade, chocolate	½ cup	3.0	67	178
Pudding, homemade, vanilla	½ cup	3.4	78	133
Pudding, commercial, chocolate	½ cup	6.7	155	150
Pudding, commercial, vanilla	½ cup	5.2	119	160
Salad dressing, French	1 tbsp	9.0	205	61
Salad dressing, Roquefort	1 tbsp	7.1	164	76
Salad dressing, 1000 island	1 tbsp	4.6	105	75
Salad dressing, Italian	1 tbsp	13.6	314	83
Salmon, regular, canned	1 oz	7.0	157	51
Sardines, canned	1 oz	10.7	247	61
Sauerkraut	½ cup	24.4	560	14
Sausage	1 oz	12.5	287	104
Soy sauce	1 tbsp	47.7	1099	10
Sweet roll	1	8.5	195	158
Tomato juice, regular, canned	½ cup	10.4	240	23
Tomato paste	½ cup	2.1	50	106
Tuna, regular, canned in oil	1 oz	10.4	240	60
TV dinner—Beef	1	34.9	820	347
Ham	1	51.2	1177	307
Pork	1	30.9	712	416
Meat loaf	1	53.1	1221.4	366
Swiss steak	1	46.7	1075	250
Chicken	1	47.1	1083	548
Fish	1	57.4	1319	326
V-8 juice	½ cup	10.4	240	20
Waffle, homemade	1 4-in. section	13.4	309	181
Worcestershire sauce	1 tbsp	10.9	250	12

The recipe for Lemon Meringue Pie is on page 187.

The recipes for Christmas cakes and cookies are in Chapter 13.

Nutritive Value of Recipes:1

RECIPES		Sodium mEq/mg	Food Energy Calories	Potas-sium mEq	Choles-terol mg	Total Fat gm	Food Group Per Serving
Angel Food Cake Supreme	16 servings	47.22/1086.10	1937.0	23.90	0.0	1.0	½ Bread II
	1 serving	2.95/67.88	121.1	1.49	0.0	0.1	
Apple Crisp	6 servings	2.18/50.11	1813.1	33.99	0.0	12.9	½ Bread I
	1 serving	0.36/8.35	302.2	5.66	0.0	2.1	1 Fruit
Apple Dumplings	6 servings	6.34/145.86	4488.2	72.43	0.0	34.3	1 Bread I
	1 serving	1.06/24.31	748.0	12.07	0.0	5.7	1 Fruit
Apple Muffins	12 servings	7.96/183.04	2371.6	59.19	2.4	90.5	Small Muffin =
	1 serving	0.66/15.25	197.6	4.93	0.2	7.5	1 Bread I
Apple Omelet	2 servings	16.02/368.42	374.0	2.86	0.0	10.2	2½ Meat
	1 serving	8.01/184.21	187.0	1.43	0.0	5.1	¼ Fruit
Apple Pie (8-inch Pie)	6 servings	0.57/13.08	3241.5	25.95	0.0	21.7	1/6 of Pie =
	1 serving	0.09/2.18	540.3	4.33	0.0	3.6	1 Fruit
Apple Pie (9-inch Pie)	8 servings	0.66/15.14	3647.9	29.92	0.0	23.8	1/8 of Pie =
	1 serving	0.08/1.89	456.0	3.74	0.0	3.0	1 Fruit
Apple Pork Chop Roast	6 servings	15.47/355.79	1807.5	64.30	475.2	109.3	1 Meat
	1 serving	2.58/59.30	301.3	10.72	79.2	18.2	
Apple Raisin Stuffing (with Low-Sodium Bread)	18 servings	11.81/271.67	3356.8	65.37	10.5	34.4	1 Bread I 3 Fat
	1 serving	0.66/15.09	186.5	3.63	0.6	1.9	½ Fruit

Nutritive Value of Recipes:2

RECIPES		Sodium mEq/mg	Food Energy Calories	Potassium mEq	Cholesterol mg	Total Fat gm	Food Group Per Serving
Apple Raisin Stuffing (with Regular Bread)	18 servings	84.70/1948.17	3356.8	65.37	10.5	34.4	1 Bread II 3 Fat
	1 serving	4.71/108.23	186.5	3.63	0.6	1.9	½ Fruit
Apple Soufflé	1 serving	2.05/47.26	106.8	2.77	0.0	0.1	¾ Meat 1 Fruit
Apple Tapioca	4 servings	3.04/69.83	1459.7	33.69	0.0	4.1	1 Fruit
	1 serving	0.76/17.46	364.9	8.42	0.0	1.0	
Applesauce Toast	8 servings	0.34/7.89	1011.7	8.65	0.0	9.9	1 Bread I
	1 serving	0.04/0.99	126.5	1.08	0.0	1.2	
Apricot Sherbet	4 servings	2.38/54.66	1306.8	51.94	0.0	1.4	1 Fruit
	1 serving	0.59/13.66	326.7	12.98	0.0	0.3	
Artichokes	1 serving	1.30/30.00	26.0	7.72	0.0	0.2	1 Vegetable
Asparagus	1 serving	0.04/1.00	20.0	4.69	0.0	0.2	1 Vegetable
Asparagus Salad	1 serving	0.23/5.38	239.1	13.80	0.0	20.5	1 Vegetable
Babka	20 servings	9.51/218.80	4779.7	45.69	0.0	60.1	½ Bread I
	1 serving	0.48/10.94	239.0	2.28	0.0	3.0	

Nutritive Value of Recipes:3

RECIPES		Sodium mEq/mg	Food Energy Calories	Potassium mEq	Cholesterol mg	Total Fat gm	Food Group Per Serving
Baked Alaska	12 servings	96.32/2215.36	6711.8	78.27	82.8	36.6	1 Bread II
	1 serving	8.03/184.61	559.3	6.52	6.9	3.0	1 Meat
Baked Apple	1 serving	0.10/2.36	133.6	4.19	0.0	1.0	1 Fruit
Baked Bananas	4 servings	0.21/4.90	350.1	26.27	0.0	0.6	1 Fruit
	1 serving	0.05/1.22	87.5	6.57	0.0	0.1	
Baked Butternut Squash	4 servings	1.63/37.45	1563.0	74.08	0.0	10.6	½ Vegetable
	1 serving	0.41/9.36	390.8	18.52	0.0	2.6	
Baked Chicken	8 servings	27.35/629.12	1805.2	78.28	696.0	77.4	1 Meat
	1 serving	3.42/78.64	225.7	9.79	87.0	9.7	
Baked Fish	6 servings	21.78/501.00	1933.2	75.64	528.0	83.7	1 Meat
	1 serving	3.63/83.50	322.2	12.61	88.0	13.9	
Baked Glazed Yams	6 servings	1.94/44.69	1299.0	63.87	0.0	1.4	1 Bread I
	1 serving	0.32/7.45	216.5	10.64	0.0	0.2	
Baked Green Peppers	2 servings	0.97/22.32	178.8	9.82	0.0	15.3	1 Vegetable
	1 serving	0.49/11.16	89.4	4.91	0.0	7.7	
Baked Haddock	6 servings	25.49/586.29	2066.1	77.17	576.0	124.5	1½ Meat
	1 serving	4.25/97.71	344.4	12.86	96.0	20.8	

Nutritive Value of Recipes:4

RECIPES		Sodium mEq/mg	Food Energy Calories	Potassium mEq	Cholesterol mg	Total Fat gm	Food Group Per Serving
Baked Pineapples	4 servings	0.37/8.50	494.5	17.46	0.0	3.0	1 Fruit
	1 serving	0.09/2.12	123.6	4.36	0.0	0.8	
Baked Pork and Apples with Caraway	8 servings	21.01/483.32	2253.0	87.89	633.6	115.2	1 Meat
	1 serving	2.63/60.41	281.6	10.99	79.2	14.4	½ Fruit
Baked Tomatoes with Savory Crumb Topping	2 servings	0.67/15.48	422.7	20.65	0.0	3.7	½ Vegetable
	1 serving	0.34/7.74	211.4	10.33	0.0	1.9	½ Bread I
Baked Tuna Fondue	5 servings	16.78/386.02	792.1	30.43	138.3	8.8	1 Meat
	1 serving	3.36/77.20	158.4	6.09	27.7	1.8	1 Bread I
Banana Cookies	18 servings	4.12/94.65	2147.3	38.24	0.0	48.9	2 Cookies =
	1 serving	0.23/5.26	119.3	2.12	0.0	2.7	¼ Bread I
Banana Nog	1 serving	6.10/140.37	199.2	18.13	3.6	1.5	¾ Meat
							¾ Milk
Banana Nut Bread	16 servings	8.55/196.64	3511.0	110.44	3.6	136.5	1 Bread I
	1 serving	0.53/12.29	219.4	6.90	0.2	8.5	
Banana Orange Drink	2 servings	0.16/3.60	210.0	22.83	0.0	0.5	2 Fruit
	1 serving	0.08/1.80	105.0	11.42	0.0	0.2	
Banana Snack Shake	2 servings	10.35/238.00	304.6	31.30	9.9	0.6	1 Milk I
	1 serving	5.17/119.00	152.3	15.65	4.9	0.3	

Nutritive Value of Recipes:5

RECIPES		Sodium mEq/mg	Food Energy Calories	Potassium mEq	Cholesterol mg	Total Fat gm	Food Group Per Serving
Bananas Foster	4 servings	1.06/24.30	692.3	29.39	0.0	2.9	1 Fruit
	1 serving	0.26/6.07	173.1	7.35	0.0	0.7	
Barbequed Fish Fillets	5 servings	16.37/376.60	1774.2	68.31	392.0	36.6	4 ounces =
	1 serving	3.27/75.32	354.8	13.66	78.4	7.3	1 Meat
Barbequed Fish in Foil	6 servings	26.28/604.45	1507.4	141.23	432.0	9.5	1 Meat
	1 serving	4.38/100.74	251.2	23.54	72.0	1.6	1½ Vegetable
Basic Brown Sauce	4 servings	0.08/1.88	98.2	15.80	0.0	0.9	2½ Tablespoons
	1 serving	0.02/0.47	24.6	3.95	0.0	0.2	½ Fat
Basic Marinade	16 servings	0.03/0.60	1598.4	0.23	0.0	180.0	1 Tablespoon =
	1 serving	0.00/0.04	99.9	0.01	0.0	11.3	2 Fat
Basic Meringue (8-inch Pie)	6 servings	7.13/164.02	227.4	3.22	0.0	0.0	⅓ Meat
	1 serving	1.19/27.34	37.9	0.54	0.0	0.0	
Basic Meringue (9-inch Pie)	8 servings	9.12/209.68	399.8	4.36	0.0	0.0	⅓ Meat
	1 serving	1.14/26.21	50.0	0.54	0.0	0.0	
Basic Pilaf	1 serving	0.23/5.31	282.6	9.66	0.0	15.3	1 Bread I
Basic Rice	1 serving	0.11/2.50	217.5	1.21	0.0	0.6	2 Bread I

Nutritive Value of Recipes:6

RECIPES		Sodium mEq/mg	Food Energy Calories	Potas-sium mEq	Choles-terol mg	Total Fat gm	Food Group Per Serving
Basic Salad Dressing	4 servings	0.07/1.65	597.4	0.09	7.5	71.5	1 Tablespoon =
	1 serving	0.02/0.41	149.4	0.02	1.9	17.9	3 Fat
Beef and Mush-room Sandwich	1 serving	3.69/84.95	304.4	7.74	47.1	11.1	1 Bread I
							⅓ Meat
Beef Fondue	4 servings	12.52/288.00	878.4	45.54	436.8	25.4	1 Meat
	1 serving	3.13/72.00	219.6	11.38	109.2	6.4	
Beef 'n' Beer Casserole	8 servings	40.01/920.14	4019.1	164.20	1274.0	139.5	1½ Meat
	1 serving	5.00/115.02	502.4	20.53	159.2	17.4	1 Vegetable
Beef Crab Dip	16 servings	18.29/420.69	1758.5	9.57	360.0	280.4	2 Tablespoons =
							⅓ Meat
	1 serving	1.14/26.29	109.9	0.60	22.5	17.5	3 Fat
Berman's Homemade Granola	20 servings	4.61/105.98	5208.8	128.04	0.0	259.9	½ Cup =
	1 serving	0.23/5.30	260.4	6.40	0.0	13.0	¼ Bread I
Black Pears Elegante	2 servings	0.58/13.41	506.5	10.43	0.0	1.4	1 Fruit
	1 serving	0.29/6.70	253.3	5.22	0.0	0.7	
Blueberry Blintzes	5 servings	17.46/401.60	818.9	15.21	26.0	10.2	1 Bread I
	1 serving	3.49/80.32	163.8	3.04	5.2	2.0	½ Milk I
Blueberry Coffee Cake	16 servings	8.51/195.78	3168.0	57.62	3.6	15.9	½ Bread I
	1 serving	0.53/12.24	198.0	3.60	0.2	1.0	

Nutritive Value of Recipes:7

RECIPES		Sodium mEq/mg	Food Energy Calories	Potas- sium mEq	Choles- terol mg	Total Fat gm	Food Group Per Serving
Blueberry Lemon Coffee Cake	18 servings	5.93/136.47	2454.9	18.38	1.2	66.2	½ Bread I
	1 serving	0.33/7.58	136.4	1.02	0.1	3.7	
Blueberry Lime Sundaes	4 servings	0.14/3.31	655.4	5.76	0.0	1.2	½ Fruit
	1 serving	0.04/0.83	163.9	1.44	0.0	0.3	
Blueberry Muffins	12 servings	6.99/160.66	1831.6	46.20	2.4	65.0	Small Muffin =
	1 serving	0.58/13.39	152.6	3.85	0.2	5.4	1 Bread I
Blueberry Pie (8-inch Pie)	6 servings	0.49/11.20	3084.1	18.02	0.0	21.8	⅙ of Pie =
	1 serving	0.08/1.87	514.0	3.00	0.0	3.6	1 Fruit
Blueberry Pie (9-inch Pie)	8 servings	0.58/13.35	3454.5	21.88	0.0	23.9	⅛ of Pie =
	1 serving	0.07/1.57	431.8	2.73	0.0	3.0	1 Fruit
Blueberry Sauce	8 servings	0.21/4.85	522.1	6.95	0.0	1.0	¼ Cup =
	1 serving	0.03/0.61	65.3	0.87	0.0	0.1	Trace Sodium
Bluefish Hampton	8 servings	31.09/715.04	1843.6	107.93	528.0	42.0	1 Meat
	1 serving	3.89/89.38	230.4	13.49	66.0	5.2	
Blushing Grapefruit	2 servings	0.15/3.55	130.3	8.48	0.0	0.2	1 Fruit
	1 serving	0.08/1.77	65.1	4.24	0.0	0.1	
Boiled Lobster	2 servings	21.91/504.00	228.0	11.08	204.0	3.6	½ Salted Meat
	1 serving	10.96/252.00	160.0	5.54	102.0	1.8	3 Fat

Nutritive Value of Recipes:8

RECIPES		Sodium mEq/mg	Food Energy Calories	Potassium mEq	Cholesterol mg	Total Fat gm	Food Group Per Serving
Boned Leg of Lamb with Stuffing	8 servings	56.26/1294.03	3314.9	177.49	1600.9	124.8	2½ Meat
	1 serving	7.03/161.75	414.4	22.19	200.1	15.6	
Bordelaise Sauce	3 servings	0.16/3.67	80.4	9.69	0.0	0.8	5 Teaspoons =
	1 serving	0.05/1.22	26.8	3.23	0.0	0.3	½ Fat
Bread Pudding	7 servings	67.88/1561.21	1680.9	38.50	15.6	16.0	1 Bread II
	1 serving	9.70/223.03	240.1	5.50	2.2	2.3	1 Milk I
Broccoli	4 servings	2.21/50.77	846.7	54.68	0.0	36.6	1 Vegetable
	1 serving	0.55/12.69	211.7	13.67	0.0	9.2	
Broccoli Polonaise	4 servings	5.03/115.75	607.5	38.29	0.4	7.0	1 Vegetable
	1 serving	1.26/28.94	151.9	9.57	0.1	1.7	
Broccoli with Lemon Margarine	4 servings	2.18/50.15	457.7	35.04	0.0	5.2	1 Vegetable
	1 serving	0.55/12.54	114.4	8.76	0.0	1.3	
Broiled Fish	6 servings	21.70/499.20	1920.0	73.95	528.0	83.6	1 Meat
	1 serving	3.62/83.20	320.0	12.33	88.0	13.9	
Broiled Lamb Chops	4 servings	11.09/255.05	702.3	29.53	360.0	27.1	1 Meat
	1 serving	2.77/63.76	175.6	7.38	90.0	6.8	
Broiled Lobster Tails with Lemon Sauce	4 servings	19.17/441.00	631.5	10.05	178.5	8.0	½ Salted Meat
	1 serving	4.79/110.25	157.9	2.51	44.6	2.0	3 Fat

Nutritive Value of Recipes:9

RECIPES		Sodium mEq/mg	Food Energy Calories	Potassium mEq	Cholesterol mg	Total Fat gm	Food Group Per Serving
Broiled Tomatoes	4 servings	9.02/207.50	505.6	34.01	1.3	32.4	1 Vegetable
	1 serving	2.26/51.87	126.4	8.50	0.3	8.1	1 Bread I
Broiled Whitefish	4 servings	11.62/267.35	1388.1	63.76	240.0	16.0	1 Meat
	1 serving	2.91/66.84	347.0	15.94	60.0	4.0	
Browned Margarine Frosting	15 servings	0.84/19.35	2050.8	1.88	0.6	6.5	Trace Sodium
	1 serving	0.06/1.29	136.7	0.13	0.0	0.4	
Brownies	32 servings	8.58/197.29	4756.5	52.23	0.0	143.4	1 Bar =
	1 serving	0.27/6.17	148.6	1.63	0.0	4.5	¼ Bread I
Brownies (Cakelike)	16 servings	4.30/98.97	2734.6	24.63	0.0	83.9	1 Bar =
	1 serving	0.27/6.17	170.9	1.54	0.0	5.2	¼ Bread I
Brunch Float	1 serving	0.37/8.50	112.8	4.08	0.0	0.6	½ Fruit
Burgundy Pot Roast	8 servings	40.80/938.45	3677.1	191.54	1310.4	134.4	1½ Meat ½ Bread I 1 Vegetable
	1 serving	5.10/117.31	459.6	23.94	163.8	16.8	
Butterscotch Brownies	16 servings	6.92/159.07	2034.3	42.34	0.0	46.4	1 Bar =
	1 serving	0.43/9.94	127.1	2.65	0.0	2.9	¼ Bread I
Butterscotch Pecan Rolls	15 servings	7.15/164.50	3542.2	32.26	1.2	114.2	1 Roll =
	1 serving	0.48/10.97	236.1	2.15	0.1	7.6	½ Bread I

Nutritive Value of Recipes:10

RECIPES		Sodium mEq/mg	Food Energy Calories	Potassium mEq	Cholesterol mg	Total Fat gm	Food Group Per Serving
Butterscotch Pudding	4 servings	16.70/384.21	1082.6	30.48	9.6	5.1	½ Milk I
	1 serving	4.18/96.05	270.7	7.62	2.4	1.3	½ Meat
Caesar Salad	8 servings	6.32/145.46	823.2	65.14	252.0	68.7	1 Vegetable
	1 serving	0.79/18.18	102.9	8.14	31.5	8.6	
Cantaloupe Surprise	6 servings	5.24/120.45	727.9	74.81	0.0	1.5	2 Fruit
	1 serving	0.87/20.07	121.3	12.47	0.0	0.3	
Caribbean Chicken	4 servings	12.60/289.70	1159.7	38.66	313.2	25.7	1 Meat
	1 serving	3.15/72.42	289.9	9.66	78.3	6.4	
Caribbean Jumble	6 servings	0.31/7.15	660.1	30.58	0.0	1.1	1 Fruit
	1 serving	0.05/1.19	110.0	5.10	0.0	0.2	
Cauliflower Parmesan	6 servings	11.10/255.36	563.5	33.02	14.8	9.3	½ Vegetable
	1 serving	1.85/42.56	93.9	5.50	2.5	1.6	1 Bread I
Cheese Omelet	2 servings	49.85/1146.50	385.6	3.46	2.5	10.1	3 Salted Meat
	1 serving	24.92/573.25	192.8	1.73	1.3	5.1	
Cherry Frosting	15 servings	0.18/4.05	2074.8	1.73	0.0	6.5	Trace Sodium
	1 serving	0.01/0.27	138.3	0.12	0.0	0.4	
Cherry Pie	8 servings	0.77/17.73	4518.4	37.50	0.0	22.6	⅛ of Pie =
	1 serving	0.10/2.22	564.8	4.69	0.0	2.8	1 Fruit

Nutritive Value of Recipes:11

RECIPES		Sodium mEq/mg	Food Energy Calories	Potassium mEq	Cholesterol mg	Total Fat gm	Food Group Per Serving
Chicken Club Sandwich	1 serving	1.11/25.51	380.8	6.87	26.1	5.8	1 Bread I ¼ Meat
Chicken Curry	4 servings	11.32/260.34	1568.6	51.28	135.3	16.7	1 Bread I
	1 serving	2.83/65.08	392.1	12.82	33.8	4.2	1 Meat
Chicken in Mushroom Sauce	4 servings	12.48/287.08	1354.0	39.30	322.8	93.1	1 Meat
	1 serving	3.12/71.77	338.5	9.82	80.7	23.3	
Chicken Noodle Soup	2 servings	2.70/62.17	219.9	46.79	60.9	5.7	½ Bread I
	1 serving	1.35/31.08	109.9	23.40	30.4	2.8	⅓ Meat
Chicken Oregano	4 servings	12.21/280.92	1140.9	39.22	313.2	28.1	1 Meat
	1 serving	3.05/70.23	285.2	9.80	78.3	7.0	
Chicken Salad	6 servings	10.72/246.57	1330.1	36.14	312.3	132.5	½ Meat
	1 serving	1.79/41.09	221.7	6.02	52.0	22.1	
Chicken Soufflé	6 servings	13.05/300.16	909.2	39.65	877.8	28.9	1 Meat
	1 serving	2.18/50.03	151.5	6.61	146.3	4.8	
Chicken Tetrazzini	4 servings	17.89/411.53	1822.4	65.92	201.7	25.2	¼ Milk I 1 Meat 1 Bread I
	1 serving	4.47/102.88	455.6	16.48	50.4	6.3	
Chili Burgers	4 servings	18.15/417.47	1658.9	118.76	676.8	82.4	1½ Meat
	1 serving	4.54/104.37	414.7	29.69	169.2	20.6	

Nutritive Value of Recipes:12

RECIPES		Sodium mEq/mg	Food Energy Calories	Potassium mEq	Cholesterol mg	Total Fat gm	Food Group Per Serving
Chili Con Carne	6 servings	37.18/855.07	2330.4	134.57	873.6	77.1	2 Meat
	1 serving	6.20/142.51	388.4	22.43	145.6	12.9	1 Bread l
Chilled Melon Balls	4 servings	0.97/22.20	55.5	11.91	0.0	0.2	½ Fruit
	1 serving	0.24/5.55	13.9	2.98	0.0	0.0	
Chocolate Cake	15 servings	18.44/424.07	4568.5	76.72	8.4	125.5	1 Bread l
	1 serving	1.23/28.27	304.6	5.11	0.6	8.4	
Chocolate Chip Cookies	18 servings	5.02/115.56	3033.7	47.77	0.0	150.1	2 Cookies =
	1 serving	0.28/6.42	168.5	2.65	0.0	8.3	¼ Bread l
Chocolate Nut Cookies	18 servings	5.14/118.24	2509.2	44.12	0.0	90.6	2 Cookies =
	1 serving	0.29/6.57	139.4	2.45	0.0	5.0	¼ Bread l
Chocolate Sauce	12 servings	3.44/79.20	1267.2	16.55	2.4	84.2	2 Tablespoons =
	1 serving	0.29/6.60	105.6	1.38	0.2	7.0	Trace Sodium
Chutney	12 servings	4.13/95.10	1209.5	64.45	0.0	2.7	1 Fruit
	1 serving	0.34/7.92	100.8	5.37	0.0	0.2	
Cinnamon Rolls	15 servings	6.22/143.11	2840.0	15.14	1.5	68.0	1 Roll =
	1 serving	0.41/9.54	189.3	1.01	0.1	4.5	½ Bread l
Cinnamon Rolls (with Salt)	15 servings	22.74/523.05	2355.9	14.30	1.2	67.9	1 Roll =
	1 serving	1.52/34.87	157.1	0.95	0.1	4.5	1½ Bread l

Nutritive Value of Recipes:13

RECIPES		Sodium mEq/mg	Food Energy Calories	Potas-sium mEq	Choles-terol mg	Total Fat gm	Food Group Per Serving
Clear Lemon Filling	15 servings	0.11/2.60	870.0	3.30	0.0	1.3	Trace Sodium
	1 serving	0.01/0.17	58.0	0.22	0.0	0.1	
Coffee Shake	1 serving	4.78/109.89	171.3	16.74	2.4	1.4	½ Milk I
							¾ Meat
Company Applesauce	4 servings	1.63/37.43	1924.2	45.72	0.0	7.0	½ Cup =
	1 serving	0.41/9.36	481.0	11.43	0.0	1.8	1 Fruit
Cookie Crust	6 servings	0.10/2.20	1099.6	2.94	0.0	8.3	⅙ of Pie =
	1 serving	0.02/0.37	183.3	0.49	0.0	1.4	Trace Sodium
Coq au Vin	4 servings	23.84/548.26	1921.2	104.36	522.0	88.5	2 Meat
	1 serving	5.96/137.06	408.3	26.09	130.5	22.1	
Corn Bread	12 servings	9.64/221.72	1720.9	84.56	4.8	10.4	1 Bread I
	1 serving	0.80/18.48	143.4	7.05	0.4	0.9	
Corn Bread Stuffing with Low-Sodium Corn Bread	18 servings	15.76/362.54	3568.3	107.28	4.8	30.6	1 Bread I
	1 serving	0.88/20.14	198.2	5.96	0.3	1.7	3 Fat
Corn Bread Stuffing with Regular Corn Bread	18 servings	167.86/3860.82	3012.4	39.00	345.0	62.2	1 Bread III
	1 serving	9.33/214.49	167.4	2.17	19.2	3.5	3 Fat
Corn Muffins	12 servings	9.64/221.72	1720.9	84.56	4.8	10.4	1 Muffin =
	1 serving	0.80/18.48	143.4	7.05	0.4	0.9	1 Bread I

Nutritive Value of Recipes:14

RECIPES		Sodium mEq/mg	Food Energy Calories	Potassium mEq	Cholesterol mg	Total Fat gm	Food Group Per Serving
Corn on the Cob	1 serving	0.0/0.0	175.2	5.11	0.0	1.9	1 Bread I 3 Fat
Cottage Cheese Bake	5 servings	36.47/838.75	380.1	14.80	9.4	8.6	½ Meat
	1 serving	7.29/167.75	76.0	2.96	1.9	1.7	1 Milk I
Coupe Louise	4 servings	0.23/5.40	487.0	19.80	0.0	0.4	1 Fruit
	1 serving	0.06/1.35	121.8	4.95	0.0	0.1	
Cranberry Banana Toast	1 serving	0.11/2.52	219.0	4.35	0.0	1.9	1 Bread I
Cranberry Gelatin	6 servings	0.69/15.80	969.6	8.20	0.0	2.5	1 Fruit
	1 serving	0.11/2.63	161.6	1.37	0.0	0.4	
Cranberry Orange Margarine	8 servings	0.09/1.96	1105.5	5.13	0.0	10.1	2 Tablespoons =
	1 serving	0.01/0.24	138.2	0.64	0.0	1.3	Trace Sodium
Cranberry Orange Muffins	12 servings	7.07/162.61	1822.6	47.06	2.4	65.3	Small Muffin =
	1 serving	0.59/13.55	151.9	3.92	0.2	5.4	1 Bread I
Cranberry Orange Nut Bread	16 servings	9.97/229.24	3437.5	97.08	4.8	137.2	1 Bread I
	1 serving	0.62/14.33	214.8	6.07	0.3	8.6	
Cranberry Orange Relish	16 servings	0.60/13.70	1074.8	17.60	0.0	3.5	¼ Cup =
	1 serving	0.04/0.86	67.2	1.10	0.0	0.2	½ Fruit

Nutritive Value of Recipes:15

RECIPES		Sodium mEq/mg	Food Energy Calories	Potassium mEq	Cholesterol mg	Total Fat gm	Food Group Per Serving
Cream of Cauliflower Soup	6 servings	4.44/102.22	425.1	48.18	2.4	3.8	½ Vegetable
	1 serving	0.74/17.04	70.8	8.03	0.4	0.6	
Creole Flounder	6 servings	26.75/615.22	1004.4	100.98	576.0	15.1	4 Ounces =
	1 serving	4.46/102.54	167.4	16.83	96.0	2.5	1½ Meat
Creole Sauce	4 servings	1.34/30.77	328.2	23.27	0.0	3.3	½ Vegetable
	1 serving	0.33/7.69	82.1	5.82	0.0	0.8	
Crêpes	12 servings	16.34/375.81	1223.9	31.35	9.6	7.8	3 Crêpe =
	1 serving	1.36/31.32	102.0	2.61	0.8	0.6	1 Bread I
Crêpes Suzette	1 serving	4.13/95.05	625.6	10.93	2.4	4.5	3 Bread I
Cresson Salad	4 servings	2.76/63.47	280.6	19.99	0.0	15.9	½ Vegetable
	1 serving	0.69/15.87	70.1	5.00	0.0	4.0	¼ Fruit
Crisscross Potatoes	2 servings	0.27/6.12	363.5	19.87	0.0	2.8	1 Bread I
	1 serving	0.13/3.06	181.7	9.94	0.0	1.4	
Cucumber Salad	6 servings	5.82/133.90	380.4	23.57	103.2	28.5	1 Vegetable
	1 serving	0.97/22.32	63.4	3.93	17.2	4.7	
Cucumber Sauce	2 servings	5.67/130.52	373.2	13.18	4.8	2.9	½ Cup =
	1 serving	2.84/65.26	186.6	6.59	2.4	1.5	½ Milk I

Nutritive Value of Recipes:16

RECIPES		Sodium mEq/mg	Food Energy Calories	Potassium mEq	Cholesterol mg	Total Fat gm	Food Group Per Serving
Cucumber Sauce with Yogurt	8 servings	5.93/136.42	142.5	15.36	19.2	4.2	¼ Cup =
	1 serving	0.74/17.05	17.8	1.92	2.4	0.5	¼ Milk I
Cumberland Sauce	24 servings	1.91/44.04	741.7	8.95	0.0	1.5	1 Tablespoon =
	1 serving	0.08/1.83	30.9	0.37	0.0	0.1	Trace Sodium
Curried Beef	4 servings	19.90/457.64	1957.3	79.76	655.2	49.2	1½ Meat
	1 serving	4.97/114.41	489.3	19.94	163.8	12.3	½ Vegetable
Curried Fruit Salad Dressing	4 servings	3.90/89.60	537.4	7.02	107.4	67.3	½ Salted Fat
	1 serving	0.97/22.40	134.4	1.75	26.8	16.8	
Curried Rice	1 serving	0.24/5.50	228.9	2.42	0.0	0.6	1 Bread I
Curry Dill Dip	16 servings	2.95/67.93	706.0	5.09	111.6	107.3	1 Tablespoon =
	1 serving	0.18/4.25	44.1	0.32	7.0	6.7	1½ Fat
Curry Sauce	2 servings	5.44/125.12	360.6	9.49	4.8	2.8	½ Cup =
	1 serving	2.72/62.56	180.3	4.74	2.4	1.4	½ Milk I
Custard Pie	8 servings	21.66/498.11	1735.1	19.79	8.4	16.4	½ Bread I
	1 serving	2.71/62.26	216.9	2.47	1.0	2.0	½ Milk I
Date Nut Bread	16 servings	4.50/103.46	3977.1	126.41	0.0	137.2	½ Bread I
	1 serving	0.28/6.47	248.6	7.90	0.0	8.6	

Nutritive Value of Recipes:17

RECIPES		Sodium mEq/mg	Food Energy Calories	Potas-sium mEq	Choles-terol mg	Total Fat gm	Food Group Per Serving
Date-Nut Squares	16 servings	4.35/99.95	2122.7	66.73	0.0	80.9	1 Bar =
	1 serving	0.27/6.25	132.7	4.17	0.0	5.1	¼ Bread I
Deep Dish Fruit Pie	8 servings	1.00/23.10	3628.6	50.20	0.0	18.4	1 Bread I
	1 serving	0.13/2.89	453.6	6.27	0.0	2.3	1 Fruit
Dijon-Type Mustard	32 servings	1.28/29.37	2109.7	26.84	0.0	158.9	1 Tablespoon =
	1 serving	0.04/0.92	65.9	0.84	0.0	5.0	½ Fat
Dill Sauce	2 servings	5.44/125.12	360.6	9.49	4.8	2.8	½ Cup =
	1 serving	2.72/62.56	180.3	4.74	2.4	1.4	½ Milk I
Double Fruit Whip	8 servings	0.90/20.72	506.5	18.08	0.0	1.1	½ Fruit
	1 serving	0.11/2.59	63.3	2.26	0.0	0.1	
Double-Quick Dinner Rolls	12 servings	38.18/878.07	1516.5	11.35	0.0	35.3	1 Roll =
	1 serving	3.18/73.17	126.4	0.95	0.0	2.9	1 Bread II
Drop Biscuits (no salt)	16 servings	5.70/131.08	1771.0	65.79	4.8	82.8	1 Biscuit =
	1 serving	0.36/8.19	110.7	4.11	0.3	5.2	½ Bread I
Dumplings	10 servings	4.28/98.40	1198.2	53.55	3.6	47.1	1 Bread I
	1 serving	0.43/9.84	119.8	5.35	0.4	4.7	
East India Peaches	5 servings	1.21/27.86	594.6	28.38	0.0	1.0	1 Fruit
	1 serving	0.24/5.57	118.9	5.68	0.0	0.2	

Nutritive Value of Recipes:18

RECIPES		Sodium mEq/mg	Food Energy Calories	Potassium mEq	Cholesterol mg	Total Fat gm	Food Group Per Serving
Easter Roast Lamb with Artichokes	8 servings	34.81/800.66	3216.1	115.70	940.8	172.9	1 Meat
	1 serving	4.35/100.08	402.0	14.46	117.6	21.6	1 Vegetable
Easy Broiled Chicken	4 servings	13.87/318.91	797.3	44.85	348.0	26.0	1 Meat
	1 serving	3.47/79.73	199.3	11.21	87.0	6.5	
Easy Grilled Chicken	1 serving	2.34/53.75	118.0	7.21	72.9	4.6	1 Meat
Easy Penuche Frosting	15 servings	4.20/96.70	2631.4	21.65	1.2	9.8	Trace Sodium
	1 serving	0.28/6.45	175.4	1.44	0.1	0.7	
Egg Salad	4 servings	19.74/454.10	598.2	7.93	30.0	56.1	1½ Meat
	1 serving	4.94/113.52	149.5	1.98	7.5	14.0	
Eggnog	1 serving	9.46/217.56	199.6	9.05	4.8	2.4	1 Milk I
							1½ Meat
Eggs and Peppers	8 servings	22.46/516.56	1121.0	25.22	2016.0	91.5	1 Meat
	1 serving	2.81/64.57	140.1	3.15	252.0	11.4	½ Vegetable
Eggs and Tomatoes	4 servings	8.48/195.05	593.1	17.93	756.0	47.8	¾ Meat
	1 serving	2.12/48.76	148.3	4.48	189.0	12.0	½ Vegetable
Emerald Ice	4 servings	0.13/3.00	339.6	1.70	0.0	0.0	Trace Sodium
	1 serving	0.03/0.75	84.9	0.42	0.0	0.0	

Nutritive Value of Recipes:19

RECIPES		Sodium mEq/mg	Food Energy Calories	Potassium mEq	Cholesterol mg	Total Fat gm	Food Group Per Serving
English Muffins	11 servings	34.23/787.34	1982.8	14.16	0.0	56.2	1 Muffin =
	1 serving	3.11/71.58	180.3	1.29	0.0	5.1	1 Bread II
Exemplary Beets	8 servings	19.12/439.79	568.7	52.08	0.0	1.1	2 Vegetables
	1 serving	2.39/54.97	71.1	6.51	0.0	0.1	
Festive Banana Crêpes	12 servings	19.29/443.76	3260.7	94.02	9.6	18.4	1 Crêpe =
	1 serving	1.61/36.98	271.7	7.84	0.8	1.5	1 Bread I ½ Fruit
Flounder with Lemon and Almonds	4 servings	16.35/376.07	736.0	48.58	240.0	17.4	1 Meat
	1 serving	4.09/94.02	184.0	12.14	60.0	4.4	
French Bread	15 servings	70.11/1612.51	1848.5	17.44	0.0	5.1	1 Bread II
	1 serving	4.67/107.50	123.2	1.16	0.0	0.3	
French Bread (no salt)	15 servings	2.70/62.19	1848.5	17.44	0.0	5.1	Trace Sodium
	1 serving	0.18/4.15	123.2	1.16	0.0	0.3	
French Dressing	6 servings	0.35/7.97	1139.6	8.18	0.0	120.9	2 Tablespoons =
	1 serving	0.06/1.33	189.9	1.36	0.0	20.2	4 Fat
French Green Beans	6 servings	3.73/85.71	687.7	60.01	0.0	5.6	1 Vegetables
	1 serving	0.62/14.28	114.6	10.00	0.0	0.9	
French Plums	6 servings	0.38/8.85	562.7	26.70	0.0	0.8	1 Fruit
	1 serving	0.06/1.47	93.8	4.45	0.0	0.1	

Nutritive Value of Recipes:20

RECIPES		Sodium mEq/mg	Food Energy Calories	Potassium mEq	Cholesterol mg	Total Fat gm	Food Group Per Serving
French Silk Frosting	15 servings	1.61/36.93	2768.8	16.20	1.2	44.8	2 Tablespoons =
	1 serving	0.11/2.46	184.6	1.08	0.1	3.0	Trace Sodium
French Toast	12 servings	124.50/2863.50	1755.2	18.01	16.8	26.7	1 Slice = ½ Meat 1 Bread II
	1 serving	10.37/238.62	146.3	1.50	1.4	2.2	
French Toast (with Low-Sodium Bread)	12 servings	22.34/513.90	1269.2	13.16	11.4	20.9	1 Slice = ½ Meat 1 Bread I
	1 serving	1.86/42.82	105.8	1.10	0.9	1.7	
Fresh Bean Salad	8 servings	2.15/49.55	1952.3	41.80	0.0	183.0	1 Vegetable
	1 serving	0.27/6.19	244.0	5.22	0.0	22.9	
Fresh Fruit Compote	6 servings	1.20/27.52	447.9	27.20	0.0	1.3	1 Fruit
	1 serving	0.20/4.59	74.6	4.53	0.0	0.2	
Fresh Lemon Sherbet	8 servings	2.49/57.26	1246.7	6.13	0.0	0.3	¾ Cup =
	1 serving	0.31/7.16	155.8	0.77	0.0	0.0	Trace Sodium
Fresh Peach Pie with Apricots	6 servings	0.66/15.13	3434.6	66.11	0.0	21.1	⅙ of Pie =
	1 serving	0.11/2.52	572.4	11.02	0.0	3.5	1 Fruit
Fresh Peach Pie with Brown Sugar	6 servings	2.63/60.40	3377.5	59.60	0.0	20.2	⅙ of Pie =
	1 serving	0.44/10.07	562.9	9.93	0.0	3.4	1 Fruit

Nutritive Value of Recipes:21

RECIPES		Sodium mEq/mg	Food Energy Calories	Potassium mEq	Cholesterol mg	Total Fat gm	Food Group Per Serving
Fresh Peach Pie (8-inch Pie)	6 servings	0.62/14.33	3300.2	45.76	0.0	20.2	1/6 of Pie =
	1 serving	0.10/2.39	550.0	7.63	0.0	3.4	1 Fruit
Fresh Peach Pie (9-inch Pie)	8 servings	0.74/16.96	3763.7	55.42	0.0	21.7	1/8 of Pie =
	1 serving	0.09/2.12	470.5	6.93	0.0	2.7	1 Fruit
Fresh Rhubarb Pie (8-inch Pie)	6 servings	0.73/16.87	3381.9	37.49	0.0	20.0	1/6 of Pie =
	1 serving	0.12/2.81	563.6	6.25	0.0	3.3	1 Fruit
Fresh Rhubarb Pie (9-inch Pie)	8 servings	0.90/20.79	3812.9	47.61	0.0	21.5	1/8 of Pie =
	1 serving	0.11/2.60	476.6	5.95	0.0	2.7	1 Fruit
Fried Corn	3 servings	0.28/6.51	320.2	9.64	0.0	3.8	1 Bread I
	1 serving	0.09/2.17	106.7	3.21	0.0	1.3	
Frittata Omelet	2 servings	6.04/138.81	660.3	10.82	504.0	64.9	1 Meat
	1 serving	3.02/69.40	330.2	5.41	252.0	32.5	1 Vegetable
Frosted Fruit	4 servings	0.50/11.55	203.9	12.71	0.0	0.4	1 Fruit
	1 serving	0.13/2.89	51.0	3.18	0.0	0.1	
Frosted Orange Rolls	15 servings	5.89/135.54	2981.4	16.43	1.2	69.1	1 Roll =
	1 serving	0.39/9.04	198.8	1.10	0.1	4.6	1/2 Bread I
Fruit Kebabs	6 servings	1.49/34.20	260.4	32.68	0.0	1.9	1 Fruit
	1 serving	0.25/5.70	43.4	5.45	0.0	0.3	
Fruit 'n' Tuna Sandwich	1 serving	0.71/16.30	300.0	4.30	33.9	24.8	1 Bread I
							1/3 Meat

Nutritive Value of Recipes:22

RECIPES		Sodium mEq/mg	Food Energy Calories	Potas- sium mEq	Choles- terol mg	Total Fat gm	Food Group Per Serving
Fruit Sundae Sauce	8 servings	0.17/3.93	249.2	8.09	0.0	0.4	2 Tablespoons =
	1 serving	0.02/0.49	31.2	1.01	0.0	0.1	Trace Sodium
Garden Patch Salad with Cabbage, Radishes, and Green Onions	6 servings	1.71/39.37	274.7	12.18	0.0	0.4	½ Vegetable
	1 serving	0.29/6.56	45.8	2.03	0.0	0.1	
Garden Patch Salad with Carrot, Cauliflower, and Green Pepper	6 servings	4.41/101.32	324.6	22.27	0.0	0.6	1 Vegetable
	1 serving	0.73/16.89	54.1	3.71	0.0	0.1	
Garden Patch Salad with Mixed Vegetables and Dill	6 servings	9.04/208.02	469.2	21.75	0.0	1.3	1½ Vegetable
	1 serving	1.51/34.67	78.2	3.62	0.0	0.2	
Garlic French Bread	28 servings	2.71/62.33	2716.1	18.30	0.0	14.8	1 Bread I
	1 serving	0.10/2.23	97.0	0.65	0.0	0.5	
Garlic Potato Balls	3 servings	0.56/12.94	458.9	33.46	0.0	2.9	1 Bread I
	1 serving	0.19/4.31	153.0	11.15	0.0	1.0	
Gazpacho	4 servings	0.93/21.40	352.3	46.69	0.0	1.4	½ Vegetable
	1 serving	0.23/5.35	88.1	11.67	0.0	0.3	1 Bread I
German Stollen	32 servings	37.10/853.41	5286.6	41.38	0.4	66.8	1½ Bread I
	1 serving	1.16/26.67	165.2	1.29	0.0	2.1	
Ginger Fruit Cup	8 servings	0.62/14.32	897.6	84.96	0.0	2.5	2 Fruit
	1 serving	0.08/1.79	112.2	10.62	0.0	0.3	

Nutritive Value of Recipes:23

RECIPES		Sodium mEq/mg	Food Energy Calories	Potassium mEq	Cholesterol mg	Total Fat gm	Food Group Per Serving
Gingerbread	9 servings	23.74/545.97	2640.7	101.93	3.6	11.5	½ Bread II
	1 serving	2.64/60.66	293.4	11.33	0.4	1.3	
Glazed Beets	6 servings	9.61/221.14	251.5	21.33	0.0	0.5	1 Vegetable
	1 serving	1.60/36.86	41.9	3.55	0.0	0.1	
Glazed Mustard Parsnips	4 servings	2.48/57.12	735.6	61.32	0.0	6.3	1 Vegetable
	1 serving	0.62/14.28	183.9	15.33	0.0	1.6	
Glow Wine	5 servings	1.79/41.14	1153.7	18.24	0.0	0.3	Trace Sodium
	1 serving	0.36/8.23	230.7	3.65	0.0	0.1	
Golden Banana Bowl	4 servings	0.60/13.85	507.0	53.94	0.0	1.5	2 Fruit
	1 serving	0.15/3.46	126.7	13.49	0.0	0.4	
Golden Pound Cake	9 servings	12.38/284.63	2662.0	47.02	3.6	16.6	1 Bread I
	1 serving	1.38/31.63	295.8	5.22	0.4	1.8	
Golden Puffs	30 servings	8.40/193.12	2236.7	64.26	3.6	66.6	1 Puff =
	1 serving	0.28/6.44	74.6	2.14	0.1	2.2	½ Bread I
Golden Waffles	3 servings	17.80/409.30	2170.9	107.11	8.4	17.1	10-inch Waffle =
	1 serving	5.93/136.43	723.6	35.70	2.8	5.7	1 Bread II
Grapefruit Mold	4 servings	0.77/17.70	736.0	11.62	0.0	0.3	½ Fruit
	1 serving	0.19/4.42	184.0	2.91	0.0	0.1	

Nutritive Value of Recipes:24

RECIPES		Sodium mEq/mg	Food Energy Calories	Potassium mEq	Cholesterol mg	Total Fat gm	Food Group Per Serving
Greek Stuffado	2 servings	6.91/158.99	616.5	31.85	218.4	25.1	1 Meat
	1 serving	3.46/79.49	308.2	15.92	109.2	12.5	
Green Beans with Dill	4 servings	0.85/19.53	246.0	19.52	0.0	2.7	1 Vegetable
	1 serving	0.21/4.88	61.5	4.88	0.0	0.7	
Green Pepper Omelet	2 servings	16.31/375.20	326.3	3.73	0.0	10.1	2½ Meat
	1 serving	8.16/187.60	163.1	1.86	0.0	5.0	¼ Vegetable
Green String Beans	4 servings	0.85/19.62	548.3	25.25	0.0	22.5	1 Vegetable
	1 serving	0.21/4.90	137.1	6.31	0.0	5.6	
Grilled Eggplant	6 servings	0.45/10.27	718.3	25.32	0.0	35.1	1 Vegetable
	1 serving	0.07/1.71	119.7	4.22	0.0	5.9	
Hamburgers	4 servings	10.21/234.72	1078.8	70.56	451.2	55.1	1 Meat
	1 serving	2.55/58.68	269.7	17.64	112.8	13.8	
Hamburger and Eggplant	4 servings	15.31/352.02	1375.7	91.77	465.4	60.7	1 Meat
	1 serving	3.83/88.00	343.9	22.94	116.4	15.2	1 Vegetable
Hamburger Casserole	4 servings	11.35/261.10	1976.1	118.35	451.2	58.3	1 Meat 1 Vegetable 1 Bread I
	1 serving	2.84/65.27	494.0	29.59	112.8	14.6	
Hamburger Stroganoff	4 servings	16.70/384.20	2430.0	95.04	567.6	67.9	1 Meat
	1 serving	4.18/96.05	607.5	23.76	141.9	17.0	1 Bread I

Nutritive Value of Recipes:25

RECIPES		Sodium mEq/mg	Food Energy Calories	Potas-sium mEq	Choles-terol mg	Total Fat gm	Food Group Per Serving
Hamburger with Horseradish and Onion Topper	4 servings	11.13/255.92	1275.9	80.86	451.2	56.6	1 Meat
	1 serving	2.78/63.98	319.0	20.22	112.8	14.1	
Hamburger with Mashed Potato Topper	4 servings	31.19/717.32	1301.4	88.68	455.2	68.7	1 Meat
	1 serving	7.80/179.33	325.4	22.17	113.8	17.2	1 Milk I
Hamburger with Pepper and Onion Topper	4 servings	11.34/260.92	1278.9	81.42	451.2	70.6	1 Meat
	1 serving	2.84/65.23	319.7	20.36	112.8	17.6	
Hamburger with Smothered Onion Toppers	4 servings	11.07/254.72	1262.8	78.70	451.2	56.5	1 Meat
	1 serving	2.77/63.68	315.7	19.67	112.8	14.1	
Hawaiian Dip	4 servings	6.04/138.90	576.9	40.91	19.2	6.5	¼ Milk I
	1 serving	1.51/34.72	144.2	10.23	4.8	1.6	2 Fruit
Hearts of Palm Salad	6 servings	13.36/307.35	797.2	156.93	0.0	53.7	2 Vegetable
	1 serving	2.23/51.22	132.9	26.16	0.0	8.9	
Herb Biscuits (no salt)	16 servings	3.89/89.48	1742.2	62.81	3.2	82.8	1 Biscuit =
	1 serving	0.24/5.59	108.9	3.93	0.2	5.2	½ Bread I
Herb Margarine	12 servings	0.39/8.92	436.5	2.22	0.0	4.9	1 Teaspoon =
	1 serving	0.03/0.74	36.4	0.18	0.0	0.4	1 Fat
Herb Omelet	2 servings	16.15/371.50	311.6	1.79	0.0	10.0	2½ Meat
	1 serving	8.08/185.75	155.8	0.89	0.0	5.0	

Nutritive Value of Recipes:26

RECIPES		Sodium mEq/mg	Food Energy Calories	Potas- sium mEq	Choles- terol mg	Total Fat gm	Food Group Per Serving
Herb-Seasoned Croutons	8 servings	0.84/19.32	1364.2	10.66	0.0	14.7	¼ Cup =
	1 serving	0.10/2.41	170.5	1.33	0.0	1.8	1 Bread I
Herbed Asparagus with Lemon	4 servings	0.27/6.30	343.5	29.42	0.0	3.7	1 Vegetable
	1 serving	0.07/1.57	85.9	7.35	0.0	0.9	
Herbed Hamburgers	4 servings	10.29/236.59	1186.5	71.85	451.2	55.6	1 Meat
	1 serving	2.57/59.15	296.6	17.96	112.8	13.9	
Herbed Tomatoes	6 servings	0.78/17.98	154.2	34.03	0.0	1.4	1 Vegetable
	1 serving	0.13/3.00	25.7	5.67	0.0	0.2	
Hollandaise Sauce	4 servings	6.09/140.10	951.2	2.51	0.0	13.1	¼ Cup =
	1 serving	1.52/35.02	237.8	0.63	0.0	3.3	½ Meat
Homestyle Pot Roast	8 servings	25.65/589.88	2339.6	98.64	873.6	111.6	1 Meat
	1 serving	3.21/73.73	292.5	12.33	109.2	14.0	
Honey Fruit Salad Dressing	8 servings	0.36/8.30	493.9	3.18	0.0	0.1	1 Tablespoon =
	1 serving	0.05/1.04	61.7	0.40	0.0	0.0	Trace Sodium
Honey Glazed Acorn Squash	6 servings	0.47/10.87	1009.0	75.61	0.0	6.4	½ Vegetable
	1 serving	0.08/1.81	168.2	12.60	0.0	1.1	
Honey Orange Cake	9 servings	11.84/272.27	2699.0	60.95	3.2	16.7	1 Bread I
	1 serving	1.32/30.25	299.9	6.77	0.4	1.9	

Nutritive Value of Recipes:27

RECIPES		Sodium mEq/mg	Food Energy Calories	Potassium mEq	Cholesterol mg	Total Fat gm	Food Group Per Serving
Honey Whole-Wheat Bread	36 servings	68.87/1584.02	3941.3	58.65	0.0	75.0	½ Bread II
	1 serving	1.91/44.00	109.5	1.63	0.0	2.1	
Honey Whole-Wheat Bread (no Salt)	36 servings	1.47/33.70	3941.3	58.65	0.0	75.0	Trace Sodium
	1 serving	0.04/0.94	109.5	1.63	0.0	2.1	
Honey Whole-Wheat Cloverleaf Rolls	12 servings	17.27/397.14	1023.1	15.44	0.0	18.8	1 Roll =
	1 serving	1.44/33.09	85.3	1.29	0.0	1.6	½ Bread II
Honey Whole-Wheat Cloverleaf Rolls (no Salt)	12 servings	0.42/9.56	1023.1	15.44	0.0	18.8	1 Roll =
	1 serving	0.03/0.80	85.3	1.29	0.0	1.6	Trace Sodium
Honey Whole-Wheat Pan Rolls	24 servings	17.27/397.14	1023.1	15.44	0.0	18.8	1 Roll =
	1 serving	0.72/16.55	42.6	0.64	0.0	0.8	1 Bread I
Honey Whole-Wheat Pan Rolls (no Salt)	24 servings	0.42/9.56	1023.1	15.44	0.0	18.8	1 Roll =
	1 serving	0.02/0.40	42.6	0.64	0.0	0.8	Trace Sodium
Honeyed Tea	6 servings	0.32/7.34	437.2	19.97	0.0	0.3	Trace Sodium
	1 serving	0.05/1.22	72.9	3.33	0.0	0.0	
Hot Bread in Foil	15 servings	2.70/62.19	2712.5	18.15	0.0	14.8	1 Bread I
	1 serving	0.18/4.15	180.8	1.21	0.0	1.0	
Hot Meatballs	16 servings	10.29/236.59	1186.5	71.85	451.2	55.6	2 Meatballs =
	1 serving	0.64/14.79	74.2	4.49	28.2	3.5	¼ Meat

Nutritive Value of Recipes:28

RECIPES		Sodium mEq/mg	Food Energy Calories	Potassium mEq	Cholesterol mg	Total Fat gm	Food Group Per Serving
Hot Pepper Relish	8 servings	6.87/158.05	203.0	42.55	0.0	3.1	¼ Cup =
	1 serving	0.86/19.76	25.4	5.32	0.0	0.4	½ Vegetable
Iced Orange Ice	4 servings	0.21/4.80	668.1	25.04	0.0	1.0	1 Fruit
	1 serving	0.05/1.20	167.0	6.26	0.0	0.2	
Italian Green Beans	4 servings	0.91/20.90	123.3	21.69	0.0	0.7	1 Vegetable
	1 serving	0.23/5.22	30.8	5.42	0.0	0.2	
Italian Greens (with Collards)	6 servings	26.74/614.91	686.2	70.18	47.5	34.8	½ Salted Vegetable
	1 serving	4.46/102.48	114.4	11.70	7.9	5.8	
Italian Greens (with Dandelion Greens)	6 servings	34.67/797.31	686.2	62.79	47.5	33.8	½ Salted Vegetable
	1 serving	5.78/132.88	114.4	10.47	7.9	5.6	
Italian Greens (with Kale)	6 servings	34.25/787.71	743.8	60.08	47.5	34.8	½ Salted Vegetable
	1 serving	5.71/131.28	124.0	10.01	7.9	5.8	
Italian Greens (with Turnip Greens)	6 servings	37.17/854.91	561.4	85.44	47.5	30.0	½ Salted Vegetable
	1 serving	6.19/142.48	93.6	14.24	7.9	5.0	
Italian Style Hamburgers	4 servings	10.21/234.72	107818	70.56	451.2	55.1	1 Meat
	1 serving	2.55/58.68	269.7	17.64	112.8	13.8	
Jeweled Fruit Cake	8 servings	13.88/319.16	4656.1	156.21	0.0	250.6	2 Bread I
	1 serving	1.73/39.89	582.0	19.53	0.0	31.3	

Nutritive Value of Recipes:29

RECIPES		Sodium mEq/mg	Food Energy Calories	Potas-sium mEq	Choles-terol mg	Total Fat gm	Food Group Per Serving
Kettle Gravy	8 servings	0.11/2.52	63.7	19.88	0.0	0.2	2 Tablespoons =
	1 serving	0.01/0.31	8.0	2.49	0.0	0.0	Trace Sodium
Lazy Day Pot Roast	6 servings	25.91/595.87	2076.0	110.49	873.6	74.5	1½ Meat
	1 serving	4.32/99.31	346.0	18.41	145.6	12.4	
Lemon Dressing	6 servings	0.03/0.59	544.7	1.35	0.0	60.2	2 Tablespoons =
	1 serving	0.00/0.10	90.8	0.22	0.0	10.0	2 Fat
Lemon Margarine Sauce	12 servings	0.01/0.30	871.5	1.79	0.0	9.8	1 Teaspoon =
	1 serving	0.00/0.02	72.6	0.15	0.0	0.8	1 Fat
Lemon Meringue Pie	6 servings	11.41/262.3	2607.1	10.49	0.0	13.8	⅙ of Pie = ½ Bread I ½ Meat
	1 serving	1.90/43.72	434.5	1.75	0.0	2.3	
Lemon Poultry Basting Sauce	28 servings	0.16/3.71	1394.1	8.99	0.0	16.3	1 Tablespoon =
	1 serving	0.01/0.13	49.8	0.32	0.0	0.6	1 Fat
Lemon Pudding	4 servings	0.13/2.88	791.1	3.16	0.0	1.6	Trace Sodium
	1 serving	0.03/0.72	197.8	0.79	0.0	0.4	
Lemon Sauce	8 servings	0.20/4.57	867.8	1.25	0.0	9.7	1 Tablespoon =
	1 serving	0.02/0.57	108.5	0.16	0.0	1.2	3 Fat
Lemon Sesame Chicken	4 servings	16.82/386.83	1219.9	51.05	435.0	63.1	1¼ Meat
	1 serving	4.20/96.71	305.0	12.76	108.8	15.8	

Nutritive Value of Recipes:30

RECIPES	Sodium mEq/mg	Food Energy Calories	Potassium mEq	Cholesterol mg	Total Fat gm	Food Group Per Serving
Lemon Squares 25 servings	8.25/189.80	2346.7	17.00	0.0	15.5	1 Bar =
1 serving	0.33/7.59	93.9	0.68	0.0	0.6	¼ Bread 1
Lime Apple Cooler 2 servings	0.48/11.10	209.2	5.19	0.0	1.1	1 Fruit
1 serving	0.24/5.55	104.6	2.59	0.0	0.6	
Macaroni Vegetable Casserole 2 servings	0.68/15.70	320.0	23.81	0.0	1.6	1 Vegetable
1 serving	0.34/7.85	160.0	11.91	0.0	0.8	1 Bread I
Macedoine of Winter Fruit with Glaze 8 servings	2.83/65.20	1768.6	75.65	0.0	5.2	2 Fruit
1 serving	0.35/8.15	221.1	9.46	0.0	0.7	
Maple Nut Frosting 15 servings	0.71/16.35	2517.4	9.64	0.0	25.7	Trace Sodium
1 serving	0.05/1.09	167.8	0.64	0.0	1.7	
Maple Syrup 6 servings	11.13/255.90	1456.6	9.69	0.0	1.2	¼ Cup =
1 serving	1.85/42.65	242.8	1.61	0.0	0.2	2 mEq Sodium
Margarine Frosting 15 servings	0.84/19.35	2050.8	1.88	0.6	6.5	Trace Sodium
1 serving	0.06/1.29	136.7	0.13	0.0	0.4	
Marinated Flank Steak 4 servings	13.49/310.34	1780.5	58.89	436.8	119.7	1 Meat
1 serving	3.37/77.58	445.1	14.72	109.2	29.9	
Mayonnaise 36 servings	3.03/69.69	1943.6	0.73	0.0	213.5	2 Teaspoons =
1 serving	0.08/1.94	54.0	0.02	0.0	5.9	1 Fat

Nutritive Value of Recipes:31

RECIPES		Sodium mEq/mg	Food Energy Calories	Potassium mEq	Cholesterol mg	Total Fat gm	Food Group Per Serving
Meat Basting Sauce	36 servings	1.67/38.30	2449.9	18.01	0.0	240.3	1 Tablespoon =
	1 serving	0.05/1.06	68.1	0.50	0.0	6.7	1 Fat
Meat Loaf	3 servings	66.88/1538.21	932.6	67.34	245.4	40.2	1½ Meat
	1 serving	22.29/512.74	310.9	22.45	81.8	13.4	1 Salted Vegetable
Meatballs and Tomato Sauce	8 servings	14.52/334.03	2242.2	159.61	451.2	73.8	⅓ Meat
	1 serving	1.82/41.75	280.3	19.95	56.4	9.2	½ Bread I
Meaty Spaghetti Sauce	4 servings	14.13/325.10	1441.3	143.74	451.2	56.8	1 Meat
	1 serving	3.53/81.27	360.3	35.93	112.8	14.2	½ Vegetable
Medium White Sauce	2 Servings	5.44/125.12	360.6	9.49	4.8	2.8	½ Cup =
	1 serving	2.72/62.56	180.3	4.74	2.4	1.4	½ Milk I
Meringue Pie Shell	16 servings	11.13/256.04	834.0	5.55	0.0	0.0	¼ Meat
	1 serving	0.70/16.00	52.1	0.35	0.0	0.0	
Mexican Relish	8 servings	2.20/50.51	199.3	40.22	0.0	1.4	¼ Cup =
	1 serving	0.27/6.31	24.9	5.03	0.0	0.2	¼ Vegetable
Middle Eastern Meatballs	24 servings	25.98/597.57	2890.8	66.45	705.6	231.6	2 Meatballs =
	1 serving	1.08/24.90	120.4	2.77	29.4	9.6	⅓ Meat
Minted Fruit Salad	8 servings	2.48/57.05	1996.9	80.21	0.0	123.3	2 Fruit
	1 serving	0.31/7.13	249.6	10.03	0.0	15.4	

Nutritive Value of Recipes:32

RECIPES		Sodium mEq/mg	Food Energy Calories	Potas-sium mEq	Choles-terol mg	Total Fat gm	Food Group Per Serving
Minted Melon Balls	6 servings	1.45/33.40	689.3	22.00	0.0	0.7	1 Fruit
	1 serving	0.24/5.57	114.9	3.67	0.0	0.1	
Minted Peas	4 servings	0.61/14.07	558.8	11.97	0.0	4.5	1 Bread I
	1 serving	0.15/3.52	139.7	2.99	0.0	1.1	
Minted Pineapple	4 servings	0.23/5.30	243.6	13.97	0.0	0.7	1 Fruit
	1 serving	0.06/1.32	60.9	3.49	0.0	0.2	
Mixed Green Salad with Lemon Dressing	6 servings	6.96/160.01	559.3	38.73	0.0	51.6	1 Vegetable
	1 serving	1.16/26.67	93.2	6.46	0.0	8.6	
Mixed Vegetable Salad	2 servings	4.64/106.64	277.9	10.86	15.0	24.5	½ Bread II
	1 serving	2.32/53.32	138.9	5.43	7.5	12.2	
Mocha Spice Cake	15 servings	18.54/426.39	5466.6	88.89	4.8	29.4	1 Bread I
	1 serving	1.24/28.43	364.4	5.93	0.3	2.0	
Mulled Pineapple Juice	4 servings	0.77/17.62	500.4	29.53	0.0	2.0	1½ Fruit
	1 serving	0.19/4.40	125.1	7.38	0.0	0.5	
Mulligatawny Soup	4 servings	9.63/221.49	1109.3	60.16	156.6	20.8	1 Vegetable
	1 serving	2.41/55.37	277.3	15.04	39.1	5.2	½ Meat
Mushroom and Radish Salad	2 servings	1.00/23.04	439.4	13.48	0.0	45.5	1 Vegetable
	1 serving	0.50/11.52	219.7	6.74	0.0	22.8	

Nutritive Value of Recipes:33

RECIPES		Sodium mEq/mg	Food Energy Calories	Potas- sium mEq	Choles- terol mg	Total Fat gm	Food Group Per Serving
Mushroom Macaroni	1 serving	1.89/43.45	229.0	4.42	4.8	2.9	1 Bread I
							½ Vegetable
Mushroom Omelet	4 servings	12.59/289.62	700.4	34.55	1008.0	54.0	1 Meat
	1 serving	3.15/72.40	175.1	8.64	252.0	13.5	1 Vegetable
Mushroom Omelet (with Imitation Eggs)	2 servings	16.34/375.75	321.4	5.72	0.0	10.1	2½ Meat
	1 serving	8.17/187.87	160.7	2.86	0.0	5.1	½ Vegetable
Near East Lamb	6 servings	19.69/452.86	1676.1	83.97	600.0	78.2	1 Meat
	1 serving	3.28/75.48	279.3	14.00	100.0	13.0	½ Vegetable
New Delhi Rice	8 servings	0.92/21.24	868.3	28.28	0.0	3.8	1 Bread I
	1 serving	0.12/2.65	108.5	3.53	0.0	0.5	
Nut Bars	24 servings	0.40/9.14	4025.4	25.13	0.0	118.0	1 Bar =
	1 serving	0.02/0.38	167.7	1.05	0.0	4.9	½ Bread I
Nut Bread	16 servings	11.17/256.84	3367.2	94.03	6.0	136.2	1 Bread I
	1 serving	0.70/16.05	210.4	5.88	0.4	8.5	
Nut Waffles	3 servings	17.80/409.30	2308.3	110.20	8.4	31.4	10-inch Waffles =
	1 serving	5.93/136 43	769.4	36.73	2.8	10.5	1 Bread II
Oatmeal Cookies	30 servings	38.47/884.92	5085.9	85.05	0.0	112.2	2 Cookies =
	1 serving	1.28/29.50	169.5	2.84	0.0	3.7	1 Bread I

Nutritive Value of Recipes:34

RECIPES		Sodium mEq/mg	Food Energy Calories	Potassium mEq	Cholesterol mg	Total Fat gm	Food Group Per Serving
Oil Pastry (8 or 9-inch One-Crust Pie)	6 servings	0.13/2.92	1238.6	3.56	0.0	81.5	1/6 of Pie =
	1 serving	0.02/0.49	206.4	0.59	0.0	13.6	Trace
Oil Pastry (8 or 9-inch Two-Crust Pie or 10-Inch One-Crust Pie)	8 servings	0.20/4.56	1890.7	5.55	0.0	122.3	1/6 of Pie =
	1 serving	0.02/0.57	236.3	0.69	0.0	15.3	Trace Sodium
Old-Fashioned French Dressing	12 servings	0.22/5.01	2242.8	4.25	0.0	241.3	2 Tablespoons =
	1 serving	0.02/0.42	186.9	0.35	0.0	20.1	4 Fat
Omelet	2 servings	15.98/367.50	308.0	0.54	0.0	10.0	2½ Meat
	1 serving	7.99/183.75	154.0	0.27	0.0	5.0	
Omelet Fines Herbes	3 servings	8.30/190.83	382.4	9.38	756.0	18.8	1 Meat
	1 serving	2.77/63.61	127.5	3.13	252.0	6.3	
Omelet Française	4 servings	12.08/277.78	616.1	9.31	1009.2	25.5	1 Meat
	1 serving	3.02/69.44	154.0	2.33	252.3	6.4	
Onion Slices Sautéed	1 serving	0.43/10.00	254.0	4.20	0.0	2.5	1 Vegetable
Open-Faced Salmon Sandwich	2 servings	3.00/68.91	383.4	10.74	39.0	11.6	1 Bread I
	1 serving	1.50/34.45	191.7	5.37	19.5	5.8	½ Meat
Orange Baked Acorn Squash	2 servings	0.18/4.20	327.0	42.73	0.0	1.6	1 Vegetable
	1 serving	0.09/2.10	163.5	21.37	0.0	0.8	

Nutritive Value of Recipes:35

RECIPES		Sodium mEq/mg	Food Energy Calories	Potassium mEq	Cholesterol mg	Total Fat gm	Food Group Per Serving
Orange Compote	8 servings	0.64/14.70	1728.3	60.23	0.0	2.3	1 Fruit
	1 serving	0.08/1.84	216.0	7.53	0.0	0.3	
Orange Eggnog	2 servings	8.53/196.14	224.3	19.88	4.8	2.5	½ Meat
	1 serving	4.26/98.07	112.2	9.94	2.4	1.2	½ Milk I
Orange or Lemon Frosting	15 servings	0.18/4.15	2029.1	2.21	0.0	6.5	Trace Sodium
	1 serving	0.01/0.28	135.3	0.15	0.0	0.4	
Orange Sauce	4 servings	0.19/4.40	1823.6	21.08	0.0	10.0	¼ Cup =
	1 serving	0.05/1.10	455.9	5.27	0.0	2.5	Trace Sodium
Orange Shake	1 serving	4.80/110.37	224.0	21.62	2.4	1.6	½ Milk I
							¾ Meat
Orange Slices Grand Marnier	1 serving	0.08/1.75	61.8	5.48	0.0	0.2	1 Fruit
Orange Spiced Tea	2 servings	0.42/9.77	273.2	12.04	0.0	0.9	Trace Sodium
	1 serving	0.21/4.88	136.6	6.02	0.0	0.4	
Orange Sweet Potatoes	4 servings	2.92/67.12	932.7	51.57	0.0	4.1	2 Bread I
	1 serving	0.73/16.78	233.2	12.89	0.0	1.0	½ Fruit
Orange Waffles	3 servings	17.82/409.90	3107.7	108.64	8.4	26.9	10-inch Waffle =
	1 serving	5.94/136.63	1035.9	36.21	2.8	9.0	1 Bread II

Nutritive Value of Recipes:36

RECIPES		Sodium mEq/mg	Food Energy Calories	Potassium mEq	Cholesterol mg	Total Fat gm	Food Group Per Serving
Oven Fried Fillets	6 servings	28.21/648.85	1392.8	80.98	578.4	7.7	4 ounces =
	1 serving	4.70/108.14	232.1	13.50	96.4	1.3	1½ Meat
Oven Poached Haddock	4 servings	19.64/451.64	674.7	77.92	432.0	1.7	1½ Meat
	1 serving	4.91/112.91	168.7	19.48	108.0	0.4	½ Vegetable
Pancakes	16 servings	16.44/378.09	1940.2	87.35	7.2	67.3	1 Pancake =
	1 serving	1.03/23.63	121.3	5.46	0.4	4.2	1 Bread I
Pan-Fried Fish	6 servings	25.84/594.41	2144.2	76.88	528.0	97.2	5 ounces =
	1 serving	4.31/99.07	357.4	12.81	88.0	16.2	1½ Meat
Parsleyed New Potatoes	3 servings	0.77/17.63	498.0	40.83	0.0	2.9	1 Bread I
	1 serving	0.26/5.88	166.0	13.61	0.0	1.0	
Parsleyed Potatoes	4 servings	1.08/24.94	507.7	36.72	0.0	3.3	1 Bread I
	1 serving	0.27/6.23	126.9	9.18	0.0	0.8	
Party Rice	4 servings	1.96/45.05	896.2	16.03	0.0	2.3	1 Bread I
	1 serving	0.49/11.26	224.0	4.01	0.0	0.6	½ Vegetable
Peaches in Port	6 servings	0.44/10.10	1316.9	31.30	0.0	0.6	1 Fruit
	1 serving	0.07/1.68	219.5	5.22	0.0	0.1	
Pepper Steak	8 servings	28.89/664.40	2303.0	189.79	902.4	80.6	1 Meat
	1 serving	3.61/83.05	287.9	23.72	112.8	10.1	1½ Vegetable

Nutritive Value of Recipes:37

RECIPES		Sodium mEq/mg	Food Energy Calories	Potassium mEq	Cholesterol mg	Total Fat gm	Food Group Per Serving
Petits Fours	35 servings	19.54/449.53	9074.4	93.01	4.8	12.9	1 Cake =
	1 serving	0.56/12.84	259.3	2.66	0.1	0.4	1 Bread I
Pineapple Carrots	2 servings	2.76/63.52	170.3	9.11	0.0	1.2	1 Vegetable
	1 serving	1.38/31.76	85.1	4.55	0.0	0.6	
Pineapple Coffee Cake	18 servings	8.47/194.84	3632.9	57.86	1.2	106.7	½ Bread I
	1 serving	0.47/10.82	201.8	3.21	0.1	5.9	
Pineapple Cranberry Relish Mold	10 servings	38.76/891.41	913.8	58.75	0.0	3.3	1 Fruit
	1 serving	3.88/89.14	91.4	5.88	0.0	0.3	½ Salted Vegetable
Pineapple Fluff	4 servings	4.03/92.62	239.2	7.84	0.0	0.2	¼ Meat
	1 serving	1.01/23.15	59.8	1.96	0.0	0.0	½ Fruit
Pineapple Frosting	15 servings	0.20/4.58	2062.9	3.87	0.0	6.6	Trace Sodium
	1 serving	0.01/0.31	137.5	0.26	0.0	0.4	
Pineapple Glacé	6 servings	0.23/5.26	983.5	18.57	0.0	1.0	1 Fruit
	1 serving	0.04/0.88	163.9	3.09	0.0	0.2	
Pineapple Sweet Potatoes	6 servings	11.91/273.90	1286.8	44.13	0.0	3.7	2 Bread I
	1 serving	1.98/45.65	214.5	7.35	0.0	0.6	
Pineapple Upside-Down Cake	9 servings	16.75/385.34	5124.5	91.98	6.0	34.9	2 Bread I
	1 serving	1.86/42.82	569.4	10.22	0.7	3.9	

Nutritive Value of Recipes:38

RECIPES		Sodium mEq/mg	Food Energy Calories	Potassium mEq	Cholesterol mg	Total Fat gm	Food Group Per Serving
Pizza	1 serving	0.72/16.61	305.1	9.81	0.0	6.4	1 Bread I
Poached Egg	1 serving	2.68/61.57	229.5	2.29	252.0	7.5	1 Meat
Poached Egg (with Imitation Eggs)	1 serving	3.00/69.09	37.6	0.08	0.0	1.6	1 Meat
Poached Fish	3 servings	11.45/263.24	800.8	43.70	264.0	40.0	1 Meat
	1 serving	3.82/87.75	266.9	14.57	88.0	13.3	
Poppy Seed Cake	15 servings	14.92/343.17	5441.8	105.00	5.4	19.4	1 Bread I
	1 serving	0.99/22.88	362.8	7.00	0.4	1.3	
Pork Chops and Rice	4 servings	10.69/245.80	1176.3	47.96	316.8	52.8	1 Meat
	1 serving	2.67/61.45	294.1	11.99	79.2	13.2	
Potato Bake	4 servings	2.03/46.62	720.4	74.54	0.0	3.7	1 Bread I
	1 serving	0.51/11.65	180.1	18.64	0.0	0.9	½ Vegetable
Potato Omelet	1 serving	2.85/65.46	272.3	8.19	252.0	21.0	1 Meat
							1 Bread I
Poulet André	4 servings	17.47/401.85	1513.7	71.20	417.6	90.9	1½ Meat
	1 serving	4.37/100.46	378.4	17.80	104.4	22.7	

Nutritive Value of Recipes:39

RECIPES		Sodium mEq/mg	Food Energy Calories	Potas-sium mEq	Choles-terol mg	Total Fat gm	Food Group Per Serving
Puffy Omelet	4 servings	10.61/244.06	366.0	6.82	1008.0	23.5	1 Meat
	1 serving	2.65/61.01	91.5	1.70	252.0	5.9	
Pumpkin Cookies	72 servings	14.67/337.51	4858.7	178.46	0.0	98.7	1 Cookie =
	1 serving	0.20/4.69	67.5	2.48	0.0	1.4	¼ Bread I
Quick Cranberry Ice	4 servings	0.63/14.50	420.2	1.92	0.0	0.5	1 Fruit
	1 serving	0.16/3.63	105.0	0.48	0.0	0.1	
Quick Dill Sauce	12 servings	3.76/86.45	1088.4	5.20	122.4	184.2	2 Tablespoons =
	1 serving	0.31/7.20	90.7	0.43	10.2	15.4	4 Fat
Quick Mix Pizza	16 servings	15.62/359.33	3066.3	162.39	451.2	92.2	⅛ of Pizza =
	1 serving	0.98/22.46	191.6	10.15	28.2	5.8	1 Bread I
Quick Orange Soufflé	1 serving	2.06/47.37	109.5	1.23	0.0	0.0	¾ Meat
Quick Peach Cobbler	6 servings	3.62/83.27	1603.0	65.50	2.4	41.3	1 Bread I
	1 serving	0.60/13.88	267.2	10.92	0.4	6.9	1 Fruit
Rainbow Float	5 servings	0.31/7.20	768.0	21.23	0.0	0.7	Trace Sodium
	1 serving	0.06/1.44	153.6	4.25	0.0	0.1	
Raspberry Melon Boats	4 servings	1.23/28.35	653.5	26.44	0.0	0.9	1 Fruit
	1 serving	0.31/7.09	163.4	6.61	0.0	0.2	

Nutritive Value of Recipes:40

RECIPES		Sodium mEq/mg	Food Energy Calories	Potassium mEq	Cholesterol mg	Total Fat gm	Food Group Per Serving
Raspberry Pineapple Ice	4 servings	0.48/11.10	638.2	18.08	0.0	1.0	2 Fruit
	1 serving	0.12/2.77	159.6	4.52	0.0	0.3	
Ratatouille	6 servings	2.45/56.28	780.9	58.90	0.0	61.9	1 Vegetable
	1 serving	0.41/9.38	130.1	9.82	0.0	10.3	
Ratatouille Omelet	2 servings	16.38/376.85	435.6	10.28	0.0	20.3	2½ Meat
	1 serving	8.19/188.42	217.8	5.14	0.0	10.1	½ Vegetable
Rice Pudding	7 servings	26.53/610.26	1738.0	36.49	12.0	7.5	½ Milk I
	1 serving	3.79/87.18	248.3	5.21	1.7	1.1	½ Meat
Roast Beef	1 serving	2.35/54.00	294.3	8.54	84.6	21.5	3 Ounces = 1 Meat
Roast Lamb	8 servings	29.35/675.09	1966.1	74.11	960.0	92.6	1 Meat
	1 serving	3.67/84.39	245.8	9.26	120.0	11.6	
Roast Turkey	1 serving	3.44/79.20	200.7	7.62	83.7	8.6	3 Ounces = 1 Meat
Roastin' Ears	1 serving	0.0/0.0	171.7	3.61	0.0	1.9	1 Bread I 1 Fat
Rum Sauce	2 servings	0.04/0.83	249.9	0.34	0.0	0.0	2½ Teaspoons =
	1 serving	0.02/0.41	125.0	0.17	0.0	0.0	Trace Sodium

Nutritive Value of Recipes:41

RECIPES		Sodium mEq/mg	Food Energy Calories	Potassium mEq	Cholesterol mg	Total Fat gm	Food Group Per Serving
Russian Teacakes	12 servings	0.36/8.27	3632.0	18.96	0.0	80.0	4 Cookies =
	1 serving	0.03/0.69	302.7	1.58	0.0	6.7	½ Bread I
Salmon Steak Alaska	4 servings	9.60/220.72	1073.2	50.19	158.4	74.9	1 Meat
	1 serving	2.40/55.18	268.3	12.55	39.6	18.7	
Salmon with Dill Sauce	4 servings	10.09/232.10	1593.6	51.99	174.3	85.2	1 Meat
	1 serving	2.52/58.02	398.4	13.00	43.6	21.3	
Sauce Provençale	16 servings	0.41/9.40	357.9	10.57	0.0	3.9	1 Tablespoon =
	1 serving	0.03/0.59	22.4	0.66	0.0	0.2	½ Fat
Sauce Stroganoff	4 servings	12.82/294.86	388.9	5.52	79.2	29.2	¼ Cup =
	1 serving	3.20/73.71	97.2	1.38	19.8	7.3	½ Milk I
Savory Lamb	2 servings	8.11/186.42	634.1	38.81	240.0	23.8	1 Meat
							1 Vegetable
	1 serving	4.05/93.21	317.0	19.40	120.0	11.9	½ Bread I
Scotch Shortbread	24 servings	0.25/5.70	2434.9	7.43	0.0	17.2	1 Cookie =
	1 serving	0.01/0.24	101.5	0.31	0.0	0.7	Trace Sodium
Scrambled Eggs	4 servings	10.61/244.12	443.8	6.97	1008.0	24.7	1 Meat
	1 serving	2.65/61.03	111.0	1.74	252.0	6.2	
Scrambled Eggs (with Imitation Eggs)	4 servings	31.96/735.00	488.4	0.90	0.0	27.5	2½ Meat
	1 serving	7.99/183.75	122.1	0.22	0.0	6.9	

Nutritive Value of Recipes:42

RECIPES		Sodium mEq/mg	Food Energy Calories	Potassium mEq	Cholesterol mg	Total Fat gm	Food Group Per Serving
Scrambled Eggs (with Imitation Eggs) Variation I	4 servings	32.19/740.27	496.8	3.28	0.0	27.6	2½ Meat
	1 serving	8.05/185.07	124.2	0.82	0.0	6.9	
Scrambled Eggs (with Imitation Eggs) Variation 2	4 servings	112.83/2595.00	666.0	4.90	6.0	27.7	3 Salted Meat
	1 serving	28.21/648.75	166.5	1.22	1.5	6.9	
Seasoned Margarine	8 servings	0.19/4.42	864.1	0.71	0.0	9.7	1 Tablespoon =
	1 serving	0.02/0.55	108.0	0.09	0.0	1.2	3 Fat
Shallot Dressing	12 servings	0.97/22.41	1871.1	12.96	0.0	196.3	2 Tablespoons =
	1 serving	0.08/1.87	155.9	1.08	0.0	16.4	3 Fat
Shish Kebabs	2 servings	3.60/82.82	291.3	24.10	81.9	6.2	½ Meat
	1 serving	1.80/41.41	145.7	12.05	40.9	3.1	1 Vegetable
Shrimp Grapefruit Shell	4 servings	13.18/303.17	967.1	29.95	360.0	94.2	1 Meat
	1 serving	3.30/75.79	241.8	7.49	90.0	23.6	1 Fruit
Sizzling Grapefruit	2 servings	0.19/4.40	183.8	7.69	0.0	1.0	1 Fruit
	1 serving	0.10/2.20	91.9	3.84	0.0	0.5	1 Fat
Skillet Pork Chops	6 servings	16.34/375.72	1620.8	75.24	475.2	78.3	1 Meat
	1 serving	2.72/62.62	270.1	12.54	79.2	13.1	
Snow Pudding	6 servings	4.50/103.60	953.2	12.77	0.0	0.8	⅓ Meat
	1 serving	0.75/17.27	158.9	2.13	0.0	0.1	½ Fruit

Nutritive Value of Recipes:43

RECIPES		Sodium mEq/mg	Food Energy Calories	Potassium mEq	Cholesterol mg	Total Fat gm	Food Group Per Serving
Spaghetti with Creole Sauce	3 servings	2.31/53.09	511.2	26.29	0.0	2.2	1 Bread I
	1 serving	0.77/17.70	170.4	8.76	0.0	0.7	
Spanish Lobster Salad	4 servings	45.37/1043.55	1099.2	41.28	415.2	84.4	1 Salted Meat
	1 serving	11.34/260.89	274.8	10.32	103.8	21.1	1 Fruit
Spanish Rice with Meat	3 servings	7.77/178.68	1205.3	70.13	225.6	29.1	⅓ Meat ½ Vegetable
	1 serving	2.59/59.56	401.8	23.38	75.2	9.7	1 Bread I
Spice Cookies	18 servings	4.90/112.59	2258.2	41.62	0.0	48.8	2 Cookies =
	1 serving	0.27/6.25	125.5	2.31	0.0	2.7	¼ Bread I
Spice 'n' Raisin Cake	9 servings	9.69/222.90	2550.2	57.07	3.6	12.0	1 Bread I
	1 serving	1.08/24.77	283.4	6.34	0.4	1.3	
Spiced Fruit Compote	6 servings	0.67/15.30	742.2	30.34	0.0	2.5	1 Fruit
	1 serving	0.11/2.55	123.7	5.06	0.0	0.4	
Spiced Fruit Mold	8 servings	1.07/24.58	556.8	32.78	0.0	2.6	1 Fruit
	1 serving	0.13/3.07	69.6	4.10	0.0	0.3	
Spiced Honeydew Melon	6 servings	3.04/69.92	475.8	51.74	0.0	2.8	1½ Fruit
	1 serving	0.51/11.65	79.3	8.62	0.0	0.5	
Spiced Minted Pears	6 servings	0.88/20.19	556.2	16.64	0.0	3.2	1 Fruit
	1 serving	0.15/3.36	92.7	2.77	0.0	0.5	

290

Nutritive Value of Recipes:44

RECIPES		Sodium mEq/mg	Food Energy Calories	Potassium mEq	Cholesterol mg	Total Fat gm	Food Group Per Serving
Spicy French Dressing	8 servings	0.65/14.97	767.5	2.06	0.0	82.1	2 Tablespoons =
	1 serving	0.08/1.87	95.9	0.26	0.0	10.3	2 Fat
Spinach and Endive Salad	8 servings	5.23/120.30	695.5	47.76	0.0	62.3	1 Vegetable
	1 serving	0.65/15.04	86.9	5.97	0.0	7.8	
Spinach Salad	6 servings	11.84/272.33	1004.8	67.79	0.0	92.5	1 Vegetable
	1 serving	1.97/45.39	167.5	11.30	0.0	15.4	
Spritz	20 servings	4.26/97.98	3238.1	8.72	0.0	24.5	3 Cookies =
	1 serving	0.21/4.90	161.9	0.44	0.0	1.2	¼ Bread I
Standard Pastry (10-inch One-Crust Pie)	8 servings	0.15/3.46	1493.7	4.92	0.0	11.4	⅛ of Pie =
	1 serving	0.02/0.43	186.7	0.62	0.0	1.4	Trace Sodium
Standard Pastry (8 or 9-inch One-Crust Pie)	6 servings	0.11/2.60	1157.2	3.73	0.0	9.0	⅙ of Pie =
	1 serving	0.02/0.43	192.9	0.62	0.0	1.5	Trace Sodium
Standard Pastry (8 or 9-inch Two-Crust Pie)	6 servings	0.23/5.20	2314.4	7.45	0.0	18.0	⅛ of Pie =
	1 serving	0.04/0.87	385.7	1.24	0.0	3.0	Trace Sodium
Starlight Cake	12 servings	17.86/410.86	3257.8	86.71	4.8	19.1	1 Bread I
	1 serving	1.49/34.24	271.5	7.23	0.4	1.6	
Steak with Mushroom Sauce	4 servings	10.56/242.94	856.4	70.48	327.6	31.5	3 Ounces =
	1 serving	2.64/60.73	214.1	17.62	81.9	7.9	1 Meat

Nutritive Value of Recipes:45

RECIPES		Sodium mEq/mg	Food Energy Calories	Potassium mEq	Cholesterol mg	Total Fat gm	Food Group Per Serving
Steamed Clams	6 servings	11.27/259.20	590.4	43.38	360.0	13.7	1 Meat
	1 serving	1.88/43.20	98.4	7.23	60.0	2.3	
Steamed Hard-Shell Crabs	6 servings	65.74/1512.00	669.6	33.23	720.0	13.7	1¼ Salted Meat
	1 serving	10.96/252.00	111.6	5.54	120.0	2.3	
Stewed Beef	12 servings	37.59/864.54	2757.6	138.18	1310.4	88.8	3 Ounces =
	1 serving	3.13/72.04	229.8	11.51	109.2	7.4	1 Meat
Stewed Chicken	10 servings	36.80/846.36	1744.2	105.80	783.0	57.5	3 Ounces =
	1 serving	3.68/84.64	174.4	10.58	78.3	5.7	1 Meat
Stewed Rhubarb	6 servings	0.54/12.50	821.3	36.46	0.0	0.6	½ Fruit
	1 serving	0.09/2.08	136.9	6.08	0.0	0.1	
Stir 'n' Roll Biscuits with Salt and Regular Baking Powder	16 servings	63.58/1462.38	1725.7	12.81	3.2	82.8	1 Biscuit =
	1 serving	3.97/91.40	107.9	0.80	0.2	5.2	1 Bread II
Stir 'n' Roll Biscuits (no Salt)	16 servings	3.89/89.48	1742.2	62.81	3.2	82.8	1 Biscuit =
	1 serving	0.24/5.59	108.9	3.93	0.2	5.2	½ Bread I
Strawberry Sparkler	4 servings	0.35/8.10	1421.7	12.88	0.0	1.5	½ Fruit
	1 serving	0.09/2.02	355.4	3.22	0.0	0.4	
Strawberry Supreme	8 servings	0.56/12.77	943.5	42.78	0.0	3.1	1½ Fruit
	1 serving	0.07/1.60	117.9	5.35	0.0	0.4	

Nutritive Value of Recipes:46

RECIPES		Sodium mEq/mg	Food Energy Calories	Potassium mEq	Cholesterol mg	Total Fat gm	Food Group Per Serving
Strawberry Turnover	6 servings	0.68/15.69	2210.7	18.48	0.3	14.2	1 Bread I
	1 serving	0.11/2.61	368.4	3.08	0.0	2.4	½ Fruit
Streamlined Batter Bread	18 servings	34.20/786.56	1774.3	12.66	0.0	34.8	½ Bread II
	1 serving	1.90/43.70	98.6	0.70	0.0	1.9	
Streusel Coffee Cake	16 servings	9.77/224.75	2913.9	81.75	3.6	54.5	½ Bread I
	1 serving	0.61/14.05	182.1	5.11	0.2	3.4	
Stuffed Cherry Tomatoes with Chicken Salad	1 serving	0.52/11.88	49.9	4.11	12.4	3.9	4 Tomatoes = ½ Vegetable ¼ Meat
Stuffed Cherry Tomatoes with Egg Salad	1 serving	1.09/25.12	39.0	2.54	2.0	3.7	4 Tomatoes = ½ Vegetable ¼ Meat
Stuffed Cherry Tomatoes with Tuna Salad	1 serving	0.24/5.52	54.3	3.26	9.0	6.3	4 Tomatoes = ½ Vegetable ¼ Meat
Stuffed Green Peppers	2 servings	7.92/182.10	828.1	64.58	225.6	28.1	1 Meat 1 Bread I 1 Vegetable
	1 serving	3.96/91.05	414.0	32.29	112.8	14.0	
Stuffing with Low-Sodium Bread	18 servings	11.60/266.82	3062.4	34.83	13.5	34.6	1 Bread I
	1 serving	0.64/14.82	170.1	1.93	0.8	1.9	3 Fat
Stuffing with Regular Bread	18 servings	105.32/2422.32	3062.4	34.83	13.5	34.6	1 Bread
	1 serving	5.85/134.57	170.1	1.93	0.8	1.9	3 Fat

Nutritive Value of Recipes:47

RECIPES		Sodium mEq/mg	Food Energy Calories	Potassium mEq	Cholesterol mg	Total Fat gm	Food Group Per Serving
Sugar Cookies	24 servings	4.35/100.00	3321.6	26.09	0.0	20.0	2 Cookies =
	1 serving	0.18/4.17	138.4	1.09	0.0	0.8	¼ Bread I
Sugar Crisp Rolls	18 servings	5.87/135.00	3895.8	34.31	1.2	161.6	1 Roll =
	1 serving	0.33/7.50	216.4	1.91	0.1	9.0	½ Bread I
Summer Cooler	10 servings	5.75/132.15	1414.5	37.86	0.0	0.1	Trace Sodium
	1 serving	0.57/13.21	141.5	3.79	0.0	0.0	
Summer Dinner Platter	12 servings	39.90/917.74	4510.9	196.22	1310.4	267.0	1 Meat
	1 serving	3.33/76.48	375.9	16.35	109.2	22.2	1 Vegetable
Summer Garden Chicken Grill	1 serving	3.78/86.92	419.3	27.11	78.3	11.4	1 Meat 1 Vegetable 1 Bread I
Summer Vegetable Skillet	4 servings	0.88/20.17	512.6	12.99	0.0	5.3	1 Vegetable
	1 serving	0.22/5.04	128.2	3.25	0.0	1.3	
Sunshine Salad	6 servings	3.49/80.17	877.9	52.45	0.0	1.6	1 Fruit
	1 serving	0.58/13.36	146.3	8.74	0.0	0.3	¼ Vegetable
Super Nog (with Egg)	4 servings	16.47/378.70	944.9	66.43	513.6	18.1	½ Milk I
	1 serving	4.12/94.67	236.2	16.61	128.4	4.5	½ Meat
Super Nog (with Imitation Eggs)	4 servings	17.17/394.88	857.1	63.29	9.6	9.9	½ Milk I
	1 serving	4.29/98.72	214.3	15.82	2.4	2.5	½ Meat

Nutritive Value of Recipes:48

RECIPES		Sodium mEq/mg	Food Energy Calories	Potassium mEq	Cholesterol mg	Total Fat gm	Food Group Per Serving
Super Tomato Salad	4 servings	1.13/26.07	800.0	32.55	0.0	62.6	½ Vegetable
	1 serving	0.28/6.52	200.0	8.14	0.0	15.6	
Surprise Muffins	12 servings	7.36/169.36	1902.4	44.24	2.4	64.3	Small Muffin =
	1 serving	0.61/14.11	158.5	3.69	0.2	5.4	1 Bread I
Swedish Broiled Lamb Chops	4 servings	11.13/256.08	739.0	31.13	360.0	28.0	1 Meat
	1 serving	2.78/64.02	184.7	7.78	90.0	7.0	
Swedish Limpa Rye Bread	16 servings	102.55/2358.67	2995.5	44.96	0.0	39.1	1 Bread II
	1 serving	6.41/147.42	187.2	2.81	0.0	2.4	
Swedish Limpa Rye Bread (no Salt)	16 servings	1.44/33.19	2995.5	44.95	0.0	39.1	Trace Sodium
	1 serving	0.09/2.07	187.2	2.81	0.0	2.4	
Swedish Sauce	24 servings	1.19/27.48	1111.6	5.04	120.0	184.6	1 Tablespoon =
	1 serving	0.05/1.14	46.3	0.21	5.0	7.7	2 Fat
Swedish Tea Ring	17 servings	8.39/193.01	3241.4	38.06	1.5	68.1	½ Bread I
	1 serving	0.49/11.35	190.7	2.24	0.1	4.0	
Sweet and Sour Pot Roast	8 servings	35.04/805.93	3602.0	257.19	1092.0	144.6	1 Vegetable
	1 serving	4.38/100.74	450.3	32.15	136.5	18.1	1 Meat
Sweet Dough	15 servings	5.78/133.00	1908.7	13.79	1.2	65.4	1 Roll =
	1 serving	0.39/8.87	127.2	0.92	0.1	4.4	½ Bread I

Nutritive Value of Recipes:49

RECIPES		Sodium mEq/mg	Food Energy Calories	Potas- sium mEq	Choles- terol mg	Total Fat gm	Food Group Per Serving
Sweet Muffins	12 servings	6.92/159.16	1738.6	43.09	2.4	64.2	1 Small Muffin =
	1 serving	0.58/13.26	144.9	3.59	0.2	5.4	1 Bread I
Sweet Potato and Apple Bake	8 servings	5.87/135.06	1865.8	98.26	0.0	7.6	1 Bread I
	1 serving	0.73/16.88	233.2	12.28	0.0	0.9	
Tahitian Hash	2 servings	3.99/91.80	631.8	22.18	106.8	29.6	½ Meat
	1 serving	2.00/45.90	315.9	11.09	53.4	14.8	½ Bread I
Tangy Fruit Juice Cocktail	8 servings	0.63/14.53	1053.2	50.16	0.0	1.3	1 Fruit
	1 serving	0.08/1.82	131.7	6.27	0.0	0.2	
Tangy Spinach	4 servings	29.65/681.91	258.1	116.56	0.0	3.0	½ Salted Vegetable
	1 serving	7.41/170.48	64.5	29.14	0.0	0.8	
Tart Coleslaw	8 servings	3.23/74.40	409.0	14.81	55.8	53.8	½ Vegetable
	1 serving	0.40/9.30	51.1	1.85	7.0	6.7	
Thick White Sauce	2 servings	5.45/125.46	638.5	10.08	4.8	5.4	½ Cup =
	1 serving	2.73/62.73	319.3	5.04	2.4	2.7	½ Milk I
Thin White Sauce	2 servings	5.43/124.92	216.2	9.16	4.8	1.5	½ Cup =
	1 serving	2.72/62.46	108.1	4.58	2.4	0.8	½ Milk I
Tomato Macaroni	1 serving	0.20/4.70	222.8	8.04	0.0	1.7	1 Bread I
							1 Vegetable

Nutritive Value of Recipes:50

RECIPES	Sodium mEq/mg	Food Energy Calories	Potassium mEq	Cholesterol mg	Total Fat gm	Food Group Per Serving
Tomato Salad 6 servings	1.69/38.98	911.0	34.26	0.0	81.4	½ Vegetable
1 serving	0.28/6.50	151.8	5.71	0.0	13.6	
Tomato Sauce 2 servings	0.66/15.21	332.6	24.26	0.0	3.6	½ Cup =
1 serving	0.33/7.60	166.3	12.13	0.0	1.8	1 Vegetable
Tomato Stuffed with Chicken Salad 2 servings	4.99/114.79	389.2	26.38	121.8	23.5	1 Vegetable
1 serving	2.50/57.39	194.6	13.19	60.9	11.7	½ Meat
Tossed Green Salad 1 serving	0.19/4.40	71.5	2.80	0.0	5.3	½ Vegetable
Tossed Salad Elegante 4 servings	4.11/94.44	756.5	52.17	0.0	67.2	1 Vegetable
1 serving	1.03/23.61	189.1	13.04	0.0	16.8	
Traditional Roll Dough 12 servings	8.69/199.97	2516.9	22.03	3.6	67.1	1 Roll =
1 serving	0.72/16.66	209.7	1.84	0.3	5.6	1 Bread I
Traditional White Bread 36 servings	152.75/3513.30	3926.2	28.66	0.0	39.5	1 Bread II
1 serving	4.24/97.59	109.1	0.80	0.0	1.1	
Traditional White Bread (without Salt) 36 servings	1.09/25.08	3926.2	28.65	0.0	39.5	Trace Sodium
1 serving	0.03/0.70	109.1	0.80	0.0	1.1	
Tropical Fizz 6 servings	3.97/91.20	370.8	35.97	0.0	0.8	1 Fruit
1 serving	0.66/15.20	61.8	5.99	0.0	0.1	

Nutritive Value of Recipes:51

RECIPES		Sodium mEq/mg	Food Energy Calories	Potassium mEq	Cholesterol mg	Total Fat gm	Food Group Per Serving
Tropical Fruit and Wine Compote	6 servings	0.62/14.25	927.6	42.99	0.0	1.3	1½ Fruit
	1 serving	0.10/2.37	154.6	7.16	0.0	0.2	
Tropical Salad Dressing	12 servings	0.17/4.00	1265.7	18.73	0.0	120.4	2 Tablespoons =
	1 serving	0.01/0.33	105.5	1.56	0.0	10.0	2 Fat
Tuna Gourmet	6 servings	27.43/630.91	2537.1	67.52	630.9	62.9	1 Meat
	1 serving	4.57/105.15	422.8	11.25	105.2	10.5	1 Bread I
Tuna Salad	6 servings	12.56/288.92	1208.6	71.16	324.6	96.7	1 Meat
	1 serving	2.09/48.15	201.4	11.86	54.1	16.1	1 Vegetable
Unsalted Tomato Paste	8 servings	0.71/16.24	118.0	31.43	0.0	0.5	1 Tablespoon =
	1 serving	0.09/2.03	14.7	3.93	0.0	0.1	½ Vegetable
Vanilla Cream Pudding	4 servings	14.91/342.88	831.0	18.19	9.6	5.1	½ Milk I
	1 serving	3.73/85.72	207.8	4.55	2.4	1.3	½ Meat
Veal Scallopine with Lemon	6 servings	25.22/579.97	2545.8	100.84	722.1	159.4	3 Ounces =
	1 serving	4.20/96.66	424.3	16.81	120.4	26.6	1 Meat
Vegetable Combo	2 servings	0.43/9.97	127.5	32.68	0.0	0.4	½ Bread I
	1 serving	0.22/4.98	63.7	16.34	0.0	0.2	1 Vegetable
Vegetable Ring Soup	8 servings	7.41/170.39	559.2	80.29	127.4	11.3	1 Vegetable
	1 serving	0.93/21.30	69.9	10.04	15.9	1.4	1 Vegetable

Nutritive Value of Recipes:52

RECIPES		Sodium mEq/mg	Food Energy Calories	Potassium mEq	Cholesterol mg	Total Fat gm	Food Group Per Serving
Vegetable Soup	10 servings	8.98/206.61	474.0	205.63	0.0	2.4	1 Vegetable
	1 serving	0.90/20.66	47.4	20.56	0.0	0.2	
Vinaigrette Dressing	10 servings	0.32/7.37	1607.1	0.78	0.0	180.0	2 Tablespoons =
	1 serving	0.03/0.74	160.7	0.08	0.0	18.0	4 Fat
Water Bagels	8 servings	17.36/399.20	1441.2	12.84	0.0	3.7	½ Bread II
	1 serving	2.17/49.90	180.1	1.61	0.0	0.5	
Water Bagels (no salt)	8 servings	0.51/11.62	1441.2	12.84	0.0	3.7	Trace Sodium
	1 serving	0.06/1.45	180.1	1.61	0.0	0.5	
Watercress and Romaine Salad	6 servings	3.42/78.61	882.4	45.89	0.0	70.5	½ Vegetable
	1 serving	0.57/13.10	147.1	7.65	0.0	11.8	½ Fruit
Western Egg Sandwich	2 servings	34.03/782.80	546.8	7.16	4.0	9.4	1½ Meat
	1 serving	17.02/391.40	273.4	3.58	2.0	4.7	2 Bread II
Whipped Margarine	4 servings	0.0/0.0	864.0	0.71	0.0	9.7	2 Tablespoons =
	1 serving	0.0/0.0	216.0	0.18	0.0	2.4	Trace Sodium
White Cake	15 servings	14.13/324.94	3290.2	91.79	4.8	12.9	1 Bread I
	1 serving	0.94/21.66	219.3	6.12	0.3	0.9	
White Mountain Frosting	15 servings	6.66/153.12	669.1	2.51	0.0	0.0	Trace Sodium
	1 serving	0.44/10.21	44.6	0.17	0.0	0.0	

Nutritive Value of Recipes:53

RECIPES		Sodium mEq/mg	Food Energy Calories	Potas- sium mEq	Choles- terol mg	Total Fat gm	Food Group Per Serving
Weiner Schnitzel (with egg)	4 servings	43.87/1008.95	2464.9	102.08	981.7	123.0	3½ Meat
	1 serving	10.97/252.24	616.2	25.52	245.4	30.8	
Wiener Schnitzel (with Imitation Eggs)	4 servings	44.22/1017.04	2421.0	100.51	729.7	118.9	3½ Meat
	1 serving	11.05/254.26	605.3	25.13	182.4	29.7	
Winter Warmer	5 servings	1.75/40.27	1258.6	20.04	0.0	0.1	Trace Sodium
	1 serving	0.35/8.05	251.7	4.01	0.0	0.0	
Yellow Cake	12 servings	15.28/351.49	4061.8	71.84	6.0	21.2	1 Bread I
	1 serving	1.27/29.29	338.5	5.99	0.5	1.8	
Zabaglione	8 servings	12.03/276.66	265.9	0.36	0.0	6.6	½ Meat
	1 serving	1.50/34.58	33.2	0.05	0.0	0.8	
Zero Salad Dressing	10 servings	0.88/20.17	227.2	19.63	0.0	15.3	2 Tablespoons =
	1 serving	0.09/2.02	22.7	1.96	0.0	1.5	½ Fat
Zesty Lettuce Salad	2 servings	1.64/37.83	405.6	16.41	0.0	38.0	1 Vegetable
	1 serving	0.82/18.91	202.8	8.20	0.0	19.0	
Zippy Potato Salad	8 servings	6.23/143.39	374.4	31.54	252.8	8.1	1 Bread I
	1 serving	0.78/17.92	46.8	3.94	31.6	1.0	
Zucchini-Cheese Casserole	4 servings	64.53/1484.15	1009.7	48.20	299.6	27.2	1 Vegetable, 1 Bread I
	1 serving	16.13/371.04	252.4	12.05	74.9	6.8	½ Meat 1½ Milk I

Index

A

Acorn Squash,
  Honey-Glazed, 164
Acorn Squash,
  Orange Baked, 164
Alaska, Baked, 174
Angel Food Cake
  Supreme, 189
Appetizer(s)
  Artichokes, 63
  Beer Crab Dip, 59
  Blushing Grapefruit, 60
  Chilled Melon Balls, 60
  Curry Dill Dip, 60
  Fruit Kebabs, 62
  Hawaiian Dip, 59
  Hot Meatballs, 64
  Ginger Fruit Cup, 62
  Golden Banana Bowl, 62
  Macedoine of Winter Fruit
    with Glaze, 62
  Middle Eastern
    Meatballs, 63
  Minted Melon Balls, 61
  Sizzling Grapefruit, 60
  Spiced Honeydew Melon, 61
  Steamed Clams, 64
  Stuffed Cherry
    Tomatoes, 63
  Tropical Fruit and Wine
    Compote, 61
Apple Bake, Sweet
  Potato and, 159
Apple, Baked, 170
Apple Crisp, 197
Apple Dumplings, 198
Apple Muffins, 99

Apple Omelet, 75
Apple Pie, 184
Apple Pork Chop Roast, 130
Apple Raisin Stuffing, 139
Apple Soufflé, 178
Apple Tapioca, 178
Applesauce, Company, 169
Applesauce Toast, 89
Apricot Sherbet, 177
Artichokes, 63
Asparagus, 160
Asparagus, Herbed, with
  Lemon, 160
Asparagus Salad, 105

B

Babka, 98
Bagels, Water, 88
Baked Alaska, 174
Balloon Cake, 190
Banana Bowl, Golden, 61
Banana Cookies, 200
Banana Crêpes, Festive, 174
Banana Nog, 67
Banana Nut Bread, 85
Banana Orange Drink, 66
Banana Shakes, 67
Banana Snack Shake, 66
Bananas, Baked, 170
Bananas Foster, 170
Barbequed Fish Fillets, 144
Barbequed Fish in Foil, 141
Batter Bread, Streamlined, 82
Bean Salad, Fresh, 104
Beef
  Casserole, with Beer, 127

Chili Burgers, 119
Chili con Carne, 121
Curried, 127
Flank Steak, Marinated, 123
Fondue, 119
Greek Stuffado, 124
Green Peppers, Stuffed, 121
Hamburger Casserole, 128
Hamburger and
  Eggplant, 118
Hamburger with Horse-
  radish and Onion
  Topper, 118
Hamburger, Italian-
  Style, 118
Hamburger with Mashed
  Potato Topper, 118
Hamburger with Peppers
  and Onion Topper, 118
Hamburger with Smothered
  Onion Topper, 118
Hamburger Stroganoff, 120
Hamburgers, 118
Hamburgers, Herbed, 119
Meatballs and Tomato
  Sauce, 120
Meat Loaf, 120
Meaty Spaghetti Sauce, 126
Pepper Steak, 122
Pot Roast, Burgundy, 123
Pot Roast, Homestyle, 123
Pot Roast, Lazy Day, 119
Pot Roast, Sweet-and-
  Sour, 126
Roast, 124
Sandwich, with
  Mushrooms, 73
Shish Kebabs, 126
Spanish Rice with Meat, 121

Steak with Mushrooms
  Sauce, 122
  Stewed, 124
  Summer Dinner Platter, 117
Beef 'n' Beer Casserole, 127
Beef and Mushroom
  Sandwich, 73
Beer Crab Dip, 59
Beets, Exemplary, 163
Beets, Glazed, 163
Bergman's Homemade
  Granola, 90
Beverage(s)
  Banana Nog, 67
  Banana Orange Drink, 66
  Banana Shakes, 67
  Banana Snack Shake, 66
  Eggnog, 66
  Eggnog, Orange, 68
  Float, Brunch, 64
  Fruit Juice Cocktail,
    Tangy, 66
  Lime Apple Cooler, 65
  Orange Shake, 67
  Pineapple Juice, Mulled, 65
  Rainbow Float, 64
  Shakes, Banana, 67
  Shakes, Coffee, 67
  Shakes, Orange, 67
  Strawberry Sparkler, 172
  Summer Cooler, 65
  Super Nog, 67
  Wine, Glow, 65
  Winter Warmer, 65
  Tea, Honeyed, 68
  Tea, Orange Spiced, 68
  Tropical Fizz, 66
Biscuits, Drop (no salt), 87
Biscuits, Herb (no salt), 87

Biscuits, Stir 'n' Roll, 86
Biscuits, Stir 'n' Roll
 (no salt), 87
Blintzes, Blueberry, 92
Black Pears Elegante, 172
Blueberry Blintzes, 92
Blueberry Coffee Cake, 95
Blueberry Lemon Coffee
 Cake, 96
Blueberry-Lime Sundaes, 175
Blueberry Muffins, 99
Blueberry Pie, 185
Blueberry Sauce, 92
Bluefish Hampton, 143
Blushing Grapefruit, 60
Bordelaise Sauce, 152
Bread(s)
 Apple Muffins, 99
 Applesauce Toast, 89
 Babka, 98
 Bagels, Water, 88
 Banana Nut, 85
 Batter Bread,
  Streamlined, 82
 Biscuits, Herb (no salt), 87
 Biscuits, Stir 'n' Roll, 86
 Biscuits, Stir 'n' Roll
  (no salt), 87
 Blueberry Blintzes, 92
 Coffee Cake, Blueberry, 95
 Coffee Cake, Blueberry
  Lemon, 95
 Coffee Cake, Pineapple, 95
 Corn Bread, 82
 Corn Muffins, 82
 Cranberry Banana
  Toast, 89
 Cranberry Orange Nut, 85
 Croutons, Herb-
  Seasoned, 90
 Date Nut, 85
 Double-Quick Dinner
  Rolls, 85
 Drop Biscuits (no salt), 87
 English Muffins, 88

 French, 83
 French, Garlic, 83
 French Toast, 89
 Honey Whole Wheat
  Rolls, 84
 Hot, in Foil, 82
 Limpa Rye, Swedish, 87
 Muffins, Apple, 99
 Muffins, Blueberry, 99
 Muffins, Corn, 82
 Muffins, Cranberry
  Orange, 99
 Muffins, English, 88
 Muffins, Surprise, 99
 Muffins, Sweet, 99
 Nut, 85
 Pancakes, 91
 Puffs, Golden, 94
 Roll Dough, Traditional, 86
 Rolls, Butterscotch
  Pecan, 97
 Rolls, Cinnamon, 97
 Rolls, Cloverleaf, 86
 Rolls, Crescent, 86
 Rolls, Double-Quick, 85
 Rolls, Orange Frosted, 98
 Rolls, Sugar Crisp, 96
 Rolls, Whole Wheat,
  Honey, 84
 Stollen, German, 93
 Streusel Coffee Cake, 94
 Sweet Dough, 93
 Tea Ring, Swedish, 96
 Toast, Applesauce, 89
 Toast, Cranberry
  Banana, 89
 Toast, French, 89
 Waffles, Golden, 91
 Waffles, Nut, 91
 Waffles, Orange, 91
 White, Traditional, 81
 Whole Wheat, Honey, 84
 Bread Pudding, 179
 Bread Stuffing, 139
 Broccoli, 165

Broccoli with Lemon
 Margarine, 165
Broccoli Polonaise, 165
Brown Sauce, Basic, 150
Browned Margarine
 Frosting, 192
Brownies, 202
Brownies, Butterscotch, 199
Brownies (Cakelike), 199
Brunch Float, 64
Burgundy Pot Roast, 123
Butternut Squash, Baked, 161
Butterscotch Brownies, 199
Butterscotch Pecan Rolls, 97
Butterscotch Pudding, 179

C

Caesar Salad, 105
Cakes [see Dessert(s),
 Cakes]
Cantaloupe Surprise, 174
Caribbean Chicken, 134
Caribbean Jumble, 171
Carrots, Pineapple, 162
Casserole, Beef 'n' Beer, 127
Casserole, Hamburger, 128
Casserole, Zucchini-
 Cheese, 147
Cauliflower Parmesan, 159
Cauliflower Soup,
 Cream of, 70
Cheese Casserole,
 Zucchini-, 147
Cheese Omelet, 75
Cherry Frosting, 192
Cherry Pie, 183
Cherry Tomatoes, Stuffed, 63
Chicken
 Baked, 135
 Caribbean, 134
 Club Sandwich, 72
 Coq au Vin, 133
 Curry, 134

 Easy Broiled, 136
 Easy Grilled, 132
 In Mushroom Sauce, 135
 In Wine, 133
 Lemon Sesame, 139
 Noodle Soup, 71
 Oregano, 136
 Poulet André, 136
 Salad, 111
 Salad, Tomato
  Stuffed with, 110
 Soufflé, 135
 Stewed, 137
 Summer Garden, 140
 Tetrazzini, 137
Chicken Club Sandwich, 72
Chicken in Mushroom
 Sauce, 135
Chicken Noodle Soup, 71
Chicken in Wine
 (Coq au Vin), 133
Chili Burgers, 119
Chili con Carne, 121
Chilled Melon Balls, 60
Chocolate Cake, 192
Chocolate Chip Cookies, 200
Chocolate Nut Cookies, 200
Chocolate Sauce, 181
Chutney, 154
Cinnamon Rolls, 97
Clams, Steamed, 64
Clear Lemon Filling, 196
Cloverleaf Rolls, 86
Cloverleaf Rolls, Honey
 Whole Wheat, 84
Club Sandwich, Chicken, 72
Coffee Cake, Blueberry, 95
Coffee Cake, Blueberry
 Lemon, 96
Coffee Cake, Pineapple, 95
Coffee Shake, 67
Coleslaw, Tart, 105
Company Applesauce, 169
Compote, Fresh Fruit, 171
Compote, Orange, 171

Cookies [*see Dessert(s), Cookies*]
Cookie Cutter Cake, 190
Cookie Crust, 186
Cookie Mix, 200
Cooler, Summer, 65
Coq au Vin, 133
Corn Bread, 82
Corn, Fried, 161
Corn Muffins, 82
Corn on the Cob, 161
Corn, Roasted (Roastin' Ears), 161
Cottage Cheese Bake, 146
Coupe Louise, 177
Crab Dip, Beer, 59
Crabs, Hard-Shell, Steamed, 144
Cranberry Banana Toast, 89
Cranberry Gelatin, 108
Cranberry Ice, Quick, 176
Cranberry Orange Margarine, 92
Cranberry Orange Muffins, 99
Cranberry Orange Nut Bread, 85
Cranberry Orange Relish, 155
Cream of Cauliflower Soup, 70
Cream Pudding, Vanilla, 179
Creative Cakes, 190
Creole Flounder, 144
Creole Sauce, 152
Creole Sauce (Spaghetti), 147
Crêpes, 173
Crêpes, Festive Banana, 174
Crêpes Suzette, 175
Crescent Rolls, 86
Cresson Salad, 107
Crisscross Potatoes, 158
Croutons, Herb-Seasoned, 90
Cucumber Salad, 107
Cucumber Sauce, 107, 151
Cumberland Sauce, 153
Curried Beef, 127
Curried Fruit Salad, 114

Curried Fruit Salad Dressing, 114
Curried Rice, 148
Curry, Chicken, 134
Curry Dill Dip, 60
Curry Sauce, 151
Custard Pie, 185

D

Date Nut Bread, 85
Date Nut Squares, 203
Decorators' Icing, 193
Deep Dish Fruit Pie, 183
Dessert(s)
  Apple Crisp, 197
  Apple Soufflé, 178
  Apple Tapioca, 178
  Apricot Sherbet, 177
  Baked Alaska, 174
  Baked Apple, 170
  Baked Bananas, 170
  Bananas Foster, 170
  Black Pears Elegante, 172
  Brownies, 202
  Brownies, Butterscotch, 199
  Brownies (Cakelike), 199
  CAKE(S) AND ICING(S)
    Angel Food, Supreme, 189
    Balloon, 190
    Chocolate, 192
    Cookie Cutter, 190
    Creative, 190
    Frosting, Browned Margarine, 192
    Frosting, Cherry, 192
    Frosting, Easy Penuche, 196
    Frosting, French Silk, 191
    Frosting, Lemon, 192
    Frosting, Maple Nut, 192
    Frosting, Margarine, 192
    Frosting, Orange or Lemon, 192

    Frosting, Pineapple, 192
    Frosting, White Mountain, 191
    Fruitcake, Jeweled, 196
    Gingerbread, 199
    Honey Orange, 195
    Icing, Decorators', 193
    Icing, Mocha, 194
    Lemon Filling, Clear, 196
    Mocha Spice, 194
    Poppy Seed, 195
    Pound, Golden, 197
    Shadow Design, 190
    Spice Raisin, 195
    Starlight, 190
    Upside-Down, Pineapple, 194
    White, 193
    Yellow, 174, 190
  Cantaloupe Surprise, 174
  Caribbean Jumble, 171
  COOKIE(S)
    Banana, 200
    Brownies, 202
    Brownies, Butterscotch, 199
    Brownies (Cakelike), 199
    Chocolate Chip, 200
    Chocolate Nut, 200
    Date-Nut Squares, 203
    Lemon Squares, 202
    Mix, Cookie, 200
    Nut Bars, 203
    Oatmeal, 201
    Pumpkin, 202
    Russian Teacakes, 198
    Shortbread, Scotch, 198
    Spice, 200
    Spritz, 201
    Sugar, 203
  Coupe Louise, 177
  Cranberry Ice, Quick, 176
  Crêpes, 173
    Crêpes, Festive Banana, 174

    Crêpes Suzette, 175
  Fruit Whip, Double, 180
  Ice, Emerald, 177
  Ice, Iced Orange, 176
  Ice, Raspberry Pineapple, 176
  Ice, Raspberry, Quick, **176**
  Orange Compote, 171
  Orange Slices, Grand Marnier, 171
  Peach Cobbler, Quick, 201
  PIE(S) AND PIE CRUST(S)
    Apple Pie, 184
    Basic Meringue, 186
    Blueberry, 185
    Blueberry, Frozen, 185
    Cherry, 183
    Cookie Crust, 186
    Custard, 185
    Deep Dish Fruit, 183
    Lemon Meringue, 187
    Meringue, Basic, 186
    Meringue Pie Shell, 186
    Oil Pastry, 188
    Peach, Fresh, 187
    Peach, Fresh, with Apricots, 187
    Peach, Fresh, with Brown Sugar, 187
    Rhubarb, Fresh, 184
    Standard Pastry, 188
  Pineapple Fluff, 178
  Pineapple Glacé, 175
  PUDDING(S)
    Apple Tapioca, 178
    Bread, 179
    Butterscotch, 179
    Lemon, 178
    Rice, 179
    Snow, 180
    Vanilla Cream, 179
  Sherbet, Fresh Lemon, 176
  Soufflé, Quick Orange, 177
  Strawberry Supreme, 172
  Strawberry Turnover, 197

Sundaes, Blueberry Lime, 175
Zabaglione, 180
Dessert Sauces: *see Sauces, Dessert*
Dijon-Type Mustard, 150
Dill Sauce, 151
Dill Sauce, Quick, 154
Dip, Beer Crab, 59
Dip, Curry Dill, 40
Dip, Hawaiian, 59
Double-Quick Dinner Rolls, 85
Double Fruit Whip, 180
Dough, Sweet, 93
Drop Biscuits (no salt), 87
Dressings [*see Salad Dressings*]
Dressings [*see Stuffing*]
Dumplings, 90
Dumplings, Apple, 198

E

East India Peaches, 154
Easter Roast Lamb with Artichokes, 129
Easy Broiled Chicken, 136
Easy Grilled Chicken, 132
Easy Penuche Frosting, 196
Egg(s)
and Peppers, 79
and Tomatoes, 79
OMELET(S)
Apple, 75
aux Fines Herbes, 76
Basic, with Imitation Eggs, 75
Cheese, 75
Française, 78
Frittata, 78
Green Pepper, 75
Herb, 75
Mushroom, 76

Mushroom (with Imitation Eggs), 75
Potato, 77
Puffy, 77
Ratatouille, 75
Poached, 79
Poached (with Imitation Eggs), 78
Salad, 109
Scrambled, 80
Scrambled, Herbed, 80
Scrambled (with Imitation Eggs), 80
Soufflé, Quick Orange, 177
Western Sandwich, 73
Eggnog, 66
Eggnog, Orange, 68
Eggplant, Grilled, 162
Emerald Ice, 177
English Muffins, 88
Exemplary Beets, 163

F

Festive Banana Crêpes, 174
Fillets, Oven Fried, 142
Filling, Lemon, Clear, 196
Fish and Shellfish
Baked, 143
Barbequed Fish in Foil, 141
Bluefish Hampton, 143
Broiled, 140
Clams, Steamed, 64
Fillets, Barbequed, 144
Fillets, Oven-Fried, 142
Flounder, Creole, 144
Flounder with Lemon and Almonds, 145
Haddock, Baked, 141
Haddock, Oven-Poached, 141
Hard-Shell Crabs, Steamed, 144
Lobster, Broiled, 145
Lobster Salad, Spanish, 114

Lobster Tails, Broiled, with Lemon Sauce, 145
Pan Fried, 140
Poached Fish, 142
Salmon with Dill Sauce, 144
Salmon Sandwich, Open-Faced, 72
Salmon Steak Alaska, 142
Shrimp Grapefruit Shell, 110
Spanish Lobster Salad, 114
Tuna Fondue, Baked, 146
Tuna Fruit Sandwich, 72
Tuna Gourmet, 146
Tuna Salad, 115
Whitefish, Broiled, 143
Fizz, Tropical, 66
Flank Steak, Marinated, 123
Float, Brunch, 64
Float, Rainbow, 64
Flounder, Creole, 144
Flounder with Lemon and Almonds, 145
Fluff, Pineapple, 178
Fondue, Beef, 119
Française Omelet, 78
French Bread, 83
French Dressing, 112
French Dressing, Old-Fashioned, 112
French Dressing, Spicy, 112
French Green Beans, 168
French Plums, 173
French Silk Frosting, 191
French Toast, 89
Frittata Omelet, 78
Frosted Fruit, 177
Frosted Orange Rolls, 98
Frosting, Cherry, 192
Frosting, Easy Penuche, 196
Frosting, French Silk, 191
Frosting, Lemon, 192
Frosting, Maple Nut, 192
Frosting, Margarine, 192
Frosting, Margarine, Browned, 192

Frosting, Orange or Lemon, 192
Frosting, Pineapple, 192
Frosting, White Mountain, 191
Fruit(s)
Bananas, Baked, 170
Cantaloupe Surprise, 174
Caribbean, Jumble, 171
Compote, Fresh, 171
Compote, Orange, 171
Compote, Spiced, 170
Compote, Tropical, and Wine, 61
Cup, Ginger, 62
East India Peaches, 154
Frosted, 177
Honeydew Melon, Spiced, 61
Juice Cocktail, Tangy, 66
Kebabs, 62
Melon Balls, Chilled, 60
Melon Balls, Minted, 61
Melon Boats, Raspberry, 172
Minted Pears, Spiced, 109
Mold, Spiced, 106
Orange Compote, 171
Orange Slices Grand Marnier, 171
Peaches in Port, 173
Pears, Black, Elegante, 172
Pineapple Glacé, 175
Pineapple, Minted, 173
Pineapples, Baked, 169
Plums, French, 173
Raspberry Melon Boats, 172
Rhubarb, Stewed, 171
Salad, Curried, 114
Salad, Minted, 109
Strawberry Sparkler, 172
Strawberry Supreme, 172
Winter, Macedoine of, with Glaze, 62
Fruit Sundae Sauce, 181
Fruit Tuna Sandwich, 72

G

Garden Patch Salad, 106
Garlic French Bread, 83
Garlic Potato Balls, 158
Gazpacho, 71
Gelatin, Cranberry, 108
German Stollen, 93
Ginger Fruit Cup, 62
Gingerbread, 199
Glacé, Pineapple, 175
Glazed Beets, 163
Glazed Mustard Parsnips, 162
Glow Wine, 65
Golden Banana Bowl, 61
Golden Pound Cake, 197
Golden Puffs, 94
Golden Waffles, 91
Granola, Bergman's
    Homemade, 90
Grapefruit, Blushing, 60
Grapefruit Mold, 108
Grapefruit Shell, Shrimp, 110
Grapefruit, Sizzling, 60
Gravy, Kettle, 153
Greek Stuffado, 124
Green Beans, French, 168
Green Beans with Dill, 168
Green Beans, Italian, 167
Green Beans Oregano, 168
Green Pepper Omelet, 75
Green Peppers, Baked, 161
Green String Beans, 167

H

Haddock, Baked, 141
Haddock, Oven-Poached, 141
Hamburger(s)
    and Eggplant, 118
    Casserole, 128

Chili Burgers, 119
Chili con Carne, 121
Hot Meatballs, 64
Herbed, 119
Italian-Style, 118
Meatballs and Tomato
    Sauce, 120
Meat Loaf, 120
Stroganoff, 120
Toppers, 118
with Horseradish and Onion
    Topper, 118
with Mashed Potato
    Topper, 118
with Pepper and Onion
    Topper, 118
with Smothered Onion
    Topper, 118
Hash, Tahitian, 134
Hawaiian Dip, 59
Hearts of Palm Salad, 105
Herb Biscuits (no salt), 87
Herb Margarine, 155
Herb Omelet, 75
Herb-Seasoned Croutons, 90
Herbed Asparagus with
    Lemon, 160
Herbed Hamburgers, 119
Herbed Scrambled Eggs, 80
Herbed Tomatoes, 102
Hollandaise Sauce, 153
Homestyle Pot Roast, 123
Honey Fruit Salad
    Dressing, 114
Honey-Glazed Acorn
    Squash, 164
Honey Margarine, 92
Honey Orange Cake, 195
Honey Whole Wheat
    Bread, 84
Honey Whole Wheat Rolls, 84
Honeyed Tea, 68
Hot Bread in Foil, 82
Hot Meatballs, 64
Hot Pepper Relish, 155

I

Ice, Emerald, 177
Iced Orange Ice, 176
Icing(s) and Frosting(s)
    Browned Margarine
        Frosting, 192
    Cherry Frosting, 192
    Decorators' Icing, 193
    Easy Penuche Frosting, 196
    French Silk Frosting, 191
    Lemon Frosting, 96, 192
    Maple Nut Frosting, 192
    Margarine Frosting, 192
    Mocha Icing, 194
    Orange Frosting, 192
    Petits Fours Icing, 193
    Pineapple Frosting, 192
    Powdered Sugar Icing, 97
    Quick White Icing, 93
    White Mountain
        Frosting, 191
Italian Greens (with Kale,
    Collards, Dandelion, or
    Turnip Greens), 167
Italian Green Beans, 167
Italian-Style Hamburgers, 118

K

Kebabs, Fruit, 62
Kebabs, Shish, 126
Kettle Gravy, 153

L

Lamb Easter Roast, with
    Artichokes, 129
Lamb, Near East, 130
Lamb, Roast, 129
Lamb, Savory, 131
Lamb Chops, Broiled, 128
Lamb Chops, Swedish,
    Broiled, 103

Lazy Day Pot Roast, 119
Leg of Lamb, Boned, with
    Stuffing, 128
Lemon Dressing, 103, 113
Lemon Filling, Clear, 196
Lemon Frosting, 192
Lemon Margarine Sauce, 63
Lemon Meringue Pie, 187
Lemon Poultry-Basting
    Sauce, 152
Lemon Pudding, 178
Lemon Sauce, 145
Lemon Sesame Chicken, 139
Lemon Sherbet, Fresh, 176
Lemon Squares, 202
Lettuce Salad, Zesty, 102
Lime Apple Cooler, 65
Limpa Rye Bread, Swedish, 87
Lobster, Broiled, 145
Lobster Salad, Spanish, 114
Lobster Tails, Broiled, with
    Lemon Sauce, 145

M

Macaroni Mushroom Cas-
    serole, 149
Macaroni, Tomato, 149
Macaroni Vegetable Cas-
    serole, 149
Macedoine of Winter Fruit with
    Glaze, 62
Maple Nut Frosting, 192
Maple Syrup, 92
Margarine, Cranberry
    Orange, 92
Margarine Frosting, 192
Margarine, Herb, 155
Margarine, Honey, 92
Margarine Sauce, Lemon, 63
Margarine, Seasoned, 155
Margarine Spreads, 83
Margarine, Whipped, 92
Marinade, 117

Marinade, Basic, 150
Marinated Flank Steak, 123
Mayonnaise, 115
Meat(s): *See also Beef*
   Hash, Tahitian, 134
   Lamb, Boned Leg, with
     Stuffing, 128
   Lamb Chops, Broiled, 128
   Lamb Chops, Swedish
     Broiled, 103
   Lamb, Easter Roast, with
     Artichokes, 129
   Lamb, Near East, 130
   Lamb, Roast, 129
   Lamb, Savory, 131
   Pork, Baked, with Apples
     and Caraway, 131
   Pork Chop Roast,
     Apple, 130
   Pork Chops and Rice, 131
   Pork Chops, Skillet, 132
   Shish Kebabs, 126
   Turkey, Roast, 138
   Veal Scallopine, with
     Lemon, 133
   Wiener Schnitzel, 132
Meat-Basting Sauce, 152
Meat Loaf, 120
Meatballs and Tomato
   Sauce, 120
Meatballs, Middle Eastern, 63
Meaty Spaghetti Sauce, 126
Melon Balls, Chilled, 60
Melon Balls, Minted, 61
Melon Boats, Raspberry, 172
Melon, Honeydew, Spiced, 61
Meringue Pie Shell, 186
Meringue, Basic, 186
Mexican Relish, 155
Middle Eastern Meatballs, 63
Minted Fruit Salad, 109
Minted Melon Balls, 61
Minted Pears, Spiced, 109
Minted Peas, 162
Minted Pineapple, 173

Mixed Green Salad with
   Lemon Dressing, 103
Mixed Vegetable Salad, 101
Mocha Icing, 194
Mocha Spice Cake, 194
Muffins [*see Bread(s),
   Muffins*]
Mulligatawny Soup, 70
Mushroom Macaroni, 149
Mushroom Omelet, 76
Mushroom Omelet (with
   Imitation Eggs), 75
Mushroom and Radish
   Salad, 104
Mustard, Dijon-Type, 150

N

Near East Lamb, 130
New Delhi Rice, 149
New Potatoes, Parsleyed, 159
Nut Bars, 203
Nut Bread, 85
Nut Bread, Banana, 85
Nut Waffles, 91

O

Oatmeal Cookies, 201
Oil Pastry, 188
Old-Fashioned French
   Dressing, 112
Omelets [*see Egg(s),
   Omelets*]
Onion Slices Sautéed, 160
Open-Faced Salmon
   Sandwich, 72
Orange Baked Acorn
   Squash, 164
Orange Compote, 171
Orange Drink, Banana, 66
Orange Eggnog, 68

Orange or Lemon
   Frosting, 192
Orange Rolls, Frosted, 98
Orange Sauce, 92
Orange Shake, 67
Orange Slices Grand
   Marnier, 171
Orange Spiced Tea, 68
Orange Sweet Potatoes, 159
Orange Waffles, 91
Oregano Chicken, 136
Oven-Fried Fillets, 142
Oven-Poached Haddock, 141

P

Pancakes, 91
Panfried Fish, 140
Parsleyed New Potatoes, 159
Parsleyed Potatoes, 157
Parsnips, Glazed Mustard, 162
Party Rice, 148
Pasta
   Macaroni, Mushroom, 149
   Macaroni, Tomato, 149
   Macaroni Vegetable
     Casserole, 149
   Spaghetti with Creole
     Sauce, 147
Pastry, Cookie Crust, 186
Pastry, Oil, 188
Pastry, Standard, 188
Peach Cobbler, Quick, 201
Peaches, East India, 154
Peach Pie, Fresh, 187
Peaches in Port, 173
Pears, Black, Elegante, 172
Peas, Minted, 162
Penuche Frosting, Easy, 196
Pepper Steak, 122
Peppers, Baked Green, 161
Peppers, Stuffed Green, 121
Petits Fours, 193

Petits Fours Icing, 193
Pies [*see Dessert(s), Pies*]
Pilaf, Basic, 148
Pineapple Carrots, 162
Pineapple Coffee Cake, 95
Pineapple Cranberry Relish
   Mold, 108
Pineapple Fluff, 178
Pineapple Frosting, 192
Pineapple Glacé, 175
Pineapple Ice, Raspberry, 176
Pineapple Juice, Mulled, 65
Pineapple, Minted, 173
Pineapple Sweet
   Potatoes, 158
Pineapple Upside-Down
   Cake, 194
Pineapples, Baked, 169
Pizza, 74
Pizza, Quick Mix, 74
Plums, French, 173
Poached Egg, 79
Poached Egg (with Imitation
   Eggs), 78
Poppy Seed Cake, 195
Pork and Apples, Baked, with
   Caraway, 131
Pork Chops and Rice, 131
Pork Chop Roast, Apple, 130
Pork Chops, Skillet, 132
Potato Balls, Garlic, 158
Potato Omelet, 77
Potato Salad, Zippy, 111
Potatoes, Crisscross, 158
Potatoes, Orange Sweet, 159
Potatoes, Parsleyed, 157
Potatoes, Parsleyed New, 159
Potatoes, Sweet, Pine-
   apple, 158
Pot Roast, Burgundy, 123
Pot Roast, Homestyle, 123
Pot Roast, Lazy Day, 119
Pot Roast, Sweet-and-
   Sour, 126
Poulet André, 136

Poultry-Basting Sauce,
  Lemon, 152
Pound Cake, Golden, 197
Provençale Sauce, 153

Q

Quick Cranberry Ice, 176
Quick Dill Sauce, 154
Quick Mix Pizza, 74
Quick Orange Soufflé, 177
Quick Peach Cobbler, 201

R

Rainbow Float, 64
Raisin Cake, Spice, 195
Raspberry Melon Boats, 172
Raspberry Pineapple Ice, 176
Ratatouille, 164
Ratatouille Omelet, 75
Relish, Cranberry Orange, 155
Relish, Hot Pepper, 155
Relish, Mexican, 155
Rhubarb Pie, Fresh, 184
Rhubarb, Stewed, 171
Rice
  Basic, 148
  Curried, 148
  Party Rice, 148
  Pilaf, Basic, 148
  New Delhi, 149
  Pudding, 179
  Spanish, with Meat, 121
Roast Beef, 124
Roast Beef Timetable, 125
Roast Lamb, 129
Roast Turkey, 138
Roastin' Ears (Roasted
  Corn), 161
Roll Dough, Traditional, 86
Rolls, Butterscotch Pecan, 97
Rolls, Cinnamon, 97
Rolls, Cloverleaf, 86

Rolls, Crescent, 86
Rolls, Double-Quick Dinner, 85
Rolls, Honey Whole Wheat, 84
Rolls, Sugar Crisp, 96
Rolls, Whole Wheat Honey, 84
Romaine and Watercress
  Salad, 103
Rum Sauce, 181
Russian Teacakes, 198

S

Salad(s)
  Asparagus, 105
  Bean, Fresh, 104
  Caesar, 105
  Chicken, 111
  Coleslaw, Tart, 105
  Cresson, 107
  Cucumber, 107
  Egg, 109
  Fruit, Curried, 114
  Fruit, Minted, 109
  Fruit Salad, Honey, 114
  Garden Patch, 106
  Gelatin, Cranberry, 108
  Grapefruit Mold, 108
  Hearts of Palm, 105
  Honey Fruit, 114
  Lobster, Spanish, 114
  Minted Fruit, 109
  Mixed Green, with Lemon
    Dressing, 103
  Mixed Vegetable, 101
  Mushroom and Radish, 104
  Pineapple Cranberry
    Relish, 108
  Shrimp Grapefruit Shell, 110
  Spiced Fruit Mold, 106
  Spinach, 104
  Spinach and Endive, 103
  Sunshine, 107
  Tomato, 101

Tomato Stuffed with
  Chicken, 110
Tomato, Super, 102
Tossed, Elegante, 104
Tossed Green, 102
Tuna, 115
Vegetable Combination, 106
Watercress and
  Romaine, 103
Zesty Lettuce, 102
Zippy Potato, 111
Salad Dressing(s)
  Basic, 112
  Curried Fruit, 114
  French, 112
  French, Old-Fashioned, 112
  French, Spicy, 112
  Honey Fruit, 114
  Lemon, 103, 113
  Shallot, 113
  Tropical, 114
  Vinaigrette, 113
  Zero, 113
  Zippy Cooked, 111
Salmon Sandwich, Open-
  Faced, 72
Salmon with Dill Sauce, 114
Salmon Steak Alaska, 142
Sandwich Ideas, 72
Sandwich(es)
  Beef and Mushroom, 73
  Club, Chicken, 72
  Pizza, 74
  Quick Pizza, 74
  Salmon, Open-Faced, 72
  Tuna Fruit, 72
  Western Egg, 73
Sauce(s)
  Basic Brown, 150
  Bordelaise, 152
  Creole, 152
  Creole (Spaghetti), 147
  Cucumber, 107, 151
  Cumberland, 153
  Curry, 151

Dill, 151
Dill, Quick, 154
Hollandaise, 153
Kettle Gravy, 153
Lemon Margarine, 63
Marinade, Basic, 150
Meat, Basting, 152
Meaty Spaghetti, 126
Poultry-Basting, Lemon, 152
Provençale, 153
Stroganoff, 73
Swedish, 154
Tomato, 151
White, 151
Sauce, Dessert
  Blueberry, 92
  Chocolate, 181
  Fruit Sundae, 181
  Lemon, 145
  Orange, 92
  Rum, 181
Savory Lamb, 131
Schnitzel, Wiener, 132
Scotch Shortbread, 198
Scrambled Eggs, 80
Scrambled Eggs (with Imita-
  tion Eggs), 80
Seasoned Margarine, 155
Shadow Design Cake, 190
Shake, Banana, 67
Shake, Coffee, 67
Shake, Orange, 67
Shallot Dressing, 113
Sherbet, Apricot, 177
Sherbet, Fresh Lemon, 176
Shish Kebabs, 126
Shortbread, Scotch, 198
Shrimp Grapefruit Shell, 110
Sizzling Grapefruit, 60
Skillet Pork Chops, 132
Snack Shake, Banana, 66
Snow Pudding, 180
Soufflé, Apple, 178
Soufflé, Chicken, 135
Soufflé, Quick Orange, 177

Soup(s)
Chicken Noodle, 71
Cream of Cauliflower, 70
Gazpacho, 71
Mulligatawny, 70
Vegetable, 69
Vegetable Combo, 147
Vegetable Ring, 69
Spaghetti with Creole
Sauce, 147
Spaghetti Sauce, Meaty, 126
Spanish Lobster Salad, 114
Spanish Rice with Meat, 121
Sparkler, Strawberry, 172
Spice Cake, Mocha, 194
Spice Cookies, 200
Spice Raisin Cake, 195
Spiced Fruit Compote, 170
Spiced Fruit Mold, 106
Spiced Honeydew Melon, 61
Spiced Minted Pears, 109
Spiced Tea, Orange, 68
Spicy French Dressing, 112
Spinach and Endive
Salad, 103
Spinach Salad, 104
Spinach, Tangy, 166
Spritz, 201
Squash, Acorn, Orange
Baked, 164
Squash, Acorn, Honey-
Glazed, 164
Squash, Butternut, Baked, 161
Standard Pastry, 188
Starlight Cake, 190
Steak with Mushroom
Sauce, 122
Steak, Pepper, 122
Steamed Clams, 64
Steamed Hard-Shell
Crabs, 144
Stir 'n' Roll Biscuits, 86
Stir 'n' Roll Biscuits (no salt), 87
Stollen, German, 93
Strawberry Sparkler, 172

Strawberry Supreme, 172
Strawberry Turnover, 197
Streusel Coffee Cake, 94
Streamlined Batter Bread, 82
String Beans, Green, 167
Stroganoff Sauce, 73
Stuffado, Greek, 124
Stuffed Cherry Tomatoes, 63
Stuffed Green Peppers, 121
Stuffing, Apple Raisin, 139
Stuffing, Regular Bread, 139
Sugar Cookies, 203
Sugar Crisp Rolls, 96
Summer Cooler, 65
Summer Garden Chicken, 140
Summer Dinner Platter, 117
Summer Vegetable Skillet, 160
Sundaes, Blueberry Lime, 175
Sunshine Salad, 107
Super Nog, 67
Super Tomato Salad, 102
Surprise Muffins, 99
Swedish Broiled Lamb
Chops. 130
Swedish Limpa Rye Bread, 87
Swedish Sauce, 154
Swedish Tea Ring, 96
Sweet Dough, 93
Sweet Muffins, 99
Sweet Potato and Apple
Bake, 159
Sweet Potatoes, Orange, 159
Sweet-and-Sour Pot
Roast, 126
Syrup, Maple, 92

T

Tahitian Hash, 134
Tangy Fruit Juice Cocktail, 66
Tangy Spinach, 166
Tapioca, Apple, 178
Tart Coleslaw, 105
Tea, Honeyed, 68

Teacakes, Russian, 198
Tea Ring, Swedish, 96
Toast, Applesauce, 89
Toast, Cranberry Banana, 89
Toast, French, 89
Tomato Macaroni, 149
Tomato Paste, Unsalted, 150
Tomato Salad, 101
Tomato Salad, Super, 102
Tomato Sauce, 151
Tomato Stuffed with Chicken
Salad, 110
Tomatoes, Baked, with Savory
Crumb Topping, 166
Tomatoes, Broiled, 166
Tomatoes, Herbed, 102
Toppers for Hamburgers, 118
Toppers for Pancakes,
Waffles, 92
Tossed Green Salad, 102
Tossed Salad Elegante, 104
Traditional Roll Dough, 86
Traditional White Bread, 81
Tropical Fizz, 66
Tropical Fruit and Wine
Compote, 61
Tropical Salad Dressing, 114
Tuna Fondue, Baked, 146
Tuna Gourmet, 146
Tuna Salad, 115
Tuna Sandwich, Fruit, 72
Turkey, Roast, 138
Turnover, Strawberry, 197

U

Unsalted Tomato Paste, 150
Upside-Down Cake,
Pineapple, 194

V

Vanilla Cream Pudding, 179

Veal Scallopine with
Lemon, 133
Vegetable(s)
Artichokes, 63
Asparagus, 160
Asparagus, Herbed with
Lemon, 160
Bean Salad, Fresh, 104
Beets, Exemplary, 163
Beets, Glazed, 163
Broccoli, 165
Broccoli Polonaise, 165
Broccoli with Lemon
Margarine, 165
Carrots, Pineapple, 162
Cauliflower Parmesan, 159
Corn, Fried, 161
Corn on the Cob, 161
Corn, Roasted, 161
Eggplant, Grilled, 162
Green Beans, French, 168
Green Beans, Italian, 167
Green Beans Oregano, 168
Green Beans with Dill, 168
Green Peppers, Baked, 161
Italian Greens (with Kale,
Collards, Dandelion and
Turnip Greens), 167
New Potatoes,
Parsleyed, 159
Onion Slices, Sautéed, 160
Parsnips, Glazed
Mustard, 162
Peas, Minted, 162
Potato Balls, Garlic, 158
Potatoes, Crisscross, 158
Potatoes, Parsleyed, 157
Potatoes, Parsleyed
New, 159
Ratatouille, 164
Spinach, Tangy, 166
Squash, Acorn,
Honey-Glazed, 164
Squash, Acorn, Orange
Baked, 164

Squash, Butternut, Baked, 161
String Beans, Green, 167
Summer Skillet, 160
Sweet Potato and Apple Bake, 159
Sweet Potatoes, Orange, 159
Sweet Potatoes, Pineapple, 158
Tomatoes, Baked, with Savory Crumb Topping, 166
Tomatoes, Broiled, 166
Tomatoes, Herbed, 102
Yams, Baked, Glazed, 158
Vegetable Combination Salad, 166
Vegetable Combo, 147
Vegetable Ring Soup, 69
Vegetable Salad, Mixed, 101
Vegetable Soup, 69
Vinaigrette Dressing, 113

Wine, Glow, 65
Winter Fruit, Macedoine of, with Glaze, 62
Winter Warmer, 65

Y

Yams, Baked, Glazed, 158
Yellow Cake, 174, 190

Z

Zabaglione, 180
Zero Salad Dressing, 113
Zesty Lettuce Salad, 102
Zippy Cooked Salad Dressing, 111
Zippy Potato Salad, 111

W

Waffles, Golden, 91
Waffles, Orange, 91
Waffles, Nut, 91
Water Bagels, 88
Watercress and Romaine Salad, 103
Western Egg Sandwich, 73
White Bread, Traditional, 81
White Cake, 193
Whitefish, Broiled, 143
White Mountain Frosting, 191
White Sauce, 151
Whipped Margarine, 92
Whole Wheat Bread, Honey, 84
Whole Wheat Rolls, Honey, 84
Weiner Schnitzel, 132